The Three-Mile Limit of Territorial Seas

The Three-Mile Limit of Territorial Seas

Sayre A. Swarztrauber
Captain, U. S. Navy

Naval Institute Press
Annapolis, Maryland

73340

Library of Congress Catalogue
card number: 72-83795.

ISBN: 0-87021-703-8

Printed in the United States of America.

Dedicated

With affection

To my family

And

With hope

To the sailors and statesmen of
all flags engaged in the search
for a workable and equitable
international law of the sea

Contents

Illustrations and Tables

Preface

During the several months between completing the manuscript and going to press, I have kept close watch on the developments in the international law of the sea, and I have noted no incident or trend which might be fairly interpreted as breathing any new life into the three-mile limit as a rule of international law. So the thesis that the three-mile limit has passed into history still stands.

However, the evolutionary political process which unfolds new relationships and concepts of international law continues. Those observers who have monitored United Nations deliberations concerning the deep sea and the sea bed have probably detected an emerging realignment of state attitudes. Whereas the East-West Cold War political confrontation played an important role in aligning states into three-mile and twelve-mile camps during the United Nations Conferences of 1958 and 1960, economic considerations seem now to be upstaging those political. Even though the antagonists of 1958 and 1960 are now close to being of one mind on a twelve-mile limit, universal agreement may still be elusive, because there is a mounting resistance among the developing states. Many of them seem reluctant to restrict voluntarily their sovereign rights and options to within a narrow twelve-mile maritime belt without some sort of assurance that theirs will be a fair share of the great natural wealth in and under the deep, high seas beyond. The industrial states appear eager to delimit a narrow territorial sea—presumably not unconscious of the fact that they possess the best available means to exploit the areas beyond the territorial sea. (But this is not plowing new ground, as history of the three-mile-limit has disclosed.) On the other hand, the non-industrial states, struggling to narrow the economic gap, apparently see little or no benefit in hastily committing themselves to a twelve-mile (or any narrow) limit, immediately beyond which the industrial states may freely help themselves, unencumbered by international conservation regulations. So the fate of the twelve-mile limit, currently in vogue, like the three-mile limit before it, may depend in no small measure upon how equitably this conflict of interests between the "have" and the "have not" states is resolved.

Be the fate of the twelve-mile limit as it will, this book on the three-mile limit is written and published. I wish to express thanks to those who extended a helping hand along the way. Since World War II, the United States' military and naval services have become increasingly sensitive to their interface with political matters. Programs have been instituted in the several services to train their officer corps in international affairs. The United States Navy, through its Doctoral Studies Program, generously granted me an academic sabbatical to study world affairs. Several admirals—Frank Vannoy, Waldemar Wendt, John Hyland, Elmo Zumwalt, Jr., and Julien Le Bourgeois, among others— were particularly instrumental in this regard, and I owe them a special debt of gratitude for their support. Although the Navy afforded me this opportunity to write, I hasten to add that these are my own views expressed herein, and not necessarily those of the Department of the Navy nor of the naval officials who so graciously provided assistance.

The academic project was undertaken at The American University, Washington, D.C., where I was given wide latitude in selecting specific disciplines to pursue. Lawrence W. Wadsworth, Grazier Memorial Professor of International Law, encouraged me to focus on the international law of the sea. Being a sailor, I found his advice easy to follow, and the work became at once a labor of love.

The international law of the sea has been in disarray since World War II, and as a result, has become a matter of basic concern to seafaring men of all flags. A key feature, and symptomatic of the disarray, has been the challenge to, and the widespread abandonment of, the three-mile limit, long dear to the hearts of Navy men. And it was for these reasons that this book, a history of the three-mile limit, came to be written.

Most of the research and writing was done in Washington. The libraries of Congress, the Supreme Court, and the Justice, State, and Defense Departments make Washington an ideal place for such study. The library of the American Society of International Law was especially useful, and Helen Philos, the Society's Librarian, has my lasting appreciation for her patient, untiring bibliographical aid. I am similarly grateful to Paul Hester of McLean, Virginia and to Glen Ruh and his staff of the U.S. Naval Institute, Annapolis, for their painstaking editorial skills. And to Professors Lawrence Wadsworth, Durward Sandifer, and Larman Wilson of The American University's School of International Service, I am deeply obligated, indeed, for they gave unselfishly and extensively of both their time and expertise, studying the manuscript and offering valuable suggestions for improvement.

Sayre A. Swarztrauber
Captain, United States Navy
Washington, D.C.
August, 1972

Introduction

To study the history of international maritime politics is to learn that the greater the maritime strength of a nation, the greater is its tendency, or at least its motivation, to control the seas. This can be, and has been, done in two ways. One method, the *mare clausum*, or closed seas, was rather crude. A state simply decreed that certain great ocean areas belonged to that state, to the exclusion of the maritime traffic of other states. A second method, *mare liberum*, or free seas, was more subtle. The seas were declared free for the navigation of all. If the declaring state's maritime assets were sufficient to protect its own interests in the face of all competition—as was the case with Rome and Britain during their respective "Pax Romana" and "Pax Britannica"—then that state controlled the seas, probably more effectively than the states that had claimed large oceans as private property.

Under this latter method, it follows that the freer the seas are, the greater the flexibility of the strong maritime powers, and the greater their opportunity to exercise control. If the coastal states of the world were to claim very narrow territorial seas along their ocean frontiers, this would maximize the area of useable seas for those states equipped to use them, whether for fishing or for commerce. Moreover, under these conditions the warships of maritime states would enjoy greater freedom of movement during hostilities or peacetime operations in the interest of their states' security.

For the simple reason that man is a land creature, the land areas are the most important to him. Likewise, those waters of the ocean nearest his coasts are the most important waters as far as he is concerned. It is there the fishing is best. The sea bottom there is more susceptible to exploitation for its sedentary sea life and mineral resources. For centuries most international trade has been conducted between coastal ports, and the important maritime battles have been fought in the vicinity of the coasts. Hence, the narrower the territorial seas of littoral states, the greater the benefits realized by the maritime powers that, using the high seas as lines of communication, have been able to take advantage of the world's coasts.

Conversely, wide territorial seas exclude ships of foreign countries from

1

the economically and strategically valuable waters closest to a state's shores. Hence, states without great naval or maritime strength have generally preferred wide territorial seas. There is an interesting trade-off in this regard between the advantages to be gained by a state in excluding foreigners from its coasts and the advantages to be gained by exploiting the coasts of other states. Periodically states have had to make this value assessment and then choose, so to speak, between *mare clausum* and *mare liberum*.

The most notable instance of *mare clausum* was the division of the world by the Pope between Spain and Portugal about half a millenium ago. And the most notable instance of *mare liberum* was the three-mile limit, the narrowest definition of the extent of territorial seas to achieve status as a rule in the law of nations.

To follow the history of the three-mile limit is, in a sense, to follow the relative power positions of the maritime states. The greatest of these states have been the most ardent defenders of the three-mile limit. The states without great fleets have been its antagonists and have argued for a wider extent of territorial seas as an alternative.

The purpose of this book is to produce a history of the three-mile limit of territorial seas as a rule of international law. The study will ascertain and document the conditions under which the rule came into existence, the course of, and reasons for, its rise to paramountcy, and the circumstances that led to its demise.

The significance of such an undertaking lies chiefly in its timing. That the three-mile limit did emerge and exist as a rule of international law scarcely needs proving, although in the course of this book that will be accomplished for reasons of completeness. The demise of the rule, however, does deserve a thorough documentation. Almost traditionally in jurisprudence, there have been laws—both national and international—that have lingered on the books long after they have served their usefulness, being ignored, sometimes even for decades, until quietly repealed. Essentially, such is the case with the three-mile limit. *De facto*, it is no longer the law of nations; *de jure*, it remains on some statute books, simply awaiting final interment.

No indication can be found that a history of the three-mile limit has been undertaken by any other writer, especially in an Italic or Germanic language. This study is believed to be the first. However, numerous valuable and comprehensive works dealing generally with the law of the sea have been written, such as those by C. John Colombos, and by Myres S. McDougal and William T. Burke.[1] Each of these devotes a generous number of pages to the matter of territorial seas. Then, too, there have been several very useful treatises focusing more closely on the more restricted topic of territorial seas. Foremost among them is that by Philip C. Jessup. The Norwegian publicist Arnold Raestad, the French publicist Joseph B. Imbart de Latour, and the British publicist Thomas Fulton produced similarly excellent works, from differing

---

1 Colombos, *The International Law of the Sea;* McDougal and Burke, *The Public Order of the Oceans.*

European points of view.[2] These works treat the subject both historically and conceptually, and each considers the three-mile rule at length. Finally, on the subject of the three-mile rule itself, several highly informative essays and papers have been published, dealing with specific aspects of the rule. In this category are those by Bernard Heinzen, Thomas Baty, and H. S. K. Kent, which have appeared in law journals.[3]

These related works, and certainly many others, were consulted in the course of the study, and in varying degrees they influenced the writer. In fact, not a great deal is written here that has not already been recorded elsewhere in different form, in related and unrelated contexts. But unlike the works which have preceded it, this book gathers pertinent information and data concerning the three-mile limit from all available sources, and organizes it in historical sequence, utilizing the three-mile rule itself as the central theme.

TERMINOLOGY

Most of the terminology in this study is common and self-explanatory, or is adequately defined in standard dictionaries. But there are instances where writers on international maritime law have used different expressions to describe the same thing. These must be mentioned in order to eliminate confusion.

TERRITORIAL SEA

The *territorial sea* is that belt of the sea adjacent to the coast of a state, beyond its land territory and its internal waters, over which the sovereignty of the state extends. However, it seems as if there have been as many attempts to apply terminology to this belt of waters as there have been attempts to establish its limits.

The term *territorial sea* (or *seas*) is very common and is also very old. Ferdinand Perels (German publicist, 1836–1903) used the term, but also employed *maritime territory* synonymously. Philip C. Jessup preferred *territorial waters;* he named his book accordingly. Certain writers object to the use of *territory*, and maintain that the state's jurisdiction over this belt of water is not quite as extensive as that exercised over land territory. Sir Travers Twiss (English jurist, 1809–1897) circumvented the notion of territory by

---

2 Jessup, *The Law of Territorial Waters and Maritime Jurisdiction;* Raestad, *La mer territoriale;* Imbart de Latour, *La mer territoriale au point de vue théorique et pratique;* Fulton, *The Sovereignty of the Sea.* The term "publicist" is used throughout this book in its traditional sense—a person who is an expert writing on international law.

3 Heinzen, "The Three-Mile Limit: Preserving the Freedom of the Seas" (this article includes a well-documented, 45-page historical summary of the three-mile rule); Baty, "The Three-Mile Limit"; Kent, "The Historical Origins of the Three-Mile Limit."

using *jurisdictional waters*. For the same reason, Henri J. F. X. Bonfils (French jurisconsult, 1835–1897) used interchangeably *jurisdictional seas* and *littoral seas*. *Littoral sea* also appears in the work of the Swiss publicist Alphonse Rivier (1835–1898) on an equal basis with *adjacent sea* or *mare proximum*. The more famous Swiss publicist, Emmerich de Vattel (1714–1767), preferred *marginal waters*. Two centuries later, William E. Masterson used similar words, *marginal seas*, in the title of a book. Another book title, *La mer côtière (The Coastal Sea)*, reflects the preference of French publicist Paul Godey. Similarly inclined, the German writer Frans von Liszt called the belt *coastal waters*. And German-born British publicist Lassa Oppenheim referred to the maritime belt simply as *maritime belt*. Examination of the texts of these writers reveals that, despite their varying terminology, they all had the same thing in mind, namely, the water defined previously as *territorial seas*.[4]

The League of Nations Preparatory Committee for the Codification Conference, in drafting the bases of discussion for the 1930 Hague Conference, selected *territorial waters*. Almost ironically, considering the failure of the Conference to reach agreement on the substantive issues, the delegates chose to manipulate semantics by enacting: "The Committee on Territorial Waters felt that the expression 'territorial sea' was more appropriate."[5] The United Nations, through its International Law Commission, has followed this lead by consistently referring to the *territorial sea* throughout its literature and conferences on the subject. This book, likewise, relies on *territorial sea* whenever confusion might result through the use of another term.

INTERNAL WATERS

A terminology problem also develops in association with those waters wholly within a state, such as lakes, harbors, bays, and rivers. *Internal waters, national waters, interior waters,* and *inland waters* are all found in contemporary usage in this regard.

Internal waters has found favor among a majority of the nations as evidenced by its inclusion in the 1958 Geneva Convention on the Territorial Sea and Contiguous Zone. Colombos, on the other hand, referred to these waters as *national* or *interior* waters. Paul Godey was of the opinion that these waters—ports, bays, and closed seas—should be called the *territorial* seas, in that they are bona fide territory. As indicated earlier, he recommended *coastal* for those waters along the coast, which are now routinely called territorial

4 Perels, *Manuel de droit maritime international*, p. 24; Twiss, *The Law of Nations Considered as Independent Political Communities*, p. 293; Bonfils, *Manuel de droit international public*, p. 322; Rivier, *Principes du droit des gens*, vol. I, p. 145; de Vattel, *The Law of Nations*, p. 109; Masterson, *Jurisdiction in Marginal Seas with Special Reference to Smuggling*; Godey, *La mer côtière*; von Liszt, *Das völkerrecht, systematisch dargestellt*, p. 86, translated in Crocker, *The Extent of the Marginal Sea*, p. 292; Oppenheim, *International Law*, vol. I, p. 255.
5 League of Nations, *Final Act, Conference for the Codification of International Law, The Hague, March-April 1930*, p. 183.

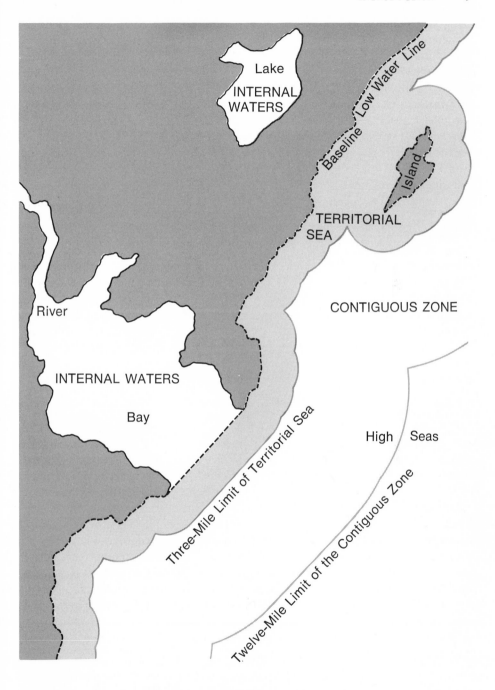

The Three-Mile Limit of Territorial Sea

seas. Herbert Briggs, among others, indicated still another preference in his choice of *inland waters*.[6]

There is ample opportunity for ambiguity in the use of the latter term, inasmuch as it is used in the United States' Inland Rules of the Nautical Road to define certain navigable waters in and near the United States. While some of these *inland waters* are well within the maritime boundary of United States territorial seas, others extend well beyond and far into the high seas, especially along the New England and Florida coasts.[7]

Further confusion arises because of certain writers' collective reference to all waters under the jurisdiction of a state as *national* waters or *territorial* waters, including both *internal* and *coastal* waters. And while there are other instances of conflicting terminology, these remarks should suffice to demonstrate that there has been no universal agreement on a standard nomenclature. In this book, *internal waters* is used wherever misinterpretation is possible.

CONTIGUOUS ZONE

During the past several decades there has come into vogue a relatively new term, *contiguous zone*, used to describe generally the waters at the maritime frontiers of littoral states. Today it is used to define a belt of water adjacent to, and extending to seaward beyond, the territorial sea, in which the state exercises certain special jurisdiction to prevent violation of its customs, immigration, navigation, and sanitary laws and regulations, to list the most important of them. While this zone is part of the high seas, it is measured from the baseline on the coast in the same manner as is the territorial sea. This is approximately the definition adopted by the United Nations Geneva Conference of 1958 and reflects little change since the earliest usage of the term. The 1958 Geneva Conference also set the maximum limit of the contiguous zone at 12 miles measured from the same baseline used to delimit the territorial seas.[8]

BASELINE

The *baseline* is the continuous point of origin along the coast from which the territorial sea is measured. Quite obviously, along a relatively straight coast, the baseline is easy to delimit; for centuries most states have agreed that it should be the low-water line. The problems arise in drawing a baseline along irregular coastlines with many indentations or fringe islands; for by

6   Colombos, *Law of the Sea*, p. 78; Godey, *La mer côtière*, pp. 7–8; Briggs, *The Law of Nations*, p. 289.
7   Farwell, *The Rules of the Nautical Road*, pp. 389–399; Wentworth, *Knight's Modern Seamanship*, pp. 297–298. See also Chapter 13.
8   United Nations, *Convention on the Territorial Sea and the Contiguous Zone*, Article 24.

definition, to landward of the baseline are the internal waters, and to seaward lies the territorial sea belt.

MEASUREMENT

Statute mile. The word *mile* comes to us from the Latin of ancient Rome, *milia passuum,* or 1,000 paces, measuring about 1,620 yards. In current English usage, the measure is slightly longer, 1,760 yards (5,280 feet or 1,609.35 meters), and is referred to as the *statute* or *English mile.*

Nautical and geographic miles. In navigation and astronomy the word *mile* was adopted because it was a familiar term, associated with measuring distances, and coincidentally, almost equal to the statute mile. Nevertheless, the nautical mile is derived from the measurement of arc on the earth's surface and is only secondarily a measure of linear distance. A nautical mile equals one minute of latitude, or one-sixtieth of a degree. This measure, also called *sea* mile, *air* mile, and in England, *Admiralty* mile, equals 2,025.37 yards (6,076.10 feet or 1,852 meters). It equals about 1.15 or one and a seventh of a statute mile. Because the earth is oblate, its equatorial diameter is slightly greater than its polar diameter. A nautical mile is sometimes erroneously defined as one minute of the arc at the equator. Rather, that unit is properly called a *geographic* mile, equal to 2,029.03 yards (6,087.08 feet or 1,855 meters). This difference between a nautical mile and a geographic mile is obviously negligible.[9]

Metric system. Infrequently, states that use the metric system have expressed the extent of their offshore customs jurisdiction in terms of that system. In such cases, the measure used has been the kilometer (1,000 meters or .621 statute miles), or the myriameter (10,000 meters or 6.21 statute miles). It should be recalled that the metric system is properly a substitute only for land measurement, a statute mile, and that states which use the metric system must still use nautical miles in matters of navigation and astronomy. In almost all cases they measure their territorial seas in nautical miles.

Marine league. The *marine league* is generally equal to three nautical miles, and consequently became virtually interchangeable with *three-mile limit* in some state papers and in the writings of several publicists. The marine league will be considered in greater detail later.

THE THREE-MILE LIMIT

The three-mile limit under international law can be defined as the limitation of the seaward extension of a coastal state's territorial jurisdiction at the outer boundary of a zone of water extending three miles from the shore of that

9 Hill, *Dutton's Navigation and Nautical Astronomy,* pp. 10–11.

state. The miles are nautical miles, and they are measured from the low-water mark.

ORGANIZATION OF THIS BOOK

History is never so simple that its writing can be reduced to a straight-line approach. Related events, occurring simultaneously, must be treated separately, in parallel, in order to avoid an utterly disjointed narrative. This has been true to a degree even with a subject as restricted as the three-mile limit. Nevertheless, wherever possible, this book follows a simple chronological narrative.

The first chapter provides the historical background from ancient times to the period of the Renaissance. The following three chapters deal respectively with three antecedents of the three-mile limit as they developed separately but concurrently during the sixteenth, seventeenth, and eighteenth centuries. Next, the three-mile limit is traced chronologically in five chapters from its eighteenth-century origins until World War II, one chapter among these being devoted to competing views and practice. The post-World War II period is dealt with in three chapters: the controversy over the extent of territorial seas, the involvement of the United Nations, and the demise of the three-mile rule. A concluding chapter completes the work.

Within each major topical or chronological subdivision, and where practical, the first things considered are the actual practice of states—court decisions, laws, treaties, and the like—and then the work of publicists and learned societies. In considering the practice of states, the relatively important maritime powers only are covered for the period up to 1930. For until that time it was solely the major maritime powers that shaped the law of territorial seas. Thereafter, the lesser powers, even nonmaritime states, began to exert an impact on that law. In considering the work of publicists, both objective and subjective materials are found. Not only do they report the *de facto* law of nations as practiced by states, citing and quoting valuable references and materials, but they also advance their opinions *de lege ferenda*, or what they believe the law should be.

In studying the events of recent times, the activity of international organizations is seen as a significant factor in the development of the law of territorial seas. The United Nations has served as a medium for the conclusion of multilateral conventions on the subject and, as such, assumes a role in the actual practice of states. Also, in the case of draft conventions or conventions that fail to receive the necessary ratifications, and in the case of the work of the International Law Commission, the United Nations can be said to be playing the role *de lege ferenda*.

SOURCES

The concept of territorial seas was developed in Europe long before the United States commenced amassing its present abundance of primary source material in the nation's capital. Primary sources for the period through the eighteenth century are located, by and large, in the archives of the capitals of Europe. For that period, the writer relied on historians and publicists who had access to and utilized those sources. For the period following the American Revolution, United States Government publications—chiefly those of the State Department and the Congress—were considered. For the period since 1920, the voluminous documentation from the prolific agencies of the League of Nations and the United Nations was used.

There are certain sources that, because of the writer's special indebtedness, should be expressly mentioned here. The ancient period was especially well examined and documented by Percy Fenn. Frances Davenport prepared a collection of documents for the Carnegie Institution of Washington that greatly facilitated the study of the fifteenth and sixteenth centuries. The cannon-shot rule, the line-of-sight doctrine, and the Scandinavian league were most effectively covered by Wyndham Walker, Paul Godey, and Arnold Raestad, respectively. H. S. K. Kent's article on the origins of the three-mile limit was very useful.[10] In 1919, Henry G. Crocker compiled for the U.S. Department of State an exceedingly valuable—over 700 pages of fine print—collection of writings, conventions, national legislative acts, decrees, regulations, treaties, and other state documents relating to the extent of territorial waters, the bulk of which covered the eighteenth and nineteenth centuries.[11] This was the most valuable of all sources of data uncovered during the course of this research. But almost as useful for the nineteenth century period was the comprehensive United States Senate twelve-volume report of the North Atlantic Fisheries Arbitration.[12]

For the early twentieth century, a most valuable work was that of William E. Masterson.[13] The League of Nations documents, especially those associated with the 1930 Hague Codification Conference, were the best sources for the interwar period. Similarly, for the post-World War II period, the documents of the United Nations, most particularly those associated with the Geneva Conferences on the Law of the Sea, provided the most lucrative and useful source of materials.

10 Fenn, "Justinian and the Freedom of the Sea"; Davenport, *European Treaties Bearing on the History of the United States and its Dependencies to 1648;* Walker, "Territorial Waters: The Cannon Shot Rule"; Godey, *La mer côtière;* Raestad, *La mer territoriale;* Kent, "Historical Origins."
11 Crocker, *Marginal Sea.*
12 United States Congress, Senate, *Proceedings in the North Atlantic Coast Fisheries Arbitration.*
13 Masterson, *Jurisdiction in Marginal Seas.*

CHAPTER 1

Historical Background of the Concept of Territorial Seas

THE MEDIEVAL PERIOD

The three-mile limit of territorial seas, as a rule of international law, did not surface until the eighteenth century, but the concept of territorial seas had developed much earlier. By way of further introduction, a summary of the pertinent world events and international political thought bearing on the development of this rubric of international law is undertaken in this and the following three chapters.

ITALIAN MARITIME SUPREMACY: THIRTEENTH AND FOURTEENTH CENTURIES

Since medieval times the issue of free seas versus closed seas has gone full cycle. Roman law laid down that the sea is *communis omnium naturali jure*, or by nature, common to all mankind, and not susceptible of possession in the same manner as land. Probably the earliest formal pronouncement concerning the legal status of seas is found in the second century writings of the Roman jurist Marcianus, as preserved in the Digest of Justinian (483–565). This pronouncement declared simply that the sea and the fish in it were open or common to all men. There was no extension of state jurisdiction from the shore to seaward, and the shore was defined as the high-water mark of the flood tide. These very liberal views were incorporated into the Justinian Code promulgated in 529 A.D.[1]

During those early times, when Rome firmly ruled the Mediterranean, the matter of control of, or sovereignty over, the seas was not particularly im-

[1] Fenn, "Justinian and the Freedom of the Sea." Fenn includes a detailed account of this period, well documented, with a generous bibliography. See also Meurer, *The Program of the Freedom of the Seas*, chap. I.

portant, or at least not contested. However, during the Middle Ages, with the growth of maritime commerce and competition, the waters of the Mediterranean and the coasts of western Europe became the subject of conflicting claims. Kings and princes of littoral states started to claim sovereignty over the waters adjacent to their land territory. Venice, which rose to dominate the Mediterranean and Near East trade routes to the Orient, demanded fees beginning in the year 1269 from all vessels sailing in the Adriatic; and they maintained control there until the seventeenth century.[2]

During the following century, there commenced the literary defense of such practice. Bartolus de Sassoferrato (1314–1357), an Italian jurist and professor at Pisa and Perugia, and one of the most famous and oft-quoted jurists of the Middle Ages, wrote a short treatise introducing a specific extent of seaward jurisdiction, 100 miles. The 100-mile limit widely attributed to Bartolus has been derived from his statements on offshore islands. He held that offshore islands belong to a province when they are within a moderate distance from the coast. He defined a "moderate" distance as 100 miles and maintained that the province should exercise jurisdiction within this distance. The coastal state's "imperium" (to use his own word) 100 miles in width, according to Bartolus, was something less than a two-day journey at sea.[3] Such a width, of course, was more than enough to make the Adriatic an Italian sea. A pupil of Bartolus, who became equally famous as a teacher, Baldus de Ubaldis (1327–1400), agreed on a wide extent of territorial waters, but held that its limit was 60 miles.[4]

Not to be outdone by their Venetian competitors, the Genoese, across the Italian peninsula, staked a claim of sovereignty over the Ligurian Gulf (now Sea). As late as the seventeenth century, a decision of the Supreme Court of Piedmont was recorded, citing Bartolus and Baldus as basis for the court's finding, which approved the action of a Savoyan man-of-war that had stopped a Spanish ship bound for Naples, in the Ligurian Sea, at a distance of 50 miles from the port of Monaco.[5]

PORTUGUESE MARITIME SUPREMACY: FIFTEENTH CENTURY

In western and northern Europe there were similar claims over large sea areas. The Danes, Swedes, and Poles claimed various parts of the Baltic; the English claimed the Narrow Seas (English Channel), the North Sea, and the waters around the British Isles within an arc drawn from Cape Finisterre

2 De Lapradelle, "Le droit de l'état sur la mer territoriale," p. 266.
3 Schücking, Das Küstenmeer im Internationalen Rechte, p. 6, quoting Bartolus' Tractatus: Tyberidis sive de fluminibus, in vol. VI of his Opera, p. 146, translated in Crocker, Marginal Sea, p. 424.
4 Imbart de Latour, La mer territoriale, p. 29; de Cussy, Phases et causes célèbres du droit maritime des nations, vol. I, p. 91; and Olivart, Tratado de derecho internacional público, vol. I, p. 203, all translated in Crocker, Marginal Sea, pp. 250, 49, and 334 respectively.
5 Schücking, Küstenmeer, p. 6, citing Cacheranus, Decisiones Senatus Pedemontani, p. 155.

in Spain to North Cape in Norway. These claims reached their greatest extravagance when Portugal, and later Spain, made their debut in maritime affairs. Under the leadership of Prince Henry the Navigator (1394–1460), the west coast of Africa was explored by Portugal. On January 8, 1455, Pope Nicholas V expressed his approval and great pleasure with the Portuguese effort by issuing the papal bull *Romanus Pontifex*, which, ". . . seeking and desiring the salvation of all . . . ," granted for the first time, to the Portuguese, the exclusive and permanent rights to the lands of Africa from Cueta to Guinea and "beyond, towards that southern shore."[6] The Portuguese did not ignore this blank check to build an empire in the name of converting heathens. By 1486, Bartholomew Diaz reached the Cape of Good Hope, and in 1498, Vasco Da Gama sailed around the Cape, up the east coast of Africa, and across the Arabian Sea to India, and thus opened up an alternate, all-ocean, trade route to the Orient.

THE SIXTEENTH CENTURY: IBERIAN MONOPOLY OF THE SEAS

SPAIN RISES TO MARITIME PARAMOUNTCY

The papal bulls. Soon the Spanish discoveries in America were to be similarly lauded and rewarded by a later Pope, Alexander VI. When news of Columbus's discoveries reached the Portuguese King, John II, the latter became suspicious that the New World lands might be within his vast, only partially explored, southern realm of "Guinea and the Guinean Sea," possibly even part of the "southern shore" mentioned in the papal bull *Romanus Pontifex*. When John II prepared an armada to take possession of Columbus's discoveries, the Spanish sovereigns, Ferdinand and Isabella, quickly notified Pope Alexander VI (Rodrigo Borgia). The Pope, in arbitrating the dispute, issued several papal bulls that were most favorable to Spain. The Pope's close ties to Spain and the Spanish crown may have influenced his decisions in issuing the bulls. Pope Alexander VI was a native of Valencia, Spain and is generally regarded as one of the most corrupt and unscrupulous of the pontiffs.[7] In the first of this series of bulls, the bull *Inter Caetera* of May 3, 1493, the Pope assigned the lands in question, and all future lands to be discovered, to Spain, but with a clause safeguarding the pontifical concessions previously made to Portugal and excepting any other lands already possessed by a Christian owner. In another bull, *Inter Caetera* of May 4, 1493, the Pope was more specific and even more favorable to Spain, granting her the exclusive right to all territories west of a demarcation line drawn ". . . from the Arctic pole, namely the north, to the Antarctic pole, namely the south . . . the said line to be distant one hundred leagues towards the west and south from any of the islands commonly known as the Azores and Cape Verde." The demarcation

---

6 For the complete text, Latin and English, see Davenport, *European Treaties*, pp. 13–26.
7 *Ibid.*, pp. 56 and "Alexander," *Encyclopaedia Britannica* (1953 edition), I, 599.

line was approximately at the 35° west meridian, passing between Greenland and Iceland and then straight south, dividing the Atlantic. This bull did not include the clause safeguarding Portugal. Moreover, it prohibited anyone, at the penalty of excommunication, ". . . to go for the purpose of trade or any other reason to the islands or mainlands, found and to be found . . ." west of the line of demarcation without Spanish permission.[8]

The Treaty of Tordesillas. That the Portuguese felt aggrieved by this partiality is not surprising. For one thing, they felt that a line only 100 leagues to the west of their Azores and Cape Verde possessions did not give them enough maneuvering room around those frequently visited island territories. Accordingly, Portugal asked Spain to agree to a line farther west, one-half way between the Cape Verde Islands and Columbus's new territories. Secretly, King John "was certain that within those limits famous lands and things must be found."[9] Apparently to obtain Portuguese recognition of their American claims, the Spanish agreed to a new demarcation meridian 370 leagues west of the Cape Verde Islands, or at approximately 45° west longitude. The Treaty of Tordesillas was concluded in June, 1494, and ratified that September. More equitable than the papal bulls, the treaty provided that all lands to the east of the line would be Portuguese and those to the west, Spanish. Although not specifically so stated, this treaty implied a division of the globe into two equal hemispheres, a feature lacking, and obviously not intended, in the papal bulls.

More important from a maritime point of view, the Treaty of Tordesillas also included language dealing with the seas, strongly implying the notion of outright ownership of the high seas by the two sovereigns. In order to reach the Americas, Spanish ships had to cross through the Portuguese waters east of the line. The treaty provided for such passage, permitting Spanish ships

> . . . to sail in either direction, freely, securely, and peacefully, over the said seas of the said King of Portugal, and within the said line . . . They shall take their courses direct to the desired region and for any purpose desired therein and shall not leave their course, unless compelled to do so by contrary weather.[10]

This wording is strikingly similar to that used today in defining the doctrine of innocent passage.

The Treaty of Tordesillas was a bonanza for Portugal, because the new, westerly displaced line of demarcation passed through eastern Brazil. When discovered some years later, it was in the Portuguese, no longer Spanish, hemisphere, confirming King John's optimistic speculation. After Tordesillas,

8 For complete texts of these bulls, see Davenport, *European Treaties,* pp. 56–63 and 71–83.
9 *Ibid.,* p. 84.
10 *Ibid.,* p. 97. For full text, Spanish and English, see pp. 86–100.

and during the sixteenth century, the Portuguese and Spanish extensively explored and colonized their territories: the Portuguese in Africa, Persia, India, the East Indies, and Brazil; the Spanish in North, Central, and South America, and the West Indies.

In spite of the broad scope of agreements reached, the sixteenth century was fraught with disputes and disagreements over the treaty's interpretation and implementation. For example, there was one quarrel concerning the number of leagues in an equatorial degree, and another concerning the exact location of the Cape Verde Islands. Later, there was a bitter disagreement when attempting to fix the exact location of the Moluccas Islands (Spice Islands) of the East Indies. These islands had been discovered in 1512 by the Portuguese captain, Magellan, who in 1518 transferred his allegiance to Spain. Both states heatedly claimed that the islands lay on their respective sides of the demarcation line.[11] (Actually, the reciprocal of the demarcation line, or the 135° east meridian, placed the islands just inside the Portuguese sector.)

Views of Vitoria. Although Italian writers had risen to the defense of Italian claims of jurisdiction over extensive sea areas, there was apparently no such move among writers in Spain and Portugal. In fact, the reverse seems true. Probably the most distinguished sixteenth-century writer on international law expressed righteous indignation at the sweeping claims of Spain and Portugal. This was, ironically, Francisco Vitoria (1480–1546), a Spanish theologian and lawyer, of the Order of the Dominicans. Although the Dominicans had generally been faithful to the Holy See,[12] Vitoria, writing in 1532, challenged the authority of the Pope to grant the New World empire; he challenged the Pope's temporal authority over the Indians in the New World; he challenged the Spanish Emperor's right to seize lands occupied by the Indians; and he held that extension of the Empire was not a just cause to wage war on the Indians. He went on to explain that

> . . . the Spaniards have a right to travel into the lands in question and to sojourn there, provided they do no harm to the natives, and the natives may not prevent them . . . [I]t would not be lawful for the French to prevent the Spanish from traveling or even from living in France, or vice versa . . . Thou shalt not do to another what thou wouldest not wish done to thyself.[13]

The spirit of free movement and commerce evident in these passages later led Grotius to invoke Vitoria as an authority when he protested the concept of sovereignty over the high seas; conversely, Selden, in defending such a concept, took exception to the views of Vitoria.[14]

11 *Ibid.*, pp. 85, 118–198. These pages contain treaties and draft treaties, annotated, documenting the attempts to settle the issues.
12 Victoria (Italian version of name), *De Indus et de Iure Belli Relectiones*, p. 75, introductory remarks by Ernest Nys.
13 Victoria, *De Indus*, pp. 129–149, 151–153.
14 *Ibid.*, pp. 96–97 (Nys' Introduction), and Nussbaum, *A Concise History of the Law of Nations*, p. 62.

NORTHERN EUROPEAN STATES CONTEST IBERIAN DOMINION OVER THE SEAS

France. Whereas Portugal had led all other states in maritime prowess during the fifteenth century, the Spanish came to the fore in the sixteenth century, with the exploitation of Mexico and Peru. But it was also during the sixteenth century that the French, English, and Dutch made their bid to wrest control of the seas from the Iberian powers. The French corsairs, in particular, began to plague both Spanish and Portuguese mariners early in the century. This, of course, brought reprisals on French shipping. The French and Spanish, especially, collided when the French attempted to establish a colony in Florida and commenced attacking Spanish treasure ships and settlements in the West Indies. The French maintained that the seas were *res communes*—free for all to use—and would not agree to being excluded on the basis of the papal bulls. The two powers concluded a treaty at Crépy-en-Laonnois in 1544 wherein the Spanish agreed that the French could sail to the West Indies for trade but not colonization.[15] Yet, the French corsairs continued to plunder the "Spanish" Indies. Likewise, British sailors scorned the Spanish claim to a monopoly of the Atlantic, and ceaselessly and increasingly committed piracy against the Spanish ships during the latter part of the sixteenth century.

It was during this Franco-Spanish rivalry that the renowned French publicist, Jean Bodin (1530–1596), published *De République.* Writing in the year 1576, he adopted the view of Baldus and fixed the limit of territorial seas at 60 miles,[16] explicitly referring to the Court of Piedmont's decision in the case of the Savoyan ship, cited earlier.

Scandinavia. The Scandinavian states of the sixteenth century numbered two: The Kingdom of Denmark and Norway and the Kingdom of Sweden. Scandinavians in general had historically been seafaring peoples; the Norwegians and Danes somewhat more so than the Swedes, probably because of their Atlantic seaboard. State papers indicate that the Dano-Norwegians were actively involved in international maritime legal matters as early as the sixteenth century. Although they did not keep pace with France, Holland, and England in naval or commercial maritime strength, their extensive fishing enterprises and their co-location with those powers on the North Sea involved

15 Davenport, *European Treaties,* pp. 205–209, 220.
16 Fenn, "Origins of the Theory of Territorial Waters," p. 479, citing Bodin, *Les six livres de république de I. Bodin Anquein,* bk. I, chap. X. There is considerable disagreement among publicists on the extent of territorial seas advocated by Bodin. In the Latin version, Bodin wrote 60 miles (". . . ut sexaginta miliaribus a littore . . ."). The French version, which appeared about the same time, reads 30 leagues (". . . iusque a XXX lieuïs loing de sa terre . . ."). The writers Bynkershoek, de Cussy, Imbart de Latour, Olivart, and Schücking cite Bodin's 60 miles. Vattel and de Lapradelle cite 30 leagues. Professor Nicholas M. Matte (*Deux frontières invisibles: de la mer territoriale à l'air territorial*) equates Bodin's 30 leagues to 90 miles. This inconsistency may stem from the varied interpretations of "league," a term often confused in writings on maritime law. In antiquity, the French league varied between two and four miles. It is now three miles.

them in matters of territorial seas. As early as May 10, 1598, the following Danish ordinance was deemed necessary and promulgated:

> If any English vessels, contrary to the orders of the king, are found hovering and fishing in the waters between Vespenø and Iceland, or two Norwegian leagues (uker sjøs) northeast from Vespenø, make all haste possible to capture them and bring them to Copenhagen.[17]

Holland. The Dutch, too, entered the international maritime scene during the sixteenth century, but with more vigor. Holland, comprised of the northernmost of the Netherlands provinces, revolted in 1567 and began a protracted war of resistance against the Spanish crown. In 1581, under William the Silent, Holland declared its independence from Spain, a status not recognized by the latter until the Treaty of Westphalia in 1648.

The revolutionary events in Holland, fortunately for that country, coincided with Spain's invasion and annexation of Portugal in 1580. For sixty years, until 1640, Spain occupied Portugal and managed her foreign affairs. This, coupled with the closing of the port of Lisbon in 1599, left certain sectors of the Portuguese empire to the mercy of the trade-hungry Dutch. Holland proceeded at once to take control of the East Indies and displace Portugal as the primary maritime power in the eastern hemisphere.

England. The British, for their part, defeated the Spanish Armada in 1588. This was clearly a turning point in maritime affairs, representing both the decline of Spain and the rise of England. Both the British and French were eager to move in and fill the vacuum left by Spain in the western hemisphere; and both did, colonizing North America throughout the seventeenth century. Joining forces with the United Netherlands (Holland), England and France formed an offensive and defensive league against Spain in 1596, designed among other things to strip Spain of her dominions.[18] Another treaty was concluded between England and the United Netherlands in 1598, this one paving the way for an English and Dutch condominium over the seas.[19] However, there were strong disagreements among Queen Elizabeth's advisors on the matter of concluding this treaty. Those opposed to the treaty foresaw the Dutch growing rich and powerful, posing a competitive threat to the British;[20] their warnings were a premonition of the Anglo-Dutch dispute over the control of the seas which was to characterize the following century.

Publicists. It was during this time, late in the sixteenth century, that the first important English writings on the matter of public maritime law were

---

17 Crocker, *Marginal Sea*, p. 513. His footnote reads: "Translation. For Norwegian text, see Arnold Raestad, *Kongens Strǿmme*, p. 195."
18 Davenport, *European Treaties*, pp. 229–234, quoting text of Treaty of the Hague, October 31, 1596.
19 *Ibid.*, pp. 239–242, quoting text of Treaty of Westminster of August 6/16, 1598.
20 *Ibid.*, p. 239.

undertaken, those of Alberico Gentili (1552–1608). Gentili was an Italian lawyer who, in 1579, fled Italy in company with his father to escape the Holy Inquisition, which later sentenced them in absentia to life imprisonment on charges of heresy. In 1580, Gentili chose England for his self-imposed exile. There he rapidly rose in favor as a teacher and jurist. In 1605, he was appointed as advocate before the English Court of Admiralty to represent the interests of Philip III of Spain. While serving as counsel for Spain, he acquired a considerable knowledge in maritime matters, especially in the mutual rights and duties of belligerent and neutral powers—especially concerning the warring Dutch and Spanish. Not only were the Dutch and Spanish in a state of war because of the Dutch declaration of independence from Spain, there was also the matter of the Dutch incursions into the Portuguese East Indies. Ironically, Spain, having occupied Portugal, had to take on the additional burden of defending the Portuguese colonies and ships against the Dutch. From this base, Gentili wrote *Pleas of a Spanish Advocate*, which he personally considered the best of his several books and manuscripts.[21]

From a twentieth-century perspective, his writings on the seas are most curious, even ambiguous. Starting from the premise of freedom of the seas, wherein ". . . it be said that the sea is common,"[22] he proceeded to impose heavy restrictions on that freedom. He invoked the prestige of Bartolus—who had advocated a 100-mile breadth—in defending the British claims to the sea areas adjacent to England (English Channel, North Sea, etc.). The following excerpts, from the same passage cited, offer a representative sampling of his views on British dominion over the coastal waters:

> . . . the word territory was applied equally to land and to water. . . .

> . . . And you see how the sway of our King extends far toward the south, the north, and the west . . . And thus, immeasurable is the broad jurisdiction of our King upon the sea.

Even over the high seas, which he maintained are "common," he attributed to his king a "jurisdiction," apparently to enable him to take measures against pirates, privateers, and possibly others:

> Nor is this jurisdiction maintained by the enforcement of a certain royal edict in which certain boundaries are laid down, beyond which the King refuses to have his territorial power extended in connection with these acts of war between the Spaniards and the Dutch.

Obviously, in the words of Arthur Nussbaum, ". . . his opinions agree perfectly with the interest of that great sea power, England."[23]

---

21 Van der Molen, *Alberico Gentili and the Development of International Law*, p. 59.
22 Gentili, *Hispanicae Advocationis Libri Duo*, p. 35.
23 Nussbaum, *Law of Nations*, pp. 81–82.

Another writer of the time, Frà Paolo Sarpi (1552–1623), Italian prelate, historian, and member of the Order of Servites, espoused the view that a state ought to exercise dominion over coastal waters to ". . . an extent equal to that which was necessary to the power of the State, but that injuries to other States were to be avoided."[24]

THE SEVENTEENTH CENTURY: OPEN OR CLOSED SEAS?

Such then, was the general background at the turn of the sixteenth century; the seventeenth century ushered in a new set of circumstances and actors. Spain and Portugal had completed their roles as the principals; now it was to be England and Holland, with the French and Scandinavians, although very interested in the proceedings, not as directly involved.

HOLLAND: MARE LIBERUM

The Dutch East India Company. As previously mentioned, the Port of Lisbon was closed in 1599, and the Dutch opportunistically seized control of the East Indies. By 1598, the Dutch had established themselves in Mauritius in the Indian Ocean, and shortly thereafter, settled in Java and the Moluccas. In 1602, the Dutch East India Company was founded. As it sought to trade in the East Indies, it met with the armed resistance of the Portuguese (then under Spanish rule), abortively attempting to hold those colonies and to exclude all others from the Indian Ocean on the authority of the papal bull of 1493. This trade confrontation led to much bitterness, culminating in the seizure by the Dutch East India Company of a Portuguese galleon as prize.[25]

Hugo Grotius. The defense of this action on the part of the Dutch East India Company came from the pen of Hugo Grotius (1583–1645), Dutch jurist, publicist, and statesman. His brilliance and works had made him famous while still an adolescent. At fifteen, he was a member of the staff of the Dutch embassy in France, where King Henry IV referred to him as "the miracle of Holland." A year later, he received the degree of Doctor of Laws from the University of Orleans.[26] There is considerable evidence that Grotius was then retained by the Dutch East India Company to write a legal opinion concerning the capture of the Portuguese galleon. There was opposition in

24 Nys, *Le droit international,* vol. I, p. 498, translated in Crocker, *Marginal Sea,* p. 325. Also Imbart de Latour, *La mer territoriale* p. 29; and Bonfils, *Manuel de droit international public,* p. 322, translated in Crocker, *Marginal Sea,* p. 11. The writers had reference to Frà Paolo Sarpi, *Domino del mar Adriatico della serenissima republica de Venetia* (vol. VI of *Opere del padre Paolo dell' ordine de' servi: e theologo della serenissima republica di Venetia*).
25 Grotius, *The Freedom of the Seas (Mare Liberum) or the Right which Belongs to the Dutch to Take Part in the East Indian Trade,* p. vii (James Brown Scott's "Introductory Note").
26 Nussbaum, *Law of Nations,* p. 97.

Holland, even within the Company, against the capture, and the Company needed a scholarly, well-documented treatise justifying the seizure in order to sway opinion favorably towards their policies. So, during the winter of 1604–1605, Grotius wrote his *On the Law of Spoils* (*De Jure Praedae*), fully vindicating the action of the East India Company.

This matter was researched extensively by Robert Fruin, a history professor at the University of Leyden. He determined that Grotius had frequent and close ties with the Dutch East India Company. *De Jure Praedae*, according to Fruin, was initially and solely a legal brief, prepared by Grotius acting as a counsel for the company at the time of the seizure of the galleon.[27]

In 1608, the Dutch entered into truce negotiations with the Spanish. The latter tried to pressure the Dutch into renouncing their East Indian trade, whereupon the Company, in a letter of November 4, 1608, requested Grotius to detach and publish Chapter XII of his manuscript, *De Jure Praedae*, which dealt with the freedom of the seas. This was done anonymously under the title, *Mare Liberum*. The remainder was not published until two and a half centuries later (1868).

In *Mare Liberum*, Grotius challenged the Portuguese title to Java and the Moluccas on the basis ". . . that the act of discovery is sufficient to give a clear title of sovereignty only when it is accompanied by actual possession." He denied the temporal power of the Pope in declaring, "Trade with the East Indies does not belong to the Portuguese by virtue of title based on the Papal Donation. . . . For no one can give away what he does not himself possess." In support of this, he argued: ". . . the Lord Jesus Christ when he said, 'My kingdom is not of this world,' thereby renounced all earthly power . . . ," citing St. Luke, St. John, and Francisco Vitoria.[28]

In Chapter V, he dealt at length with the sea:

> . . . since the sea is just as insusceptible of physical appropriation as the air, it cannot be attached to the possession of any nation.
>
> But if the Portuguese call *occupying* the sea merely to have sailed over it before other people, and to have, as it were, opened the way, would anything in the world be more ridiculous? . . . There is not a single person in the world who does not know that a ship sailing through the sea leaves behind it no more legal right than it does track.[29]

Concerning the Papal right to grant title to the sea, Grotius wrote:

> . . . the sea and the right of navigating it, are concerned only with money and profits, not with piety; surely every one with any brains at all will agree that the Pope has no jurisdiction here.[30]

27 Grotius, *Mare Liberum;* Scott's "Introductory Note," p. vi; see also Nys' introduction to Grotius, *De Jure Belli ac Pacis*, pp. xv–xxiii, citing Fruin.
28 Grotius, *Mare Liberum*, pp. 12, 16, and 66.
29 *Ibid.*, pp. 38–40.
30 *Ibid.*, pp. 44–46.

Although *Mare Liberum* was probably written for the relatively limited purpose of justifying the Dutch activities in the east, its relevance increased with time, and its impact was felt more by the British than by the Spanish. For the seventeenth century became one of Anglo-Dutch rivalries, worldwide. During the course of the century, for example, the Dutch wrested control of Surinam from the British in the west, and the British similarly established themselves in India and Malaya at the expense of the Dutch. As early as the first decade of the seventeenth century, a London East India Company had been formed to compete directly not only with the Portuguese, but also with the Dutch East India Company.

Grotius was one of four deputies sent to England in 1613 by the Dutch East India Company in an unsuccessful attempt to resolve the quarrels between the two companies.[31] Ten years later he resumed writing, again addressing the subject of jurisdiction over the seas. In 1623 and 1624 he produced his great work *On the Law of War and Peace*. In this epoch-making work, he refined his earlier position on the extent of a state's dominion over the seas:

> Now the Lordship over a portion of the sea is acquired in the same way as other lordships—that is, as we have said above, by means of persons and by way of territory. By way of persons, when a fleet, which is a sea army, is established somewhere on the sea; by way of territory, insofar as those who navigate in that part of the sea nearest the land can be held in restraint from the land, no less than if they were found upon the land itself.[32]

Here, introduced by Grotius, was the concept that jurisdiction over the adjacent seas was a function of the effective extent of control from the land, a concept which would capture the fancy of statesmen for the next 300 years.

ENGLAND: MARE CLAUSUM

Although Grotius' thesis—that the sea is a territory open and free to all—was not directed at the English, the latter were quite wary of it. For if his argument were sound, then the English claims to the surrounding seas would fail. Moreover, as she moved into the vacuum of declining Spanish influence, England stood to gain through "inheriting" vast areas previously claimed by Spain.

John Selden. Not long after *Mare Liberum* was published, the English seized several Dutch cargos of walrus, taken in Greenland waters, on the basis the Dutch lacked British authority to fish there. The Dutch government complained. It was probably King James I himself, who at this point requested that a treatise be prepared as a direct rebuttal to that of Grotius. Because of his renown as a scholar, lawyer, and historian, John Selden (1584–1654), was asked to perform the task, which he did in 1618. Because of some passages

---

31   Clark, "Grotius's East India Mission to England," pp. 45 ff.
32   Grotius, *De Jure Belli ac Pacis*, pp. 129–130.

that the King considered offensive to his friend, the Danish King, the work was shelved until it was published in 1635.[33]

The work was published under the Latin title, *Mare Clausum, seu de Dominio Maris*. A rather wordy second subtitle on this edition reveals much of Selden's purpose:

> The right and dominion of the sea in two books. In the first the sea is proved by the law of nations, not to be common to all men, but to be susceptible of private dominion and propriety as well as the land. In the second, it is asserted that the most serene King of Great Britain is the Lord and proprieter of the circumfluent and surrounding sea, as an inseparable and perpetual appendix of the British Empire.[34]

Comparing Selden's work to that of Grotius, James Kent writes:

> He fell far short of his great rival in the force and beauty of his argument, but he entirely surpassed him in the extent and variety of his citations and researches.[35]

Although far more scholarly, thorough, and complete than Grotius, Selden was at a distinct disadvantage. Selden was writing an apologia of the *status quo* in an age of widespread liberalization. He accurately reported the maritime practice and concepts of nations at the time, using Venice, Genoa, Portugal, Spain, and all the English kings as authoritative examples. "If the *Mare Liberum* was the inspired harbinger of the future, the *Mare Clausum* was the faithful mirror of the actual and the exhaustive record of the past."[36]

Regarding the substance of the disagreement between Grotius and Selden, de Lapradelle had this to say:

> . . . The disagreement between Grotius and Selden did not bear on the right of passage which Selden acknowledged, but on the right of fishing, the right to maritime honors of the flag, the right of neutrals to forbid naval war. With the concession by Selden of the right of passage, great progress was accomplished. In the other parts of his doctrine, the *Mare Clausum*, after its first breach, gradually crumbled. The monopolies of fishing on the high seas were extinguished by purchase. In 1636, Holland obtained from England the exemption from licenses for fishing in the North Sea by the payment of thirty thousand pounds sterling. The right to salute, by which maritime sovereignty was symbolized, continued much longer. Its persistence caused in part the war of 1652, and furnished a pretext for that of 1672 . . . The regulations of the English admiralty, up to 1805, preserved traces of these pretensions. But at the beginning of this century, Great Britain finally renounced them.[37]

33 Fletcher, "John Selden (Author of *Mare Clausum*) and his Contribution to International Law," pp. 8–9.
34 Selden, *Mare Clausum*.
35 Kent, *Commentaries on American Law*, p. 27; in Crocker, *Marginal Sea*, pp. 178–180.
36 Fletcher, "John Selden," p. 11.
37 De Lapradelle, "Le droit de l'état," pp. 266–267.

The teachings of Selden provided the official basis for English policy on the matter of the seas for over 100 years. The English legal writer, Charles Molloy, writing in 1676, reaffirmed the view:

> After the writing of the illustrious Selden, certainly 'tis impossible to find any prince or republic or single person imbued with reason or sense that doubts the dominion of the British Sea to be entirely subject to that imperial diadem.[38]

If Molloy seriously believed what he wrote here, it must have been from a position of strength, i.e., the ability of the British by force to impose their will, for certainly the other maritime states at this time, notably Holland, France, and Denmark and Norway had ideas of their own as to the extent of territorial seas. These will be examined in the next chapter.

38 Molloy, *De Jure Maritimo et Navali*, p. 75, translated in Crocker, *Marginal Sea*, pp. 297–298.

CHAPTER 2

The Cannon-Shot Rule

Thus far, sovereignty over the seas has been treated in general terms with an emphasis on the involvement of early nation states, one with another, on matters concerning the seas. Too, the term *territorial seas* has been taken for granted. However, at this point, brief mention must be made concerning the concept of territorial seas. As states gradually abandoned their extravagant, vague claims over vast expanses of the high seas in favor of more modest claims to coastal waters, they also became more definitive and selective about the purposes and justifications behind their maritime claims. This is especially true in the case of the cannon-shot rule, which made its debut for virtually the sole purpose of identifying neutral coastal zones in which warlike acts were not to be committed.

The Notion of Territorial Seas

As pointed out in Chapter 1, the Romans did not extend their state jurisdiction to seaward. Later, however, the Glossators, who were commentators on the text of Roman law or civil law, especially Azo (Azolinus Porcius, 1150?–1230?), an Italian jurist and professor at Bologna, advanced the doctrine that the state exercised punitive powers over offenses committed on the high seas.[1] Here the Glossators were attributing extraterritorial authority to state vessels, for there was no concurrent claim whatsoever to territorial seas.

In the following century, the renowned Bartolus expanded on the notion of state authority. He taught that the prince was lord of his territory and of the sea subject to him. He defined the part of the sea which was subject to the prince as that portion immediately adjacent to his territory—which, according to Bartolus, extended seaward 100 miles. The prince, therefore, was to exercise his jurisdiction in this adjacent area, which Bartolus termed

1 Fenn, "Origins of the Theory of Territorial Waters," p. 480.

a "judicial district." A few years later, Baldus introduced these concepts into feudal law.[2] The importance and extent of this territorial jurisdiction is more readily appreciated when it is considered in light of the fundamental land-tenure relationship (fief holding) between lord and vassal under the feudal system.

One hundred years after Baldus, a commentator on feudal law by the name of Matthaeus de Afflictis recorded the existence of a new officer of the law, the admiral, who was appointed by the sovereign and who ranked as the third officer of the realm. The admiral's duty was to punish those guilty of offenses committed at sea and to suppress piracy. The sea for this purpose was still a district of the nation or kingdom.[3] Thus, it would seem that the first meaningful purpose in claiming certain territorial sea was that of judicial jurisdiction over offenses that might be committed therein.

It would have been quite logical at this period of time to identify these seas as jurisdictional seas or waters (see pages 3–4). But it was only a matter of a few decades until Gentili produced his *De Jure Belli* (first published in 1598), in which he gave us the basis for the more comprehensive term "territorial seas." He credited Baldus with elaborating the theory of *mare adiacens*—adjacent seas—and Bartolus with the 100-mile limit, both of which he espoused in part. He then applied the term *territorium* to these adjacent seas,[4] and implied that the sovereign's jurisdiction within these seas was authority *in toto*, just as if it were his land territory. Thus, after Gentili, publicists began writing of *territorial* seas or waters.

The theory or notion of territorial seas, then, had been evolved, but the matter of determining the extent of the territorial sea and defining the purpose or purposes to be served by such seas was left to further evolutionary processes. It has already been pointed out, in connection with the Grotius-Selden controversy, that the British had attached by as early as the seventeenth century certain other significances to the "British" seas, such as the rendering of honors to their flag, and others (see page 21). The Spanish and Portuguese, for their part, had considered their claims over the seas as reserving for themselves an expanse of "private property," a "private road" so to speak, through which foreigners could not pass without obtaining special permission (see pages 11, 13).

DEVELOPMENT OF THE CANNON-SHOT RULE

Three antecedents can be claimed as the basis, in varying degrees, for the three-mile limit. Each of these, the line-of-sight doctrine, the Scandinavian league, and the cannon-shot rule, will be examined. The cannon-shot rule, which is certainly the most famous, will be considered first.

The cannon-shot rule, simply stated, is that a state exercises sovereignty over its coastal waters as far as its cannons can shoot. The French have a

---

2 *Ibid.*, p. 472, quoting Baldus de Ubaldis, *Usus Feudorum Commentaria*, p. 85.1.2.
3 *Ibid.*, p. 473, citing M. de Afflictus, *Sanctiones, et Constitutiones Novissima Praelectio*.
4 Gentili, *De Jure Belli Libri Tres*, p. 384.

better term for it, *portée du canon*. *Portée* conveys the impression of distance more so than the English term *shot*, and it might have been more accurate if the rule had been called the *cannon-range rule* in English. The cannon-shot rule served the statesmen who favored it for about three hundred years, during the period 1610 until 1911. It was paramount during the eighteenth century, especially from 1702 until 1793, during which effective cannon range was relatively constant, increasing from about one to two miles.[5]

The cannon-shot rule was a most practical rule. There was never any problem in determining the extent of state control at any given location; one needed only to shoot the cannon and measure the distance to the fall of the shot. There was, of course, no uniform extent of seaward boundaries provided by the rule. In each location, cannon range depended on height, position, and caliber of the cannon or cannons emplaced. But as will be seen, for the purpose intended, this was irrelevant.

SEVENTEENTH-CENTURY PRACTICE OF STATES

Holland. The Dutch were the first to advance the cannon-shot idea. On May 6, 1610, a Dutch delegation visited England to complain about a British proclamation of a year earlier forbidding "strangers" to fish in waters claimed as British seas. The Dutch argument, submitted in the form of a note, included the following:

> 2. For that it is by law of nations, no prince can challenge further into the sea than he can command with a cannon except gulfs within their land from one point to another.[6]

Interestingly, this Anglo-Dutch fishing disagreement and the Dutch cannon-shot argument occurred concurrently with the publication of Grotius' *Mare Liberum*. It may even be that there was some connection between Grotius and the cannon-shot note. Although several writers have assumed on fairly substantial grounds that it was Grotius himself that composed the note, it has not been proven that he was directly involved.[7] And while the possibility has been suggested, it is reasonably certain that Grotius was not a member of the 1610 delegation. G. Norman Clark writes that the only time Grotius visited England was in 1613.[8] It can be said, however, that Grotius' later writings, while not specifically mentioning cannon range in connection with territorial seas, strongly suggest that he favored the cannon-shot concept (see Chapter 1, note 32).

5 Manucy, *Artillery Through the Ages*, pp. 5–12, 32.
6 Fulton, *The Sovereignty of the Sea*, p. 156, quoting Great Britain, *State Papers, Domestic*, vol. 47, p. 111. See also Walker, "Cannon Shot Rule," p. 222.
7 De Pauw, *Grotius and the Law of the Sea*, p. 43, citing Ledeboer, "Een nota uit het jaar 1610" (A Note Dating from 1610), in *Grotiana IV*, pp. 38–40.
8 Clark, "Grotius's East India Mission to England," p. 45.

Again in 1671, Holland showed partiality for the cannon-shot rule in international diplomacy by issuing regulations to Dutch ships requiring them to salute foreign fortresses and towns when they approached to within cannon range.[9]

Belgium. Another instance noted wherein the cannon-shot rule figured in state affairs occurred between Belgium and Algiers in 1662. Ships returning to port from long voyages would stop for inspection ". . . at a distance at which a ship could be struck by cannon shot . . . ," in order that port authorities could determine if the ship was still in the hands of its registered owner.[10]

France. Within a few years, the cannon-shot concept began to take root in France. Without a doubt, the French had everything to gain in championing any concept that espoused narrow territorial seas, because the British claimed all the waters on France's Atlantic coasts: The North Sea, the English Channel, and the Bay of Biscay. The English based their claim to the entire Channel, right up to the shores of France, on their former title to Brittany and Normandy.[11] The French resented this claim and Louis XIV even refused to allow the Channel to be called the English Channel or British Sea.[12] To this date in French cartography and literature, the English Channel is referred to as *la Manche* or simply the Channel.

As early as 1685 the French were treating the cannon-shot rule as established law in France. The capturing of ships as prizes of war had become a matter of significance during the seventeenth century and the French adapted the cannon-shot doctrine to suit this particular situation. They held that the range of cannon was the limit of territorial waters in matters of capture at sea, and that maritime acts of war would not be committed within range of neutral states' guns.[13] In 1691, the French ambassador at Copenhagen, protesting a Danish claim to a greater extent of territorial seas, tendered the following to the Dano-Norwegian Government: "Respect of the coasts of any part of Europe whatsoever has never been extended further than cannon range, or a league or two at the most."[14]

In 1693, the French had cause to complain to the Portuguese Government. The British had captured two French ships within range of the guns of Lisbon, and France was seeking redress from Portugal on the grounds that Portugal should have prevented the seizure. They offered the argument that they them-

9   Crocker, *Marginal Sea*, quoting Raestad, *La mer terrioriale*, p. 114.
10 "Amended treaty of peace between the Federated States of Belgium and the Kingdom of Algiers," translated in Crocker, *Marginal Sea*, p. 511, citing Dumont, *Corps universel diplomatique du droit des gens*, vol. 6, pt. 2, p. 445.
11 Boroughs, *The Sovereignty of the British Seas*, pp. 61–62.
12 De Vattel, *The Law of Nations*, p. 108.
13 Walker, "Cannon Shot Rule," p. 215, citing a letter to M. De Croissy of 19 January 1685, French National Archives, *Collection de la Marine*, F2.7.
14 Crocker, *Marginal Sea*, p. 519. Crocker's footnote reads, "Translation. For the French text, see Arnold Raestad, *La mer territoriale*, p. 111."

selves had previously captured a Dutch ship under the guns of a Portuguese fortress, but after having reflected on the matter, they had concluded that it had been illegal under the law of nations and had released the Dutch ship.[15]

The French, then, had formulated a rule of maritime law, at least for their own purposes, making it illegal in wartime to capture a ship in a neutral port or under guns actually emplaced in a neutral fortress, consequently offering protection for belligerent vessels seeking refuge *sous les canons des forteresses* of neutrals. There was apparently no objection to such capture or warlike acts along undefended coasts. Further, there was apparently no intention to extend territorial jurisdiction uniformly to seaward in order to form a belt of territorial seas equal to the range of theoretical cannons emplaced all along the coast. The theory, rather, was one of zones or areas of fire, near and around guns actually in place.

SEVENTEENTH-CENTURY PUBLICISTS

This cannon-shot rule of France was developed without the aid of any known publicists on international law. Those who had written on coastal waters and who might have mentioned the cannon-shot concept, did not. Nevertheless, a few of the more important and interesting seventeenth century commentators on the subject of territorial seas must be considered.

Richard Zouche (1590–1660), an Englishman, published his most important work in 1650. He cited several authors in a bibliographical attempt to justify England's claim to the Channel. He quoted Grotius out of context to strengthen this position, and even discovered a Frenchman, John du Tillet, writing in *De Rebus Gallicis*, who ". . . frankly admits that the kings of France had no sovereignty over the sea. . . ."[16]

Joannes Loccenius (1598–1677), a Swedish jurist and publicist, writing in 1651, declared that the sovereignty of the sea can belong to no man. Then he defeated his own purpose by adding that a part of the adjacent sea may be subjected to the ownership of a king, that part being equal to a two-day journey at sea[17]—this latter phrase having appeared in the works of Bartolus. This extent of territorial seas, of course, is indeterminable; it depends on the speed of the vessel, and could be as little as 50 miles or as great as 500, depending on the force of the wind. But Loccenius's theory was so novel that it is mentioned by many writers, including Bonfils, de Cussy, Hall, de Lapradelle, Imbart de Latour, Nys, and Schücking.

Franz Stypmann (1612?–1650), a German, is quoted by German publicists and others as claiming the 100-mile limit to be the only one commonly ac-

15 Walker, "Cannon Shot Rule," p. 217, citing a letter to M. D'Estrées, of 1 April 1693, French National Archives, *Collection de la Marine*, F2.11, folio 263, and letters to De L'Escole of 22 April and 3 June 1693, same collection F2.11, folio 449.

16 Zouche, *An Exposition of Fecial Law and Procedure*, pp. 74–75.

17 Loccenius, *De jure maritimo libri tres*, bk. I, chap. IV; Latin text excerpted in de Lapradelle, "Le droit de l'état," p. 275; and Imbart de Latour, *La mer territoriale*, p. 29.

cepted. Stypmann, of course, drew mainly on Bartolus, but also acknowledged the 60-mile claim of Baldus and Bodin.[18]

Samuel Pufendorf (1632–1694), a most prolific Saxon publicist, published his main work in 1672. He wrote that dominion of the high seas would be useless—even unjust—obviously following very closely the writing of Grotius, not only for his views, but also for his manner of presenting them. On the subject of territorial seas he wrote:

> . . . any maritime people which has any use of navigation is master of the sea which washes its shores, in so far as it is held to serve as a defence, and especially of parts or places where any easy landing can be made. (Bodin, *On the Republic*, Bk. I, the last chapter, states on the authority of Baldus: "By a kind of right common to all rulers whose territories border upon the sea, it has been agreed that a ruler can impose his law upon those who approach within sixty miles of his shore."). . .[19]

Pufendorf made no comment on his quotation of Bodin, leaving the reader with the impression that he approved, or at least had no objection to, a 60-mile territorial sea.

Johann Wolfgang Textor (1638–1701), a third German writer of the period, added nothing new to the concept or extent of territorial seas, but concurred generally with Grotius that the whole ocean cannot properly be owned.[20] Textor is mentioned here only because of the elevation of his work to the status of a "classic" by James Brown Scott, a status since questioned by several writers.

CORNELIUS VAN BYNKERSHOEK AND HIS DISSERTATION

Certainly the name that has been most commonly associated with the cannon-shot rule is that of Bynkershoek (1673–1743). Born of a Zeeland family of merchants, he devoted his life to the law and writings on the law. He sat for 40 years on the Supreme Court of Appeals at The Hague, 19 years of which he served as the President (Chief Justice). He is most famous for the dissertation *Dominion of the Sea*, written in 1702, early in his legal career.

Bynkershoek, opposing the British pretensions on sovereignty over the seas, took up and elaborated on the doctrine of Grotius and Pufendorf of the common rights of all peoples to navigation, trade, and fishing on the high seas. His most celebrated contribution to international maritime law is found in his dissertation, in chapter II, which is entitled, "Whether a Maritime Belt Can Be Occupied and Held Under Sovereignty, and If So, in What Way It May Be Done." In this chapter, he addressed the matter of the possession of seas

---

18 Schücking, *Küstenmeer*, p. 7, quoting Stypmann, *De jure maritimo*, sec. 56, translated in Crocker, *Marginal Sea*, p. 425.
19 Pufendorf, *De Jure Naturae et Gentium Libri Octo*, p. 565.
20 Textor, *Synopsis of the Law of Nations*, pp. 66–67.

close to the shore. First he critically examines the claims of states to a maritime belt:

> But indeed since by the law of nations we do not recognize ownership without possession, we must examine how far the ownership of a maritime belt seems to have extended . . . For according to that law, possession is not acquired, unless the entire "res" in question is brought under the control of the man who wishes to possess it . . . .

> I should think, therefore, that the possession of a maritime belt ought to be regarded as extending just as far as it can be held in subjection to the mainland, for in that way, although it is not navigated perpetually, still the possession acquired by law is properly defended and maintained . . . Hence we do not concede ownership of a maritime belt any farther out than it can be ruled from the land, and yet we do not concede it that far . . . .

> . . . [Y]ou may see that the early jurists who ventured to recognize dominion over a maritime belt wander about in great uncertainty in regulating its limits.

> Some authorities extend it to a hundred miles, some to sixty . . . Others again set various other limits . . . But no one could easily approve the reasoning on which all these rules are based, or that reasoning either by which it is accepted that dominion over the sea extends as far as the eye can reach.[21]

Bynkershoek then introduces what he believes to be an acceptable alternate, the cannon-shot rule:

> Wherefore on the whole it seems a better rule that the control of the land [over the sea] extends as far as cannon will carry; for that is as far as we seem to have both command and possession.[22]

Thirty-five years later, Bynkershoek completed his main work, *Questions of Public Law*. In his chapter entitled "Whether it is Lawful to Pursue or Attack an Enemy in a Neutral Port or Territory," he reaffirms his earlier view:

> . . . for I hold that the territorial domain ends where the power of weapons terminates. . . .

> Following this principle, it is not permitted to begin a battle on the seas so near land that it is within reach of the cannons of the forts. . . .[23]

Nowhere in Bynkershoek's writing did he suggest an exact measurement or width of a territorial sea, rather he seemed to write disapprovingly of

21   Van Bynkershoek, *De Domino Maris*, p. 42–43.
22   *Ibid.*, p. 44.
23   Van Bynkershoek, *Quaestionum Juris Publici Libri Duo*, pp. 54, 57.

it. To him, the width of the territorial sea was clearly a function of the range of a cannon, which, of course, varied from place to place and from cannon to cannon. Moreover, nowhere did he say that states ought to claim a maritime belt along their coasts the width of which would equal cannon range, nor did he say they should not claim such a belt. Literally scores of well-known writers since Bynkershoek have drawn the inference from his words that he envisioned such a belt and have accorded this interpretation to his writings. Likewise, many writers have accepted the view that Bynkershoek himself conceived of the cannon-shot rule. The evidence, however, suggests that the former is probably incorrect and that the latter is certainly untrue. It would be safer to speculate, as does Wyndham Walker, that Bynkershoek was merely recording, approvingly, the current practice of certain states—notably Holland and France—in recognizing the protection afforded to belligerent ships by the series of coastal "safe havens" within firing range of actual guns in forts on the shore.[24] Certainly this view is consistent with Bynkershoek's strong advocacy of free seas as found through the rest of his writings.

There is no doubt that Bynkershoek deserves continued recognition as the first publicist to record and to recommend the cannon-shot rule; indeed, he popularized it. That he was successful and convincing in his argument is evidenced by the number of states that soon accepted the cannon-shot rule and by the number of writers that have attributed even more to him than perhaps he ever intended to say or imply.

EIGHTEENTH-CENTURY PRACTICE OF STATES

France. France, of course, continued to adhere to the cannon-shot rule. In treaties of 1786, 1787, and 1795 with England, Russia, and Tunis respectively, she established the range of cannon shot as the extent of the neutral zone for warships.[25]

England. During the eighteenth century, England gravitated away from her claims to "British seas" and as early as 1762 had concluded the following:

> Article II. It is also agreed that if any ships or vessels of Christian nations, in enmity with the King of Great Britain, &c., shall, at the time hereafter be met with or forced upon the coast of the Kingdom of Algiers, either at anchor or otherwise, and not within the reach of cannon shot of the shore, that it shall and may be lawful for any of His Britannic Majesty's ships or vessels of war, or any English privateers, or letters of marque, to take and seize as prizes, any such ships or vessels. . . .[26]

24 Walker, "Cannon Shot Rule," pp. 230–231. This view is also shared by Brierly, *The Law of Nations*, p. 202.
25 For texts, see Crocker, *Marginal Sea*, pp. 521–523.
26 Great Britain and Kingdom of Algiers, "Treaty of Peace and Commerce, May 14, 1762," *British and Foreign State Papers*, vol. 1, pt. 1, p. 372, reproduced in Crocker, *Marginal Sea*, p. 537.

Italian States. Between 1778 and 1787, the Grand Duchy of Tuscany, the Vatican, the Republic of Genoa, the Republic of Venice, the Kingdom of the Two Sicilies, and the Kingdom of Naples issued edicts, passed laws, or concluded treaties barring maritime hostilities within range of their cannons.[27] Following the unification of Italy, the new Italian government reaffirmed the cannon-shot rule of its several predecessors in instructing its naval officers:

> IV. You will bear in mind that you must abstain from any act of hostility whatever in the ports and in the territorial waters of neutral Powers; remembering that the limits of the territorial waters extend to the distance of a cannon shot from the shore.[28]

Spain and Portugal. Spain and Portugal, in treaties with Algiers (1786) and with Russia (1787), respectively, adopted the cannon shot rule for purposes of neutrality and taking of prizes.[29]

United States. In January, 1787, the United States concluded a treaty of peace and friendship with the Sultan of Morocco, protecting American vessels ". . . within gunshot of his forts. . . ."[30] Seven years later, the United States and England agreed that:

> Article 25 . . . Neither of the said parties shall permit the ships or goods belonging to the subjects or citizens of the other, to be taken within cannon shot of the coast, nor in any of the bays, ports or rivers of their territories. . . ."[31]

Russia. In 1787, Russian entered into the treaty with the Two Sicilies, cited above, the first in a series of similar treaties with other states, recognizing the range of cannon shot as the extent of protective, neutral waters. During

27 Regulations of the Grand Duchy of Tuscany Relating to Navigation and Commerce in Time of War, August 1, 1778; Edict of the Pope Relating to Navigation and Commerce in Time of War, March 4, 1779; Edict of the Republic of Genoa Concerning Navigation and Commerce in Time of War, July 1, 1779; Edicts of the Republic of Venice Concerning Navigation and Commerce in Time of War of July 1, and September 9, 1779; Treaty of Commerce Between Russia and the Two Sicilies of January 6/17, 1787; and Treaty Between Naples and Russia of January 17, 1787; pertinent articles translated in Crocker, *Marginal Sea*, pp. 596–598.
28 Kingdom of Italy, "Instructions from the Minister for Marine Affairs to all general, superior and subaltern officers, commanding the navy, the squadrons and the vessels on service, June 20, 1866," *British and Foreign State Papers*, vol. 58, p. 307, reproduced in Crocker, *Marginal Sea*, p. 598.
29 Spain and Algiers, Treaty of June 14, 1786, and Portugal and Russia, Treaty of Commerce of December 9/20, 1787, applicable articles translated in Crocker, *Marginal Sea*, pp. 618 and 623, quoting G. F. von Martens, *Recueil des traités*, vol. IV, pp. 128, 328.
30 French language version: ". . . *la portée du canon des chateaux* . . . ," see Crocker, *Marginal Sea*, p. 632 for full text.
31 United States and Great Britain, "Treaty of Amity, Commerce, and Navigation, November 19, 1794," *U.S. Statutes at Large*, vol. 8, pp. 116, 128, reproduced in Crocker, *Marginal Sea*, p. 637. This article expired October 28, 1807.

the nineteenth century, Russia experimented with several other limits—3 miles, 10 miles, 30 miles, and 100 miles—for various purposes of neutrality, fishing, and territorial jurisdiction[32]—but abandoned them all in 1911, and reverted to the cannon-shot rule. This will be treated more fully in Chapter 8.

From this it can be seen that within a century of Bynkershoek's dissertation, all the important maritime states except for Scandinavia, together with some not-so-important maritime states, had adopted in actual practice the cannon-shot rule for purposes of neutrality. Nothing in this eighteenth century practice seems to indicate that the states considered the cannon-shot rule as applying to purposes other than neutrality and prize law, for example, such as fishing. Whenever fishing is considered, it seems to be in terms of some other means of measuring the limits; these will be considered in the following chapters.

EIGHTEENTH-CENTURY PUBLICISTS

The writers, too, considered the cannon-shot rule as applying exclusively to neutrality and prize law.

Giuseppe Casaregi (1675–1737), an Italian authority on maritime and commercial law, whose major work was published in 1740, accepted the cannon-shot rule for neutrality, holding that ships may not be taken as prizes in a neutral prince's ports or in the adjacent sea within the range of shore batteries. However, he adhered to the old 100-mile rule of Bartolus for other purposes, such as criminal or civil jurisdiction.[33]

Christian Wolff (1676–1756), a German publicist, who produced a vast work on international law between 1740 and 1748, with a condensation of it in 1749, did not mention the cannon-shot rule. He upheld the freedom of the sea for navigation and fishing, and considered that the sea was not subject to ownership by anyone. Wolff wrote that the extent of the marginal sea was a matter of mutual protection. "Parts of the sea can be occupied by nations which dwell near it, so far as they are able to protect the same." The mutuality was explained by Wolff:

> . . . since the sea furnishes a means of protection to maritime countries, and therefore it is to the advantage of the inhabitants that no one should be allowed to remain there with armed ships.[34]

Félix Joseph de Abreu y Bertodano (1700?–1775), a Spanish publicist writing in 1746, like Casaregi, concluded that capture under neutral guns was illegal.

---

32   Ukase of September 4/16, 1821, establishing territorial seas of Russian Asia and America at 100 sea miles; Russian Prize Law of 1869, establishing neutral zone as cannon range or 3 miles; Russian instruction to cruisers of 1893 establishing 3-mile territorial waters; Rules and Treaties of 1893 establishing 10-mile fishing zone on Russian sea coast and 30-mile fishing zone around Komandorsky Islands, reproduced in Crocker, *Marginal Sea*, pp. 620–622.

33   Walker, "Cannon Shot Rule," p. 224, citing Casaregis (Latin version of name), *Discursus Legales de Commercio*.

34   Wolff, *Jus gentium methodo scientifica pertractatum*, pp. 69–72.

Also, like Casaregi, Abreu contended that states, like Spain, with expansive ocean frontages should extend their jurisdiction 100 miles to seaward. He added, however, that states which fronted on narrow seas (presumably less than 200 miles wide), should share the sea, sound, channel, or strait as the case may be, on an equal basis with the other littoral state or states also bordering that sea.[35]

Emmerich de Vattel (1714–1767), a well-known Swiss diplomat and philosopher, published his most important work in 1758. In it he followed generally the principle of free seas, but accepted claims to wide marginal seas such as those of Britain and Venice, provided they were maintained by force. Concerning the cannon-shot rule he wrote:

> Today, all the sea space within cannon range all along the coasts is regarded as being part of the national territory, and for this reason, a vessel captured under the cannons of a neutral fortress, is not a legal prize.[36]

Vattel's words in the first part of the sentence can be interpreted as advocating a uniform belt of territorial seas, the width of cannon range, all along (. . . *le long de* . . .) the coast. But the latter part of the sentence clouds the issue, and there is no amplifying indication of exactly what Vattel had in mind.

René Josué Valin (1695–1765), a French Admiralty official, produced two important works concerning the extent of jurisdiction over coastal waters. The first of these, in 1760, dealt extensively with fisheries. After discussing the diverse claims to coastal waters, he offered his own suggestion, namely, that for purposes of fishing, the coastal state should claim exclusive rights as far out to sea as bottom soundings can be obtained, or to two leagues, whichever is farther.[37] The most eminent of Valin's critics on this theory was the Argentinian publicist Carlos Calvo. He attacked the theory on its impreciseness, specifically its failure to define suitably the sea bottom. He pointed out that the floor of the sea drops off precipitously in some places and that it inclines slightly elsewhere, all of which would produce an unacceptably nonuniform extent of territorial seas.[38]

The second of Valin's works, in 1763, dealt with the law of prizes. Like Casaregi and Abreu writing before him, he believed in different limits for different purposes, and upheld the cannon-shot rule in cases of prizes and neutral rights and duties.[39]

---

35 Walker, "Cannon Shot Rule," pp. 224–225, citing Abreu y Bertodano, *Tradato Juridico-Politico sobre Pressas de Mar*, chaps. IV–VI.
36 Vattel, *Law of Nations*, p. 108–109. This translation, by the author, is from the French text and is more literal than the one furnished in Scott's *Classics of International Law* series.
37 Valin, *Commentaire sur l'ordonance de la marine*, vol. II, p. 687, cited by Imbart de Latour, *La mer territoriale*, p. 30, and translated in Crocker, *The Marginal Sea*, p. 250.
38 Calvo, *Le droit international théorique et pratique*, vol. I, pp. 477–478.
39 Valin, *Traité des Prises*, vol. I, chap. IV, sec. 3–6, cited by Walker, "Cannon Shot Rule," pp. 225–226.

RANGE OF CANNON

One of the main difficulties in dealing with the cannon-shot rule is that cannons have varied so much in range throughout history from country to country. Another difficulty is in overcoming the common misconception that cannon range was about three miles at the time of Bynkershoek. International lawyers of no less stature than James Brown Scott and C. John Colombos have stated this to be the case;[40] so have many others.

Cannons came into general use during the Hundred Years' War (1339–1453). The fifteenth century became the age of the large bombards, the largest caliber gun ever built. Edinburgh Castle boasted a cannon named Mons Meg, which could throw a 19½-inch iron ball 1,400 yards, and a stone ball twice as far.[41] Many such guns were built in the fourteenth, fifteenth, and early sixteenth centuries.

The only state that is reported to have constructed a cannon capable of shooting three miles is Spain. The sixteenth century Spanish mathematician and historian, Luis Collado, claimed that the Spanish had culverins capable of randomly throwing a 24-pound ball as far as 6,666 yards; however, their effective range was only something on the order of 1,742 yards. Albert Manucy pointed out that the fall of shot of these mammoth guns was completely unpredictable and uncontrollable beyond 1,742 yards, or approximately one mile. Moreover, these guns could only be serviced to fire a few times a day, and there was an inordinate possibility on each firing that the gun itself would blow up. None of the other European states, it appears, built culverins as large as did the Spanish. The smallest Spanish culverin was larger than the largest French or British model. Moreover, the French, British, and Germans soon abandoned the heavy, immobile, and inaccurate guns for lighter, trainable, and maneuverable pieces; and the big guns of the fifteenth century became obsolete. The Germans, under Maximilian I, with guns of 1,500-yard range, earned the reputation as the best gunners in sixteenth-century Europe.[42]

English guns of the mid-seventeenth century were capable of firing a 40-pound ball about 1,700 yards,[43] and the largest caliber French cannon carried about 1,200 yards.[44] Thus, at the time of Bynkershoek's *De Domino Maris*, the maximum range of a cannon was about one mile. At least one well-known publicist attributed a lesser range to cannons at this time. The Belgian publicist Ernest Nys estimated that cannon range at the time of Bynkershoek was 700 meters, or just under half a mile.[45] Ranges increased slowly during the century. In 1740, during negotiations between Denmark

---

40 Scott, "Introductory Note" in Bynkershoek, *De Domino Maris*, p. 17; Colombos, *Law of the Sea*, p. 83.
41 Manucy, *Artillery*, p. 3.
42 *Ibid.*, pp. 31–35, and 6. Concerning the Spanish culverins, Manucy cited Collado, *Platica Manual de la Artilleria*.
43 Norman and Pottinger, *A History of War and Weapons, 449 to 1660*, pp. 213–214.
44 Favé, *Études sur le passé et l'avenir de l'artillerie*, vol. IV, p. 9.
45 Nys, *Le droit international*, vol. I, p. 504.

and Holland, in which Holland was disputing a Danish claim to a territorial sea of four leagues, one Dutch diplomat is quoted as saying, "I do not believe that there is any cannon in the world that can carry even one league, let alone four leagues."[46] And toward the end of the eighteenth century, the Spanish king made the following contribution:

> 1. The immunity of the coasts of all my dominions is not to be marked as hitherto by the doubtful and uncertain range of cannon, but by the distance of two miles of 950 toises each.[47]

This is particularly noteworthy, coming from Spain, whose gunners claimed their cannons to have the longest range.

During the Napoleonic wars, French artillery ranges increased to just under three miles,[48] and during the United States Civil War, the maximum range of artillery and naval rifles was three and one-half miles.[49] In the early years of the twentieth century, the range of field artillery increased spectacularly. By World War I, standard field artillery of Great Britain had a five-mile range; that of France and Germany, a little greater. The British had one gun, the Mark III 14-inch gun that could shoot 20 miles, and the Germans developed the "Big Berthas," mammoth guns that dropped 265-pound shells on Paris from gun sites 76 miles distant in Germany.[50] Standard field artillery ranges rose to 20 miles in World War II, but this was eclipsed by the development of the V-2 rockets and the post-World War II intercontinental ballistic missiles.

To review, while technology had been such that three-mile guns could have been manufactured during Bynkershoek's time, such guns were considered impractical and hence were not built. Cannon range was about one mile in 1702 when *De Domino Maris* was published; it increased to about two miles at the end of the century, and to about three miles by the end of the Napoleonic wars. It did not reach 12 miles until the twentieth century during the pre-World War I arms race.

46 Walker, "Cannon Shot Rule," p. 227.
47 "Spanish regulations to be observed in prize cases, June 14, 1797," translated in Crocker, *Marginal Sea*, p. 624, citing A. Riquelme, *Apéndice al derecho internacional de España*, vol. 2, p. 252. *Toise* is the French word for fathom, or six feet.
48 Favé, *Études*, vol. V, p. 59.
49 Manucy, *Artillery*, pp. 20 and 52.
50 "Artillery," *Encyclopaedia Britannica* (1953 edition), II, 468 and 470; "Ordnance," *Encyclopaedia Britannica* (1953 edition), XVI, 860–861.

CHAPTER 3

The Line-of-Sight Doctrine

—————◆—————

While the cannon-shot rule was growing on the north central European mainland, a competing formula was being developed by the peripheral maritime states—Spain, England, and Scandinavia—that of the line-of-sight doctrine. A most flexible concept, the line-of-sight doctrine can furnish the logic necessary to satisfy claims to a territorial sea as narrow as three miles or as wide as 50 miles. The rule has been most commonly associated with claims to three miles, six miles, and with the Scandinavian claims, all of which will be considered in this chapter.

THE PRACTICE OF STATES

SPAIN

The first government to associate itself with the line-of-sight doctrine was that of Spain in the year 1565. It must be recalled that this was a period when Spain was desperately trying to resist the French and British inroads into her western hemisphere realm. Maritime competition, both in commerce and naval strength, was growing. These realities must have occasioned some pragmatic thinking in the Courts of Spain, for in October, 1565, King Philip II of Spain proclaimed:

> No one can come to our coasts, harbors, roadsteads or rivers, or within sight of our land to wait for or damage the ships of our allies, under any pretext whatsoever, on pain of seizure of crew and goods.[1]

This is a considerable watering down of the restrictive provisions in the Treaty of Tordesillas and in the papal bulls prohibiting transit on the "Spanish and Portuguese oceans" except by special permission. This proclamation certainly

1 Crocker, *Marginal Sea*, p. 622, quoting Nys, *Le droit international*, vol. I, p. 499.

reflects the apparent serious doubts of the Spanish government as to its ability to continue to enforce its claims over those vast ocean areas.

ENGLAND

The next state to adhere to the line-of-sight doctrine in diplomatic relations was England. As might be expected, England did not abandon her claims to the waters surrounding the British Isles, but applied the line-of-sight rule to other areas of the world. Between 1676 and 1751, Great Britain concluded eight treaties with Tripoli, Algiers, and Tunis establishing line-of-sight protective zones around her Mediterranean dominions, i.e., Tangier, Minorca, and Gibraltar. The following treaty excerpt is typical:

> Article VIII. That none of the ships or other smaller vessels of Tripoli shall remain cruising near His Majesty's city and garrison of Tangier, or in sight of it, nor other way disturb the peace and commerce of that place.[2]·

SCANDINAVIA

Just 15 years later, in June 1691, the King of Denmark and Norway established a protective zone within sight of Norway and Jutland, prohibiting captures therein.[3] That same year the King promised protection to British and Dutch ships sailing "within sight of the dominion of the Dano-Norwegian King. . . ."[4] In implementing these 1691 policies of the Dano-Norwegian monarchy, Denmark ordered the following:

> If our cruising frigates encounter any man of war or privateer from any of the belligerents, that might have been captured in Nessed or Rifved, or within sight of our coasts, which is computed as four or five leagues (*mil*) from the outlying rocks, they shall courteously demand their freedom, considering them as invalid captures. . . .[5]

This is the earliest instance found equating the line of sight to a specific measure, namely, 16 or 20 nautical miles. The Norwegian coast is mountainous, which gives the observer an enhanced height of eye and consequently a more

---

2 Great Britain and Tripoli, "Treaty of Peace and Commerce, March 5, 1676," *British and Foreign State Papers*, vol. I, pt. I, p. 715, reproduced in Crocker, *Marginal Sea*, p. 534. The other treaties in this series, Treaties of Peace and Commerce with Algiers of April 10, 1682, April 5, 1686 and August 17, 1700; Treaties of Peace with Tripoli of July 19, 1716 and September 19, 1751; and Treaties with Tunis of August 30, 1716 and October, 19, 1751, also quoted from *British and Foreign State Papers*, are reproduced in Crocker, *Marginal Sea*, pp. 534–537.

3 King of Denmark and Norway, "Royal Decree Regarding Prizes, June 9, 1691," translated in Crocker, *Marginal Sea*, p. 518, quoting Raestad, *Kongens Strømme*, p. 245.

4 Great Britain, Netherlands, and Denmark and Norway, Treaty of December 8/18, 1691, Article 6, translated in Crocker, *Marginal Sea*, p. 518.

5 King of Denmark, "Kings Order in Council, Regarding Maritime Prizes, June 13, 1691," Crocker, *Marginal Sea*, p. 514.

extensive view. However, this was not the whole logic underlying the Dano-Norwegian claim. They held that the distance of 16 to 20 miles was the distance, on a clear day, that the uppermost parts of the rigging of a large ship would first come into the view of an observer on the shore.[6]

ITALY

At least one other line-of-sight case is recorded, involving the Kingdom of the Two Sicilies and the Ottoman Empire:

> Article 16. We, on our part, will not permit the vessels of the Ottoman Empire to be pursued or molested within sight of the coasts of our states. Likewise, the vessels of the Ottoman Empire may not molest the vessels of our friends within sight of our coasts.[7]

THE VIEW OF PUBLICISTS

These occasions wherein the line-of-sight doctrine was incorporated into the laws and treaties of various states were by no means as numerous as those of the cannon shot. Nevertheless, there is virtually no book on international maritime law that does not mention the line-of-sight doctrine, referring specifically to one or more of the above state papers or to one of three writers on the subject: Bynkershoek, de Rayneval, and Godey.

BYNKERSHOEK

Apparently the earliest writer to take a position on the line-of-sight doctrine was Cornelius van Bynkershoek. He specifically challenged the proclamation by King Philip II of Spain, cited above, on the basis that it was ". . . too loose and variable a rule." He then rhetorically queried:

> For does he mean the longest possible distance a man can see from the land, and that from any land whatever, from a shore, from a citadel, from a city? As far as a man can see with the naked eye? or with the recently invented telescope?[8]

Bynkershoek then rejected the line-of-sight doctrine in favor of the cannon-shot rule.

6 Jessup, *Territorial Waters,* p. 416, quoting Löfgren, legal advisor to the Swedish Foreign Office, in an opinion rendered February, 1925, to the Swedish Minister for Foreign Affairs.
7 Crocker, *Marginal Sea,* p. 629, translating and quoting from Wenck, *Codex juris gentium recentissmi,* vol. I, p. 525.
8 Van Bynkershoek, *De Domino Maris* p. 44. Bynershoek cited the proclamation as being issued in October, 1563, instead of 1565.

The line-of-sight doctrine did not have a champion such as Bynkershoek had been for the cannon-shot rule in 1702. As a matter of fact, a whole century passed before a Frenchman, Joseph M. G. de Rayneval (1736–1812), came to the doctrine's defense. Writing in 1803, Rayneval took the reverse of Bynkershoek's position:

> . . . Authors generally adopt the rule of the cannon shot, but their opinion is based neither upon a general rule nor upon practice. According to some the most just standard would be the visual horizon, as seen from the shore.[9]

Then, after considering the several other historic and contemporary claims to territorial seas, Rayneval agreed with those who advocated the line-of-sight doctrine.

GODEY

Another century passed before the doctrine had a second major sponsor, also a Frenchman, Paul Godey. Godey, writing in 1896, was under secretary of the French Navy and adapted the line-of-sight doctrine to suit the needs of a specific project of his, that of justifying a six-mile limit of territorial waters. Godey is the first writer to explain and elaborate upon the line-of-sight doctrine; hence, his work will be discussed here, even though per se, it bore no direct relation to the origin of the three-mile limit.

His most convincing argument lay in the fact that cannon range had increased to the point that it exceeded visual range. Agreeing in principle with the cannon-shot rule, he contended that shore gunners could not effectively control their guns beyond human sight, and therefore the range of human sight, and not the range of cannon, should be the governing criterion.

Godey argued that neither the cannon-shot rule nor the three-mile limit had provided states with adequate protection for their fishing and fiscal interests and suggested that the range of human sight would be sufficient to meet those needs. Godey admitted that the exact distance that one could see varied with the height of eye, the time of day, the season, atmospheric conditions, the size and color of the object to be seen, and other factors. But he offered a solution: states could adopt as a limit the mean extreme range of human eyesight, translated into precise figures.[10] Godey arranged to conduct the

---

9 de Rayneval, *Institutions du droit de la nature et des gens*, vol. I, p. 301; translation by the author.
10 Godey, *La mer côtière*, pp. 17, 20–21.

necessary experiments and computations. A series of horizon sightings were taken, using a height of eye of 10 meters above the surface. His findings:

> From personal information that we have been able to procure from professional men, it seems that this mean very closely approaches six marine miles (about 11 kilometers).[11]

Finally, Godey packaged the several needs of coastal states—fishing, customs, neutrality, security, and jurisdiction—neatly within a six-mile territorial limit:

> The single zone of 6 miles, seems to us, fully sufficient in time of war as in time of peace; to extend it beyond—which would be to adopt a rule without sanction—would be to expose one's self to the most serious dangers, without receiving in return, any appreciable advantages.[12]

Godey's advocacy of the line-of-sight doctrine and the six-mile rule was not warmly received. One of his critics, de Lapradelle, humorously accused Godey of favoring the line-of-sight doctrine because, as a man of the sea, he would rather have his territorial sea measured by seaman's eye than by army artillery.[13]

ANALYSIS OF THE LINE-OF-SIGHT DOCTRINE

EXTENT OF TERRITORIAL SEAS BASED ON LINE OF SIGHT

For a man standing on the beach at sea level, the seaward horizon is about three nautical miles away. This alone gives the line-of-sight doctrine some right to the title of forerunner of the three-mile limit. The writers Brittin and Watson agree with this view: "The theory that it [the three-mile limit] originated from the line of sight, which from the shoreline at sea level is approximately three miles, contains substantial validity."[14] Too, as will be pointed out in Chapter 5, there is ample evidence that the statesmen who formulated the three-mile rule gave consideration to the line-of-sight doctrine. But as Godey pointed out, a man on the beach 10 meters above sea level has a horizon of approximately six nautical miles. And, a man atop a 500-foot cliff overlooking the beach can see 26 miles. Moreover, a ship with a 100-foot mast approaching the beach can be seen 11 miles farther away by all three men. In other words, given a clear atmosphere, the distance things can be seen at sea is a function of two variables—the height of the viewer and

11   Godey, "Les limites de la mer territoriale," p. 232; translation by the author.
12   *Ibid.*, p. 237; translation by the author.
13   De Lapradelle, "Le droit de l'état," p. 330.
14   Brittin and Watson, *International Law for Seagoing Officers*, p. 54.

the height of the object viewed. The following table lists horizon distances for several selected heights:[15]

Height Feet	Nautical Miles	Height Feet	Nautical Miles
1	1.1	80	10.2
3	2.0	100	11.4
6	2.8	110	12.0
7	3.0	310	20.1
10	3.6	500	25.6
20	5.1	1,000	36.2
30	6.3	2,000	51.2
33 (10 meters)	6.6	50,000	255.8
50	8.1	100,000	361.8

Using the figures in the above table, a man enjoying the vantage point of a 100-foot sand dune can see to a horizon 11.4 miles distant. On a clear day, he could see the 110-foot sail or smokestack of an approaching ship at 23.4 miles away, an addition of the two heights. Similarly, he could see the top of a 1,000-foot island almost 48 miles away.

CONFIGURATION OF TERRITORIAL SEAS BASED ON LINE OF SIGHT

The human eye, unlike a cannon, is very portable. And whereas most sea-coasts have not been rimmed with cannons, almost all seacoasts are populated. Hence, unlike the cannon-shot rule, which defines territorial seas only within the arcs of fire of cannons in place, the line-of-sight doctrine provides a continuous belt of territorial seas along the coast; out to the range of visibility of those who live and work there. Moreover, the wording of the state papers, e.g., "within sight of our land" or "within sight of our coasts" (see above), clearly implies a continuous visual surveillance belt of waters, whether or not there are lookouts posted all along the shoreline.

In criticizing the line-of-sight doctrine, Bynkershoek classified it along with the other maritime belts—the 100-mile and 60-mile belts—both of which he rejected.[16] Rayneval claimed that the waters that washed the coasts of a state were part of it, not all the way out to a hundred miles or to sixty miles, but only out to the horizon, thereby strongly implying a belt.[17] Godey defined his marginal sea as ". . . that part of the open sea which lies along the coasts. . . ."[18]

---

15 U.S. Navy Hydrographic Office, *American Practical Navigator*, p. 1254; and Hill, *Dutton's Navigation and Piloting*, pp. 147–148.
16 Bynkershoek, *De Domino Maris*, p. 43.
17 de Rayneval, *Institutions*, p. 300.
18 Godey, *La mer côtière*, p. 8.

The actual configuration of the belt could vary depending on one's opinion as to where the viewer should stand. Godey chose to position his viewer everywhere along the coast at an elevation of 10 meters. The Scandinavians, who claimed the horizon was 16 to 20 miles distant, obviously were considering their viewer as taking advantage of the geographic elevations along their shores. Hence, Godey's continuous belt was quite uniform; the seaward boundary was at all points six miles from the nearest land. The Scandinavian concept, conversely, would cause the width of the belt to vary, bulging to seaward in areas of mountainous or high shoreline and shrinking where the coast was low and flat.

PURPOSE OF TERRITORIAL SEAS BASED ON LINE OF SIGHT

Thus, the continuous belt feature of the line-of-sight doctrine distinguishes it from the cannon-shot rule. But it is also different in its purpose. Whereas the cannon-shot rule was developed for purposes of neutrality, the line-of-sight doctrine's primary function was to provide a protective or security belt around the littoral state. True, the line-of-sight belt was considered also in terms of customs, fishing, and neutrality zones, but the prevailing theme of the documents and publicists was that of protection. Both the Spanish declaration and the Anglo-Tripoli Treaty, quoted above, read as creating a protective belt.

It seems quite possible and logical that the instinctive human need for protection and security prompted the early claims to a territorial sea based on the visual horizon. For the same reasons, security lookouts have traditionally been posted on exposed perimeters to provide early warning. It is human nature that those dangers that are not visible are the ones feared most.

In any event, as indicated earlier, the Dano-Norwegian king in 1691 promised protection to British and Dutch ships sailing within sight of his lands. It was at the same time that the pirates of the Barbary states (Morocco, Algiers, Tunis, and Tripoli) achieved their greatest strength and became a significant menace to the ships of the maritime states plying the Mediterranean. This occasioned the conclusion of the eight British treaties noted previously that established a line-of-sight protective zone around the British possessions in the area. It was also at this time that Christian Wolff described the territorial sea as a protective zone (see page 32). De Rayneval, too, envisioned coastal waters within visual range as a protective zone:

> A state should be master of its adjacent waters for two equally important reasons: first, protection against all surprise and violation of its territory; the second, defense against smugglers.[19]

19   de Rayneval, *Institutions*, p. 300; translation by the author.

Finally, Godey wrote of the marginal seas:

> They are free for innocent passage, under condition, nevertheless, of respecting the military and police ordinances enacted by the adjacent state for the protection of its territory, of its coastal population, and of its economic and fiscal interests.[20]

In brief summary, the cannon-shot rule contributed the notion of territorial seas within range of cannon for purposes of neutrality. The line-of-sight doctrine added the notion of a continuous belt along the coast for the protection of the state. Neither of these concepts dealt, except in an ancillary context, with fishing, one of the most important of the reasons that states claim territorial seas. This will be considered in the next chapter.

20 Godey, *La mer côtière*, p. 8, translation by the author.

CHAPTER 4

The Marine League

The first apparent application of the line-of-sight doctrine was by the King of Spain in 1565. Likewise, it was the Dutch who first invoked the cannon-shot rule in the year 1610. And, it was during the intervening period that the Danes instituted the use of an exactly fixed extent of territorial seas—in marked contrast to the variable distance of cannon or visual range—measured in marine leagues. This took the form of a 1598 Danish ordinance ordering the seizure of any English ships hovering or fishing within two leagues of the coast (for text, see page 16). Thereafter, with only very few exceptions, most of which have already been noted, the Scandinavian states consistently measured their territorial sea boundaries in leagues. Granted, in earlier times, Bartolus and Baldus had fixed the limit of territorial seas at 100 and 60 miles; however, the narrower limits which evolved in Scandinavian practice were the first claims to specifically measured seas that were consistent with the principle of free seas and enforceable.

EARLY SCANDINAVIAN CLAIMS

The foregoing is not to say that Denmark had always been a consistent champion for the cause of free seas. For 500 years she collected "Sound Dues," tolls collected from ships passing through the straits between the Baltic and North Seas. This she reluctantly gave up at the Treaty of Copenhagen of 1857, because she found herself no longer powerful enough to enforce the practice.[1] Moreover, the Danes had claimed as closed seas, the "Northern Seas," i.e., the water between Norway, Iceland, and Greenland, now known as the Norwegian Sea. This claim was made in order to reserve exclusive fishing grounds for Dano-Norwegian citizens. Licenses were sold authorizing foreigners to fish on the high seas there during the seventeenth century and

---

1 Lawrence, *The Principles of International Law*, p. 192.

as late as the eighteenth century.[2] This boldness inevitably led to confrontation with Holland and France, and even strained relationships with otherwise amicable England.

ICELAND AND THE FAEROES

Research reveals that not all the early Scandinavian coastal claims were as liberal as the two-league ordinance of 1598, especially as concerned their insular colonial possessions. The Dano-Norwegian government decreed some rather exorbitant private fishing zones before finally being forced to retreat before the diplomatic pressure of the great maritime powers during the eighteenth century. The first of these restrictive zones appeared as a decree by the King of Denmark and Norway on December 16, 1631:

> And if any foreigners, whether whale hunters or English sea fishermen, come within four geographic leagues (*mil*), or if those from other nations come within six leagues of the coast, they shall be attacked.

This decree, addressed to Dano-Norwegian maritime enforcement authorities, and showing partiality toward England, was apparently designed to avoid friction with England. Nevertheless, a state message from Danish King Christian IV to Charles I of England politely requested that English fishermen also be cautioned to remain at least six leagues from the coast.[3] During the course of the seventeenth century, Denmark claimed several successive fishing belts around Iceland and the Faeroes, varying between two and six leagues. Finally, in 1682 the limit was fixed at four leagues,[4] and remained so until 1836, when it was reduced to one league.[5]

GREENLAND

In the case of Greenland, Dano-Norwegian claims were even more selfish, as evidenced by the following declaration of 1738:

> All foreign vessels which come within a distance of four leagues of the coasts of our colonies or land within a distance of thirteen leagues of the colonies (of Greenland) shall be attacked.[6]

2 Kent, "Historical Origins," p. 538.
3 King of Denmark and Norway, "Decree of December 16, 1631, Establishing a Protective Zone in Territorial Waters," in Crocker, *Marginal Sea*, p. 517. See p. 514 for text of state message.
4 King of Denmark, "Manifesto regarding the management of the trade and fishing along Iceland and the Faerø group, of May 13, 1682," translated in Crocker, *Marginal Sea*, p. 514, quoting Stephensen and Sigurdson, *Lovsamling for Island*.
5 Denmark, "Decision of the exchequer regarding fishing privileges in Iceland of March 19, 1836," translated in Crocker, *Marginal Sea*, p. 515.
6 "Norwegian consular declaration establishing a protective zone along the coasts of Greenland, of February 22, 1738," translated in Crocker, *Marginal Sea*, p. 608, quoting Raested, *Kongens strømme*, p. 238. Raestad's *La mer territoriale* is an abbreviated French language edition of the original Norwegian version of *Kongens strømme*.

This thirteen-league prohibited zone was widened to fifteen leagues by royal orders in 1740 and 1751, before being reduced to four leagues by royal decree of October 22, 1758.[7] Fifteen leagues, although a short-lived claim, seems to be the widest Scandinavian fishing zone on record—fifteen leagues being 60 nautical miles.

EUROPEAN MAINLAND

The Dano-Norwegian king, surprisingly, was somewhat more generous toward foreign fishermen with respect to his mainland coasts. By royal order in 1692 he reserved the fjords and a ten-league whaling belt along the coast of Norway for his own subjects.[8] (By way of clarification, the three Scandinavian monarchies underwent many historical power realignments. From 1397 to 1523, the Danish monarch served also as that of Norway and of Sweden; from 1523 to 1814, the Danish King served also as King of Norway; from 1814 to 1905 the King of Sweden served also as King of Norway. Nevertheless, royal decrees, regulations, and proclamations continued to be issued in the name of all three states, e.g., in the present case, this Norwegian Royal Concession was issued by the King of Denmark and Norway in his capacity as King of Norway.)

In all these ordinances, decrees, and concessions reserving exclusive rights along Scandinavian coasts, there were two common elements: the claims were consistently measured in leagues and most of them dealt solely with fishing rights. Certain writers maintained that there is a relationship between this Scandinavian practice of measuring fishing zones in leagues and the doctrine of line of sight. Norwegian Supreme Court Judge Thorvald Böye traced the Dano-Norwegian fishing claims to the 1691 line-of-sight neutrality decree,[9] discussed in the previous chapter. Similarly, Thorsten Kalijarvi maintained that even modern-day Scandinavian claims originated with the principle of sight.[10] However, the tie between the line-of-sight doctrine and the Scandinavian league is probably less valid than a tie between the line-of-sight doctrine and the three-mile rule or the six-mile rule. The argument tracing the practice of measuring Scandinavian territorial seas in leagues to the 1691 line-of-sight decree is defeated by the existence of the two-league fishing ordinance of 1598, which was 93 years its senior. The point that Böye and Kalijarvi tried to make is that the Scandinavian league, as a measure of territorial waters, developed independently of either the cannon-shot rule (in the case of Kali-

---

7   Kent, "Historial Origins" pp. 543–544, quoting Vahl and Andrup, *Greenland*, p. 21.
8   "Norwegian Royal Concession for Whale Fishing of December 3, 1692," translated in Crocker, *Marginal Sea*, p. 608, quoting Raestad, *Kongens Strømme*, p. 242.
9   Böye, "Territorial Waters, with Special Reference to Norwegian Legislation," pp. 298–300.
10 Kalijarvi, "Scandinavian Claims to Jurisdiction over Territorial Waters," pp. 59–60, 64.

jarvi),[11] or the three-mile rule (in the case of Böye).[12] Both these assertions are undoubtedly true. The Danish two-league fishing ordinance of 1598 predated by 12 years the Dutch argument based on cannon shot. Moreover, the earliest mention of a three-mile limit did not occur until the eighteenth century.

Definition of Marine League

The Scandinavians were the first to measure their territorial seas with the marine league. Other states followed; by the nineteenth century France, England, Holland, Spain, the United States, Germany, and others had incorporated the term *marine league* into state papers defining the various limits of their territorial seas. But in each of these cases, they were referring to the more widely accepted definition of the term *marine league*, the one that has persisted to present times.

CONTEMPORARY MARINE LEAGUE

This contemporary marine league is equivalent to three nautical miles, 6,076 yards, or 5,556 meters. It is also referred to as a *sea league* and often simply as a *league*. It is the same measurement known as the English *league*, the French *lieue*, and the Spanish *legua*.[13] All these measurements are based on the length of a nautical mile, or an arc of one minute, defined previously. Hence, the marine league, three times as long, equals three minutes or one twentieth of a degree of latitude.[14]

GERMAN LEAGUE

Arnold Raestad also reports the existence of another league—a measurement known as the Low German *mil*, which was approximately 6,600 meters.[15] Kalijarvi cites Swedish "Instructions" to the fleet dated 1779 calling for naval jurisdiction out to a distance of one German mile, or four English miles.[16] This correlates closely to Raestad's German *mil*, in that four English, or statute miles equal approximately 6,500 meters. This measure equals about three and one-half nautical miles.

SCANDINAVIAN LEAGUE

The most difficult measure to understand is the Scandinavian league. The term has been derived from *uke sjøs*, a medieval Nordic measure equal to

11 *Ibid.*, p. 64.
12 Böye, "Territorial Waters," p. 298.
13 Raestad, *Kongens Strømme*, p. 186, translated in Crocker, *Marginal Sea*, p. 513.
14 Hill, *Dutton's Navigation and Piloting*, pp. 10–11.
15 Raestad, *Kongens Strømme, loc. cit.*
16 Kalijarvi, "Scandinavian Claims," p. 60.

one twelfth of a degree or five nautical miles. In the sixteenth century it was considered to be about seven or eight kilometers or about four nautical miles, and it took the name *mil, norsk mil,* or Norwegian mile. Then, in the seventeenth century it was interpreted variously in Dano-Norwegian writings as: one league (*mil*), one marine league, one old marine league, and one geographic league of 7,420 meters.[17]

There are three sources of difficulty here. First, Scandinavian measurements, in contrast to those of southern Europe, are based on geographic measurements, or degrees of longitude at the equator. Because the earth is flattened at the poles, an equatorial degree is slightly longer than a degree of latitude. Therefore, the Scandinavian navigational mile was a "geographic" mile, three meters longer than the standard nautical mile.[18]

Second, the *uke sjøs* became known as both *mil* and league. Some publicists have translated *mil* as "mile," and others have translated it as "league." Third, the Scandinavian league (*mil*) of 7,420 meters contains four nautical miles (plus 12 meters) instead of three miles as is the league of southern Europe. As such, it equals one-fifteenth of a degree in lieu of one-twentieth of a degree.

All of this leads to difficulty in reconciling the writings of different publicists. In some cases *geographic mile* will be correctly defined as one mile or 1,852 meters, and in others, the 7,420-meter length will have been intended.

In summary, *marine league,* when used by Scandinavian publicists or by others referring to Scandinavian territorial waters, generally refers to a distance of four nautical miles; otherwise, the term usually means three nautical miles.

Adoption of the One-League Limit

The eighteenth century became a major turning point regarding the specific claims of the Dano-Norwegian kingdom. In attempting to put teeth into their extensive claims around Iceland and Greenland, the Danes made a series of seizures of Dutch vessels found fishing along the Iceland and Greenland coasts. These occurred between 1737 and 1740.[19] But by this time, the Danes could no longer count on the support of the British, who were shifting from a policy of *mare clausum* to *mare liberum.* An armed clash between Denmark and Holland was avoided only after the British, French, and Swedish jointly applied pressure on Copenhagen to abandon the large Danish claims.[20]

The outcome of this diplomacy was the reduction of Scandinavian claims over territorial seas to one marine league (four nautical miles). On June 18, 1745, a royal rescript was issued that fixed four miles as the extent of the Dano-Norwegian fishing monopoly.[21] On the same day, a royal decree estab-

---

17   Raestad, *Kongens Strømme,* loc. cit.
18   Böye, "Territorial Waters," p. 301; Hill, *Dutton's Navigation,* p. 11.
19   Kent, "Historical Origins," p. 542.
20   *Ibid.,* p. 543.
21   De Lapradelle, "Le droit de l'état," p. 338; Aubert, "La mer territoriale de la Norvège," p. 432; and Crocker, *Marginal Sea,* p. 608.

lished one league as the neutrality zone.[22] Two years later another rescript was issued:

> Russian fishermen are hereby permitted to fish off the coasts of Finmarken . . . providing they remain at a distance of one league (*mil*) from the land.[23]

Sweden followed suit for purposes of neutrality in 1779 when Prince Carl the Younger promulgated an instruction proclaiming Swedish jurisdiction over a maritime belt one "German Mile" wide, within which hostilities would not be tolerated.[24]

Thus, by the middle of the eighteenth century, there had evolved the Scandinavian one-league limit of territorial seas, primarily for fishing purposes but also for neutrality. Most Scandinavian states tenaciously defended their one-league limit in the face of repeated diplomatic attempts to obtain their agreement to the later three-mile limit. In defending their one-league (four-mile) claim, they reasonably argued that it enjoyed legal seniority over all claims made subsequent to 1745.

Miscellaneous Claims

The Dano-Norwegian 15-league claim around Greenland was not the only 15-league fishing zone on record. The Treaty of Paris between France and England, terminating the French and Indian War, prohibited French fishermen within 15 leagues of Cape Breton Island (Nova Scotia) and within three leagues of the mainland coast.[25] Granted that 15 Dano-Norwegian leagues are 60 miles and 15 English leagues are only 45 miles, this demeaning treaty provision clearly reflected the defeat rendered France by England in that war. But not to be completely outdone, four years later France imposed similarly restrictive treaty terms on the Emperor of Morocco. In the Franco-Moroccan Treaty of Peace and Commerce of May 28, 1767, a 30-mile territorial sea was established around France insofar as Moroccan vessels were concerned.[26]

Some really odd proposals on how to measure the territorial sea have been uncovered by the research of publicists. The German publicist Johann Ludwig Klüber (1762–1837) mentioned an ancient proposal that the territorial sea should be no wider than a stone's throw.[27] Another writer, Johann Kaspar

---

22 See Crocker, *Marginal Sea, loc. cit.* for text translated from Norwegian.
23 *Ibid.* Footnote reads, "Translation. For the Norwegian text, see J. A. S. Schmidt, *Rescripter, resolutioner og collegial-breve for Kongeriget Norge for tidsrumemt 1660–1813,* vol. I, p. 315."
24 Jessup, *Territorial Waters,* pp. 36–37, translating an article by von Holstein in *Stockholms Dagblad,* Dec. 10, 1924.
25 France and Great Britain, Treaty of Paris, Article 5 of the Definitive Treaty of Peace, February 10, 1763. The full English text is in Crocker, *Marginal Sea,* p. 520, quoting from *British and Foreign State Papers,* vol. I, part 1, p. 422.
26 Article 6 of Treaty, translated in Crocker, *Marginal Sea,* p. 521.
27 Klüber, *Droit des gens moderne de l'Europe,* p. 180, translated in Crocker, *Marginal Sea,* p. 183.

Bluntschli (1808–1881), without citing his sources, explained the proposal this way:

> . . . The sovereignty of States over the sea originally extended a stone's throw from the shore, subsequently to an arrow shot; firearms were then invented, and by rapid progress we have arrived at the long-range cannon of today, but the principle has still been retained—"dominion over the territory ends where the force of arms ends. . . ."[28]

The French publicist Paul Pradier-Fodéré (1826–1904) compiled a list of the various extents of the territorial sea. Among those listed was the very vague proposal that the territorial sea be as wide as the length of a race course. Also among his listings is the equally vague proposal that the measure of territorial seas be based on the maximum range that the human voice could be heard from the shore.[29] Imbart de Latour also mentioned the human voice limit and, like Pradier-Fodéré, rejected it as too vague and arbitrary.[30]

One final ancient claim should be mentioned before moving on to an examination of the three-mile limit—and this one is no doubt the strangest of them all. Strange, because in a century when states had greedily divided the entire earth's ocean surfaces, there was stated what must have been the most modest claim ever: ". . . In 1594, the Baltic Sea was considered as belonging to the Duke of Pomerania only to the extent of half a mile from the shore. . . ."[31]

28 Bluntschli, *Le droit international codifié*, para. 302, translated in Crocker, *Marginal Sea*, p. 8.
29 Pradier-Fodéré, *Traité de droit international public européen et américain*, vol. II, para. 630, p. 152, translated in Crocker, *Marginal Sea*, p. 394.
30 Imbart de Latour, *La mer territoriale* p. 29, translated in Crocker, *Marginal Sea*, p. 250.
31 Schücking, *Küstenmeer*, p. 7, translated in Crocker, *Marginal Sea*, p. 425.

CHAPTER 5

Genesis of the Three-Mile Limit

EARLY THREE-MILE PRACTICE

The three-mile limit quietly crept into international practice and then crept back out again virtually unnoticed on at least two occasions before it emerged as a long-term fixture in the maritime affairs of state.

PORT OF YARMOUTH

Probably the first instance of the three-mile limit occurred in connection with the British so-called "hovering acts." The first of these acts was passed in 1709 and was designed to prevent the smuggling of dutiable items such as pepper, raisins, and mace, under penalty of treble the value of not only the goods themselves but also the means of conveyance, whether watercraft or horse and carriage.[1] This law was found to lack the requisite clarity and definition for proper enforcement and a second hovering act was passed by Parliament in 1718, "An Act against clandestine running of uncustomed goods, and for the more effectual preventing of frauds relative to the customs."[2] This law noted that ships laden with coffee, tea, brandy, spirits, and other goods, ". . . pretending to be bound for foreign ports, do frequently lie hovering on the coasts of this kingdom, with intentions to run the same privately on shore as opportunity offers . . . ," and granted authority to British customs officers to visit and search:

> Any ship or vessel of the burthen of 50 tons, or under, laden with customable or prohibited goods, . . . found hovering on the coasts of this Kingdom, [or] within the limits of any port, ...[3]

---

1 Masterson, *Jurisdiction in Marginal Seas,* p. 6, citing 8 Anne, chap. 7, sec. 17, "An Act for granting to Her Majesty new duties of excise and upon several imported commodities . . . ."
2 *Ibid.,* citing 5 Geo. I, chap. XI.
3 *Ibid.,* pp. 7–8.

The Act did not specify the extent of customs officers' authority along the coasts, and left the matter of determining the limits of the various ports up to the respective port authorities. The ports of King's Lynn, Newcastle-on-Tyne, and Whitby were delimited at the 14, 16, and 30-fathom lines, respectively; but the Customs Collector at Yarmouth established a three-mile limit for his port. In his letter of October 31, 1728, he advised the Board of Customs that the port of Yarmouth extended:

> . . . from Cromer church in the County of Norff, and by an imaginary line bearing north into the sea to the distance of 3 miles from the land and then bearing by an imaginary line at the same distance from the shoar East South East 3 miles and by the same line and same distance bearing South till it falls opposite Lewestoff Ness and from thence from the same line and same distance bearing South and by West till it falls opposite to a place commonly called Covehithe, Cove Kitts or Cothy in the County of Suffolk, 3 miles from the shoar and from the said bounds and limits West in at the Peer commonly called Yarmouth Peer and so North up the River Yarmouth to Yarmouth Bridge.[4]

This three-mile limit at Yarmouth survived only eight years. The problem of smuggling became so acute in the view of the English that in 1736 another hovering act was enacted establishing a customs zone of two leagues, all along the coast, which extended the previous limits established by individual ports. The three-mile limit did not appear again in British customs matters for almost a century and a half.

SWEDISH NAVAL INSTRUCTIONS

Something of an anomaly in Scandinavian practice is reported by Lage Stael von Holstein in his account of a short-lived Swedish experiment with the three-mile limit. Von Holstein wrote that there were numerous privateers operating off the coast of Sweden in 1758. The Governor of Göteborg requested instructions from the Crown as to how far out to sea he might legally seize the vessels of privateers. King Adolf Frederick, after consulting with the Boards of Chancery, Commerce, and Admiralty issued instructions that:

> A distance of three miles from the Swedish waters (coast) in the open sea undeniably belongs to the jurisdiction of Sweden and consequently no hostilities should be allowed there.[5]

There is disagreement as to whether or not this Swedish three-mile neutrality zone did in fact measure three nautical miles. H. S. K. Kent supported the view of von Holstein that the Swedish mile was equal to the modern nautical mile.[6] Conversely, Eliel Löfgren, Swedish Foreign Office, believed that the three miles in the 1758 neutrality zone was equal to 12 nautical miles.[7] Torsten

---

4 *Ibid.*, p. 10. (*Norff*: Norfolk County.)
5 Swedish Royal Order of October 9, 1758, in Jessup, *Territorial Waters*, p. 36, citing an article by von Holstein in *Stockholms Dagblad*, December 10, 1924.
6 Kent, "Historical Origins," p. 550.
7 Jessup, *Territorial Waters*, pp. 413–416, quoting from Löfgren.

Gihl supported this latter view, holding that the three miles equaled either 12 or 18 nautical miles.[8] Both positions are entirely plausible.

As in the case of the port of Yarmouth, this three-mile limit was superseded by a wider limit several years later. In 1779, Prince Carl the Younger fixed the extent of Swedish jurisdiction at one German mile. Von Holstein laments this abandonment of the three-mile limit as he writes:

> Hastily and seemingly without cause the three-mile limit was given up for the German mile . . . . The reason for this change was probably the desire to have similar regulations to those in force in Denmark.[9]

From a practical point of view, it is difficult to see why this substitution of the German mile troubled von Holstein. Assuming Arnold Raestad and Thorsten Kalijarvi are correct (see page 47), the German mile was equal to 3.48 nautical miles, representing a difference of only about 900 yards, quite insignificant considering the 30-mile French-Moroccan territorial sea and the 45-mile British-French fishing zone in effect at that time (see page 49).

THE *Joanna Katherina*

Although the difference between the German mile and three miles was worrisome to von Holstein, to Thomas Baty the difference was irrelevant. In fact, he considered a Scottish legal case of 1761 that upheld the "German mile limit" as being tantamount to an historic affirmation of the three-mile limit.[10]

The case in question was that of the *Joanna Katherina*, a British ship that had been seized by a French privateer on the Norwegian coast. The British owner of the ship attempted, through court action, to block the sale of the ship by its French captors. He alleged that it had been illegally captured within the territorial waters of the Kingdom of Denmark and Norway. The court in reaching its decision, however, determined the extent of Dano-Norwegian seas to be one German mile and accordingly decided in favor of the captors.[11]

THE EQUATION OF CANNON SHOT AND THREE MILES

THE *Ellen* AND THE *Squirrel*

The seizure of the *Joanna Katherina* had been only one of many during the then-current war between England and France (Seven Years' War, [1756–1763] fought in Europe and India, and the French and Indian War,

---

8   Gihl, "The Limits of Swedish Territorial Waters," pp. 121–122.
9   Jessup, *Territorial Waters*, pp. 36–37, quoting von Holstein.
10   Baty, "The Three-Mile Limit," p. 517.
11   *Benton v. Briork: The Joanna Katherina, ibid.,* citing *Folio Decisions,* vol. IV, p. 143, Faculty Collection, No. 49, p. 104.

[1754–1763] fought in North America). During the same year, 1761, there occurred two other seizures, under similar circumstances, which brought to light the first apparent evidence that governments might be thinking in terms of equating the then widely accepted cannon-shot rule to a specific distance. A French privateer had captured two British ships, the *Ellen* and the *Squirrel*, in the Kattegat off Jutland—waters claimed by Denmark as territorial seas. The British complained on behalf of the owners to the Dano-Norwegian government, which protested the seizures in turn to the French.

There had been considerable error or deliberate distortion of truth in the testimony as to the exact location of the captures. The problem was further complicated in that the Danes claimed a four-mile league and the French recognized only the cannon shot for purposes of neutrality. The case came before the French *Conseil des Prises*, which rejected the testimony of the British ship captains in favor of the deposition of the French privateer. In her ensuing memorial to the Danish government, France asserted that the seizures had been legal as far as France was concerned. But curiously the memorial went on to indicate a French willingness to depart from their previous position and concede to a continuous belt of territorial seas as claimed by the Scandinavians. The French, however, could not agree to the Danish four-mile belt, but perhaps to one of three miles.[12]

The Danish foreign minister, Baron Bernstorff, then prepared a report concerning this French reply, which he considered unsatisfactory, and delivered it to British Ambassador Titley. Titley, in turn, forwarded it to London, commenting on the French memorial:

> Besides this chicane about sufficient Testimony, the French make another Difficulty concerning the Distance. They seem indeed to think that the Territorial Right may extend to Three Miles, the possible Reach of Cannon Shot from Land; but this Measure is short of the League (of Fifteen to a Degree) required by Denmark.[13]

For whatever motive, this equation of cannon shot to three miles reflected a capacity for progressive thinking in the Quai d'Orsay. It is reasonably certain that French artillery was not effective beyond two miles in 1761. Possibly the French were planning ahead and heeding the forecasts of ordnance experts—three-mile cannons were developed and placed in service within a few decades. But in any event, they had formulated an equation between cannon shot and three miles and had communicated it diplomatically to a foreign power.

THE PUBLICIST FERDINANDO GALIANI

A score of years passed before the cannon-shot three-mile equation is again noted in the literature. In 1782 the monograph, *The Duties of Neutral Princes*

12 Kent, "Historical Origins," pp. 548–549.
13 *Ibid.*, citing Great Britain, *State Papers, Foreign, Denmark*, vol. 112, Titley to Lord Holdernesse [British Secretary of State for the Northern Department], despatch of January 6, 1761, with enclosures.

towards Belligerent Princes,[14] was published by the Abbé Ferdinando Galiani (1728–1787). An Italian, Galiani was known primarily as an economist. He had written books on practical economics, international trade, monetary matters, and even on the arts, but he climaxed his literary career with an excursion into international law.

This interest in international law was probably occasioned by Galiani's diplomatic service. From 1759 to 1769, he was secretary of the Neopolitan Embassy (Kingdom of the Two Sicilies) in Paris, where he also served frequently as chargé d'affaires.[15] This period happened to coincide with the latter years of the war between England and France just discussed. It is noteworthy that Galiani was serving in Paris at the time the French Foreign Office made its cannon-shot three-mile equation. Galiani's subsequent book on neutrality is a fair indication that he put to good use his Paris exposure to the maritime affairs among England, France, and Denmark. In his book he analyzed the cannon-shot practice wherein states claimed as territorial waters the areas covered by the guns of shore batteries. Then he concluded:

> It would appear reasonable to me, however, that without waiting to see if the territorial sovereign actually erects some fortifications, and what caliber of guns he might mount therein, we should fix, finally, and all along the coast, the distance of three miles, as that which surely is the utmost range that a shell might be projected with hitherto known gun powder.[16]

This passage is remarkably consistent with the position advanced by France in 1761. Galiani does not credit the French with equating cannon shot to three miles, nor does he claim it as his own original idea. But it would be naive to assume that Galiani could have remained unaware of the French position after ten years in Paris diplomatic circles. He may well have borrowed the idea from the French. Or he may have been trying to strike a compromise. His own government, the Kingdom of the Two Sicilies, favored the cannon-shot rule. Cannon range was approximately two miles at the time. The Scandinavians claimed a league of four miles. Galiani selected a standard league of three miles. But whatever the basis for his convictions, he approved of

---

14 Galiani, *De' doveri de' principi neutrali verso i principi guerregianti, e di questi verso neutrali.*
15 "Galiani, Ferdinando," *Dizionario Enciclopedico Italiano,* vol. V, pp. 183–184.
16 Galiani, *De' doveri*, p. 422. The writer was assisted in this translation by Lieutenant Colonel Salvatore Martire, Doctor of Aeronautical Engineering, Italian Air Force, Assistant Attache for Air, Italian Embassy, Washington, D.C., October 27, 1969. The original Italian version reads:

> Mi parrebbe peraltro ragionevole, che senza attendere a vedere se in atto tenga il Sovrano del territorio costrutta taluna torre o batteria, e di qual calibro di cannoni la tenga montata, si determinasse fissamente, e da per tutto la distanza di tre miglia dalla terra, come quella, che sicuramente è la maggiore ove colla forza della polvere finora conosciuta si possa spingere una palla, o una bomba.

three miles as the limit for territorial seas and he published it. So even if Galiani's only contribution were to publish a concept that had recently been introduced, having done so, he must be credited with being the first three-mile-limit publicist. What is said of Bynkershoek in popularizing the cannon-shot rule must also be said of Galiani with respect to the three-mile rule. Arnold Raestad wrote of Galiani, "After him, the authors began to identify cannon range and the three-mile limit. . . ."[17]

The United States' Adoption of the Three-Mile Limit

POLITICAL PRESSURES ON THE UNITED STATES

Galiani had written his book during the American Revolution. For England, that had been just another in a long series of wars that kept her occupied throughout the eighteenth century. The powers of Europe, notably France, took advantage of England's involvement in America to harass British colonial possessions in other regions of the world. France's support of the Americans, both direct and indirect, built up a considerable reservoir of goodwill between the two countries and placed the fledgling United States in France's debt.

The American Revolution was followed within a few years by the French Revolution, and in 1793 the British found themselves in coalition with the other powers of Europe, again fighting France. The ensuing hostilities between France and the Coalition were embarrassing to the United States, because they placed the latter in the position of maintaining her neutrality in the face of Anglo-French and Franco-Spanish maritime hostilities along the American coast, for all three—England, France, and Spain—still held possessions in North America.

George Washington's administration not only faced the serious internal problems of the infant republic but also had to walk a political tightrope between the great powers. France especially applied political pressure on the American government. On September 13, 1793, French Minister Edmond Charles Genet sent a letter to Secretary of State Thomas Jefferson asking that the United States define the extent of territorial protection along its coasts, noting that governments and jurists had differing views on the subject.[18] Genet, meanwhile, attacked Washington's policy of neutrality and tried to cash in on goodwill by drawing America into France's war against England and Spain. The following is an example of Genet's pressure tactics:

> I have passed one year at London, two at Vienna, one at Berlin, five in Russia, and I am too well initiated in the mysteries of these cabinets, not to tremble at the fate which menaces America, if the cause of liberty should not triumph, everywhere; for everywhere there is a throne, I warrant that you have an enemy. All the princes look upon you as our

17   Raestad, *La mer territoriale*, p. 125.
18   United States Government, *The American State Papers*, vol. I (1789–1794), p. 195.

teacher; almost all consider you as rebels, who must sooner or later be chastised; almost all have *sworn your ruin as well as ours.* . . .[19]

THE JEFFERSON NOTES

Although neither Washington nor Jefferson wished to be hurried into establishing a limit for United States territorial seas, they had no choice but to respond to Genet. On November 8, 1793, Jefferson sent notes, almost identical in substance, to Genet and to the British minister, Mr. G. Hammond, fixing "provisionally" United States' territorial seas at three miles:

The President of the United States, thinking that, before it shall be finally decided to what distance from our seashores the territorial protection of the United States shall be exercised, it will be proper to enter into friendly conferences and explanations with the powers chiefly interested in the navigation of the seas on our coasts, and relying that convenient occasions may be taken for these hereafter, finds it necessary in the meantime to fix provisionally on some distance for the present government of these questions. You are sensible that very different opinions and claims have been heretofore advanced on this subject. The greatest distance to which any respectable assent among nations has been at any time given, has been the extent of the human sight, estimated at upwards of twenty miles, and the smallest distance, I believe, claimed by any nation whatever, is the utmost range of a cannon ball, usually stated at one sea league. Some intermediate distances have also been insisted on, and that of three sea leagues has some authority in its favor. The character of our coast, remarkable in considerable parts of it for admitting no vessels of size to pass near the shores, would entitle us, in reason, to as broad a margin of protected navigation as any nation whatever. Reserving, however, the ultimate extent of this for future deliberation, the President gives instructions to the officers acting under his authority to consider those heretofore given them as restrained for the present to the distance of one sea league or three geographic miles from the seashores. This distance can admit of no opposition, as it is recognized by treaties between some of the powers with whom we are connected in commerce and navigation, and is as little, or less, than is claimed by any of them on their own coasts.

For the jurisdiction of the rivers and bays of the United States, the laws of the several States are understood to have made provision, and they are, moreover, as being landlocked, within the body of the United States.[20]

---

19 "The Minister of the French Republick with the United States, to Mr. Jefferson, Secretary of State of the United States, New York, Nov. 15, 1793, 2d year of the Republick of France," *ibid.,* p. 194.

20 "Mr. Jefferson to Mr. G. Hammond, Germantown, Nov. 8, 1793," in United States Congress, House of Representatives, *The Counter Case of Great Britain as Laid Before the Tribunal of Arbitration, Convened at Geneva Under the Provisions of the Treaty Between the United States of America and Her Majesty the Queen of Great Britain, Concluded at Washington May 8, 1871,* 42nd Cong., 2nd Sess., Ex. doc. 324, pp. 553–554.

This note to Mr. Hammond is slightly longer than the one sent to Mr. Genet.[21] The version sent to the French did not include the first sentence, emphasizing the temporary nature of the U.S. position. It appears from the modest and cautious—almost apologetic—language of the note, that the United States not only did not want to offend the British by seeming greedy, but also wanted to keep the door open for a later claim to a wider limit of territorial seas when strong enough to defend it. This interpretation is confirmed by John Quincy Adams in his *Memoirs*, who at the same time reveals something of Jefferson's annoyance with Genet:

> The President [Jefferson] mentioned a late act of hostility committed by a French privateer near Charleston, S.C., and said that we ought to assume as a principle that the neutrality of our territory should extend to the Gulf Stream, which was a natural boundary, and within which we ought not to suffer any hostility to be committed. M. Gaillard observed that on a former occasion, in Mr. Jefferson's correspondence with Genet, and by an act of Congress at that period, we had seemed only to claim the usual distance of three miles from the coast; but the President replied that he had then assumed that principle because Genet by his intemperance forced us to fix on some point, and we were not then prepared to assert the claim of jurisdiction to the extent we are in reason entitled to; but he had then taken care expressly to reserve the subject for future consideration, with a view to this same doctrine for which he now contends. I observed that it might be well, before we ventured to assume a claim so broad, to wait for a time when we should have a force competent to maintain it. But in the meantime, he said, it was advisable to squint at it, and to accustom the nations of Europe to the idea that we should claim it in the future.[22]

From the foregoing statement, made by Jefferson on November 30, 1805, when John Quincy Adams was a U.S. senator, it is apparent that the 1793 three-mile claim—the first formal three-mile claim made by a state—was not envisioned by its architects as the enduring rule of international law which it became. Moreover, it was seen as serving only a single purpose: a neutrality zone. There are good reasons to believe—these will be mentioned later—that the idea of a three-mile zone for fishing or customs would have been repugnant to American statesmen at the time.

The text of the Jefferson three-mile-limit notes to England and France is evidence enough that the Secretary of State and his staff had considered the cannon-shot rule, and line-of-sight doctrine, and the marine league before selecting a three-mile limit; all three are specifically mentioned in the notes. Cannon range was being equated to three miles at the time; a man standing on the beach could see about three miles; and the one-league limit—albeit a league of four miles—was currently claimed in Scandinavia. It is not known which of these influenced Jefferson the most, although one of his later writings

---

21 "Mr. Jefferson, Secretary of State, to Mr. Genet, Minister of France, Germantown, Nov. 8, 1793," in *American State Papers*, pp. 195–196.
22 Adams, *Memoirs of John Quincy Adams*, ed. Charles Francis Adams, vol. I, pp. 375–376.

indicates that he looked with favor on the line-of-sight doctrine.[23] Nor can there be found any direct tie between the writings of Galiani and the Jefferson notes. The point was apparently too obscure to have been commented on by Jefferson's biographers, although Thomas Baty suggests that the United States' decision was influenced by Galiani's writings.[24]

Although there seems to be no concrete evidence that Jefferson was specifically aware of Galiani's equation of cannon shot with three miles, it may well have been that the equation was known in diplomatic circles at the time. As pointed out earlier, the French Foreign Office had considered three miles as the equivalent of cannon range as early as 1761. Hence, it is not inconceivable that Genet, in his enthusiasm to influence the young American republic, had arranged to have this view communicated to Jefferson or to his staff. With respect to Jefferson's statement about the range of human sight and twenty miles, it can be fairly assumed that the Dano-Norwegian Royal Order of June 13, 1691 (see page 37) equating the range of sight to five Scandinavian leagues had received wide diplomatic dissemination. Concerning Jefferson's mention of the three-league practice, it must be assumed that as Secretary of State he was familiar with the provisions of the 1763 Treaty of Paris between England and France, fixing a three-league fishing zone along the North American mainland. (See Page 43.) Moreover, four years earlier, in 1789, the publicist G. F. von Martens had written: "A custom, generally acknowledged, extends the authority of the possessor of the coast to a cannon shot from the shore; that is to say, three leagues from the shore. . . ."[25] Jefferson is known to have been familiar with this view advanced by von Martens, by virtue of marginal cross-reference notes which he made in his personal copy of Vattel's *Le droit des gens.*[26]

In any event, it is reasonably certain that the choice of three miles was made reluctantly, under pressure; that it was intended to be a stopgap measure to provide a temporary solution; and that it was a compromise, blending elements of three historic antecedents: the line of sight (a continuous coastal belt), the marine league (of a specific, uniform width), and the cannon shot (for purposes of neutrality).

THE ACT OF 1794

Seven months after the Jefferson notes were delivered to Genet and Hammond, the three-mile limit became the law of the land, enacted by the Congress of the United States:

> Section 6. And be it further enacted and declared, that the district courts shall take cognizance of complaints, by whomsoever instituted, in

23 Letter from President Jefferson to the Secretary of the Treasury, dated September 8, 1894, in Ford, *The Writings of Thomas Jefferson*, vol. VIII, p. 319.
24 Baty, "Three-Mile Limit," p. 516.
25 von Martens, *Précis du droit des gens moderne de l'Europe*, p. 165.
26 See Heinzen, "Three-Mile Limit," pp. 615–616; and Riesenfeld, *Protection of Coastal Fisheries under International Law*, pp. 25–28.

cases of captures made within the waters of the United States or within a marine league of the coasts or shores thereof.[27]

The United States thus became the first state to incorporate the three-mile limit into its domestic laws.

THE THREE-MILE LIMIT IN EARLY COURT DECISIONS

THE *Twee Gebroeders* (1800)

Curiously, it was the British High Court of Admiralty, and not the U.S. Supreme Court, that first based a decision on the three-mile limit. Four Dutch ships had been captured off the Prussian coast. The Prussian chargé d'affaires sought restitution in the English courts, contending that the ships had been seized in Prussian territorial waters. Sir William Scott delivered the opinion that the seizure was illegal and that the vessels should be restored, on the grounds that the seizing ship

> . . . was lying in the Eastern branch of the Eems, within what may I think be considered as a distance of three miles, at most, from East Friesland . . . I am of the opinion, that the ship was lying within those limits, in which all direct hostile operations are by the law of nations forbidden to be exercised.[28]

THE *Anna* (1805)

Five years later, the British High Court of Admiralty handed down another decision invoking the three-mile limit, this time involving the United States. The *Anna*, sailing under the American flag, was captured by a British privateer at a distance of a mile and a half from the alluvial islands of silt built up at the mouth of the Mississippi River. The defense held that the silt islands were not part of the territory of the United States, but were "no man's land." It was again Sir William Scott that delivered the opinion of the Court:

> We all know that the rule of law on this subject is "*terrae dominium finitur, ubi finitur armorum vis*," and since the introduction of fire arms, that distance has usually been recognized to be about three miles from the shore . . . I am of the opinion that the right of territory is to be reckoned from those islands. That being established, it is not denied that the actual capture took place within the distance of three miles from the islands . . . .[29]

27 "An Act in addition to the Act for the punishment of certain crimes against the United States, June 5, 1794," United States Congress, *The Public Statutes at Large*, ed. Richard Peters, vol. I, p. 384.

28 *Twee Gebroeders* (Alberts, Master), 3 C. Robinson 162 (1800), in Dickinson, *A Selection of Cases and Other Readings on the Law of Nations*, pp. 778–780.

29 *The Anna* (La Porte, Master), 5 C. Robinson 373 (1805), in Fenwick, *Cases on International Law*, pp. 482–483.

The seizure was held illegal, and restitution was ordered, with costs and damages.

THE *Tilsit* CAPTURES (1808)

Thomas Baty described a French case of 1808 in which the *Tilsit* captured some American ships in the Baltic Sea off Pillau on the Prussian coast. The French prize court upheld the captures as legal prize, because the ships had been taken more than three miles from the shore.[30]

THE BRIG *Ann* (1812)

The first major case in United States Courts involving the three-mile limit, was that of the brig *Ann*, decided by the U.S. Circuit Court, Massachusetts, May term, 1812. Circuit Justice Story, in his decision, referred to the three-mile limit in such a clever way as to make it, rather than the cannon-shot rule, appear as established international law:

> As the *Ann* arrived off Newburyport, and within three miles of the shore, it is clear that she was within the acknowledged jurisdiction of the United States. All the writers upon public law agree that every nation has exclusive jurisdiction to the distance of a cannon shot, or marine league, over the waters adjacent to its shore.[31]

His several citations and references were to cases and publicists that had upheld the cannon-shot rule. Apparently he had not yet learned of the foreign cases, *Twee Gebroeders*, the *Anna*, or the *Tilsit*, which certainly would have enhanced the documentation of the opinion.

THE FISHING CONVENTION OF 1818

With these several court cases, the three-mile limit had been advocated by publicists, adopted as foreign policy, incorporated into domestic statutes, and upheld by the courts. All that was lacking was the recognition of the three-mile limit between governments in the form of an international treaty. This came in 1818.

TREATY OF PARIS (1783)

Before the American Revolution, the North Atlantic seaboard was fished on the basis of equal rights for all British subjects whether from New Jersey, New Hampshire, Nova Scotia, or Newfoundland. The best fishing was found along the shores and banks of Nova Scotia and Newfoundland. By the Treaty

---

30 Baty, "Three-Mile Limit," p. 518, citing de Cussy, *Phases et Causes* vol. II, p. 71.
31 *The Brig Ann*, 1 Gallison 62 (1812), in United States Government, *The Federal Cases*, vol. I, case number 397, pp. 926–928.

of Utrecht (1713), the French had lost Nova Scotia (Acadie) and Newfoundland to the English, but retained fishing rights there.[32] Then as a result of the French and Indian War, France lost all the rest of Canada except for the islands, St. Pierre and Miquelon, off the coast of Newfoundland, again retaining fishing rights in Newfoundland but losing them in Nova Scotia.[33]

Thus, colonial fishermen had little competition. Wide fishing zones were claimed by Great Britain, and the colonists exploited them with British protection and blessing. But American independence threatened to change this. The fishermen from New Jersey and New Hampshire would no longer be British subjects, able to enjoy the fishing off Newfoundland and Nova Scotia. They feared a 45-mile exclusion similar to that imposed on the French. Hence, the American peace negotiators, being briefed for Paris, were given strict instructions to preserve to their utmost ability the fishing privileges they had traditionally enjoyed.[34]

During the Paris negotiations of 1782, the British strongly resisted the American fishing demands, wishing instead to exclude completely the rebels from the fisheries of the remaining British colonies in Canada. It was a distinct victory for the Americans, and a tribute to the negotiating skill of Benjamin Franklin, that the British yielded on this point. The final version of the peace treaty provided that the Americans should ". . . continue to enjoy unmolested the right to take fish of every kind . . . where the inhabitants of both countries used at any time heretofore to fish. . . ." In effect, the Americans won the right to continue to enjoy the wide territorial seas of the British colonies without having to defend those seas—the Royal Navy would take care of that—and without having to make any formal commitments to define or defend their own newly acquired coastline! As something of a face-saving *quid pro quo*, in Article VIII of the Treaty, the United States agreed that British ships could freely navigate the length of the Mississippi River.[35]

TREATY OF GHENT (1814)

Things went smoothly until after the War of 1812. The Treaty of Ghent, December 24, 1814, settling that war, had made no mention of either the fisheries or the navigation of the Mississippi. Then in June, 1815, an American

---

32 United States Congress, Senate, *Proceedings in the North Atlantic Coast Fisheries Arbitration*, vol. IV, pp. 5–6.

33 *Ibid.*, p. 6, and "Definitive Treaty of Peace, Great Britain and France, February 10, 1763," in Crocker, *Marginal Sea*, p. 520, citing *British and Foreign State Papers*, vol. I, pt. 1, p. 422. Also see Chapter 4, p. 49.

34 Extract from "Report of a Committee of Congress, consisting of Mr. Lovell, Mr. Caroll, and Mr. Madison, to which had been referred certain papers relative to the fisheries and Proceedings in Congress in regard thereto on 22nd January and 20th August, 1782," in Senate, *North Atlantic Coast Fisheries Arbitration*, vol. VII, p. 46.

35 Great Britain and the United States, Article III of "Definitive Treaty of Peace, September 3, 1783," *Public Statutes at Large*, vol. VIII, pp. 82, 83.

cod fisherman, 45 miles from the Nova Scotia coast, was warned by a British sloop that he was trespassing and was ordered not to come within 60 miles of the coast. The American Minister in London, John Quincy Adams, protested the act and maintained that the War of 1812 in no way affected the fishery provisions of the treaty of 1783. The British rejected this and averred that the treaty of 1783, like all treaties in similar circumstances, was annulled by the subsequent war between England and the United States.[36]

CONVENTION OF 1818

This triggered a bitter controversy, which lasted three years.[37] British naval ships were ordered by the Admiralty to seize American fishing vessels found in the contested waters. Negotiations were arduous and long; neither side would yield to the reasoning of the other. The Americans wished to fish Canadian waters right up to the shore; the British wished to exclude them entirely. A compromise was inevitable, and again it was a three-mile limit that became the compromise solution. The key sentence in the Convention of 1818 reads:

> And the United States hereby renounces, for ever, any liberty hereto-fore enjoyed or claimed by the inhabitants thereof to take, dry, or cure fish on or within three marine miles of any of the coasts, bays, creeks, or harbors of His Britannic Majesty's dominions in America. . . .[38]

It had been obvious to the American negotiators that they were going to have to give up something. Their rights to fish in British waters had been a case of "having one's cake and eating it too." More important, it had been an unpallatable affront to British dignity, and the British utilized the War of 1812 to put an end to it. While the Americans would have preferred a wider territorial sea along their own coast, they felt they had more to gain by exploiting the British fisheries up to within three miles, than they might lose if foreigners were to fish within three miles of the American coast.

Thus, illogically, it was a struggling, infant republic that launched the three-mile rule, for purposes of neutrality and for fishing, and for reasons quite beyond its control. Concurrently, Britain, having defeated Napoleon, became the strongest of the great powers and the uncontested "Mistress of the Seas." She had already seen the advantages in scaling down the world's territorial seas. She willingly followed the American lead, and shortly became the champion of the three-mile limit.

36 Moore, *A Digest of International Law*, vol. I, p. 771.
37 This controversy is dealt with at length in Adams, *The Duplicate Letters, the Fisheries, and the Mississippi.*
38 Great Britain and the United States, "Convention Respecting Fisheries, Boundary, and the Restoration of Slaves, October 20, 1818," *Public Statutes at Large*, vol. VIII, p. 249.

CHAPTER 6

The Nineteenth Century:
Growth of the Three-Mile Limit

———◆———

The year 1815 represents one of the truly important watersheds of history. With the defeat of Napoleon and the Congress of Vienna, there commenced a century of relative calm—at least by the standards of the foregoing centuries—throughout Europe and the world. The "Concert of Europe," a peace-keeping alliance, was organized among the great powers. But it was soon discovered that the great powers could not always agree on how to keep the peace, and the Concert of Europe fell into disuse. It was Great Britain, instead, with her great strength and her "balance of power" diplomacy, which provided the stabilizing influence that kept the peace from 1815 to 1914, which has come to be known by many as the "Pax Britannica."

GREAT BRITAIN AS CHAMPION OF THE THREE-MILE LIMIT

Of the so-called great powers of 1815—Austria, France, Great Britain, Prussia, and Russia—Great Britain was supreme. Her empire extended to every continent, and British interests were manifest on the shores of every ocean and principal sea. She had developed an intricate network of islands and enclaves that served as communication and coaling stations. The Royal Navy boasted ninety-five capital ships after 1815, enough according to Lord Strang, ". . . to meet any conceivable combination . . ." of foreign opposition. Lord Strang continued:

> In manufacture, in merchant marine, in foreign trade, in international finance, we had no rival. . . . As we came, by deliberate act of policy, to adopt the practice of free trade and to apply the principle of "all seas freely open for all," we moved towards the *Pax Britannica*, using the Royal Navy to keep the seas open for the common benefit, to suppress

piracy and the slave trade, and to prepare and publish charts of every ocean. No other of our western rivals now had an empire.[1]

It was this situation—a superpower, in control of the seas, adopting the three-mile limit—that was chiefly responsible for the rise of the three-mile limit to status as a rule of international law. During the nineteenth century, Britain took many deliberate steps to put the three-mile rule into effect, and other states commenced to follow suit.

BRITISH TREATIES AND CONVENTIONS

Twenty-one years after the 1818 convention with the United States, England concluded the first in a series of five treaties with France, establishing a three-mile limit for fisheries. The Convention of 1839 established the three-mile limit along the coast of the two states.[2] The Convention of 1857 relaxed some of the eighteenth century treaty restrictions imposed on French fishermen in Canada, establishing a three-mile limit for Newfoundland.[3] Another convention was concluded at Paris in 1859, refining the provisions of that of 1839; however, the treaty was not ratified by France, and its provisions were placed in effect only in British waters.[4] Then, in 1867, another convention between the two states, with similar terms, did receive the necessary ratifications.[5] Finally, in 1882, Britain and France both became signatories to the multilateral three-mile North Sea Fisheries Convention, to be discussed subsequently.

These international instruments all contained similar provisions, namely that the limit was fixed at three nautical miles, to be measured from the low-water mark. In the case of bays, the mouths of which did not exceed 10 miles in width, the three miles were to be measured from a line drawn from headland to headland.

BRITISH DOMESTIC LEGISLATION

Between 1819 and 1852 there were enacted a series of acts, parliamentary and colonial, establishing a three-mile limit for the Canadian colonies: New-

---

1 Strang, *Britain in World Affairs*, pp. 99–100.
2 Great Britain and France, "Convention for defining and regulating the limits of the exclusive right of the oyster and other fisheries on the coasts of Great Britain and France, August 2, 1839," reproduced in Crocker, *Marginal Sea*, p. 524, citing *British and Foreign State Papers*, vol. 27, pp. 986, 988–989.
3 Great Britain and France, "Convention relative to the rights of fishing on the coast of Newfoundland and the neighboring coasts, January 14, 1857," reproduced in Crocker, *Marginal Sea*, p. 525.
4 Calvo, *Le droit international théorique et pratique*, vol. I, para. 358, pp. 480–481, citing unratified treaty between Great Britain and France of August 2, 1859.
5 Great Britain and France, "Convention relative to fisheries in the seas between Great Britain and France, November, 11, 1867," reproduced in Crocker, *Marginal Sea*, pp. 525–526, quoting from *British and Foreign State Papers*, vol. 57, pp. 9–10.

foundland and Labrador, 1819;[6] Nova Scotia, 1836;[7] Prince Edward Island, 1843;[8] and New Brunswick, 1853.[9] Likewise, in 1877, the British fixed a three-mile territorial sea limit for the Empire's Pacific islands.[10] In 1881, a one-league fisheries limit was enacted for New South Wales, Australia,[11] and a three-mile neutrality zone was ordered for Cyprus.[12]

Not only did Britain meticulously legislate a three-mile limit throughout the Empire, but also she took care to advise her subjects concerning the three-mile limits of other states. For example, in 1866, the British government issued instructions to all owners and masters of British fishing vessels not to fish within three miles of the Belgian coast.[13] Similar instructions were issued for the German coasts in 1868, 1874, and 1880.[14]

As far as the British Isles themselves were concerned, several important acts of Parliament were passed that enhanced the legal status of the three-mile rule in England. The Act of July 31, 1868, conferred admiralty jurisdiction on British county courts, so far as maritime jurisdiction, salvage, collisions

6   Great Britain, "Act of Parliament, to enable His Majesty to make regulations with respect to the taking and curing of fish on certain parts of the coasts of New-foundland, Labrador, and His Majesty's other possessions in North America, according to a convention made between His Majesty and the United States of America; June 14, 1819," reproduced in Crocker, *Marginal Sea*, pp. 544–545.

7   Province of Nova Scotia, "An Act relating to the fisheries, and for the prevention of illicit trade in the Province of Nova Scotia, and the coasts and harbors thereof, March 12, 1836"; Statute of Nova Scotia, 6 William IV, chap. 8, reproduced in United States Congress, Senate, *North Atlantic Coast Fisheries Arbitration*, vol. V, p. 1033.

8   Council and Assembly of Prince Edward Island, "Act relative to the American right of fishing under the Convention of illicit trade in the Province of Nova Scotia, and the America, April 15, 1843," (confirmed by British Order in Council, Sept. 3, 1844), reproduced in Crocker, *Marginal Sea*, pp. 547–548.

9   Government of New Brunswick, "Act relating to the coast fisheries, and for the prevention of illicit trade, May 3, 1853," 16 Victoria, chap. 69, reproduced in Crocker, *Marginal Sea*, p. 549.

10 Great Britain, "Order in Council, for the Regulation of British Jurisdiction in the Western Pacific Islands (Friendly Islands, Navigators' Islands, Union Islands, Phoenix Islands, Ellice Islands, Gilbert Islands, Marshall Islands or Archipelago, Caroline Islands, Solomon Islands, Santa Cruz Islands, Rotumah Island, part of Island of New Guinea, Islands or Archipelago of New Britain and New Ireland, Louisade Archipelago, etc.) and the Water within Three Miles of Every Island or Place above Mentioned, August 13, 1877," reproduced in Crocker, *Marginal Sea*, p. 567, quoting from Hertslet, *Commercial Treaties*, vol. XIV, p. 874.

11 "The Fisheries Act of New South Wales, 1881," reproduced in Crocker, *Marginal Sea*, p. 569.

12 Great Britain, "Order in Council, for regulating the conduct of the inhabitants of Cyprus and others during hostilities between States with which Her Majesty is at peace, and for the control by the High Commissioner over recruiting in Cyprus for the service of any State, May 18, 1881," reproduced in Crocker, *Marginal Sea*, p. 570, quoting from *British and Foreign State Papers*, vol. 73, p. 358.

13 "Notice of June 20, 1866," reproduced in Crocker, *Marginal Sea*, p. 553, citing Hertslet, *Commercial Treaties*, vol. XIV, p. 167.

14 "Notices of November 1868, December 1874, and July 1880," reproduced in Crocker, *Marginal Sea*, pp. 555, 558, and 569, citing Hertslet, *Commercial Treaties*, vol. XIV, pp. 1055 and 1057, and vol. XV, p. 209.

at sea, and slave trade were concerned, out to a distance of three miles.[15] The Territorial Waters Jurisdiction Act of August 16, 1878, extended the Common Law to all offenses committed in British waters within the three-mile limit.[16] The Sea Fisheries Act of August 2, 1883, made it a criminal offense for a foreign fishing vessel to enter the three-mile territorial waters of the British Isles.[17]

BRITISH COURT CASES

The courts, too, took an active role in the strengthening of the three-mile rule throughout the nineteenth century. In several cases, the bench emphasized in its dictum the territorial or property right of the Crown out to the three-mile limit:

The King v. 49 Casks of Brandy (1836?). Admiralty Judge Sir John Nicoll found: "As between nation and nation, the territorial right may, by a sort of tacit understanding, be extended to three miles."

The Leda (1860). In his dictum, Dr. Lushington declared that the term "United Kingdom" included the waters to a distance of three miles from the shore.

Gammell v. Commissioners of Woods and Forests (1861?). Lord Wensleydale referred to the distance of three miles as belonging, by the acknowledged law of nations, to the coast of the country.

Whitstable Fishery Case (1865). Ex-Lord Chancellor (Chelmsford) was quoted as saying:

> The three-mile limit depends upon a rule of international law, by which every independent state is considered to have territorial property and jurisdiction in the sea which washes their coast within an assumed distance of cannon-shot from the shore.[18]

---

15 Reproduced in Crocker, *Marginal Sea*, p. 555, citing Hertslet, *Commercial Treaties*, vol. XIII, p. 1115 (31 and 32 Victoria, chap. 71).
16 Reproduced in Moore, *Digest*, vol. I, p. 714, citing 41 and 42 Victoria, chap. 73. (This Act applied also to the dominions.)
17 Reproduced in Crocker, *Marginal Sea*, p. 573, citing *British and Foreign State Papers*, vol. 74, p. 200.
18 *The King v. 49 Casks of Brandy*, 3 Haggard's Admiralty Reports 259 (1836?), cited in Creasy, *First Platform of International Law*, p. 241; *The Leda*, Swabey's Reports, 40 (1860), cited in Baty, "The Three-Mile Limit," p. 520; *Gammell v. Commissioners of Woods and Forests*, 3 McQueen's House of Lords Reports 419 (1861?), Baty, "Three-Mile Limit," p. 522; *The Company of Free Fishers of Whitstable v. Gann*, 11 Common Bench Reports [New Series] 387 and 11 House of Lords Cases 192 (1865), Baty, "Three-Mile Limit," pp. 521–522; and Creasy, *First Platform*, p. 241.

In other decisions, the court stressed the point that the three-mile boundary was the maximum limit of the coastal state's jurisdiction, particularly in admiralty matters:

The General Iron Screw Collier Company (1860). Vice Chancellor Sir W. Page Wood held that:

> . . . every country may, by the common law of nations, legitimately exercise jurisdiction over that portion of the high seas which lies within the distance of three miles from its shores.

The Annapolis (1864). Dr. Lushington described British territorial waters as those ". . . within British jurisdiction, namely, within British territory, and at sea within three miles of the coast."

The Franconia (1876). Sir Robert Phillimore's dictum included this language:

> As I understand the contention on behalf of the Crown, the answer is, international law; in other words, by the consent of all civilized states, England has become entitled to include within her realm a marine league of sea, and therefore has jurisdiction over a foreign vessel within that limit.

The Chishima and the Ravenna (1895). This case was decided

> . . . upon the ground that the collision had occurred within three miles of the coast of Japan, in the territorial waters of that country; that the liability of the Emperor of Japan, as owner of the Chishima, for the negligent acts of the officers and crew of that vessel must therefore be regulated by the law of Japan . . . .[19]

BRITISH PUBLICISTS

The British publicists were just as consistent as the British courts in defending the three-mile rule. In fact, there were no well-known British publicists writing during the nineteenth century period who did not endorse the three-mile rule. The earlier writers, such as Sir Robert Phillimore (1810–1855) and Sir Edward Creasy (1812–1878) understandably equated the three-mile rule with cannon shot.

---

19 *General Iron Screw Collier Company v. Schurmanns*, 1 Johnson and Hemming's Reports 180 (1860), reproduced in Crocker, *Marginal Sea*, p. 551; *The Annapolis*, 1 Lushington's Reports 356, (1864), Baty, "Three-Mile Limit," p. 522; *The Franconia* (*Regina v. Keyn*), Law Reports, 2 Exchequer Division 63 (1876), reproduced in British Institute of International and Comparative Law, *British International Law Cases*, vol. II, p. 704; *The Imperial Japanese Government v. the Peninsular and Oriental Steam Navigation Company* (on appeal from the Supreme Court for China and Japan at Shanghai, in Admiralty), *Law Reports*, 20 *Appeal Cases* 644 (1895), reproduced in part in Crocker, *Marginal Sea*, pp. 579–581.

Phillimore served as a member of Parliament, as a judge of the High Court of Admiralty and as Judge Advocate General. His 1879 edition of *Commentaries* reads:

> But the rule of law may be now considered as fairly established—namely, that this absolute property and jurisdiction does not extend, unless by the specific provision of a Treaty or an unquestioned usage, beyond a marine league (being 3 miles), or the distance of a cannonshot, from the shore at low tide. . . . [20]

Sir Edward Shepherd Creasy, an accomplished historian and professor of history, was appointed and served as Chief Justice of Ceylon, following which he wrote on the subject of government and international law. In his work on international law, published in 1876, he observed that the extent of territorial waters, as a function of artillery range, had been fixed at three miles. He then speculated that a territorial sea limit of five miles might be adopted in the future as a result of improvements in cannons.[21]

The later publicists, however—Sir Travers Twiss (1809–1897), William Edward Hall (1836–1894), and Thomas Joseph Lawrence (1849–1919)—came to the conclusion that the three-mile rule had become established on its own merits and that the extent of territorial waters was no longer a function of cannon range.

Twiss was so highly esteemed and renowned as a jurist, professor, and public servant that the King of Belgium requested Twiss to draw up the constitution for the Congo Free State. Writing on territorial seas, Twiss declared: "Beyond the distance of a sea-league from its coast the territorial laws of a nation are, strictly speaking, not operative."[22]

Hall's *Treatise* was first published in 1880 and has gone through eight editions. In it, he concluded that the three-mile limit is so well-fixed that it must be assumed that a state adheres to it in the absence of an express notice to the contrary. In a footnote, however, he acknowledged the existence of foreign claims to great limits:

> It is felt, and growingly felt, not only that the width of three miles is insufficient for the safety of the territory, but that it is desirable for a state to have control over a larger space of water for the purpose of regulating and preserving the fisheries in it. . . .

At the same time, Hall seemed quite satisfied with the consistency of British adherence to the three-mile limit by pointing out a singular departure, the Treaty of Washington of 1846, dividing the 15-mile wide Strait of Juan de Fuca equally between Britain and the United States.[23]

20 Phillimore, *Commentaries*, vol. I, p. 263.
21 Creasy, *First Platform*, p. 241.
22 Twiss, *The Law of Nations*, p. 292.
23 Hall, *A Treatise on International Law*, pp. 154, 156.

T. J. Lawrence taught international law first at the Royal Naval College, Cambridge, and later at the University of Chicago. On the extent of territorial seas, he succinctly stated that ". . . a state's territory includes the sea within a 3-mile limit of its shores." He then considered certain contemporary proposals for a six-mile and a ten-mile territorial sea, but predicted that the British Government would probably successfully resist any change.[24]

THE CUSTOMS CONSOLIDATION ACT OF 1876

Of all the factors influencing the growth of the three-mile rule—treaties, laws, court decisions, and writings of the experts—the Customs Consolidation Act of 1876 probably went the furthest in establishing the three-mile limit as a rule in the law of nations. The significance of this legislation, however, cannot be fully appreciated without a brief review of the events which led up to it.

The early "Hovering Acts" were mentioned in Chapter 5, where it was noted that the Act of 1736 established a customs zone of two leagues. The two-league zone was strictly enforced by customs officials and upheld in court, but Great Britain found that even so, smuggling was on the increase. Tobacco, alcoholic beverages, and tea were the major items involved, and the smugglers were especially busy on and around the Isle of Man. Accordingly, Parliament passed an act in 1765 that extended customs jurisdiction to three leagues around the Isle of Man.[25] But this act, too, was ineffective against the amazingly efficient and complex organization between the smugglers afloat and their armed gangs ashore. To give enforcement authorities even greater flexibility, Parliament, by its Act of 1784, increased the customs zone to four leagues.[26] Still, smuggling continued unabated, and in 1802 another in the series of "Hovering Acts" was passed, increasing the zone to eight leagues.[27] Yet in spite of this act, which extended customs jurisdiction to 24 miles, the first quarter of the nineteenth century saw smuggling reach its zenith; Masterson called it the "Golden Age of Smuggling." In seeming exasperation, Parliament enacted legislation in 1805 extending the zone to 100 leagues![28]

But then, the situation began to change. During the next half-century, the

24 Lawrence, *The Principles of International Law*, pp. 141–142. First edition published in 1895.
25 The Act, 5 George III, chap. XXXIX, sec. VII, "An Act for more effectively preventing the mischiefs arising to the revenue and commerce of Great Britain and Ireland, from the illicit and clandestine trade to and from the Isle of Man," in Masterson, *Jurisdiction in Marginal Seas*, pp. 31–34, 41–42.
26 The Act, 24 George III (2^d session), chap. XLVII, "An Act for the more effectual prevention of smuggling," *ibid.*, pp. 58–60; Crocker, *Marginal Sea*, pp. 539–540.
27 The Act, 34 George III, chap. L, "An Act to alter, amend, and render more effectual an act, made in the 24th year of the reign of His present Majesty, for the more effectual prevention of smuggling in Great Britain" [The Act of 1784], Masterson, *Jurisdiction in Marginal Seas*, pp. 73–74; Crocker, *Marginal Sea*, p. 541.
28 The Act, 45 George III, chap. CXXI, July 12, 1805, "An Act for the more effectual prevention of smuggling," Masterson, *Jurisdiction in Marginal Seas*, pp. 72–78.

British Coast Guard greatly improved its record of dealing with smugglers. In a report of 1851, the Commissioners of Customs noted that smuggling was on the decline in most districts and had been entirely suppressed in others.[29] Also, by midcentury the 100-league customs zone had become a source of friction and disagreement—both externally and internally—for the British Government. For example, in 1850, the Coast Guard seized a French smuggler, the *Petit-Jules*, 25 miles from England, laden with spirits and bound for the English coast. A fight ensued and the craft escaped. The Lords of the Treasury asked the Queen's Advocate General for an opinion as to what steps Britain might take to apprehend and prosecute the French crew. The Advocate General surprisingly advised the Treasury that such would be illegal on the basis that British jurisdiction extended to sea only a distance of three miles.[30]

Moreover, the extensive customs legislation of Great Britain had not gone unnoticed abroad. Laws extending domestic customs jurisdiction to ten or twelve miles appeared in Belgium, France, and the United States, to mention a few. These actions concerned the British Foreign Office, which began to press for revision of the maritime limit down to one league. The British merchant fleet was large, and on the basis of reciprocity, it might be expected that British merchant ships could be subjected to the annoyance of being stopped and searched outside the three-mile limit of foreign states.

In the end, the issue was decided in favor of the Foreign Office in the form of the Customs Consolidation Act of 1876. The act repealed all the customs or "hovering" acts in force up to that time. In their stead, the new act adopted a three-league customs zone applicable only to vessels belonging in whole or in part to British subjects and vessels of which half the persons on board were British subjects. The act excluded from the three-league authority vessels that were not British, applying to those vessels a zone of one league, or three miles.[31]

By this act, together with the Territorial Waters Jurisdiction Act of 1878 and the Sea Fisheries Act of 1883, Britain publically and intentionally limited herself to a three-mile limit for all purposes. From that time, she maintained the policy that the territorial sea within three miles was the maximum extent for state jurisdiction, irrespective of the state's ability or power to extend its authority farther. This position, taken by the "Mistress of the Seas" was held out as the legal standard for the other states to follow.

NINETEENTH-CENTURY STATE PRACTICE

GREAT POWERS

France. As noted in the preceding section on England, France became a subscriber to the three-mile limit with respect to fishing. In addition to the

29 *Ibid.*, p. 115, citing *Parliamentary Papers*, 1851, vol. LIII, no. 454.
30 *Ibid.*, pp. 125–127.
31 The Act, 39 and 40 Victoria, chap. 36 (July 24, 1876), "An Act to Consolidate the Customs Laws," *ibid.*, pp. 150, 155; Crocker, *Marginal Sea*, 563–564.

five conventions fixing a limit of three miles for fishing, regulations issued in 1843, an imperial decree of 1862, and laws of 1885 and 1888 confirmed the French position.[32] The law of 1888 is representative:

> Article 1. Fishing is forbidden to foreign boats in the territorial waters of France and Algeria within a limit set at three nautical miles from low-water mark.[33]

With respect to customs, in 1817 France established a zone of two myriameters (approximately 11 nautical miles).[34] She, unlike Britain, maintained this limit the rest of the century. For purposes of neutrality, on the other hand, France continued to adhere to her very old cannon-shot practice. As late as 1854 this was confirmed by the Minister of Marine.[35] Not until 1896 was the practice modified. In that year, a decree was issued, regulating the approach, during war, of vessels within three miles of the French coast;[36] and four years later instructions were issued to naval officers that expressly redefined neutral waters as those within a three-mile limit.[37]

Austria (after 1867, Austria-Hungary). Austria's only sea frontier was on the Adriatic. During the nineteenth century, her interests focused on the Balkans and the decaying Ottoman Empire. There is very little record of Austrian pronouncements and practice in matters of territorial seas; but that which is available indicates that Austrian claims were quite modest.

By an ordinance of 1803, Austria established cannon range as the extent of her seas for neutrality purposes.[38] However, in a decree of August 23, 1846, and then in a circular of April 28, 1849, the government explained that the expression "within cannon range" was equivalent to the distance of

---

32 "Regulations for the guidance of the fishermen of Great Britain and of France in the seas lying between the coasts of the two countries, May 24, 1843," reproduced in Crocker, *Marginal Sea*, p. 524, citing *British and Foreign State Papers*, vol. 31, p. 166; "Decree of the French Emperor relative to coastal fishing, May 10, 1862," translated in Crocker, *Marginal Sea*, p. 525, quoting Hertslet, *Commercial Treaties*, vol. XIII, p. 400; "Law prohibiting fishing privileges to foreigners in the territorial waters of Algeria and France, for a distance of three miles, November 24, 1885," Crocker, *Marginal Sea*, p. 526.

33 "Law in regard to fishing in territorial waters, March 1, 1888," translated in Crocker, *Marginal Sea*, p. 527, citing Hertslet, *Commercial Treaties*, vol. XVIII, p. 393.

34 "Law establishing a customs zone of two myriameters, March 27, 1817," translated in Crocker, *Marginal Sea*, p. 523. The customs zone had previously been four leagues, or 12 nautical miles, under a law of March 24, 1794. *Ibid.*, p. 522.

35 "Instructions addressed by the Minister of Marine and the Colonies to general naval officers, etc., March 31, 1854," translated in Crocker, *Marginal Sea*, pp. 524–525.

36 "Decree regulating conditions of admission to, and sojourn at, the anchorages and ports of the French coast for ships, French and foreign, in time of war, June 12, 1896," translated in Crocker, *Marginal Sea*, p. 527.

37 Jessup, *Territorial Waters*, pp. 20–21; Crocker, *Marginal Sea*, p. 528; Raestad, *La mer territoriale*, p. 148, note 1.

38 "Ordinance respecting the observance of neutrality, August 7, 1803," translated in Crocker, *Marginal Sea*, p. 509, citing von Martens, *Recueil de traités* vol. VIII, p. 109.

three marine miles.[39] In 1881 a customs zone of four miles was adopted,[40] and in 1884 an exclusive fishing zone of three miles was ordered.[41]

Prussia (German Empire after 1871). In 1866 Prussia adopted the cannon-shot limit for her territorial waters.[42] Then in 1882, Germany became a signatory to the North Sea Fisheries Convention, and in 1888, to the Suez Convention, both of which featured the three-mile limit. (These will be discussed more fully subsequently.)

Russia. In 1821 Tsar Alexander I took a radical departure from the cannon-shot rule:

> Paragraph 2. It is therefore prohibited to all foreign vessels not only to land on the coasts and islands belonging to Russia as stated above, but also, to approach them within less than 100 Italian miles. The transgressor's vessel is subject to confiscation along with the whole cargo.[43]

This Ukase was occasioned by Russia's fear that foreign fishermen would deplete the seal fisheries in Alaska and Siberia, and especially those in the Bering Sea. (The term *Italian mile* was used here to specify a standard nautical mile as opposed to the longer *German mile* or *Norwegian mile*.) In another paragraph the Ukase barred all foreign vessels from the Bering Sea, the Gulf of Alaska, and the Sea of Okhotsk by prohibiting them north of a line drawn between 45° north on the Asian shore and 51° north on the American shore. The Russian representative in Washington advised the United States government that the entire sea area involved was considered Russian territory.[44] This aroused heated resistance not only in Washington, but also in London, for the British had fishing interests in western Canada. Meanwhile, in 1822, a Russian sloop seized the United States brig *Pearl* en route to Sitka.[45] Negotiations between the three states resulted in conventions between the U.S. and Russia (1824) and Britain and Russia (1825) in which Russia gave up her 1821 Ukase pretentions.[46] In 1829 the *Pearl* was released by Russia with com-

---

39 Barclay (reporter), "Report of the Third Commission: "Définition et régime de la mer territoriale," *Annuaire de l'Institut de Droit International*, vol. XIII (1894, Paris session), p. 361.
40 "Order of the Minister of Finance, establishing a customs zone of four marine miles, March 23, 1881," translated in Crocker, *Marginal Sea*, p. 510.
41 "Decree of the Ministry of Commerce, December 5, 1884," Fulton, *Sovereignty of the Sea*, p. 659.
42 "Decree of the Supreme Court of Prussia establishing the extent of the territorial sea at cannon range, November 28, 1866," translated in Crocker, *Marginal Sea*, p. 619.
43 "Ukase establishing Russian sea boundaries at a distance of 100 Italian miles from the Asiatic and American continents, September 4/16, 1821," United States Congress, Senate, *Proceedings of the Alaskan Boundaries Tribunal*, vol. I, pt. 2, pp. 9–10.
44 Hall, *Treatise*, p. 149.
45 Baty, "Three-Mile Limit," p. 520.
46 Hall, *Treatise*, p. 150.

pensation; this appears to be the only case in which Russia attempted to enforce the Ukase.[47]

During the remainder of the century, Russia conformed generally to the three-mile rule. This was manifested on a number of occasions in a number of ways. In 1868, the Russian Foreign Minister informed the United States that foreign whalers were forbidden within a distance of less than three miles from the Russian shore, where whaling was reserved for Russian subjects.[48] In 1869, Russia legislated the three-mile limit with respect to neutrality.[49] This was reaffirmed by Russia's 1893 Instructions to Cruisers, which established Russian territorial waters at three miles, but in the same paragraph claimed the entire White Sea as a closed Russian territorial sea within an 89-mile cape-to-cape baseline.[50] Then, finally, in May of the same year, Russia succeeded in obtaining a degree of international approval of her efforts to protect the seal fisheries. In agreements negotiated with the United States and Great Britain, those powers agreed to a prohibition against seal fishing within ten miles of the Russian mainland and within thirty miles of the Komandorsky Islands and of Tulénew Island.[51]

THE LESSER POWERS

Europe. Many of the lesser states of Europe followed Britain's lead. Denmark, which had traditionally measured her territorial sea at one league of four miles, became a party to the three-mile North Sea Fisheries Convention in 1882. She thereby accepted the three-mile limit—for fishing—with regard to the six other littoral signatory states. (See page 85.) Belgium and the Netherlands, also signatories, had previously adopted the three-mile limit in 1832 and 1874, respectively.

In 1832, Belgium enacted a rather complicated customs law which called for two seaward boundaries: one at one myriameter (about six miles), and one at one-half myriameter (about three miles). Within the outer zone, visit and search was authorized, but vessels could be seized only in the inner zone when within two and one-half kilometers of the land, and then only if they

---

47 Baty, *loc. cit.*

48 United States Government, *Fur Seal Arbitration: Proceedings of the Tribunal of Arbitration Convened at Paris under the Treaty Between the United States of America and Great Britain, Concluded at Washington, February 29, 1892,* British Case, p. 88.

49 Mr. Lothrop to Mr. Bayard, St. Petersburg, April 11, 1887, quoting Article 21, chap. III, of Russian Prize Law of 1869, in United States Department of State, *Papers Relating to the Foreign Relations of the United States, 1887,* p. 957.

50 "Instructions to Cruisers," *Revue générale de droit international public* I (1894), p. 440, translated in Crocker, *Marginal Sea,* p. 621.

51 Great Britain and Russia, "Agreement of May 10, 22, 30, 1893 relative to Seal Fisheries," Hertslet, *Commercial Treaties,* vol. XIX, p. 818; and United States and Russia, "Agreement for a modus vivendi in relation to the fur-seal fisheries in Bering Sea, May 4, 1894," *British and Foreign State Papers,* vol. 86, p. 272.

were under 30 tons.[52] Nevertheless, this multiple-zone arrangement has been evaluated as a three-mile territorial sea by a number of publicists.[53]

The Dutch advised Great Britain in 1874 that they regarded the seaward limit as being fixed at three miles under international law.[54] Eight years later, the Netherlands signed the 1882 North Sea Fisheries Convention. The Dutch government then issued a Royal decree, confirming its earlier actions and fixing three miles as the limit of its territorial waters.[55]

Greece declared a three-mile fishing limit in 1869.[56] Italy signed the three-mile Suez Convention of 1888, but that was her only nineteenth century association with the three-mile limit. Italy adhered closely to the cannon-shot rule throughout the century. At the time of the North Sea Fisheries Convention, the Italian Fisheries Commission had recommended adoption of the three-mile limit, but the government did not implement the recommendation until after the turn of the century, and then only with respect to coastal dredging in the Tyrrhenian Sea.[57] For customs, Italy preferred a wider zone. In 1874, Italy advised Great Britain that

> . . . the political dominion which creates complete jurisdiction extends over the sea to a distance within reach of cannon shot; but that following the example of most other states, including England, Italy has carried the limits within which operations for the protection of the Customs Revenue may be effected to a distance of ten thousand meters from the coast.[58]

This was formally confirmed in 1892 when Italy concluded a convention with Egypt, calling for a ten-kilometer customs zone.[59]

The Ottoman Empire was also a signatory to the Suez Convention, and in 1893 she went a step further and fixed a three-mile fishing limit around the island of Crete.[60] Spain, too, experimented with a three-mile limit, but only briefly, between 1828 and 1830. On March 31, 1828, a Spanish Royal order was issued adopting a three-mile antismuggling zone.[61] Only two years later, however, the law of May 3, 1830 was passed, adopting a six-mile zone

52 Belgium, "Law of June 7, 1832," translated in Crocker, *Marginal Sea*, p. 511.
53 Calvo, *Le droit international*, p. 477; Jessup, *Territorial Waters*, pp. 87–88; Baty, "Three-Mile Limit," p. 520; and Fulton, *Sovereignty of Sea*, p. 658.
54 Meyer, *The Extent of Jurisdiction in Coastal Waters*, p. 204, citing an intergovernmental letter from the Foreign Minister of Norway and Sweden, dated November 17, 1874; and Smith, *Great Britain and the Law of Nations*, vol. II, p. 206.
55 "Royal Decree of March 20, 1884," cited in Fulton, *Sovereignty of Sea*, p. 658.
56 Fulton, *Sovereignty of Sea*, p. 661; Jessup, *Territorial Waters*, p. 45; and Baty, "Three-Mile Limit," p. 523.
57 Fulton, *Sovereignty of Sea*, p. 660, citing Decree of September 4, 1908.
58 Italian diplomatic note of October 15, 1874, in Smith, *Great Britain*, vol. II, p. 206.
59 "Commercial Convention of February 1, 1892," translated in Crocker, *Marginal Sea*, p. 599, citing *British and Foreign State Papers*, vol. 83, pp. 165–166.
60 "Notice by the Governor General of Crete respecting the coast fishing, April 10, 1893," *British and Foreign State Papers*, vol. 85, p. 1286.
61 Smith, *Great Britain*, pp. 183–184.

in its place.[62] Thomas Fulton reported that Spain and Portugal later concluded a treaty, in 1885, prescribing a three-mile limit for exclusive fishing rights with respect to the coasts and fishermen of the two states.[63] But Fulton's statement about the 1885 treaty cannot be corroborated with any other source and is doubtful. His footnote cites the Treaty of October 2, 1885, which contains no three-mile provision. (See page 91.)

The Orient. Colonization of the Orient by the three-mile maritime powers of Europe reached its peak during the nineteenth century. The few oriental states that retained their independence and made claims to territorial seas opted for three miles. Japan proclaimed a three-mile neutrality zone during the Franco-Prussian War. The Japanese proclamation of July 28, 1870, reads:

> The two nations may not engage in battle between ports and inland seas, nor within three miles from land on the high seas. Their warships or merchant vessels may, however, pass as heretofore.

Although the proclamation was later revised, changing "three miles" to "three *ri* [about 6 miles] . . . such being the range of the cannons," subsequent decisions by the Sasebo Prize Court upheld the three-mile limit.[64]

Hawaii, an independent monarch between 1844 and 1898, did likewise. During both the Crimean War and the Russo-Turkish War (1877–1878), King Kamehameha issued proclamations declaring neutrality and advising that the extent of Hawaiian jurisdiction over the sea was one league from low water.[65]

The Western Hemisphere. Possibly because of Chile's particularly extensive maritime frontier, she led the way for the other Latin American states in making pronouncements concerning the territorial seas. The Civil Code of Chile, enacted in 1855, provided for the dual-zone concept—an inner zone of territorial seas and an extended zone for other purposes—practiced by several of the northern hemisphere countries:

> Article 593. The contiguous sea to the distance of a marine league counted from the low-water line is a territorial sea appertaining to the national domain; but the right of police, in all matters concerning the security of the country and the observance of the customs laws, extends to the distance of 4 marine leagues counted in the same manner.[66]

62 *Ibid.*, pp. 174, 176.
63 Fulton, *Sovereignty of Sea*, p. 666.
64 Crocker, *Marginal Sea*, pp. 603–604.
65 "Proclamation of the King of the Hawaiian Islands declaring the neutrality of his dominions in the war between Great Britain, France, Turkey, and Russia, May 16, 1854," Hertslet, *Commercial Treaties*, vol. XIV, p. 380, reproduced in Crocker, *Marginal Sea*, pp. 595–596; "Proclamation of neutrality in the war between Russia and Turkey, May 29, 1877," *British and Foreign State Papers*, vol. 68, p. 785.
66 Chilean Civil Code, December 14, 1855, translated in Crocker, *Marginal Sea*, p. 512; and the United Nations, *Laws and Regulations on the Regime of the High Seas*, vol. I, p. 61.

During the Franco-Prussian War of 1870, Chile declared a neutrality zone of 150 miles.[67] This nineteenth-century anomaly in Chilean practice is more interesting when considered in the light of Chile's 200-mile claim the following century. (See Chapters 10 and 11.)

Within the next twenty-five years, four other Latin American states followed suit with civil codes in language virtually the same as Chile's Code of 1855: Ecuador in 1857; El Salvador in 1860; Argentina in 1869; and Honduras in 1880.[68] Without giving a date, Jean Pierre François stated that Brazil, too, adopted the three-mile limit during the "nineteenth century."[69]

In the north, the Dominion of Canada was constituted in 1867 with the merger of New Brunswick, Nova Scotia and Quebec (formerly Upper and Lower Canada). One year later, Canada adopted a three-mile limit for fisheries.[70] In 1888, the Dominion proposed to the British Foreign Office that ". . . all salt water within three miles of the shore . . . should be considered within the absolute jurisdiction of Canada."[71] The Foreign Office responded that ". . . the right of the American [Canadian] Government to make regulations . . . in the waters within the three-mile limit, is not disputed."[72]

United States. Although the United States did not become an avid proponent of the three-mile limit until the twentieth century, she did not waver, at least on a formal, official basis, from her 1793 position. On several occasions, in fact, she protested violations of, or departures from, the three-mile limit. The protest against the Russian Ukase of 1821 has already been mentioned.

During the American Civil War, Secretary of State William Seward chided the British chargé for what he considered to be a veiled suggestion by the British to turn back the clock to the cannon-shot rule:

> . . . Her Majesty's government have through you, expressed a hope that the United States will concur with the British government in opinion that vessels should not fire towards a neutral shore at less distance than that which would insure shot not falling in neutral waters, or in neutral territory. . . .

67 De Lapradelle, "Le droit de l'état," p. 338.
68 Ecuadorian Civil Code of November 21, 1857, Article 582, United Nations, *Laws and Regulations on the High Seas*, vol. I, p. 67; El Salvadorian Civil Code of 1860, Article 574, *ibid.*, p. 71; Argentinian Civil Code of September 29, 1869, Article 2340, *ibid.*, p. 51; Honduran Civil Code of August 27, 1880, Article 671, *ibid.*, p. 80.
69 United Nations, *Second Report on the Regime of the Territorial Sea*, in United Nations, *Yearbook of the International Law Commission, 1953*, p. 60.
70 "Act by the Government of Canada Respecting Fishing by Foreign Vessels, May 22, 1868," Hertslet, *Commercial Treaties*, vol. XIII, p. 1107.
71 Memorandum, General Cameron to Colonial Secretary, 1888, in Baty, "Three-Mile Limit," pp. 525–526.
72 Letter, Sir Charles Tupper (Canadian High Commissioner in London) to Colonial Secretary, August 9, 1889, *ibid.*, p. 525.

> . . . Are Her Majesty's government to be understood as proposing that cannon shot shall not be fired within a distance of eight miles from neutral territory?[73]

The United States was also concerned that its fishing interests might clash with those of Russia in the North Pacific. In a diplomatic note, the United States reminded the Russians of the practice of nations whereby:

> . . . No nation would claim exemption from the general rule of public law which limits its maritime jurisdiction to a marine league from its coast. We should particularly regret if Russia should insist on any such pretension.[74]

On a later occasion in 1879, the United States protested to Mexico a Mexican attack on an American merchant vessel more than three miles distant from the Mexican coast.[75] An even stronger protest had been made in 1862 against Spain; this will be considered in the next chapter.

Nineteenth-Century Publicists

The English publicists have already been noted. Unlike them, the publicists of other states were not generally so unanimous in their approval of the three-mile limit. Those who acknowledged the three-mile limit—whether they approved of it or not—will be mentioned here. They are more numerous than those who did not acknowledge it, who will be considered in the next chapter.

PUBLICISTS PREFERRING THE CANNON-SHOT RULE

Quite a number of the nineteenth century publicists—other than British—were still partial to the cannon-shot doctrine of the previous century. Although this group acknowledged that the three-mile rule had become commonly accepted in the practice of states, they recommended that territorial waters should be extended proportionally with the increase in the range of coast artillery. One of the most distinguished publicists in this group was the Russian professor, diplomat, arbitrator, and member of the Permanent Court of Arbitration, Fedor Fedorovich de Martens (1845–1909). He advocated increasing the territorial seas from three miles to ten miles. In 1882, de Martens had written that ". . . the majority of treaties and authors recognize as a formal limit

---

73 Secretary of State Seward to Mr. Burnley, British Chargé, October 16, 1864, reproduced in Crocker, *Marginal Sea*, pp. 662–664, quoting *U.S. Diplomatic Correspondence,* 1864, vol. 2, p. 708.

74 Secretary of State Fish to the United States Minister to Russia, December 1, 1875, Moore, *Digest,* vol. I, pp. 705–706.

75 Secretary of State Evarts to Mr. Foster, April 19, 1879, Wharton, *Digest,* vol. I, p. 106.

of the littoral seas a distance of three English miles."[76] A few years later, in 1894, de Martens wrote:

> We must recognize, however, that the limits of the territorial sea ought to change with the modification in the range of cannon. . . . If at present cannons carry to 12 or 15 miles, the territorial sea of modern adjacent States ought also to extend to 15 miles. . . . In our opinion the limit of 10 miles is more in accord with the mean range of modern cannon, and a more efficacious protection of the interests of the adjacent population which live upon maritime fishing.[77]

About the same time (1887), the Spanish publicist, Marquis de Ramón de Dalmau y de Olivart (1861–1928), also used the logic of increasing cannon range to justify Spanish and Portuguese claims to six miles. Like de Martens, de Olivart, a Madrid lawyer, admitted that generally practiced international law had set the limit at three miles, but he argued that the limit should not be considered as invariable.[78]

The Argentinian publicist, Carlos Calvo (1824–1906), probably the leading modern-day Spanish language publicist, had similarly suggested a five-mile territorial sea based on the contemporary cannon range in 1868. Calvo, who had served successively as Argentinian Minister to Paris and to Berlin, acknowledged that the ". . . general doctrine of international law concerning the coastline is that territorial jurisdiction ceases 3 miles from shore." He then held that the three-mile limit was not unalterable, as it no longer agreed ". . . with the range of the newly perfected guns, whose balls can be projected to a distance of 5 miles; it is only just, then, that this limit should be proportionally extended."[79]

Most of the French publicists of the century, including Jean Félicité Théodore Ortolan (1808–1874), Antoine Louis Nuger, Paul Louis Ernest Pradier-Fodéré (1826–1904), and Joseph J. B. Imbart de Latour (1859–1924), shared much the same opinion on the matter. And at least one German language publicist, the Austrian Franz von Liszt (1851–1919), numbers among the group.

Théodore Ortolan, a French naval officer, noted that the range of cannon shot had been commonly accepted as three miles. He believed, however, that the rule of cannon shot was better founded, and advocated the idea that when cannon range increased, that the treaties and laws ought also to increase proportionally.[80]

Nuger wrote only one book, a doctor's dissertation, which has been cited

---

76 de Martens, *Traité de droit international*, vol. I, p. 500, translated in Borchardt, *North Atlantic Coast Fisheries Arbitration: Coastal Waters*, p. 225.
77 de Martens, "Le tribunal d'arbitrage de Paris et la mer territoriale," pp. 39, 43.
78 Olivart, *Tratado de derecho internacional publico*, vol. I, pp. 204–205; translated by the author.
79 Calvo, *Le droit international*, pp. 478, 484; translated by the author.
80 Ortolan, *Règles internationales et diplomatie de la mer*, vol. I, p. 169, translated in Borchardt, *Fisheries Arbitration*, pp. 284–285.

with approval by many publicists since. He shared the view of Ortolan, above, but felt more strongly about it:

> We are satisfied to have shown that the fixed measure of 3 miles is common to all nations, and has a tendency to become more generally adopted every day. . . . The truth is that this identification, correct at one time when the range of cannon did not exceed 3 miles, is today nonsense.[81]

Pradier-Fodéré, professor of international law, wrote an eight-volume treatise on European and American international law. Writing concurrently with Nuger, he took almost the same position, but in terms not quite as harsh:

> The distance adopted by the majority of States, calculated from low-water mark, is 3 geographic miles, 60 to the degree of latitude, and one may therefore see how, in view of the perfection in the art of artillery, it would become necessary to modify this mode of limiting the maritime territory. . . . [N]othing prevents States from fixing among themselves by treaty a different limit to the territorial sea.[82]

Joseph J. B. Imbart de Latour, French advocate and doctor of law, acknowledged the popularity of the three-mile rule but preferred a seaward boundary, which would vary with the increases in cannon range.[83]

In 1898, von Liszt wrote that the three-mile limit had become established in modern practice as a result of the laws and treaties of states. He felt, however, that territorial seas had as a purpose the defense of a state and were reckoned as a function of the state's ability to defend itself. He pointed out that cannon range had increased to from five to seven miles and that it would be ". . . advisable to return to the old rule . . ." of cannon shot.[84]

The German, Georg Friedrich von Martens (1756–1821), also seemed to favor the cannon-shot principle, but his work preceded the period of popular acclaim for the three-mile rule. Moreover, he equated cannon shot with three leagues, probably through a printing or translating error, which makes it difficult to ascertain and assess von Martens' position.

A prolific publicist and jurist, von Martens is most well known for his monumental, multivolume *Recueil des traités*. He published the first edition of his *Précis* in 1789, only seven years after Galiani. In it there appears a most interesting passage:

> The sea surrounding the coast, as well as those parts of it which are land-locked, such as the roads, little bays, gulphs, &c. as those which are

81 Nuger, *De l'occupation: Des droits de l'état sur la mer territoriale*, pp. 178–179, translated in Borchardt, *Fisheries Arbitration*, pp. 237–238.
82 Pradier-Fodéré, *Traité de droit international public europeen et américain*, vol. II, p. 154, translated in Crocker, *Marginal Sea*, p. 396.
83 Imbart de Latour, *La mer territoriale* p. 34, translated in Borchardt, *Fisheries Arbitration*, p. 178.
84 von Liszt, *Das Völkerrecht, systematisch dargestellt*, pp. 86–87, translated in Borchardt, *Fisheries Arbitration*, pp. 216–217.

situated within cannon shot of the shore (that is, within the distance of three leagues), are so entirely the property, and subject to the dominion, of the master of the coast. . . . In short, these parts of the sea surrounding the coast, ought to be looked upon as forming a part of the territory of the sovereign. . . .[85]

This equation of cannon shot to three leagues is inconsistent with everything that can be determined from available documents concerning artillery and ordnance of that period. As pointed out in Chapter 2, artillery range of von Martens' day was just under three miles. Wyndham Walker, in his essay on the cannon-shot rule, commented on this paragraph of von Martens, stating ". . . it appears that in the first edition of the *Précis* (1789) a curious error has crept in, making three leagues equivalent to cannon shot."[86] Bernard G. Heinzen observed that this appeared to have been straightened out by 1796, when there was published a German language edition of *Précis*, acknowledging that no cannon could shoot as far as three leagues.[87] In any event, the French second edition reads: "Can a nation acquire an exclusive right over . . . parts of an adjacent sea which exceed the range of cannon or even the distance of 3 miles?"[88] This edition, although edited and published after von Martens' death, seems to resolve the problem. The latter rhetorical question, incidentally, was answered in the affirmative with the proviso that in order to do so, the coastal state must possess a maritime police force or fleet strong enough to guarantee the extended claim.

PUBLICISTS PREFERRING THE THREE-MILE RULE

An even greater number of the nineteenth century publicists wrote approvingly of the three-mile rule. Certain of them such as the Italian Domenico Alberto Azuni (1760–1827) and the Austrian Felix Stoerk (1851–1908) espoused the position that the three-mile rule was a substantial improvement over the cannon-shot rule, which they considered obsolete.

Azuni, jurisconsult and expert on maritime affairs, followed closely, as might be expected, the lead of his countryman, Galiani. He commented very favorably on Bynkershoek's opinion that a territorial sea the width of human sight was too variable. Azuni examined the *mare clausum* claims of the Venetians and English, but sided with the *mare liberum* concept held by the Dutch and French: "In this conflict of opposite opinions, I adopt that of Galliani [sic]. . . ." Then, in language practically identical to that of Galiani, he

---

85   von Martens, *Summary of the Law of Nations* (*Précis du droit des gens*), pp. 165–166.
86   Walker, "Cannon Shot Rule," p. 229.
87   Heinzen, "Three-Mile Limit," p. 616.
88   von Martens, *Précis*, translated in Borchardt, *Fisheries Arbitration*, p. 219.

faulted the cannon-shot rule for its imprecision, and adopted the three-mile rule:

> It would be reasonable, then, in my opinion, without enquiring whether the nation, in possession of the territory, has a castle, or battery, erected in the open sea, to determine, definitively, that the jurisdiction of the territorial sea shall extend no farther than three miles from the land, which is, without dispute, the greatest distance to which the force of gunpowder can carry a ball, or bomb.[89]

Stoerk earned renown as the translator and editor of von Martens' epic *Nouveau recueil des traités*. He also wrote considerably on his own and contributed several essays to von Holtzendorff's *Handbook*. In one of these essays he pointed out that submarines, mines, dirigibles, and torpedoes have made the principle of cannon shot obsolete and that the three-mile limit has logically taken its place.[90]

Others, including the American Henry Wheaton (1785–1848), and the Germans, August Wilhelm Heffter (1796–1880), Heinrich Bernard Oppenheim (1819–1880), and Ludwig Gessner (1828–1890), observed that the states had abandoned the cannon-shot rule in favor of the three-mile rule as a matter of simple evolution.

Wheaton, American diplomat and lawyer, wrote his first edition of *Elements* in 1836. It has since been acclaimed as one of the *Classics of International Law*. On the subject of territorial waters, he wrote that the general usage of nations extends ". . . territorial jurisdiction a distance of a marine league, or as far as a cannon-shot will reach from the shore, along all coasts of the state." Within these limits, Wheaton declared, the rights of property and territorial jurisdiction of a state are absolute.[91]

Heffter, a Saxon professor and jurist, as early as 1844 cited the practice of Great Britain, France, the United States, and Belgium as evidence that the three-mile limit had become law.[92]

Heinrich Oppenheim, German publicist and political economist, wrote in 1845 (one year after Heffter) that territorial seas had traditionally been measured by cannon shot, but, citing the 1818 Anglo-American and the 1839 Anglo-French treaties, observed the trend toward fixing the territorial sea at three miles.[93]

---

89 Azuni, *The Maritime Law of Europe*, p. 204, 205.
90 Stoerk, "The Legal Regulation of the International Maritime Traffic outside of the Territory of the Adjacent State," in von Holtzendorff, *Handbuch des Völkerrechts*, vol. II, p. 473, translated in Borchardt, *Fisheries Arbitration*, p. 95.
91 Wheaton, *Elements of International Law*, p. 255.
92 Heffter, *Le droit international de l'Europe*, p. 171, translated in Borchardt, *Fisheries Arbitration*, p. 80.
93 Oppenheim, *System des völkerrechts*, p. 127, translated in Borchardt, *Fisheries Arbitration*, p. 277.

Gessner's logic concerning the evolution of the three-mile limit is difficult to follow. He stated that the

> . . . proposition of Bynkershoek has been generally adopted. This is why the rights of riparians have been augmented by the invention of rifled cannon. Formerly this distance was estimated at two leagues. To-day we ordinarily take as a basis three geographic miles.[94]

This remark about two leagues could have been prompted by any one of several two-league claims of the seventeenth or eighteenth centuries, but, appearing where it does in this passage, it seems to be a *non sequitur*.

Still others, such as the Swiss publicist Johann Kaspar Bluntschli (1808–1881), the Italian Pasquale Fiore (1837–1914), and the Frenchman B. Castel, strongly supported the three-mile rule on the basis that it was an all-purpose rule serving well all the national requirements for territorial waters.

Bluntschli, legal scholar, statesman, professor, and founder and president of the Institute of International Law, took exception to Calvo's views on extending the territorial sea with increases in cannon range:

> The perfecting of cannon is of importance for the defense of the country and has no effect upon the utilization of the territorial waters for fishing, oyster beds, etc. In this respect we must consider the distance of . . . 3 English miles, as continuing to exercise its effect and the extension of the sovereignty of the State over the high seas is not justified.[95]

Fiore, writing in 1890, agreed expressly with Bluntschli's codification efforts, and similarly "codified" the law concerning the extent of the territorial sea: "By customary law, the territorial sea extends to three miles from low water mark."[96]

Castel, in his doctor's dissertation published in 1900, declared the limit of three miles to be adequate for all the needs of a state.[97]

PUBLICISTS PREFERRING VARIOUS LIMITS FOR SPECIAL PURPOSES

There was still a third group of publicsts, who approved of the three-mile rule, but only for certain purposes. They believed that states' needs would be best served by various limits for various purposes. The most articulate of these was Albert Geouffre de Lapradelle (1871–1955). Writing in 1898, he departed from the traditional French adherence to the cannon-shot rule. In its place he elaborated a sophisticated system including a three-mile limit

---

94 Gessner, *Le droit des neutres sur mer*, p. 17, translated in Borchardt, *Fisheries Arbitration*, p. 70.
95 Bluntschli, *Le droit international codifié*, para. 302, translated in Crocker, *Marginal Sea*, p. 8.
96 Fiore, *International Law Codified and its Legal Sanctions*, p. 181.
97 Castel, *Du principe de la liberté des mers et de ses applications dans le droit commun international*, p. 86, translated in Borchardt, *Fisheries Arbitration*, p. 43.

for neutrality, "three or four" miles for fishing—accommodating the Scandinavians—and four leagues for customs.[98] At least two United States publicists should be listed in this category. James Kent (1763–1847) recommended a much wider belt—over 100 miles in certain coastal areas—for purposes of security and neutrality. Likewise Henry Wagner Halleck (1815–1872) advocated that a state was competent to exercise customs and security jurisdiction beyond the three-mile limit.

Kent, professor of law and later Chief Justice of the Supreme Court of New York, published the first edition of *Commentaries* in 1826. It has since gone through fourteen editions. He recognized the marine league to be the established legal extent of territorial seas. But he was not satisfied with so narrow a limit in view of the extensive American coasts and the problems of defending them. He suggested that the government assume control of all coastal waters

> . . . within lines stretching from quite distant headlands, as, for instance, from Cape Ann to Cape Cod, and from Nantucket to Montauk Point, and from that point to the capes of Delaware, and from the south cape of Florida to the Mississippi[!][99]

Such a baseline would enclose waters of the Gulf of Mexico as far as 140 nautical miles from land.

General Halleck served as Secretary of State of California and as Chief of Staff of the Army in addition to writing many volumes on politico-military matters and international law. On territorial waters, he stated the cannon-shot maxim poetically:

> Far as the sovereign can defend his sway,
> Extends his empire o'er the wat'ry way:
> The shot sent thundering to the liquid plain
> Assigns the limits of his just domain.

Halleck then noted that the cannon-shot range, by general usage, had become standardized at a distance of one marine league or three miles. Then he added: "And even beyond this limit States may exercise a qualified jurisdiction for fiscal and defensive purposes—that is, for the execution of their revenue laws and to prevent 'hovering on their coasts'."[100]

INTERNATIONAL ARBITRATIONS AND MULTINATIONAL CONVENTIONS

In addition to the writings of publicists and the practice of individual states, several international arbitrations and multilateral conventions of the nineteenth century contributed to the growth of the three-mile rule.

98 de Lapradelle, "Le droit de l'état," pp. 340–343.
99 Kent, *Commentaries on American Law*, vol. I, p. 29.
100 Halleck, *Halleck's International Law*, vol. I, p. 168. The poem also appears in Azuni's *Maritime Law of Europe*, p. 204, credited to an anonymous author.

THE SCHOONER *Washington* (1855)

The three-mile limit was supported by international arbitration as early as 1855. A United States-British Claims Commission was appointed under a convention of February 8, 1853, between the two countries. The Commission was to consider the case of the American fishing schooner *Washington*, which, on May 10, 1843, had been seized while fishing ten miles from the shore in the Bay of Fundy, taken to Yarmouth, Nova Scotia, forfeited to the Crown by the vice-admiralty judge, and ordered sold. The United States was pressing a claim on behalf of the owners. The United States' contention was simply that the *Washington* had been fishing on the high seas outside the three-mile limit specified in the Convention of 1818. The British contention was that the Bay of Fundy was one of the bays that the United States had renounced its right to fish in under the terms of that treaty.

The umpire, Mr. Joshua Bates, pointed out that the Franco-British fishing treaty of 1839 had defined closed bays as those which measured ten miles or less from headland to headland. Conversely, he noted that the Bay of Fundy was 65 to 75 miles wide and therefore could not be considered as a bay under the treaty of 1818, but rather as high seas, just as the Bay of Bengal and the Bay of Biscay are considered as high seas. Accordingly, on January 13, 1855, he decided the case on the basis of the three-mile rule in favor of the American owners of the *Washington*.[101]

THE NORTH SEA FISHERIES CONVENTION (1882)

Earlier in this chapter several references were made to the North Sea Fisheries Convention. The full, formal title is: "Hague Convention of 1882 for the Regulation of the Police of the Fisheries in the North Sea outside Territorial Waters." The convention had an important influence on the views and practices of its signatories. For example, Denmark, the only Scandinavian signatory to the convention, later adopted a three-mile territorial limit, the only Scandinavian country to do so. Other signatories, too, adopted the three-mile limit, if they had not already done so, or clarified ambiguities in their practice.
The important provisions of the convention are as follows:

> Article 2. The fishermen of each country shall enjoy the exclusive right of fishery within the distance of 3 miles from low water mark along the whole extent of the coasts of their respective countries, as well as of the dependent islands and banks.
> As regards bays, the distance of 3 miles shall be measured from a

101 Moore, *History and Digest of the International Arbitrations to which the United States has been a Party*, vol. IV, p. 4342.

straight line drawn across the bay in the part nearest the entrance, at the first point where the width does not exceed 10 miles. . . .

Article 3. The miles mentioned in the preceding article are geographic miles whereof sixty make a degree of latitude.[102]

The signatory powers included Great Britain, Germany, Belgium, France, Denmark, and the Netherlands. Norway and Sweden (one state under the Swedish king at the time) was the only North Sea state that did not sign the convention.

Under the convention all fishing vessels were to be registered and were to display an identifying emblem, which was to distinguish them from vessels of nonsignatory states. The convention went as far as to authorize the naval vessels of all six signatories reciprocally to visit, search, and seize vessels of their several nationalities in order to enforce the rules.[103]

THE SUEZ CANAL CONVENTION (1888)

Not as significant in its development of the three-mile rule, but nevertheless worthy of mention, is the Suez Canal Convention. The most important provision of this convention was its neutralization of the Suez Canal, guaranteeing that the Canal would be open in time of peace as well as in time of war to the merchantmen and warships of all states. In doing so it recognized the three-mile rule:

> 4. The Maritime Canal remaining open in time of war as a free passage, even to the ships of war of belligerents, according to the terms of Article 1 of the present Treaty, the High Contracting Parties agree that no right of war, no act of hostility, nor any act having for its object to obstruct the free navigation of the Canal, shall be committed in the Canal and its ports of access, as well as within a radius of three marine miles from those ports, even though the Ottoman Empire should be one of the belligerent Powers.[104]

The convention was signed on October 29, 1888, in Constantinople. Great Britain, Austria-Hungary, France, Germany, Russia, Italy, the Netherlands, Spain, and Turkey ratified the convention.

THE BERING SEA ARBITRATION (1893)

By the Seward Convention of 1867, Tsar Alexander II sold to the United States all the Russian territory and dominions on the continent of America, together with the adjacent islands. The western boundary of the ceded area passed south through the Bering Strait, and then southwesterly so as to pass

---

102 *Foreign Relations of the United States*, 1887, p. 439.
103 *Ibid.;* and *British and Foreign State Papers*, vol. 73, p. 39.
104 Crocker, *Marginal Sea*, p. 487.

midway between Attu (the westernmost of the Aleutians) and the Koman-dorskie Islands.[105]

By this treaty, Russia ceded not only Alaska, but also half of her problems in the conservation of the fur seals. The substance of the problem was this: open sea (or *pelagic*) sealing was a most efficient way of catching the seals, very valuable for their fur. Yet because of the habits of the animals, 80 to 90 percent of a catch consisted of females (cows), searching the surface of the high seas for food for their pups, which died if their mothers did not return. The fur seals were in real danger of complete extinction as a result of unrestricted pelagic fishing.[106]

Both the Russians, in 1835,[107] and the United States, in 1869,[108] passed laws that strictly forbade the taking of cows. But the Japanese and British (Canadians) were not affected by Russian and American domestic legislation and continued to take seals. In a bold attempt to exclude foreigners, the U.S. Treasury Department in 1881 interpreted the U.S. conservation legislation as applying to all waters of the Bering Sea east of the 1867 treaty boundary and sent Coast Guard cutters to enforce the new interpretation.[109] At first, foreign seal fishermen who violated the conservation laws were only warned. But in 1886, the Coast Guard commenced seizing British vessels. Fourteen were seized between 1886 and 1890 at distances from 15 to 115 miles from land, in the United States "sector" of the partitioned Bering Sea.[110] The ships were confiscated and their crews were fined and imprisoned. The British protested vigorously, and the United States agreed to negotiate the matter. A *modus vivendi* was concluded in 1891, and renewed in 1892, to the effect that the British would not permit seal fishing in the Bering Sea and that the United States would not confiscate British vessels until the matter could be arbitrated.[111]

An arbitration convention was concluded in 1892. The two governments submitted five questions to arbitration, the key question being:

> 5. Has the United States any right, and if so, what right of protection or property in the fur-seals frequenting the islands of the United States

105 United States and Russia, "Convention ceding Alaska, March 30, 1867," Malloy, *Treaties, Conventions, International Acts, Protocols and Agreements between the United States of America and Other Powers, 1776–1909*, vol. II, pp. 1521–1522.
106 Williams, "Reminiscences of the Bering Sea Arbitration," p. 569.
107 Ireland, "The North Pacific Fisheries," p. 400.
108 *Fur Seal Arbitration Proceedings*, vol. I, pp. 38–39, quoting text of legislation.
109 Williams, "Bering Sea Arbitration," p. 563.
110 U.S. Treasury Department, *Acts of Congress, Presidents' Proclamations, Regulations Governing U.S. Vessels, Acts of Parliament, Orders in Council, Pertaining to the Fur Seal Fisheries in Bering Sea and North Pacific Ocean*, pp. 21–22.
111 "Agreement between the Government of the United States and the Government of Her Britanic Majesty for a Modus Vivendi in Relation to the Fur-Seal Fisheries in Behring Sea, June 15, 1891," and "Convention Between the United States of America and Great Britain for the Renewal of the Existing 'Modus Vivendi' in Behring's Sea, April 18, 1892," *ibid.*, pp. 4–5, and 11–13.

in the Behring Sea when such seals are found outside the ordinary three-mile limit?[112]

The tribunal met in 1893, handing down its award in August, and deciding that the United States ". . . has not any right . . ." in the seals of the Bering Sea when ". . . found outside the ordinary three-mile limit."[113] The tribunal recommended certain conservation measures, which were put into practice, but were discovered to have little effect in saving the seal herd. Only the two United States members of the seven-member tribunal, Justice John Harlan and Senator John Morgan, dissented from the award. The French, Italian, Swedish, and British members constituted the five-man majority. The award was at once a defeat for the Americans and for the fur seals and a victorious step forward in the development of the three-mile rule.

Thus, the nineteenth century saw the three-mile rule become a fairly well-established rule of international law. All the great powers, and most of the lesser ones, had adopted the rule in some form. Those states that had not yet accepted it will be considered in the next chapter.

112 "Convention Between the Governments of the United States and Her Britanic Majesty, Submitting to Arbitration the Questions which Have Arisen Between those Governments Concerning the Jurisdictional Rights of the United States in the Waters of Behring Sea, February 29, 1892," *ibid.*, pp. 6–10.
113 "Award of the Tribunal of Arbitration Constituted under the Treaty Concluded at Washington, the 29th of February, 1892, Between the United States of America and Her Majesty the Queen of the United Kingdom of Great Britain and Ireland," *Fur Seal Arbitration Proceedings*, vol. I, p. 78.

CHAPTER 7

Early Resistance and Contradictions to the Three-Mile Limit

The nineteenth century witnessed a steady rise in the acceptance of the three-mile rule. Resistance to the rule and deviations from it steadily decreased. Some counterpractices were abandoned as having served their purpose. A few competing claims were suppressed by great-power politics, only to surface again in the twentieth century. But even so, the contradictions to the three-mile limit did not disappear entirely. Those which most directly related to the history of the three-mile limit will be discussed in the ensuing sections.

CLAIMS OF STATES TO DIFFERENT LIMITS

FOUR-MILE LIMIT

The four-mile limit was conceived by the Scandinavians, as pointed out in Chapter 4. It was adopted by those states and only by those states. Denmark alone abandoned it in 1882 when she signed the North Sea Fisheries Convention. For most of the nineteenth century, the four-mile limit served Norway and Sweden as an all-purpose limit—fishing, customs, neutrality—just as the three-mile limit served England.

The governing document read:

> We will most graciously to establish as a rule in all instances where there is question as to the limit of our territorial sea, that it shall extend to a distance of one marine league from the outermost islands or islets which are not submersed by the sea.[1]

---

1 "Norwegian Resolution of February 22, 1812," translated in Crocker, *Marginal Sea,* p. 609.

This policy was maintained until 1877 when the Swedish monarch approved a customs zone of approximately six miles. This Swedish law, following the example of most continental states, extended the territorial sea for customs purposes:

> Article 1 counts as territorial waters in all customs matters . . . a distance of one Swedish league (one and one-half geographical league) from the coasts or from its outermost rocks.[2]

This zone amounted to six nautical miles in width, inasmuch as the geographical league in Scandinavian usage was equal to four nautical miles.

SIX-MILE LIMIT

Spain was the recognized leading protagonist for the six-mile limit, with Portugal giving her support. The Spanish six-mile (two-league) claim, interestingly, antedates the three-mile rule. In royal decrees of 1760, 1775, and 1852 repressing contraband trade, and in a 1799 treaty with Morocco establishing a neutrality zone, Spain adopted a two-league or six-mile limit.[3] In 1830, Spain enacted a new fiscal law which, among other things, defined the crime of smuggling as the mere approach within six miles of the Spanish coast by any vessel under 200 tons that had on board any dutiable goods.[4] This led to direct confrontation with England in 1840 and 1841, during which time Royal Navy warships were deployed to protect British ships outside the one-league distance from the Spanish coast. As a result of this British pressure, Spain capitulated.[5]

The Spanish government cancelled its contract with a private Spanish firm, which was hired to enforce the Spanish law of 1830 and which had been overzealous in doing its job. The coastal protective function was assumed by a government agency, and an informal modus vivendi between Spain and England was reached wherein Spain stopped seizing British vessels. But the Spanish did not make any formal change in their laws or treaties that claimed a six-mile limit. The dispute lay dormant until 1853 when Spain again seized a British craft beyond the three-mile limit. In reply to the British protest, Spain claimed that hot pursuit had commenced within the three-mile limit.[6]

But the situation was never formally resolved. The Spanish ignored pressure from England and France to change their laws from six to three miles, and the great maritime powers ignored the Spanish six-mile limit. Knowing they would be protected by the Royal Navy, French, German, and English fisher-

---

2 "Customs Statute of November 2, 1877," translated in Crocker, *Marginal Sea*, p. 627.

3 Crocker, *Marginal Sea*, pp. 622–625, quoting decrees of December 17, 1760, May 1, 1775, and June 20, 1852; and the Spanish-Moroccan Treaty of March 1, 1799.

4 Spanish law of May 3, 1830, cited in Smith, *Great Britain*, vol. II, pp. 174, 176.

5 *Ibid.*, pp. 178–181, citing a British Foreign Office Memorandum of April 14, 1853.

6 *Ibid.*, pp. 193–194, citing an Opinion of the Queen's Advocate, dated August 10, 1853.

men fished the Spanish coast up to within three miles during the rest of the nineteenth century and into the twentieth. Philip Jessup nicely summarized the situation as one in which Spain was desirous of extending the three-mile rule but unable to do so.[7]

The Spanish, unable to defend a six-mile claim in Europe, then tried to do so in America; this led to a protracted dispute (1856–1882) with the United States. The claim by Spain to a six-mile maritime belt around Cuba led to confrontation between the two powers, particularly during the American Civil War. The Spanish complained to the United States that American warships had committed hostilities within Spanish territorial waters—between three and six miles—basing their claim to six miles on the range of modern cannon. The United States vigorously and emphatically rejected the Spanish claim to six miles and advised the Spanish Minister that the United States would not recognize jurisdiction over any waters beyond the customary three-mile limit.[8] The Spanish threatened to use their navy to enforce the claim, and during the period May through July, 1880, boarded and/or fired upon four American vessels on the Cuban coast. The two states agreed to submit the matter to arbitration by the King of Belgium, but the question was never submitted.

Undaunted by the consistent international opposition to her six-mile claim, Spain negotiated a six-mile treaty with Portugal in 1885.[9] The arrangement provided for exclusive fishing rights for Portuguese and Spanish subjects within six miles, and for conservation measures that prohibited certain types of injurious trawling within 12 miles. (This was apparently Portugal's first formal adoption of the six-mile limit. As indicated in Chapter 2, Portugal adopted the cannon-shot rule in 1787. In 1842, she concluded a treaty with Great Britain dealing with the suppression of slave trade and again fixed her territorial seas at the range of cannon.[10]) The treaty of 1885 was renegotiated, retaining these six- and twelve-mile provisions in 1893.[11] A year later, Spain enacted a new six-mile customs law.[12]

NINE-MILE LIMIT

Unlike the Scandinavian and Iberian states, Mexico stood alone in her claim to a nine-mile territorial sea. Her claim dates to 1848, with the signing of

7 Jessup, *Territorial Waters*, pp. 42–43.
8 Secretary of State Seward to Mr. Tassara, Spanish Minister, letters of December 16, 1862 and August 10, 1863, reproduced in Moore, *Digest*, vol. I, pp. 706–714.
9 Spain and Portugal, "Convention Regulating the Exercise of Fishing Rights on the Coast, October 2, 1885," Crocker, *Marginal Sea*, p. 547, citing Great Britain, Foreign Office, *British and Foreign State Papers*, vol. 77, p. 1182.
10 Portugal and Great Britain, "Treaty of July 3, 1842," translated in Crocker, *Marginal Sea*, p. 547, citing *British and Foreign State Papers*, vol. XXX, p. 533.
11 Spain and Portugal, "Treaty of Commerce and Navigation, March 27, 1893," *ibid.*, p. 626, citing *British and Foreign State Papers*, vol. 85, pp. 420 and 455.
12 Customs Law of October 15, 1894, cited by League of Nations, Committee of Experts for the Progressive Codification of International Law, *Report of the Sub-Committee on Territorial Waters*, pp. 71–72.

the Treaty of Guadalupe Hidalgo, settling the Mexican War. The treaty specified that the U.S.-Mexican boundary commenced ". . . in the Gulf of Mexico, 3 leagues from land, opposite the mouth of the Rio Grande. . . ."[13] The British protested the Treaty, suggesting that the boundary should have commenced one league from land and not three. The United States defended its actions, explaining that the treaty only applied to U.S.-Mexican relations and did not affect British rights.[14] The three-league boundary terms were repeated, almost verbatim, in the treaty formalizing the Gadsden Purchase of 1853.[15] It is almost humorous that a few years later the British concluded a nine-mile customs-zone treaty with Mexico. With respect to customs, this Anglo-Mexican treaty provided that

> . . . the two contracting parties agree to consider, as a limit of their territorial waters on their respective coasts, the distance of three marine leagues, reckoned from the line of low-water mark.[16]

Similar treaties were also negotiated by Mexico with Germany, the Kingdom of Norway and Sweden, France, El Salvador, and China.[17] The treaties with France and El Salvador called for a zone of twenty kilometers, or about 11 nautical miles.

UNITED STATES PRACTICE

The American rejection of the Spanish six-mile claim was one of several instances wherein the United States defended the three-mile rule during the nineteenth century. Others were noted in Chapter 6. But American practice was ambivalent during the century. Thomas Jefferson's opinion that the territorial seas of the United States should extend to the Gulf Stream, James Kent's view that extensive baselines should be drawn to delimit the Atlantic coast territorial sea, the three-league boundary treaty of 1848 with Mexico, and the United States claims in the Bering Sea have already been mentioned. These, coupled with several other cases, acts, and pronouncements lead logically to

13 United States and Mexico, "Treaty of Peace, Friendship, Limits, and Settlement, February 2, 1848," Article 5, United States Congress, *U.S. Statutes at Large*, vol. IX, p. 926.
14 Secretary of State Buchanan to Mr. Crampton, the British Minister, August 19, 1848, Moore, *Digest*, pp. 730–731.
15 United States and Mexico, "Treaty of Boundary, Cession of Territory, etc. . . .", December 30, 1853," Malloy, *Treaties*, vol. I, p. 1121.
16 Great Britain and Mexico, "Treaty of Commerce and Navigation, November 27, 1888," Hertslet, *Commercial Treaties*, vol. XVIII, p. 857.
17 Germany and Mexico, "Treaty of Friendship, Commerce and Navigation, December 5, 1882," Crocker, *Marginal Sea*, p. 532; Kingdom of Norway and Sweden and Mexico, "Treaty of July 29, 1885," *ibid.*, p. 605; France and Mexico, "Treaty of Amity, Commerce, and Navigation, November 27, 1886," von Martens, *Nouveau recueil général de traités*, vol. XV, p. 844; El Salvador and Mexico, "Treaty of Friendship, Commerce, and Navigation, April 24, 1893," *British and Foreign State Papers*, vol. 95, p. 1362; China and Mexico, "Treaty of Friendship, Commerce, and Navigation, December 14, 1899," *ibid.*, vol. 92, p. 1061.

the conclusion that the United States spent the nineteenth century unofficially "repenting at leisure" for the hasty decision of adopting a three-mile limit in 1793.

Bays. In 1793 when Jefferson delivered his notes adopting a three-mile limit, there occurred the first of several inconsistencies. The French frigate *L'Embuscade* had captured the British ship *Grange* in Delaware Bay. The capture took place near the mouth of the Bay, between headlands ten miles apart, and not within cannon shot or three miles of the land. United States Attorney-General Randolph rendered an opinion that, in view of American proprietorship of both the New Jersey and Delaware headlands and shores, the entire Bay was territorial. He argued that in the days of British rule, navigation of the Delaware had been "peculiar to the British Empire" and with the American Revolution this right had passed to the Americans. He concluded that in such a situation there was justification in ". . . attaching to our coasts an extent into the sea beyond the reach of cannon shot."[18] On this basis, he held that the capture of the *Grange* had been a violation of the neutrality of the United States. Randolph's opinion was not consistent with the concept of delimitation of Bays prevailing at the turn of the eighteenth century, namely, that bays could be closed off as part of a state's territory at the point where their mouths narrowed to a point equal to twice the extent of the territorial sea.

The publicist Thomas Balch claimed that the six-mile closing line for bays was formulated as a natural corollary to the three-mile rule.[19] In the early years of the three-mile limit, the British shared this view. They applied it in their interpretation of the Convention of 1818 with the United States. As late as 1870, instructions to this effect were issued by the Foreign Office to the Governor General of Canada:

> Her Majesty's Government hopes that the United States fishermen will not be for the present prevented from fishing, except within three miles of land, or in bays which are less than six miles broad at the mouth.[20]

However, in her dealings with other states, Britain was shifting to the ten-mile bay closing line. (See pages 85–86.) In any event, it appears that the United States 1793 contention was not disputed by either England or France, thus assuring Delaware Bay its status as an "historical" territorial bay.

Customs. The United States in 1799, during John Adams' administration, enacted legislation extending its customs jurisdiction to a distance of four leagues. This was in keeping with the desire of Thomas Jefferson—then vice

18 "Opinion of Attorney General Randolph on the Capture of the *Grange* by the *L'Embuscade* for the Secretary of State, May 14, 1793," Crocker, *Marginal Sea*, pp. 632–636.
19 Balch, "Is Hudson Bay a Closed or an Open Sea?" p. 417.
20 Dispatch from Lord Granville, British Foreign Secretary to the Governor General, June 16, 1870, Crocker, *Marginal Sea*, p. 556.

president—for a wider maritime zone. The new law prohibited transshipment of foreign goods once inside the four-league limit and authorized United States officials to board vessels at four leagues (twelve miles) for inspection of manifests and examination of cargos.[21] Five years later, the United States Supreme Court upheld this law by its decision in *Church v. Hubbart*, which also acknowledged the right of other states to a similar zone. An American trading ship, the *Aurora*, had been seized four leagues off the coast of Brazil and confiscated for having engaged in illicit trade in violation of Portuguese law. The Supreme Court upheld the seizure as legal, holding that a state's ". . . powers to secure itself from injury may certainly be exercised beyond the limit of its territory," and offered as an example, ". . . the right given to our own revenue cutters, to visit vessels four leagues from our coast. . . ."[22]

Neutrality. Two years after *Church v. Hubbart*, the United States negotiated a treaty with England that called for a five-mile neutral zone off the American coast. The United States, most anxious to avoid involvement in the Anglo-Napoleonic hostilities, signed the treaty with England on December 31, 1806.[23] But influential forces in England, notably in the Admiralty, resisted ratification on the grounds that three miles was the greatest extent justifiable under the law of nations.[24] In 1807, Great Britain refused to ratify the treaty, and it never became effective.

This notwithstanding, the United States remained interested in a wider neutrality zone throughout the century. In 1896, the secretary of state advised the Dutch that the United States was interested in a six-mile neutral zone. The previous year the Netherlands minister had delivered a letter to the American secretary of state, suggesting the adoption of a six-mile limit.[25] The United States replied favorably:

> This Government would not be indisposed, should a sufficient number of maritime powers concur in the proposition, to take part in an endeavor to reach an accord having the force and effects of international law as well as of conventional regulation, by which the territorial jurisdiction of a State, bounded by the high seas, should henceforth extend 6 nautical miles from low water mark, and at the same time providing that this six-mile limit shall also be that of the neutral maritime zone.[26]

21 Sections 27 and 54 of the Act of March 2, 1799, "An Act to Regulate the Collection of Duties on Imposts and Tonnage," United States Congress, *The Public Statutes at Large,* vol. I, pp. 647 and 668.

22 *Church v. Hubbart,* 2 Cranch 187 (1804), pp. 187, 234, Briggs, *The Law of Nations,* p. 356; Fenwick, *Cases,* p. 496; and Hudson, *Cases and Other Materials on International Law,* p. 627.

23 Great Britain and the United States, "Treaty of Amity, Commerce and Navigation, December 31, 1806" (unratified), reproduced in Senate, *North Atlantic Coast Fisheries Arbitration,* vol. IV, appendix, p. 42.

24 Riesenfeld, *Protection of Coastal Fisheries,* p. 138.

25 G. de Weckherlin, Netherlands Minister to Secretary of State Olney, Washington, November 5, 1895, reproduced in Crocker, *Marginal Sea,* pp. 606–607.

26 Secretary of State Olney to the Netherlands Minister, G. de Weckherlin, Washington, February 15, 1896, reproduced in Moore, *Digest,* vol. I, p. 734.

After the turn of the century, the U.S. Naval War College proposed the adoption of such a limit. Responding to the stimuli of the 1899 and 1907 Hague Conferences, the Naval War College conducted a study, "Marginal Seas and Other Waters," to determine what regulations should be made in regard to the use of marginal seas in time of war. The study proposed codifying the extent of the territorial sea: "(a) Marginal Sea.—The jurisdiction of an adjacent State over the marginal sea extends to 6 miles (60 to a degree of latitude) from the low water mark." The study cautioned that such an extension would necessarily involve a corresponding reduction in the area of the high seas, and accordingly, that it could not be accomplished except by the general agreement of the maritime states.[27]

Navigation. In 1897, the United States enacted the Inland Rules of the Road, governing the navigation of ships in and near the United States and her territories. The boundary limits wherein the rules were to apply did not conform to the three-mile limit; rather they extended to seaward as far as 15 miles in some areas. This will be covered in more detail in Chapter 13.

Claims of States for Special Purposes

Claims to different limits such as the six-mile limit, discussed previously, were not the only type of contradiction to the three-mile limit. Another type of contradiction was that of claiming an area of the sea for a special purpose. Claims over special zones for customs—four miles, four leagues, ten kilometers, two myriameters, etc.—contradict the three-mile limit and have already been mentioned in connection with the practice of several states. Special-purpose claims did not, in the eyes of the claimant states, necessarily conflict with the three-mile limit. In fact, Great Britain, the most persistent defender of the three-mile limit, advanced the greatest number and the widest variety of claims for special purposes.

SEABED SEDENTARY LIFE

Legislation to protect fisheries, the sea-grass feeding grounds, and the sea bottom life is not new. As early as 1829, the French enacted an ordinance to restrict harmful trawling within three leagues of the French coast.[28] This ordinance prohibited trawling within three leagues of the shore between April 15th and September 1st, and within two leagues from September 1st to April 15th. Thomas Fulton wrote that the law was enforced against foreigners, but did not cite the instances.[29] In 1868, the British Parliament empowered the Irish Commissioner to regulate or restrict oyster dredging as far as 23 miles

---

27 United States Naval War College, *International Law Topics and Discussions, 1913*, p. 11.
28 "French Marine Department Ordinance of January 15, 1829," Baty, "Three-Mile Limit," p. 534.
29 Fulton, *Sovereignty of the Sea*, p. 608.

from the coast through the Sea Fisheries Act. The act protected oyster beds and banks located

> . . . within the distance of twenty miles measured from a straight line drawn from the eastern point of Lambay Island to Carnsore Point on the Coast of Ireland, outside of the exclusive fishing limits of the British Islands. . . .[30]

The protected area included 1,300 square nautical miles outside the three-mile limit, and projected in places as far as twenty miles beyond that limit.[31] A similar act in 1895 enabled the Fishery Board to prohibit ". . . the methods of fishing known as beam trawling and otter trawling . . . within thirteen miles of the Scottish coast. . . ."[32] The act provided that there would be no enforcement of the act against subjects of signatories of the North Sea Fisheries Convention of 1882 without the express prior agreement of the signatories.

Not all of the special-purpose claims extended beyond three miles. Austria-Hungary and Italy modestly claimed exclusive sponge and coral fishing zones only one mile wide. A treaty between them provided that the subjects of Austria-Hungary and those of Italy were authorized to fish along the coasts of each state

> . . . with the exception, however, of coral and sponge fishing, as well as the fisheries, to the distance of one nautical mile, which are reserved exclusively to the inhabitants of the coasts.[33]

The British, however, were not so modest in their efforts to protect the pearl and chank fisheries of Ceylon. Those fisheries were claimed from early times, first by the Rajahs, and then successively by their Portuguese, Dutch, and British colonial masters. By a series of three acts, Great Britain laid claim to the Ceylonese pearl, chank, coral, bêche-de-mer, and shell fishing grounds—excluding all foreigners—within the twelve-fathom curve, the twelve-mile limit, and the twenty-mile limit, successively. The fisheries are located in the Gulf of Manaar and Palk's Bay, the two coral bays that separate India from Ceylon. These bays in turn are separated by the long stretch of islets between India and Ceylon known as Adam's Bridge. The British Colonial Act of 1811 authorized the seizure and confiscation of any boat hovering or anchoring in the pearl banks or in waters between four and twelve fathoms deep.[34]

---

30 "Sea Fisheries Act of July 13, 1868," 31 and 32 Victoria, chap. 45, reproduced in Crocker, *Marginal Sea*, p. 554.
31 Hurst, "Whose is the Bed of the Sea?" p. 41; and Jessup, *Territorial Waters*, p. 13.
32 "Act for the Better Regulation of Scottish Sea Fisheries, July 6, 1895," 58 and 59 Victoria, chap. 42, Hertslet, *Commercial Treaties*, vol. 20, p. 608.
33 Austria-Hungary and Italy, "Treaty of Commerce and Navigation, December 6, 1891," translated in Crocker, *Marginal Sea*, p. 599, citing *British and Foreign State Papers*, vol. 83, p. 655.
34 "Regulation No. 3 of 1811 for the Protection of H. M. Pearl Banks of Ceylon, March 9, 1811," reproduced in Crocker, *Marginal Sea*, p. 544; see also Jessup, *Territorial Waters*, pp. 14–16; and Hurst, "Bed of the Sea," pp. 40–41.

Another protective ordinance was passed in 1843 prohibiting chank fishing or even the possession of fishing and dredging equipment within twelve miles of the low-water mark between the towns of Talaivilla and Talaimanaar.[35] A third, even more restrictive, ordinance was passed in 1890, making it unlawful to fish, dive for, or collect chanks, bêche-de-mer, coral, or shells in the area ". . . eastward of a straight line drawn from a point six miles westward of Talaimanaar to a point six miles westward from the shore two miles south of Talaivilla."[36] This ordinance created an irregularly shaped geographic protective area extending as far as 20 miles from the shore.[37] But the British did not feel that these claims conflicted with the three-mile limit, as they were based on long standing prescriptive rights. Even Vattel, the Swiss publicist, supported this view: "Who can doubt that the pearl fisheries of Bahrein and Ceylon may be lawful objects of ownership?"[38] In Australia, too, Great Britain instituted protective measures for the pearl shell and bêche-de-mer fisheries. Acts of Parliament in 1888 and 1889 authorized the respective colonial parliaments in Queensland and in Western Australia to regulate fisheries in the Coral Sea to a distance of 250 miles and in the Indian Ocean to a distance of 600 miles.[39] Neither of these two acts was applicable to any except British ships and boats.

SUBSOIL MINERALS

Another special-purpose claim to maritime areas arose as a result of the very rich and important tin and copper mines at Cornwall, England.[40] The tin mines of Cornwall had been worked as early as the Bronze Age. Later, Cornish copper became equally important, and by the middle of the nineteenth century, the area was producing one-third of the copper mined in Europe. The ore there was found in veins along the coast, beneath both the peninsula and the seabed. As the veins were exploited, the tunnel complex gradually worked its way beyond the shoreline and beneath the open sea. A dispute arose between the Crown and the Duchy of Cornwall over the ownership of the minerals taken from beneath the seabed. The matter was arbitrated by Judge John Peterson of the Court of Queen's Bench, and his award was enacted as the Cornwall Submarine Mines Act of 1858. The act assigned the right to all mines and minerals between the high- and low-water marks in

35 "Ordinance to Declare Illegal the Possession of Certain Nets and Instruments within Certain Limits, November 30, 1843," reproduced in Crocker, *Marginal Sea,* pp. 548–549.
36 "Chank Ordinance of November 19, 1890," reproduced in Crocker, *Marginal Sea,* p. 577.
37 Baty, "Three-Mile Limit," p. 512.
38 Vattel, *Law of Nations,* p. 107.
39 "The Queensland pearl-shell and bêche-de-mer fisheries (extraterritorial) Act of January 20, 1888," reproduced in Crocker, *Marginal Sea,* pp. 574–575; and "The Western Australia pearl-shell and bêche-de-mer fisheries 'extraterritorial' Act of February 4, 1899," reproduced in *ibid.,* pp. 576–577.
40 See "Cornwall," *Encyclopaedia Britannica* (1953 edition) VI, 452–453.

the County of Cornwall to the Prince of Wales and the right to all mines and minerals seaward of the low-water mark and under the open sea to the Queen.[41] The act did not set a seaward limit to the Queen's mineral rights. In defense of this action, the British publicist Lassa Oppenheim explained that the subsoil under the open sea is "no-man's-land" and can be acquired by occupation; occupation, he wrote, takes place *ipso facto* by a tunnel or mine being driven from the shore, through the subsoil of the territorial sea, and beyond, into the subsoil of the open sea.[42] An interesting sidelight is that this 1858 case was almost a blueprint for the century-later contests in the United States between the Federal Government and the states of California, Louisiana, and Texas over offshore petroleum resources wherein the Supreme Court similarly decided that the mineral rights beyond the low-water mark were vested not in the individual states, but in the U.S. Federal Government.[43]

Although the Cornish tin and copper mines did not extend beyond the three-mile limit, underwater coal mines elsewhere in England did. The publicist Paul Fauchille (1858–1926) wrote

> . . . Great Britain . . . exploits beneath the sea, to several [*plusieurs*] kilometers from her coast, tin and copper mines in Cornwall, and coal mines in Cumberland County as well as between Folkestone and Dover.[44]

Burdick Brittin wrote: "Coal mines of Great Britain, whose tunnels commence on dry land, extend far beyond the 3-mile limit."[45] With respect to the Cornish copper and tin mines, British geologist G. Bisson reported that

> [t]he Levant Mine worked just less than one mile to seaward of the extreme west coast of Cornwall in the vicinity of St. Just, and this I believe was the greatest seaward penetration by any of the mines. . . .[46]

With respect to the coal mines, Mr. W. B. Evans wrote that

> . . . [t]he maximum extension of coal mining beneath the sea-bed from collieries near Whitehaven is a little over 3½ miles, (nearly 6 Km). Although reserves exist beyond this line, it seems unlikely that it will ever be economic to develop them.[47]

41 Hurst, "Bed of the Sea," pp. 34–35, quoting from Cornwall Submarine Mines Act of August 2, 1858.
42 Oppenheim, *International Law, a Treatise*, vol. I, p. 630.
43 *United States v. California*, 332 U.S. 19 (1947); *United States v. Louisiana*, 339 U.S. 699 (1950); and *United States v. Texas*, 399 U.S. 707 (1950); Whiteman, *Digest of International Law*, vol. IV, pp. 769–783.
44 Fauchille, *Traité de droit international public*, vol. I, pt. 2, p. 205, translated by the author.
45 Brittin, *International Law for Seagoing Officers*, p. 80.
46 Letter by Mr. G. Bisson, District Geologist, Institute of Geological Sciences, Exeter, Devon, England, to author, dated 5 December 1969.
47 Letter by Mr. W. B. Evans, Institute of Geological Sciences, Leeds, Yorkshire, England, to author, dated 5 January 1970.

This is corroborated by the *Encyclopaedia Britannica*, which diagrams the coal deposits at Whitehaven, Cumberland County, as extending about nine statute miles to seaward and those at Dover, Kent County, to about five statute miles.[48]

CRIMINAL AND ADMIRALTY JURISDICTION

In 1833 and 1843, Great Britain established courts of justice in Canton and Hong Kong, respectively, to try British subjects for criminal and admiralty offenses committed in China or within 100 miles thereof.[49] The result was a very unique type of maritime jurisdiction wherein a British subject might commit a crime in violation of Chinese law, aboard a Chinese ship, against a Chinese citizen, 100 miles off the Chinese coast, but still be subject to British, rather than Chinese, jurisdiction. British courts had authority to try British subjects for offenses committed ". . . within the dominion of the Emperor of China, or being within any ship or vessel at a distance of not more than one hundred miles from the coast of China."[50] Here again, Britain did not consider herself departing from the three-mile limit. The arrangement for extraterritorial jurisdiction or "capitulations," dating from the Middle Ages, was still commonly practiced by European powers in non-Christian states, generally of the Near East and Far East, as late as the nineteenth and early twentieth centuries. Hence, no maritime or great power would have had occasion to protest the British 100-mile jurisdiction law.

VIEWS OF PUBLICISTS AND LEARNED SOCIETIES

The several nineteenth century publicists whose writings were reviewed in the preceding chapter all recognized that the three-mile limit had been generally accepted as the law of nations. The present chapter will consider those nineteenth-century publicists who did not acknowledge that the three-mile limit had become law, but either rejected it in favor of another limit of territorial seas, or ignored it altogether. These writers, by and large, were still loyal to the rule of cannon shot, which had been very popular. A general tendency can be detected among the nineteenth-century publicists to adhere fairly closely to the contemporary practice of their native states. There were several exceptions, of course, and the publicists of landlocked Switzerland had to base their opinions on the practice of other states—which incidentally might well make them the most objective of all.

48 "Coal and Coal Mining," *Encyclopaedia Britannica* (1953 edition), V, 873.
49 British Order in Council, Appointing a Court of Justice at Canton, for the Trial of Offenses Committed by British Subjects in China, December 9, 1833," *British and Foreign State Papers*, vol. XX, p. 262; and Act of Parliament, "For the Better Government of Her Majesty's Subjects Resorting to China, August 22, 1843," *ibid.*, vol. XXXI, p. 1231.
50 *Ibid.*

PUBLICISTS WHO REJECTED THE THREE-MILE LIMIT

The Swiss publicist Alphonse Rivier (1835–1898) rejected not only the three-mile limit, but also the four- and six-mile limits in favor of a standard, scientifically and internationally determined cannon range.[51] Rivier, professor of international law and Swiss consul general in Brussels, proposed a belt of territorial seas the width of a standard cannon range, as determined by ". . . the state of science and industry . . ." on a worldwide basis, and not left up to the various cannon ranges of the several individual maritime countries.[52] He did not go into any further detail on how this standard cannon range would be determined.

The Frenchman, Laurent Basile Hautefeuille (1805–1875), believed it impractical to attempt to quantify cannon range at any fixed "mathematical" distance.[53] Hautefeuille, a jurist and prolific authority on maritime law, published the first edition of his major work on the subject in 1848. In it, he made an articulate defense of the classic cannon-shot doctrine. He then commented on the prospect of equating cannon range to a fixed distance:

> A modern author (Boucher) has expressed the wish that all nations may agree to determine exactly and mathematically the extent of the territorial sea or rather the range of cannon shot. . . . It would certainly be very desirable . . . that the territorial seas of each country be fixed in a definite manner. However, I do not believe that it is possible to reach this result. Besides, the experienced eye of mariners and coast guards can pretty well determine the range of cannon shot.[54]

Hautefeuille was quoting the French publicist Pierre B. Boucher (1758–1814?), author of *Institution au droit maritime,* diplomatic official, jurisconsult, and professor of maritime law.

Four other French publicists, Théophile Funck-Brentano (1830–1906), Albert Sorel (1842–1906), Robert Piédelièvre (1859–1939), and Baron Ferdinand de Cussy (1795–1866), maintained that it was the range of cannon shot, and not three miles, which was the basic, universal rule. The Germans, Ferdinand Paul Perels (1836–1903) and Walther Schücking (1875–1935), were of the same opinion, holding that the territorial sea should be extended as the range of cannons increased.

Funck-Brentano, professor of political science, and Sorel, professor and historian, collaborated in 1877 to produce a work on international law, strongly

---

51 Rivier, *Principes du droit des gens,* vol. I, p. 146, translated in Crocker, *Marginal Sea,* pp. 419–420.
52 *Ibid.,* p. 420.
53 Hautefeuille, *Des droits et des devoirs des nations en temps de guerre maritime,* vol. I, 52, translated in Borchardt, *North Atlantic Coast Fisheries Arbitration, Coastal Waters,* p. 76.
54 *Ibid.,* pp. 52–53.

oriented towards European practice.[55] Concerning the three-mile limit treaties, they wrote:

> Conventions concluded between States may more exactly delimit the territorial seas on their respective coasts. This has, for example, been effected between France and Great Britain in the matter of fisheries. These conventions naturally bind only the States which contract them. For other States the territorial sea is determined by usage.[56]

Piédelièvre, professor of international law and essayist wrote:

> This extreme range of cannon is usually considered by treaties both of fishing and neutrality as 3 miles, but this is neither general nor universal. . . . It is certain that in the absence of all conventions the extent of the marginal sea is measured by the greatest range of cannon placed on shore, whatever that range may be.[57]

Baron de Cussy, who served as French consul general in Palermo, rejected the three-mile limit in favor of the cannon-shot rule for purposes of neutrality. But he agreed that ". . . the surveillance which ought to be exercised in the matter of customs to prevent smuggling, may extend still further."[58]

Perels, professor at the Imperial Naval Academy, legal advisor to the admiralty and privy councilor, published his first important work in 1882. In it, he stated that it is a mistake to equate cannon shot with three miles on the grounds that it is the cannon shot, and not three miles, which is the rule of law. He congratulated the "German publicists and the majority of French and Italian" publicists who ". . . have not fallen into this error." He believed, like Rivier, that:

> The extent of the territorial sea is therefore fixed according to the cannon range of each epoch; but in each epoch it is the same for all seas, for the matter cannot depend upon each particular country's establishing batteries upon its coast. . . .[59]

Schücking, member of the Reichstag and a judge of the Permanent Court of International Justice, wrote a great number of volumes on law, including one on the territorial sea (*küstenmeer*). He examined the various claims, includ-

---

55 Funck-Brentano and Sorel, *Précis du droit des gens*, p. 375, translated in Borchardt, *Fisheries Arbitration*, p. 68.
56 *Ibid*.
57 Piédelièvre, *Précis de droit international public ou droit des gens*, vol. I, p. 336, translated in Borchardt, *Fisheries Arbitration*, p. 299.
58 De Cussy, *Phases et causes*, vol. I, p. 93, translated in Borchardt, *Fisheries Arbitration*, p. 50.
59 Perels, *Manuel de droit maritime international*, p. 26, translated in Borchardt, *Fisheries Arbitration*, p. 292.

ing the three-mile rule, and then recommended a definition of the law of territorial seas:

> . . . [E]very adjacent State has the right to extend its boundaries as far over the sea as it thinks necessary for its protection against disease, smuggling, etc., but it shall not trespass in the limit marked by a cannon's range [at the time, about ten miles].[60]

PUBLICISTS WHO IGNORED THE THREE-MILE LIMIT

The German publicists Theodor Schmalz (1760–1831) and Johann Klüber (1762–1837) both supported the cannon-shot rule. Neither of them mentioned the three-mile limit, even though Great Britain had already adopted it at the time of their writings. Schmalz, an appellate judge and professor of jurisprudence, must have been influenced either by the 1789 edition of von Martens' *Précis* or by the three-league provision of the 1763 Treaty of Paris, because in 1817 he wrote that

> . . . the sea ought to belong to the nation as far as the defence of the coasts may extend, taking as the standard of measurement the range of cannon shot, but since then it has been fixed quite arbitrarily at three marine leagues.[61]

Klüber, whose first edition was published in 1809, was a professor of law, a ranking civil servant, and a member of the Prussian delegation to the Congress of Vienna. His writings adhere strictly to the cannon-shot rule.[62]

The French publicist Eugène Cauchy (1802–1877), even though writing several decades later, took the same approach as Schmalz and Klüber. Cauchy, a ranking civil servant in the French Ministry of Justice and a maritime lawyer, asked rhetorically ". . . will not the improvements made daily in this formidable art of artillery modify in the future the limit of the imaginary line which is thus drawn upon the seas?"[63]

The Italian, Giuseppe Carnazza-Amari (1837–1911), proposed a belt of territorial waters, the width of cannon range, measured from a series of straight cape-to-cape baselines. Carnazza-Amari, a judge and professor, formulated a system (84 years ahead of its time) of measuring the territorial sea using these baselines:

> In order to stifle all contests which the irregularities of the shore might give rise to, we measure the range of cannon fire as if they were discharged from

---

60 Schücking, *Küstenmeer*, p. 10, translated in Borchardt, *Fisheries Arbitration*, p. ·328.
61 Schmalz, *Le droit des gens européen*, p. 144, translated in Borchardt, *Fisheries Arbitration*, p. 322.
62 Klüber, *Droit des gens moderne de l'Europe*, p. 180, translated in Borchardt, *Fisheries Arbitration*, p. 103.
63 Cauchy, *Le droit maritime international*, vol. I, p. 40, translated in Borchardt, *Fisheries Arbitration*, p. 54.

the headlands which project into the sea. We thus obtain a curved or straight line without any sinuosities mapped out from one promontory to another. The territorial sea extends from this line as far as the range of cannon.[64]

The Portuguese writer, Carlos Testa (1823–1891), also ignored the three-mile limit but utilized the doctrine of cannon shot to justify the Iberian six-mile claims. Testa, a naval officer and professor at the Lisbon Naval Academy, referred to the limit of territorial waters at extreme cannon range as the "line of respect," i.e., the limit to which a state could command the respect of other states. Then, presumably in defense of Portugal's six-mile fishing convention with Spain, he added that

> although the greatest range of cannon is the measure usually adopted, nothing prevents powers from conventionally agreeing upon a greater extent to their territorial sea, with the object of common utility or for the better regulation of their respective commercial interests.[65]

LEARNED SOCIETIES

Institute of International Law. The Institute of International Law was organized in Ghent in September, 1873. Its work has included extensive research and codification on nearly all aspects of international law. Its members are specialists in international law. Most of the nineteenth-century publicists mentioned heretofore were members of the Institute. At its Paris session in 1894, the Institute adopted a set of rules on the territorial sea, proposing a six-mile limit. The proposed article on the territorial sea read:

> The Institute: Considering that there is no reason to confound in a single zone the distance necessary for the exercise of sovereignty and for the protection of coastwise fishing and that which is necessary to guarantee the neutrality of non-belligerents in time of war; That the distance most generally adopted of three miles from low-water mark has been recognized as insufficient for the protection of coastwise fishing; That this distance, moreover, does not correspond to the actual range of guns placed on the coast; Has adopted the following provisions: . . . Art. 2. The territorial sea extends 6 marine miles (60 to a degree of latitude) from the low-water mark along the full extent of the coasts.[66]

International Law Association. The International Law Association was also organized in 1873, but in Brussels. Its object was to reform and codify interna-

64 Carnazza-Amari, *Traité du droit international public en temps des paix,* translated from the Italian *Trattado di diritto internazionale pubblico* by Revest, vol. II, p. 64, translated in Borchardt, *Fisheries Arbitration,* pp. 39–40. *Cf. post,* Anglo-Norwegian fisheries dispute, Chapters 9 and 11.

65 Testa, *Le droit public international maritime,* translated in Borchardt, *Fisheries Arbitration,* p. 342.

66 Institute of International Law (Barclay, reporter), "Report of the Third Commission: Définition et régime de la mer territoriale," pp. 517–519.

tional law, but most of its efforts were directed towards popularizing questions of international law by public discussion. Its membership was not limited to international law specialists, but included men of any profession who were interested in international affairs. Many international lawyers, of course, were members of both organizations. Sir Thomas Barclay, who had been reporter of the Territorial Sea Commission of the Institute, served also as secretary of the Special Committee on Territorial Waters of the Association. The Association adopted in 1895 a set of rules identical, for all practical purposes, to the 1894 rules of the Institute.[67]

INTERNATIONAL TRIBUNALS AND MULTILATERAL AGREEMENTS

THE SAINT HELENA HOVERING ACT OF 1816

Certainly one of the most unique contradictions to the three-mile rule was the Saint Helena Hovering Act of 1816. It might fairly be said that this was not a genuine contradiction to the three-mile rule inasmuch as the three-mile rule had not yet become established at that early date. However, the Saint Helena Act would have been a contradiction to any of the three-mile limit's antecedents, so it is noted here.

Napoleon had escaped from the Mediterranean island of Elba in January, 1815, and returned to Europe to lead France against the other Great Powers. After his defeat at Waterloo, he was banished to the South Atlantic British island of St. Helena. On this occasion the powers took more effective precautions to prevent another escape. With the approval of the "Concert of Europe," the British enacted the Act of 1816. The act prohibited British vessels from approaching St. Helena without license, and non-British vessels from remaining within twenty-four miles of St. Helena, after being warned to leave.[68] Apparently no state ever objected to the arrangement, and in any event, it only lasted five years until Napoleon's death in 1821.

THREE-LEAGUE DECLARATION OF 1874

Henry Crocker's State Department compilation of documents on the extent of the territorial sea cites a multilateral declaration by seven states in 1874. The declaration, signed by the United States, Germany, Austria, Italy, Denmark, Holland, and Belgium, provided ". . . that if the limit of the territorial sea should be determined by an international agreement three sea leagues should be the minimum."[69] The year 1874, was also the year that the British Government, exasperated with Spain's claim to six miles, sent out a circular inquiry

---

67 The International Law Association, *Report of the Seventeenth Conference of the International Law Association*, pp. 102, 109–110.
68 Baty, "Three-Mile Limit," p. 513, and Hilbert, "The Three-Mile Limit of Territorial Waters," p. 809.
69 Crocker, *Marginal Sea*, p. 485.

to the several maritime states requesting their views toward the Spanish six-mile claim.[70] This writer found no direct tie between the British circular inquiry and the Declaration of 1874, but the timing of the two suggests a possible connection. Walther Schücking wrote that the Declaration of 1874 was made on the occasion of an international conference on the regulation of the Sound fisheries.[71] Hence, it seems possible that the circular inquiry may have triggered the interest, and the conference forum provided the opportunity.

THE *Alleganean* (1885)

During the century that followed the seizure of the *Grange* (1793), the three-mile rule and the ten-mile bay baseline rule had become fairly well established among the maritime states. Then in 1885, there came before the bench a very similar test case, that of the *Alleganean*. During the American Civil War, Confederate naval officers had captured the ship *Alleganean*, anchored in Chesapeake Bay more than four miles from the nearest land. The *Alleganean* was a cargo ship registered in New York. Her cargo was destined for London and consigned to British subjects. The injured parties claimed that her New York registry entitled the vessel to U.S. protection against the action of Confederate rebels on the high seas. The mouth of Chesapeake Bay is twelve miles wide. Consequently, the claimant contended the ship was seized on the high seas, and thus, the seizure was illegal. The United States, defendent in the case, held that the Chesapeake Bay was entirely within U.S. territory. The case was referred to international arbitration. The tribunal was that which had convened in the case of the *Alabama* claims in 1872, and was reestablished to sit in the case of the *Alleganean*, with United States, British, Swiss, Italian and Brazilian members on the court. The arbitral tribunal decided in favor of the United States:

> The [Chesapeake Bay] headlands are about twelve miles apart and the bay is probably nowhere more than twenty miles in width. The length may be two hundred miles. To call it a bay is almost a misnomer. It is more a mighty river than an arm or inlet of the ocean.[72]

The tribunal then examined the case of the *Grange*, seized in Delaware Bay, and compared the two cases:

> It will hardly be said that Delaware Bay is any less an inland sea than Chesapeake Bay. Its configuration is not such as to make it so. . . .[73]

---

70 *Ibid.*, p. 557, reproduces the copy of the circular inquiry sent to the United States, citing *British and Foreign State Papers*, vol. 70, p. 186; and Heinzen, "The Three-Mile Limit: Preserving the Freedom of the Seas," p. 633, notes 154 and 155.
71 Schücking, *Küstenmeer*, pp. 9–10.
72 *The Alleganean, Stetson v. United States*, No. 3993, Class 1, Second Court of Commissioners of *Alabama* Claims, Moore, *Arbitrations*, vol. IV, p. 4332.
73 *Ibid.*, p. 4341.

Finally, after citing the British claim to Conception Bay, Newfoundland, with its twenty-mile entrance, the tribunal held that Chesapeake Bay was not part of the high seas, a distinct victory for the United States, but a contradiction to the three-mile limit.

CONGRESS OF MONTEVIDEO (1889)

The first South American Congress on Private International Law met in Montevideo from August, 1888, to February, 1889, on the invitation of Argentina and Uruguay. Five other states accepted the invitation, Bolivia, Brazil, Chile, Paraguay, and Peru. The Congress approved eight draft treaties and a protocol on several aspects of private international law.[74] Some of the draft treaty articles touched on public international law. In particular, Article 12 of the Treaty on International Penal Law adopted a territorial sea of five miles:

> For the purpose of penal jurisdiction, declared as territorial waters, are those which are included within the extent of five miles from the terra firma and from the islands which are part of the territory of each State.[75]

The treaty was signed by Argentina, Bolivia, Paraguay, and Uruguay, but only Uruguay followed through on the five-mile limit, declaring the same in a neutrality decree: "Article 2. In accordance with the principles established by the Treaty of Montevideo in 1889 (Penal Law, article 12), and with the principles generally accepted in these matters, the waters will be considered as territorial waters to a distance of five miles from the coast. . . ."[76] This claim by Uruguay encountered British opposition during World War I.[77] Nevertheless, Uruguay has upheld her five-mile claim for neutrality purposes since that time.

Costa Rica Packet CASE (1897)

In 1891, the Australian master of the whaling ship *Costa Rica Packet* was arrested by order of a Dutch court in the Dutch East Indies for an offense committed in 1888, and later shown to have been committed outside Dutch territorial seas. The claim for damage was referred by England and Holland to an arbitrator, Fedor F. de Martens, the well-known Russian publicist, diplo-

74 Inter-American Institute of International Legal Studies, *The Inter-American System*, p. xix.
75 "Article 12, Traité de droit pénal international, Treaty of Montevideo, January 25, 1889," reproduced in Pradier-Fodéré, "Le Congrès de droit international Sud-Américain et les traités de Montevideo," p. 563, translation by the author; and Bustamente y Sirven, *La Mer Territoriale*, p. 41.
76 "Presidential Decree Establishing Rules of Neutrality to Be Observed in the Ports, Roadsteads and Territorial Waters of Uruguay, 7 August 1914," reproduced in United Nations, *Law and Regulations of the High Seas*, vol. I, p. 130.
77 Jessup, *Territorial Waters*, p. 49.

mat, and jurist. His award properly called upon Holland to pay damages. But the case attained some notoriety because of the dictum rendered with the award. De Martens, fully aware that both England and Holland claimed a three-mile limit of territorial waters, completely ignored the three-mile limit, and decided the case on the basis of the rule of cannon shot.[78] That he used the arbitration to give effect to his well-known personal view was all the more obvious because the alleged offense had taken place outside both the three-mile limit and the ten-mile limit, which de Martens claimed the range of cannon shot currently to be.

In summary, by the end of the nineteenth century, Mexico, Spain, Portugal, and Sweden and Norway were still resisting the mounting pressures to adopt the three-mile limit. All other countries had adopted the three-mile limit in one or more of its forms. A majority of publicists recognized the three-mile rule as law, but a considerable number still preferred the rule of cannon shot. There were several instances of special claims for special purposes, but in most cases the claimants believed their claims not to be in contradiction of the three-mile limit. Lastly, towards the end of the century, there was evidence of significant interest in the possibility of a six-mile limit.

78 Great Britain and Netherlands, Claims Arbitration, February 13/24, 1897, Crocker, *Marginal Sea*, pp. 582–584; Moore, *Arbitrations*, vol. 5, pp. 4952–4954.

CHAPTER 8

The Early Twentieth Century: The Three-Mile Limit Becomes Paramount

It was noted in Chapter 6 that Britain enjoyed maritime supremacy in 1815. She continued to enjoy that position throughout the century, and even at the outbreak of World War I there was no state that approached Britain in strength of either merchant or naval shipping. It must be pointed out, however, that Britain's maritime strength vis-à-vis the other powers was declining. Whereas in 1815, Britain's navy was larger than all others combined, by 1914 the combined navies of Germany, France, and the United States exceeded that of England, as indicated in Table 1.

The decline of the Royal Navy in relative numerical superiority was just

Table 1
Comparative Naval Strengths of Selected States in 1914*

State	Capital Ships and Battle Cruisers	Cruisers	Total Major Warships	(Major Warships under Construction)
Great Britain	72	120	192	(19)
Germany	39	50	89	(16)
United States	35	32	67	(4)
France	25	27	52	(8)
Japan	20	21	41	(6)
Italy	11	17	28	(5)
Russia	9	14	23	(17)

* From "Great Britain," *Encyclopaedia Britannica* (1953 edition), X, 688. Figures for Great Britain include three major warships of Australia.

that, and only that—a relative decline. The nineteenth century, with the invention of the Armstrong gun, the naval steam boiler, and steel armored ships, sounded the death knell for the wooden battleships and navies of 1815. By 1914 the Royal Navy had been converted to steam and steel with the construction of the well-known *Dreadnaught* battleship fleet. In fact, in 1914 the British fleet was at its highest state of efficiency and strength.[1] But the other powers were able to take advantage of the midcentury mass obsolescence of the British wooden fleet, and commenced building modern fleets of their own late in the nineteenth century. Although they did not keep pace with Great Britain, as the figures show, they did narrow the gap.

The merchant shipping picture was much the same as the naval fleet situation in 1914. In 1886, over half the merchant tonnage of the world sailed under the Union Jack.[2] Of the world's total tonnage at that time, about one-half was still under sail. By 1914, however, when the world's total tonnage had more than doubled to 49 million gross tons, 92 percent of it was steam powered. The British claimed 21 million tons of that 1914 total, or four times as much as either of her closest competitors, Germany and the United States, as shown in Table 2.

By 1914, two non-European countries, the United States and Japan, were among the top maritime powers. Whereas only European states had figured as important maritime powers at the beginning of the nineteenth century, events at the end of the century heralded the debut of non-European states as principal members of the cast on the stage of world politics. First, there was the Spanish-American War of 1898. During much of the nineteenth century, the United States pursued her policy of "manifest destiny" which, in the end, provided her with frontiers on two oceans. That accomplished, she was ready, in the words of Rudyard Kipling, to "take up the white man's burden"; and the United States' adventure in the Spanish-American War added her to the roster of imperial powers. In losing that war, Spain forfeited most of her remaining colonies. The Spanish claims to six-mile territorial seas around Cuba, the Philippines, and Puerto Rico were replaced by the United States' three-mile claims.

In the far east, there followed shortly a similar event. The Japanese surprised the world with a brilliant military victory over Russia in the Russo-Japanese War of 1904–1905. For the second time in seven years, a non-European state had defeated a European state. Not only did this war serve as the harbinger of the development of the Japanese Empire, but also it signaled the decline of Imperial Russia as a leading world power; and the government of the Tsars never recovered from that blow. Interestingly, to settle the war Russia accepted the mediation of the United States, further enhancing the international prestige of the latter country. The Peace of Portsmouth in 1905 resulted in Russia's cession of the southern half of Sakhalin to Japan; consequently, roughly

1 "Great Britain," *Encyclopaedia Britannica* (1953 edition), X, 688.
2 "Shipping: Merchant Ships of the World," *Encyclopaedia Britannica* (1953 edition), XX, 548, table I.

Table 2
World's Merchant Ships of 100 Tons or More in 1914*

| States Where Owned | (In Thousands of Tons) | | Total |
	Steam	Sail	
United Kingdom	18,892	364	19,256
British Dominions	1,632	157	1,789
Empire Total	20,524	521	21,045
Germany	5,135	325	5,460
United States	4,330	1,038	5,368
Norway	1,951	547	2,504
France	1,922	397	2,319
Japan	1,708	—	1,708
Italy	1,430	238	1,668
Netherlands	1,472	25	1,497
Sweden	1,015	103	1,118
Spain	884	15	899
Greece	821	16	837
Denmark	770	50	820
Other States	3,436	411	3,847
Grand Total	45,404	3,686	49,090

* From "Shipping: Merchant Ships of the World," *Encyclopaedia Britannica* (1953 edition), XX, 548, Table I, citing various editions of *Lloyd's Register*. The United States did not take the lead in merchant shipping until World War II.

a thousand miles of Russian coastline with a ten-mile fishing limit became Japanese coast with a three-mile limit.

A glance at a world map of 1900 reveals that most of the world's coastlines were three-mile-limit coastlines. England, France, Germany, and the Netherlands—three-mile states—had colonized or absorbed within their spheres of influence most of the coasts of Africa, southern Asia, and Oceania. The countries that did not adhere to the three-mile rule—Uruguay, Scandinavia, Iberia, and Mexico—accounted for very little of the world's total coastline, and the ships of those states accounted for less than 10 percent of the global aggregate. The events of the first quarter of the twentieth century strengthened even more the three-mile rule, bringing it to its zenith in the 1920s. These events will be taken up in the remainder of this chapter.

THE PRACTICE OF STATES

GREAT BRITAIN

The British continued to press those states that favored greater limits than the three-mile rule. Uruguay had asserted a claim to control fishing in the mouth of the Rio de la Plata, an area more than 60 miles wide that included some 5,000 square miles. A Canadian sealer, the *Agnes G. Donohoe* was arrested in 1905 for fishing in those "Uruguayan" waters in violation of a presidential decree. The British protested the Uruguayan claim to exercise jurisdiction beyond the usual three-mile limit, and the vessel was released.[3]

The same year, 1905, the British reaffirmed their earlier position against the Spanish and Portuguese six-mile limit. Bolstering the activities of British, French, and German fishermen, still fishing up to within three miles of the Iberian coast in defiance of local regulations, the British Foreign Office declared ". . . that His Majesty's Government did not recognize any claims of the Spanish or Portuguese Governments to exercise jurisdiction over British vessels beyond the three-mile limit."[4] In July, 1908, Sir Edward Grey, the British Foreign Secretary, summed up the policy of Great Britain in this regard as being not only ". . . to uphold the three-mile limit, but to protect against and to resist by every means in our power the pretension of any foreign country to enforce its own jurisdiction on the sea beyond the three-mile limit."[5]

However, the British government was careful to insure that her diplomatic pressure abroad was matched by reciprocal treatment of foreigners in British waters. For example, the Herring Fishery (Scotland) Act had been passed in 1889 prohibiting "otter-trawling" or "beam trawling" in certain areas. These areas were extended in 1892 by the Fishery Board for Scotland to include all of Moray Firth, the headlands of which are over seventy miles apart. In 1906, the Danish master of a Norwegian fishing vessel was convicted by the Scottish High Court of Justiciary for "otter-trawling" in Moray Firth, even though beyond the three-mile limit. Six more Norwegian trawlers were similarly arrested and fined in 1907. The Norwegian and Swedish governments protested the practice to the British government, which in turn directed that those arrested be released. The Foreign Office held that the conviction violated international law and thenceforth the act was interpreted as applying only to British subjects.[6]

In marked contrast to the case of the *Alleganean*, wherein Chesapeake Bay was held to be an "historic" territorial bay, was the case of the *Fagernes*. In 1926, a collision occurred between the steamship *Cornish Coast* and the *Fagernes*, the latter being sunk. The collision took place in the Bristol Channel, about midway between the English and Welsh coasts, where the width of the channel was 20 miles. In 1927, a British court of appeals, following an instruction from the home secretary, held that the point at which the collision

---

3 Fulton, *Sovereignty of the Sea*, p. 663.
4 *Ibid.*, p. 667, citing the National Sea Fisheries Protective Association, *Twenty-fourth Annual Report of the Committee of Management* (1905), p. 7.
5 *Ibid.*, p. 732, citing Great Britain, Parliament, [*Hansard's*] *Parliamentary Debates*, vol. 170, p. 1383.
6 *Mortensen v. Peters*, 8 *Session Cases, 5th Series*, 93 (1906), Briggs, *The Law of Nations*, pp. 52–57; and 14 *Scots Law Times Reports* 227 (1906), Fenwick, *Cases*, p. 25.

occurred was not within territorial jurisdiction.[7] This was a most striking instance of upholding the three-mile rule. There had been many precedents wherein such bodies of water had been assimilated as national territory; Britain herself had done it earlier in the case of Conception Bay. Yet in this case, out of ardor for the three-mile limit, Britain abstained from claiming as territorial waters, waters which by legal standards of the 1960s would be considered not only territorial waters, but *internal waters.*

GERMANY

Although Germany had been a signatory to the 1882 North Sea Fisheries Convention and the 1888 Suez Convention, she had not formally legislated the three-mile limit during the nineteenth century. The cannon-shot decree of 1866 remained effective until 1909 when Germany redefined her neutral territorial waters as those ". . . within the sea area 3 nautical miles in breadth from the coast line at low water, extending along the coast and the islands and bays belonging thereto."[8] The three-mile limit was upheld by the German Supreme Prize Court at Berlin in 1915 in the case of the *Elida.* The Swedish ship *Elida* had been captured between three and four miles from the Swedish coast. Germany claimed three miles; Sweden claimed four. The Court rejected Sweden's claim to four miles, noting that the German three-mile limit was more in accord with international law, inasmuch as the Swedish claim was supported only by one other state, Norway.[9]

Following the war, Germany continued to observe the three-mile limit. In 1924, she protested a Finnish customs zone beyond three miles, which Germany regarded as the only limit recognized under international law.[10] That same year, in a treaty with the United States, Germany pledged her ". . . firm intention to uphold the principle that 3 marine miles . . . constitute the proper limits of territorial waters."[11]

ITALY

Italy, too, had waited until the twentieth century to declare specifically a three-mile limit. This came in 1908 in the form of naval instructions:

> . . . [F]or the purposes of the law of war territorial waters have the extent to cannon range from the shore. The said extent, by customary

---

7   The *Fagernes,* Probate 311 (1927), British Institute of International and Comparative Law, *British International Law Cases,* vol. II, pp. 907–923.

8   German Naval Prize Regulations of September 30, 1909, translated in Crocker, *Marginal Sea,* p. 533.

9   *The Elida,* German Imperial Supreme Prize Court, I *Entscheidungen des Oberprisengerichts,* 9 (1915), Briggs, *Law of Nations,* pp. 278–280.

10   Note of February 24, 1924 cited in Jessup, *Territorial Waters,* p. 24.

11   United States and Germany, "Convention for the Prevention of Smuggling of Intoxicating Liquors, May 19, 1924," cited in *ibid.*

law must be held to be fixed at three marine miles from the coast, beginning at low water mark.[12]

NETHERLANDS

Like Germany and Italy, Holland confirmed her nineteenth century treaty commitments to the three-mile limit by domestic acts in the twentieth century, namely the neutrality declarations of 1904[13] and 1914, the latter of which reads:

> The State territory comprises the coastal waters to a distance of three nautical miles . . . .[14]

PORTUGAL

The diplomatic pressure from the great powers, most notably England, finally influenced Portugal to adopt the three-mile limit. In 1909, she "accepted the inevitable," in the words of Thomas Fulton,[15] and passed a new law which read:

> Article 1. Foreign vessels are prohibited from fishing in Portuguese territorial waters within the limit of three nautical miles measured from the line of extreme low water.[16]

Portugal did not, however, abandon her six-mile claim with respect to customs[17] and neutrality.[18]

SPAIN

Although Portugal had adopted a three-mile fishing limit while retaining a six-mile zone for neutrality, the Spanish government did just the opposite. Spain tenaciously held on to her six-mile fishing limit but adopted a neutrality zone of three miles early during World War I.[19] Three years later she an-

12 Office of the Chief of Staff, Italian Ministry of the Navy, "Rules of International Maritime Law in Time of War, 1908," translated in Crocker, *Marginal Sea*, pp. 600–601, quoting paragraph 14 of the rules.
13 "Proclamation of Neutrality in the Russo-Japanese War, February 12, 1904," United States Department of State, *Foreign Relations of the United States*, 1904 vol., p. 27.
14 "Declaration of Neutrality in the War between Belgium and Germany, and between Great Britain and Germany, August 5, 1914," Crocker, *Marginal Sea,* p. 607.
15 Fulton, *Sovereignty of Sea*, p. 668.
16 Portuguese Fishery Law of October 26, 1909, translated and reproduced in Crocker, *Marginal Sea*, p. 619.
17 Portuguese customs decree of May 27, 1911, articles 211 and 216, cited in Raestad, "Tableau des lois et règles actuellement en vigueur dans les pays d'Europe en aux Etats-Unis d'Amérique en ce qui concerne l'étendue de la mer territoriale," p. 418.
18 U.S. Naval War College, "Marginal Sea and other Waters," p. 24.
19 Heinzen, "Three-Mile Limit p. 635; and Riesenfeld, *Protection of Coastal Fisheries*, p. 176.

nounced a similar three-mile maritime boundary for the neutrality of Spanish Morocco.[20]

DENMARK

As pointed out in Chapter 6, the Danes departed from the historic Scandinavian league practice with their signing of the three-mile North Sea Fisheries Convention of 1882. Denmark went a step further and adopted the three-mile rule for Danish territorial waters in her domestic legislation in 1900.[21] Then, the following year, she gave up her long-standing claim to a greater extent of exclusive fisheries in her colonies by granting the British permission to fish within three miles of Iceland and the Faeroes.[22]

SWEDEN

The case of the *Elida* had been unpleasant for Sweden. (See page 112.) Wishing to maintain her neutrality during World War I, Sweden chose to come into line with the laws of the belligerent states so as to reduce the chances of friction and possible hostile involvements. In 1916 she adopted a three-mile neutral zone:

> Submarines belonging to foreign Powers and equipped for use in warfare may not navigate or lie in Swedish territorial waters within three nautical minutes (5,556 meters) from land. . . .[23]

NORWAY

The personal union of Sweden and Norway under the King of Sweden was dissolved in 1905 and Norway became an independent monarchy. The new Norwegian monarchy also remained neutral in World War I and found the four-mile limit too difficult to defend. In 1918 she followed the lead of Sweden and declared:

> 1. The Norwegian Government, who have in the past claimed that the territorial waters of Norway extend to 4 miles from the shore, have recognized the difficulty of upholding this claim during the war, since it is not recognized by either the British or the German Governments.[24]

20 Neutrality Regulations for the Spanish Zone in Morocco, July 18, 1917, cited in Jessup, *Territorial Waters*, p. 42.
21 Denmark, "Law Respecting Illegal Trawling in Territorial Waters, April 7, 1900," translated in Crocker, *Marginal Sea*, pp. 516–517.
22 Great Britain and Denmark, "Convention for Regulating the Fisheries outside Territorial Waters in the Ocean Surrounding the Faerø Islands and Iceland, June 24, 1901," Hertslet, *Commercial Treaties*, vol. XXIII, p. 425.
23 "Royal decree, comprising additions to the Royal decree of December 20, 1912, with certain regulations with respect to the neutrality of Sweden during war between foreign Powers, July 19, 1916," translated in Crocker, *Marginal Sea*, p. 628.
24 Norwegian Declaration of June 18, 1918, United States Naval War College, "Maritime Jurisdiction," p. 29.

The declaration went on to redelimit the Norwegian territorial sea at three miles for neutrality purposes.

MEXICO

Even Mexico, which had claimed a three-league limit for many decades, adopted the three-mile limit at the beginning of the twentieth century. In 1902—just after the United States had defeated Spain in the Gulf of Mexico and Caribbean—a three-mile act was passed by the Mexican government.[25] This was probably done reluctantly, under the mounting international pressure in favor of the three-mile rule; at least the fact that she later reverted to her nine-mile claim, when the opportunity presented itself, makes it seem so.

UNITED STATES

As the United States grew stronger as a maritime power, her interest in the three-mile limit seemed to grow. Following her success in the war with Spain, the United States took several steps indicating this to be the case. In 1900, a code of naval warfare was adopted that featured the three-mile limit.[26] In 1901, incident to the planned construction of the Panama Canal, a treaty was concluded with Britain specifying a three-mile limit off the proposed canal zone.[27] In 1902, the United States issued a policy declaration on the three-mile rule:

> The Government of the United States claims and admits the jurisdiction of any State over its territorial waters only to the extent of a marine league, unless a different rule is fixed by treaty between two States: even then the treaty States are alone affected by the agreement.[28]

Several years later, the United States brought Cuba and Panama formally into the three-mile "club" by signing smuggling treaties with those states, each treaty affirming the three-mile limit.[29]

25 "Law of Immobile Properties of the Nation, December 18, 1902," Article 4, section I, Heinzen, "Three-Mile Limit," p. 634; Reisenfeld, *Protection of Coastal Fisheries*, p. 235.
26 "United States Naval War Code, June 27, 1900," in United States Naval War College, *International Law Discussions 1903*, pp. 18, 101, 103.
27 United States and Great Britain, "Treaty to Facilitate the Construction of a Ship Canal, November 18, 1901," Malloy, *Treaties*, vol. I, p. 783.
28 "Declaration Relative to the Extent of Jurisdiction Claimed over the Bordering Waters of the Bering Sea, July 4, 1902," (Declaration of Mr. Herbert H. D. Peirce, agent of the United States, in the *C. H. White* case, Russian Arbitration, in reply to the question asked by Mr. T. M. C. Asser, arbitrator. It was made under the specific authority received by him from the Secretary of State of the United States on July 3, 1902), Crocker, *Marginal Sea*, pp. 680–681; *Foreign Relations of the United States 1902*, Appendix, I, pp. 440–461.
29 Jessup, *Territorial Waters*, p. 49, citing Treaty of June 6, 1924 with Panama, *U.S. Treaty Series* No. 707, and Treaty of March 4, 1926 with Cuba, *U.S. Treaty Series* No. 738.

INTERNATIONAL ARBITRATIONS AND MULTILATERAL AGREEMENTS

The practice of individual states during the first quarter of the twentieth century clearly attested to the paramountcy of the three-mile limit. Virtually all opposition to, and deviation from, the three-mile limit either disappeared or was effectively suppressed by the unanimity of the great powers. International and multilateral practice, too, strongly enhanced the status of the three-mile rule. The period leading up to World War I was one of great popularity for the practice of international arbitration. The Permanent Court of Arbitration had been established at the First Hague Peace Conference of 1899. Subsequently, dozens of bilateral and multilateral arbitration treaties were signed. Scores of international disputes were submitted to arbitration, and several of them involved territorial waters and the three-mile limit. The most pertinent of these, *inter alia*, will be considered in this section.

SECOND HAGUE PEACE CONFERENCE (1907)

Although the Second Hague Peace Conference did not have as one of its purposes the codification of the law of territorial waters, the issue of the three-mile limit did arise. The conference met at The Hague with the task of codifying the rules of war and neutrality. The conference's Third Commission was to prepare the Eighth Convention, dealing with the laying of automatic submarine contact mines. The Committee of Examination, in preparing the draft convention, included several references to the territorial sea. The article concerning the three-mile limit appeared as follows:

Article 2
It is forbidden to lay anchored automatic mines, beyond a distance of three nautical miles from low-water mark, throughout the length of the coast-line, as well as along the islands and islets adjacent thereto.[30]

This draft was essentially the British version which, surprisingly, encountered the resistance of the United States. Rear Admiral Charles S. Sperry, speaking for the U.S. delegation, proposed that references to any specific width, such as three miles, be deleted. While Admiral Sperry and the United States may have regretted this later, they had their reasons for this position at the time. They argued that the draft convention was not specific enough on baselines and that until the determination of baselines could be agreed upon, there was no point in fixing an exact limit. It must be recalled that the United States had recently acquired the Philippines. Admiral Sperry pointed out the problem of delimiting and measuring territorial seas in an area like the Philippines with its extensive labyrinth of coral islets and reefs, some of which appear only at low tide. Sperry added that it had not been

30 "Report to the Third Commission of the Second Hague Peace Conference, September 17, 1907," in Scott, *The Reports to the Hague Conferences of 1899 and 1907*, p. 664.

ascertained under international law or under the draft convention whether or not these partially and occasionally submerged islets and reefs were considered part of the territory of the United States, and consequently, that "low-water mark" was too elusive a term upon which to construct baselines.[31]

There was also the matter of the contemporary dispute with Great Britain over how to measure baselines off eastern Canada. In this dispute, to be discussed presently, the United States was attempting to obtain a more favorable British interpretation of the Convention of 1818 as regarded the baseline along the coast, bays, and inlets of the Canadian maritime provinces. The Americans were fully aware of the British fondness for the three-mile limit, and the negotiating tactic employed by Sperry may well have been intended to apply additional pressure for the sake of the Canadian dispute.

The American argument prevailed and the final version adopted by the conference contained no reference to three miles. The term "territorial waters," however, was used frequently in the language of the convention, in effect deferring the issue of extent until the baseline problem was solved. Article 2 of the conference's eighth convention simply reads: "It is forbidden to lay automatic contact mines off the coasts and ports of the enemy. . . ."[32] In the final act of the conference, provision was made to schedule a Third Hague Peace Conference. Preparations and preliminary work were interrupted by World War I and the third conference was never held.

INTERNATIONAL SETTLEMENT OF THE PELAGIC SEALING CONTROVERSY

As noted in Chapter 6, the Bering Sea Arbitration of 1893 provided only a partial, and ineffective, solution to the problem of pelagic sealing. In their subsequent enthusiasm and determination to prevent the extinction of the fur seals, U.S. authorities boldly and liberally interpreted the Bering Sea Award and Regulation as authorizing the seizure of any vessel or person having on board or in his possession any of several forbidden seal-fishing apparatus. (The Bering Sea Regulation, in fact, only prohibited the ". . . *use* of nets, firearms, and explosives . . . in the fur seal fishing" [emphasis added].)[33] This interpretation inevitably led to a confrontation with the British. In June, 1909, three Canadian sealing schooners were hunting sea otters outside the three-mile limit near the Cherikof Islands. The craft were boarded by an over-zealous U.S. revenue officer who locked up their hunting weapons. The revenue officer had searched the three craft for seal skins but found none. Even so, he then placed all the firearms found on board under seal and ordered that they not be reopened as long as the vessels remained north of 35° north latitude and east of 180° west latitude—a vast ocean area. The British protested the action on behalf of the owners, and the case was submitted to arbitration. The arbitra-

31 *Ibid.*, pp. 664–665.
32 *Ibid.*, p. 645.
33 Bering Sea Fur Seal Arbitral Award and Regulations of August 15, 1893, reproduced in Moore, *Arbitrations*, vol. I, p. 945.

tion tribunal decided that the American revenue officer had committed an error in judgment, and awarded indemnities for each of the British vessels.[34]

Nevertheless, the controversial situation continued to deteriorate. Several other Canadian sealers were actually seized on the high seas by American cutters attempting to enforce seal conservation measures.[35] After many fruitless attempts at settlement, differences were resolved by means of a multilateral convention between Britain, Russia, Japan, and the United States, whereby a long-needed effective conservation program was placed into effect. In so doing, the so-called Fur Seal Convention of 1911 acknowledged the three-mile limit:

> Article V. Each of the contracting parties agrees it will not permit its citizens or subjects or their vessels to kill, capture, or pursue beyond the distance of three miles from the shore of its territories sea otters. . . ."[36]

This Convention did solve the fur seal problem; the seal herd thrived, and within a few years its normal population was restored.

THE NORTH ATLANTIC COAST FISHERIES ARBITRATION

Just as the year 1911 brought solutions to the fur seal fisheries problem in the Pacific, the following year witnessed the solution of the long-standing North Atlantic coast fisheries rivalry. The North Atlantic fisheries dispute culminated in the second famous arbitration in as many decades between the United States and Great Britain over fishing rights. Both disputes had their roots in the same two issues: conservation of fisheries and the delimitation of territorial jurisdiction to seaward. Positions, however, were reversed in the two cases. Whereas in the Bering Sea Arbitration, it was the United States that was attempting to exercise controls to preserve the fur seals, in the latter instance it was the Canadians who were trying to preserve their fisheries against American encroachment.

Background. The early background events, i.e., the Treaty of Paris (1783), the Treaty of Ghent (1814), and the Convention of 1818, have already been discussed. It will be recalled that in the Convention of 1818, the United States ". . . renounce[d] forever, any liberty heretofore enjoyed . . . to take, dry, or cure fish on or within three marine miles of any of the coasts, bays, creeks

34 *The Jessie, the Thomas F. Bayard, and the Pescawha, Great Britain v. United States,* Claims Arbitration, 1921, Neilsen's *Report* 479, reproduced in part in Briggs, *Law of Nations,* pp. 327–328.

35 The *Wanderer,* the *Favorite,* and the *Kate, Great Britain v. United States,* Claims Arbitration, 1921. Nielsen's *Report* 459, 472, 515, cited in Briggs, *Law of Nations,* p. 328.

36 "Convention between Japan, Great Britain, Russia, and the United States for the Protection of Fur Seals and Sea Otters in the North Pacific Ocean, Washington, July 7, 1911," reproduced in Supplement to *American Journal of International Law,* V (October, 1911), Supplement, pp. 267–274.

or harbors . . ." of the British American provinces. (See page 63.) This wording caused more problems than it solved. In the century which followed there were arrests, seizures, abortive negotiations, unratified treaties, charges of breach of faith, and vexed diplomatic relations. The Canadians felt they had sovereign rights to protect and regulate the fishery, provided American and British subjects shared the same restrictive conservation measures "in common," as the terms of the treaty suggested. The Americans, instead, interpreted the "in common" feature of the treaty to invest them with a share of the sovereign control of these waters. In the absence of agreement on this issue, the Canadians and Newfoundlanders resorted to imposing and enforcing discriminatory regulations against U.S. fishermen.

The case of the *David J. Adams* provides a remarkable example of both the extent of the deterioration of diplomatic relations, and of the pettiness in the interpretation and implementation of the 1818 Convention by the British authorities. In that case, the American schooner *David J. Adams* had entered the port of Digby, Nova Scotia, in 1886 to purchase bait. This right had not been expressly permitted under the Convention of 1818, and the authorities at Digby seized, condemned, and disposed of the vessel.[37] There occurred many other disagreeable instances such as this one before the two powers agreed to submit the issue to The Hague Permanent Court of Arbitration; a treaty was concluded to that effect in 1908.

The contentions. The *compromis d'arbitrage* posed seven questions for the tribunal to consider. Only one of them is closely germane to a study of the three-mile limit, that being Question 5 of the *compromis* which dealt with baselines.

> Question 5. From where must be measured the "three marine miles of any of the coasts, bays, creeks, or harbors" referred to in the said Article [Article I of the Convention of 1818]?[38]

This question referred to the coasts, the territorial waters of which the United States had renounced its right to fish. In order to obtain the greatest fishing area, the United States desired a strict application of the three-mile rule, thus holding to a minimum the territorial waters from which it would be excluded.

The British naturally espoused the position that would enclose as great an area within exclusive jurisdiction as possible, namely that the three-mile limit should be measured from baselines drawn from headland to headland across all bays, regardless of size and configuration. She had earlier advanced this

---

37 The *David J. Adams, United States v. Great Britain*, Claims Arbitration, 1921, Nielsen's *Report 526*, reproduced in part in Briggs, *Law of Nations*, pp. 892–896.

38 "Special agreement for the submission of questions relative to fisheries on the North Atlantic coast under the general treaty of arbitration concluded between the United States and Great Britain on the 4th day of April, 1908," Senate, *North Atlantic Coast Fisheries Arbitration*, vol. I, p. 27.

interpretation in the case of the Bay of Fundy in defending her seizure of the schooner *Washington*. (See page 85.) Having failed in that attempt, she was now applying the interpretation to all the remaining, lesser bays. The United States countered with the argument that American fishermen could not, under the treaty, be excluded from bays or indentations that did not narrow to six miles, excepting of course "historical" bays, such as Delaware Bay, which was cited as an example.

The tribunal had been asked to address a western hemisphere problem that had already found a solution among the European powers. The North Sea Fisheries Convention had adopted the ten-mile bay baseline formulated earlier in the 1839 Anglo-French Treaty. But the United States and Britain, between themselves, had been unable, or unwilling, to agree on the basis of that earlier formula. True, they had made an attempt in this direction. In 1888 they had signed a treaty, featuring the ten-mile baseline, but the treaty was never ratified.[39] At the time, the ten-mile baseline was at once too long for the Americans and too short for the British.

One other of the seven questions of the *compromis* was indirectly related to this study, namely Question 1, which asked the tribunal to determine whether or not the British had the right, independent of the United States, to regulate the taking of fish, i.e., setting seasons and hours for fishing, and controlling the methods and implements to be used.

The award. The Permanent Court decided the latter question in favor of Great Britain, by affirming the British right to issue regulations which were "appropriate or necessary for the protection and preservation" of the fisheries. Seeing the desirability of international cooperation in conservation, the court exercised its right of recommendation conferred in the *compromis* and recommended the establishment of a Permanent Mixed Fishery Commission to determine the reasonableness of regulations which might arise and create friction in the future.[40]

In its dictum as to Question 5, the court paved the way for a compromise solution:

> The negotiators of the treaty of 1818 did probably not trouble themselves with subtle theories concerning the notion of "bays"; they most probably thought that everybody would know what was a bay. In this popular sense the term must be interpreted in the treaty. The interpretation must take into account all the individual circumstances which, for any one of the different bays, are to be appreciated; the relation of its width to the length of penetration inland . . . [etc.][41]

39 United States and Great Britain, "Treaty for the Settlement of the Fishery Question on the Atlantic Coast of North America, February 15, 1888," (unratified), *British and Foreign State Papers*, vol. 79, p. 267.
40 Senate, *North Atlantic Coast Fisheries Arbitration*, vol. I, p. 87.
41 *Ibid.*, p. 97.

Offering that introductory explanation, the tribunal decided and awarded:

> In the case of bays, the three marine miles are to be measured from a straight line drawn across the body of water at the place where it ceases to have the configuration and characteristics of a bay. At all other places the three marine miles are to be measured following the sinuosities of the coast.[42]

Realizing that this solved nothing, the court again drew on its recommendatory powers. Considering the multilateral precedent of the North Sea Fisheries Convention, the tribunal suggested that Britain and America adopt like procedures:

> Now therefore this tribunal recommends for the consideration and acceptance of the High Contracting Parties the following rules and method of procedure for determining the limit of the bays hereinbefore enumerated:
> 1. In every bay not hereinafter specifically provided for the limits of exclusion shall be drawn three miles seaward from a straight line across the bay in the part nearest the entrance at the first point where the width does not exceed ten miles.[43]

The court went on "specifically to provide" for Conception Bay, confirming its "historic" status. But the court failed to define the term "bay," i.e., configuration, characteristics, depth-to-breadth ratio, etc. Only the width of the mouth of a bay was established. Nothing would have prevented a littoral state from drawing a series of ten-mile lines across even the shallowest indentations all along its coast, if it chose arbitrarily to ascribe to them the status of bays. Fortunately, this did not occur; and the ten-mile bay practice gained wide acceptance among nations during the next several decades.

The recommendations made by The Hague tribunal were carefully considered by the contracting parties. On July 20, 1912, the two governments signed an agreement embodying both the recommendation on the Permanent Mixed Fisheries Commission and the ten-mile rule for bays.[44]

The arbitration enjoyed wide publicity and acclaim and not only strengthened the three-mile rule but also enhanced the prestige of arbitration as a means of pacific settlement of disputes.

EL SALVADOR V. NICARAGUA (1917)

In 1914, the United States concluded a treaty with Nicaragua, which granted the United States the right to construct a transoceanic canal through Nicaragua

---

42 *Ibid.*
43 *Ibid.*, pp. 97–98.
44 "Agreement between the United States and Great Britain Adopting with Certain Modifications the Rules and Methods of Procedure Recommended in the Award of September 7, 1910, of the North Atlantic Coast Fisheries Arbitration, Washington, July 20, 1912" (Ratifications exchanged November 15, 1912), reprinted in Supplement to *American Journal of International Law*, Vol. VI, pp. 41–46.

and to build and operate a naval base on the Nicaraguan coast of the Gulf of Fonseca.[45] The Gulf of Fonseca is surrounded by the coastlines of Nicaragua, Honduras, and El Salvador. The Gulf opens to the Pacific with its western headland in El Salvador and its eastern headland in Nicaragua. Because of a number of islands and sand banks between headlands, the 19-mile headland distance is reduced, in effect, to four miles. The bay is fifty miles long and averages thirty miles in width.

Certain Central American states opposed the 1914 treaty on the grounds that the Gulf of Fonseca was a closed "historical" bay, owned jointly by the three littoral states. They held that any rights granted to nonlittoral states must have the approval of all littoral states, and could not be conferred unilaterally as Nicaragua had. Costa Rica and El Salvador brought the matter before the Central American Court of Justice to ascertain the legal status of the Gulf with a view to having the treaty nullified.

Several questions were placed before the court concerning the status of the Gulf. The judges' replies to the questions reflected unanimous approval of the three-mile rule but they did not agree regarding the application of the three-mile rule.

To the Ninth Question, the judges unanimously agreed that the Gulf of Fonseca was an historic bay, possessing the characteristics of a closed sea. The Fifteenth and Thirteenth Questions, respectively, asked if there need be a marine league belt of territorial sea on the Gulf coast in view of the Gulf's co-ownership, and if so, what should be the configuration of the zone of territorial waters and the adjacent customs inspection zone. The Fifteenth Question was:

> [a]nswered in the affirmative by Judges Medal, Oreamuno and Castro Ramírez; and in the negative by Judge Gutiérrez Navas, on the ground that in the interior of closed bays there is no littoral zone; Judge Bocanegra answered in the affirmative on the ground that the high parties litigant, having accepted the Gulf of Fonseca as a closed bay, the existence of the marine league of exclusive ownership becomes necessary, since the Gulf belongs to three nations instead of one.[46]

With respect to the Thirteenth Question:

> Judges Medal, Oreamuno, Castro Ramírez and Bocanegra answered that the zone should follow the contours of the respective coasts, as well within as outside the Gulf; and Judge Gutiérrez Navas that, with respect to the Gulf of Fonseca, the radius of a marine league zone of territorial sea should be measured from a line drawn across the bay at the narrowest part of the entrance towards the high seas, and the zone of inspection extends three leagues more in the same direction.[47]

45 Bryan-Chamorro Treaty of August 5, 1914, Malloy, *Treaties*, vol. II, pp. 2740–2741.
46 *The Republic of El Salvador v. the Republic of Nicaragua, Central American Court of Justice, Opinion and Decision of the Court*, San Jose, Costa Rica, March 9, 1917, reproduced in *American Journal of International Law*, vol. XI, p. 694.
47 *Ibid.*, p. 693.

The majority opinion of the court, then, held that the Gulf is a closed sea, co-owned by the three littoral states, except for the littoral belt of a marine league, which is the exclusive property of each state. In the nonlittoral portion of the Gulf, the three states share jurisdiction in matters of customs and national security. Hence, for Nicaragua to invite U.S. warships—subject exclusively to U.S. jurisdiction—would nullify or restrict the jurisdictional rights of Honduras and of El Salvador.

EFFECTS OF WORLD WAR I ON THE THREE-MILE LIMIT

NEUTRALITY CLAIMS

By deleting references to the three-mile limit, the Hague Peace Conference of 1907 produced something of a problem for states that had traditionally adhered to the cannon-shot rule for neutrality purposes. The pertinent article of the 1907 Hague Convention on rights and duties of neutral powers reads:

> Belligerents are bound to respect the sovereign rights of neutral Powers and to abstain in neutral territory or neutral waters, from any act which would, if knowingly permitted by any Power, constitute a violation of neutrality.[48]

Such vagueness left questions unanswered and invited reevaluation and liberal interpretation. The United States Naval War College described the situation this way:

> The World War made it necessary for many States to pronounce what limits they proposed to fix for their neutral territorial waters as regards belligerent and neutral rights.[49]

France, a three-mile state for fishing and a cannon-shot state for neutrality, seems to have been the first to react. In 1912 she decreed:

> For the application of the rules of the 13th Hague Convention, dated October 18, 1907;—French territorial waters extend out to a limit fixed at six marine miles. . . .[50]

Italy followed suit. The Italian ambassador in Washington, in a note of November 6, 1914, to the secretary of state, stated that his government had established a six-mile neutral zone.[51] Similarly, Uruguay proclaimed a five-mile neutral zone the same year. But as noted earlier in this chapter, World War I had

---

48 Article 1, Convention XIII concerning the Rights and Duties of Neutral Powers in Naval War, Scott, *Reports to the Hague Conferences*, p. 832.
49 U.S. Naval War College, "Maritime Jurisdiction," p. 27.
50 "Decree Determining Certain Rules of Neutrality in Case of Maritime War, October 18, 1912, translated in Crocker, *Marginal Sea*, p. 529.
51 U.S. Naval War College, "Maritime Jurisdiction," pp. 29–30.

the opposite effect on certain other states, notably Spain, Norway, and Sweden, which reduced their neutral zones to three miles.

THE RUSSIAN TWELVE-MILE CLAIM

The Soviet claim to a twelve-mile territorial sea had its origin in certain acts taken by the Tsarist government in its last declining years just before World War I. Although Russia had adopted a three-mile territorial sea, she was dissatisfied with that limit for fishing purposes. Professor de Martens had long been advocating the extension of the territorial sea. In an official capacity within the Tsarist Government in 1898 he had urged the Tsar to extend Russian waters to keep up with the increasing range of cannon, insisting that there was no good reason to hold territorial waters at three miles when states' best interests would be served by controlling areas beyond, especially inasmuch as this was clearly within their capabilities.[52]

The first step was the conclusion with Romania, in 1907, of a treaty establishing a ten-mile exclusive fishing zone between the two states.[53] Two years later the Russians enacted a new customs law:

> The surface of the waters for twelve marine miles from extreme low-water mark from the seacoasts of the Russian Empire, whether mainland or islands, is recognized as the marine customs area, within the limits of which every vessel, whether Russian or foreign, is subject to supervision by those Russian authorities in whose charge is the guarding of the frontiers of the Empire.[54]

This drew an immediate protest from the British government, whereupon the Russian ambassador in Washington inquired of the State Department whether the British had made such a protest concerning the similar United States twelve-mile customs law ". . . either when it was originally passed or at a later date." The State Department reply was in the negative.[55] Whereas the British had repealed their twelve-mile customs laws in 1876, the U.S. Act of 1799 was still on the law books.

This Russian customs law was followed in 1911 by a bill to reserve exclusive fishing rights for Russians out to twelve miles. Russian Foreign Minister Sazanov stated the Tsar's position to the American Ambassador:

> [T]erritorial jurisdiction over marginal seas is based on the theory of control from the land, and . . . the delimitation of this area of control at twelve miles now corresponds more nearly with actual conditions than

52 Shapiro, "The Limits of Russian Territorial Waters in the Baltic," p. 444.
53 Baty, "Three-Mile Limit," p. 536.
54 Enclosure to a dispatch from Mr. Rockill, American Ambassador at St. Petersburg, to the United States Secretary of State, September 30, 1910, quoted in Jessup, *Territorial Waters*, p. 29.
55 *Foreign Relations of the United States, 1912*, p. 1287.

does the three-mile limit which represented the effective range of cannon at the time when this limitation of control over the seas was recognized as a principle of international law.[56]

The bill went into effect in May, 1911, but applied only to Pacific and not to European waters. It should be recalled that in 1893 the Russians had successfully negotiated American and British approval of a ten-mile fishing zone on the Russian Pacific mainland. (See Chapter 6.) Another bill was drafted which would have created a similar twelve-mile fishing zone along Russian European coasts; British protests again followed and the bill failed to pass in the Duma.[57] The American ambassador to Russia interpreted the situation in St. Petersburg in a message of February 3:

> M. Sazanov in a long interview last night assured me that Russia proposed to maintain the 12-mile limit as a permanent policy. . . . Russia contends that the 3-mile limit is obsolete. The distance of 3 miles having been set as the conventional range of a cannon, it is claimed that with the extension of the range of modern ordnance the limit of jurisdiction should be increased to correspond.[58]

These Russian intentions became reality, not under the Tsars, but under their successors, the Soviets. In 1921, the Soviet government decreed the twelve-mile European exclusive fishing zones which had failed to pass in the Duma.[59] Then in 1927, a statute was promulgated decreeing the Soviet seaward boundary to include a twelve-mile belt of waters.[60]

POLITICAL CONSEQUENCES OF THE WAR

The Russian twelve-mile claim must be considered in the context of its timing with relation to the events just before, during, and just after World War I. The Russian claims between 1907 and 1912, while they at first annoyed the maritime powers, especially the United States, Britain, and Japan, were soon eclipsed by the pre-World War I naval rivalries among the Western powers over armaments and tonnage. Russia may have been considered a nineteenth century great power in terms of land, army, and population, but never in terms of naval or maritime strength. Russia had been interested in the

---

56 Dispatch from Mr. Rockill, American Ambassador at St. Petersburg to the Secretary of State, February 13, 1911, Jessup, *Territorial Waters*, p. 27.
57 Jessup, *Territorial Waters*, p. 28. See Crocker, *Marginal Sea*, pp. 592 and 593 for a record of the February 9 and 13, 1911, debates in the House of Commons concerning the proposed Russian law and the British protests.
58 Dispatch from Mr. Guild, American Ambassador at St. Petersburg to the Secretary of State, February 3, 1912, reproduced in U.S. Naval War College, *International Law Situations with Solutions and Notes, 1928*, pp. 26–27.
59 Soviet decree of June 1, 1921, Jessup, *Territorial Waters*, p. 28.
60 Soviet Statute of June 15, 1927, cited in de Hartingh, *Les conceptions soviétiques du droit de la mer*, pp. 18–19.

sea strictly for fishing purposes. Then came World War I. Russia suffered a military defeat at the hands of the German and Austrian armies in 1917 and accepted the humiliating terms of the Treaty of Brest-Litovsk on March 3, 1918. Simultaneously, the country was undergoing the bloody and disruptive Bolshevik Revolution. Following that, from 1918 to 1920, the Bolsheviks were engaged in civil war with the pro-tsarist counterrevolutionaries, who were abetted by the expeditionary forces of France, Great Britain, Japan, the United States, and Romania. Too, Estonia, Latvia, Lithuania, Finland, and the Trans-caucasian states revolted against the Bolsheviks and declared their independence. The new Soviet government had such monumental internal problems, conditioned by external fears, that it withdrew into diplomatic isolation. The government had no means whereby to give effect to its twelve-mile decrees of 1921 and 1927; hence, the decrees were meaningless at the time, and went virtually unnoticed by the great powers, most of which had not even extended diplomatic recognition to the Soviet regime. Hence, with Russia's collapse, the twelve-mile limit disappeared, so it seemed, leaving the three-mile limit supreme, virtually without competition or challenge.

Other political consequences of World War I included the defeat and break-up of the Austro-Hungarian, German, and Ottoman Empires. The dominions of those empires were either granted independence or were mandated to the victors. Once-powerful Austria even lost its seacoast, becoming a small, land-locked state. Among the imperial remnants, there commenced a movement which may well be termed the era of self-determination among colonial populations. This, too, as will be shown in a later chapter, was to play an important role in the history of the three-mile limit.

Moreover, once again the two non-European powers, the United States and Japan, had played key roles in the affairs of Europe. Many historians agree that although the world did not realize it, Europe had collapsed politically, and the future lay in the hands of non-European powers.[61] This was especially significant in view of the gradual assumption by the United States of the maritime and great power role once played by Great Britain. It remained to be seen how enthusiastically the United States would carry on the defense of the three-mile limit.

VIEWS OF LEARNED SOCIETIES AND PUBLICISTS

LEARNED SOCIETIES

So widely accepted was the three-mile limit by 1924, the International Law Association revised its 1895 Draft Convention which had proposed setting the limit at six miles. The Association's 1924 annual report included the following language:

61 For a brief but lucid presentation of this thesis, see Holborn, *The Political Collapse of Europe, passim.*

With regard to the extent of territorial waters, your Committee, by a majority, have adopted the three-mile limit, as, in their opinion, it has been so generally approved by the usage of states that it ought to be preserved.[62]

Article 6 was modified to read as follows: "The territorial jurisdiction of each state shall extend over the waters along its coast for three marine miles from low-water mark at ordinary spring tide."[63] The Institute of International Law, too, four years later modified its 1894 position to provide for a "qualified" three-mile limit:

> Article 2. The extent of the Territorial Sea is three marine miles. International usage may justify the recognition of an extent greater or less than three miles.[64]

PUBLICISTS

Well-known British and American publicists of the first quarter-century, such as John Westlake (1828–1913) and Hannis Taylor (1851–1922), emphatically declared the paramountcy of the three-mile limit.

Westlake, English legal scholar, professor of law at Cambridge, and member of the Hague Permanent Court of Arbitration, wrote that the three-mile limit "as a minimum is universal: no State claims less." He claimed that only Spain and Norway stood in the way of the three-mile limit being universal also as a maximum, and added:

> Of course a power which had admitted the 3-mile limit by international engagements could not extend it in its own favor without the consent of the parties to those engagements.[65]

Hannis Taylor, lawyer, publicist, and U.S. Minister to Spain, represented the United States before international tribunals. Writing in 1901, he adhered closely to the three-mile limit, much more so than Kent, Halleck, and Wheaton before him, writing:

> It is asserted by a few publicists that with the increasing range of great guns States should have the right of their own motion to extend the limits of their jurisdiction over littoral seas. . . . It is very difficult to conceive upon what theory or by what authority any State acting alone could do any such thing, as the existing jurisdiction rests solely upon common consent as manifested by usage.[66]

62 International Law Association, C. John Colombos, reporter, "Report of the Neutrality Committee," *Report of the Thirty-Third Conference of the International Law Association*, vol. XXXIII, p. 260.
63 "Amended Draft Convention: Laws of Maritime Jurisdiction in Time of Peace," *ibid.*, p. 286.
64 Institute of International Law, "Project de règlement relatif à la mer territoriale en temps de paix," p. 755. Translation by the author.
65 Westlake, *International Law*, vol. I, p. 189.
66 Taylor, *A Treatise on International Public Law*, pp. 137–138.

Other publicists, like Lassa Oppenheim (1858–1919) and Philip Jessup (born 1897), although equally impressed with the popularity and strength of the three-mile rule, speculated that territorial seas might be extended in later years by general agreement between the states.

Lassa Francis Lawrence Oppenheim, born and educated in Germany, became a naturalized English citizen in 1900. A professor both on the continent and in England, and a prolific writer in both English and German, he noted that three miles had become generally recognized as the breadth of the maritime belt. He prophesied:

> And although Great Britain, France, Austria, the United States of America, and other States, in municipal laws and international treaties still adhere to a breadth of one marine league, the time will come when by a common agreement of the States such breadth will be very much extended.[67]

Philip C. Jessup, contemporary publicist, wrote many volumes on international law, and until 1970, served as the United States member on the International Court of Justice. Commenting on the three-mile limit in 1927, Jessup wrote:

> When it ceases to be generally convenient, it will probably be changed by general convention. But today, it is believed, the three-mile limit for the marginal sea stands as a rule of international law.[68]

This is believed to be a fair statement of the condition of things in 1927.

It was also during this period that the French publicist Alexander Giraud Jacques Antoine Mérignhac (1857–1927) broke with the traditional view of his predecessors which favored, recommended, or predicted the extension of territorial waters as a function of cannon range. Rather, he seemed completely content with the three-mile limit. Mérignhac observed:

> The older jurists extended the limit excessively, which, in our day, has been reduced by a sorts of tacit international understanding to three marine miles or a marine league.

Although he looked with approval on the 1894 proposal of the Institute of International Law to extend the limit to six miles, he balked at the idea of extending the limit up to the range of cannon shot ". . . as leading to an uncertainty in the [maritime boundary] line, by reason of the essentially variable range of cannon."[69]

The distinguished Belgian, Ernest Nys (1851–1920), wrote in much the same vein, rejecting the cannon-shot rule. A professor of international law,

---

67 Oppenheim, *International Law, a Treatise*, vol. I, p. 256.
68 Jessup, *Territorial Waters*, p. 7.
69 Méringhac, *Traité de droit public international*, pp. 378–379, translated in United States Congress, Senate, *Supplement to British Extracts: Coastal Waters and Territorial Sovereignty, Proceedings in the North Atlantic Coast Fisheries Arbitration*, p. 2.

member of the Permanent Court of Arbitration, and associate author of *Revue de Droit International,* Nys wrote:

> The greatest range of cannon shot has been criticized as uncertain, changeable, and as necessarily subservient to the improvements of inventions in the art of ballistics. . . . Thus . . . in our day, authors insist on having a definite measurement adopted, and governments in their decrees and international conventions have established such a measurement. . . . It is to this measurement of this number of miles that we must have recourse when there is no special convention. . . . The greatest range of cannon has ceased to be in force as the general rule. . . . Up to the present time the distance of 3 miles has been most generally adopted.[70]

And the Norwegian, Arnold Christopher Raestad (1878–1945), prolific publicist and Norwegian Foreign Minister, while acknowledging the three-mile limit as a rule of law, wrote a scholarly defense of the Scandinavian four-mile fishing limit. Writing in 1912, Raestad pointed out that the Scandinavian four-mile limit antedated the three-mile limit. He conceded to the great maritime powers their option voluntarily to restrict themselves to a three-mile exclusive fishing zone but argued on behalf of the four-mile zone:

> [W]hen a reserved fishery zone more than 3 miles wide existed and was recognized before the adoption by the Powers of the 3-mile limit, then they are really obliged to respect it, for a rule which was originally legal does not become illegal simply because a majority of the Powers adopted another one.[71]

Probably no publicist, however, before or since, has written so enthusiastically and eloquently in favor of the three-mile limit as the Briton, Thomas Baty (1869–1954):

> After any close inquiry into the present authority of the rule of the three-mile limit of territorial waters, the candid observer will probably come to the conclusion that the rule, while not infrequently attacked in theory, is supreme in practice. Diplomatists seldom or never question it; professors occasionally do. In the actual conduct of affairs, it is seldom challenged, and never successfully so. . . . It has, what is still more important, sunk into, and become firmly rooted in, the consciousness of all seafaring men, who are not experts in law and whose ideas it is dangerous to unsettle.[72]

Baty was writing in 1928, one of the years the three-mile rule was enjoying its peak of popularity. The events of the following two years were to deal

---

70 Nys, *Le droit international: les principes, les théories, les faits,* vol. I, pp. 504–505, translated in Borchardt, *Fisheries Arbitration:,* pp. 266–276.
71 Raestad, *La mer territoriale,* pp. 169, 173, translated in Crocker, *Marginal Sea,* pp. 410, 414.
72 Baty, "Three-Mile Limit," p. 503.

a crippling blow to the three-mile limit, triggering its decline. These will be discussed in the next chapter.

It would seem that the greatest years for the three-mile limit were those from 1876 to 1926, quite coincidentally exactly half a century. The year 1876 brought Great Britain squarely in support of the three-mile limit with the passage of the Customs Consolidation Act. After that, the rule grew steadily and surely, overcoming virtually all opposition and competition. If domestic legislation, international instruments, court decisions, and the writings of publicists are a fair measure, then by 1926, the three-mile limit was in every sense a rule of international law.

CHAPTER 9

The Interwar Period: The Three-Mile Rule Commences Its Decline

———————◆———————

Historians are generally in agreement that the period between the two world wars was characterized by several paradoxes in international affairs. One of these paradoxes was the concurrent growth of nationalism on the one hand and internationalism on the other.

The four defeated empires—Russian, Ottoman, Austro-Hungarian, and German—were dissected. From the remains, there emerged several independent states—Finland, Latvia, Estonia, Lithuania, Poland, Arabia (Nejd and Hedjaz), Egypt, Yemen, Czechoslovakia, and Yugoslavia. Elsewhere, the imperial spoils were partitioned into mandates—Iraq, Palestine, Transjordan, Syria, and Tanganyika for example—pending their readiness and preparation for later independence.

The victorious powers, of course, retained their possessions. But one of the ironical necessities of World War I had been the introduction onto European soil by the Western powers of non-Western colonial troops in considerable numbers: Senegalese, Indian, Algerian, and Indo-Chinese, for example, not to mention those from the Western British Dominions. These troops fought side by side with, dug in with, and slept in trenches with, the armies of their colonial masters. When they returned to their native colonies, they did not forget what they had seen, heard, and learned about the strengths, weaknesses, and institutions of their European overlords. Moreover, President Wilson's Fourteen Points, notably as they concerned self-determination, had become indelibly imbedded in the minds of the leaders of colonial populations. Nationalism flourished widely as both newly independent states and motivated colonists sought greater freedom of action and control in determining their future.

Simultaneously, among the great powers there had developed a dissatisfaction with the traditional means of conducting foreign affairs. International law and diplomacy had failed to prevent the world from being plunged into its most costly and devastating war to date. A new approach was sought whereby the states might settle their differences by peaceful means, and the League of Nations was created as the instrument for the new experiment in internationalism. Each sovereign state would have its due say, and decisions would not be taken on any major issue without the unanimous approval of the members. It was hoped that states could mutually agree on the rules by which they were to conduct their relations with one another, renounce the use of force, and achieve lasting peace.

THE HAGUE CONFERENCE OF 1930

This concurrent growth of nationalism and internationalism had its impact upon the three-mile limit: young states wished to assert their independence from the old system, and in some instances from its rules, and the old states—the great powers—agreed to invite them into their councils and hear them out. Previously, many rules of international law, such as the three-mile limit, had essentially been dictated through the consensus of the great powers. But to illustrate how rapidly this "international democracy" grew following World War I, at the Hague Conference of 1930 a new, nonmaritime, landlocked state—Czechoslovakia—was given an equal voice in the attempt to codify the international law of the territorial sea. As a result, the Hague Conference opened up the previously fairly well-settled issue of the extent of territorial seas like Pandora's box, and served as the first of five major developments that contributed directly and substantially to the demise of the three-mile rule.

THE PREPARATORY ROLE OF THE LEAGUE OF NATIONS

With utopian hopes, the members of the League of Nations set about the task of codifying the law of nations. The first step was taken by the Assembly of the League in September, 1924. The Assembly requested the League Council to convene a committee of experts that would carefully determine those rubrics of international law which should be considered for codification.[1]

The Committee of Experts. This was done, and the Committee of Experts for the Progressive Codification of International Law, thus organized, met for its first session in April, 1925, and selected eleven subjects for investigation. A subcommittee was appointed to conduct an inquiry into each subject. *Ques-*

---

1 Fifth Assembly of the League of Nations, Resolution of September 22, 1924, "Development of International Law," reproduced in Special Supplement to *American Journal of International Law*, (*A.J.I.L.*) vol. XX, pp. 2–3.

tion (*b*) dealt with territorial seas and its subcommittee was directed ". . . to examine whether there are problems connected with the law of the territorial sea . . . which might find their solution by way of conventions. . . ."[2] The subcommittee was chaired by publicist Walther Schücking of Germany and included Professor Barbosa de Magalhaes of Portugal (formerly Portuguese minister of foreign affairs, justice and education), and George W. Wickersham of the United States (formerly U.S. attorney general). The full committee met for its second session in January, 1926, to study the reports of its subcommittees. The result of that study was a decision to send questionnaires concerning seven of the subjects to the various governments, both League members and nonmembers. Questionnaire number two dealt with territorial waters. Attached to the questionnaire was a draft convention which proposed the codification of the three-mile rule:

ARTICLE 2
Extent of the rights of the riparian State
The zone of the coastal sea shall extend for three marine miles (60 to the degree of latitude) from low-water mark along the whole of the coast. Beyond the zone of sovereignty, States may exercise administrative rights on the ground either of custom or of vital necessity. . . .[3]

This three-mile draft convention notwithstanding, it was the questionnaire itself that opened the "Pandora's box." The basic question asked of the governments was essentially whether or not the law of the territorial sea should be made the subject of an international convention. However, the members of the Subcommittee on Territorial Waters had not been able to agree on the extent of the territorial seas. The choice of subcommittee members had been most unfortunate as far as the three-mile rule was concerned. Professor Schücking for years had opposed the three-mile limit as being inadequate. (See pages 101–2.) Instead, in keeping with the 1894 codification by the Institute of International Law, in which he had participated, he recommended a six-mile territorial sea with a customs, sanitary, and police zone beyond.[4] Professor de Magalhaes, reminiscent of the traditional Portuguese preference for a six-mile fishing zone with additional conservation jurisdiction out to twelve miles (see page 9), proposed one single zone of twelve miles in order to satisfy all the needs of states. It was only the articulate arguments of Mr. Wickersham that resulted in a draft convention incorporating the three-mile limit. But because of the divergence of opinions, the dissenting views of Schücking and de Magalhaes were appended to the questionnaire, with the explanation that

---

2 League of Nations, *First Session of the Committee of Experts for the Progressive Codification of International Law*, p. 14.
3 League of Nations, *Second Session of the Committee of Experts for the Progressive Codification of International Law* ("Report of the Sub-Committee on Territorial Waters"), p. 141.
4 *Ibid.*, p. 79.

if an international conference were to be called, certain questions would have to be resolved:

> (a) Whether several zones of diverse legal character should be recognized as territorial waters or this designation be reserved for the zone within which the powers of the coastal State are most complete. . . .
> (c) What should be the width of the territorial seas and possibly of other zones.[5]

As a result, a lengthy, controversial questionnaire was circulated to the governments of the world, under League auspices, which, in effect, invited them to take sides in the debate between the members of the subcommittee. This 1926 decision to circulate such a questionnaire marks, in this writer's view, the dividing watershed in the rise and decline of the three-mile rule.

One other of the seven questionnaires impinged on the matter of territorial seas. Questionnaire number seven asked simply "[w]hether it is possible to establish by way of international agreement rules regarding the exploitation of the products of the sea."[6]

The replies to these questionnaires were studied in detail by the Committee of Experts at their third session in March and April, 1927. Twenty-five states replied that a convention to codify the law of territorial waters would be possible and desirable. These included Great Britain, Germany, the United States, and Japan. (The other 21 states were Australia, Brazil, Bulgaria, Cuba, Denmark, Egypt, Estonia, Finland, Greece, India, Irish Free State, Netherlands, New Zealand, Norway, Portugal, Romania, El Salvador, Yugoslavia, Sweden, Czechoslovakia, and Venezuela.)[7]

Three states—France, Italy, and Poland—replied that they felt the time was inopportune for such a convention. Landlocked Austria and Switzerland abstained, and Spain objected to the questionnaire because it included a three-mile draft convention, ". . . contrary to Spanish Law."[8]

On the question of the exploitation of the products of the sea, twenty-two states, including the United States, France, and Italy, favored a convention. But six states, including Great Britain—because of her strict interpretation of the three-mile limit—and Japan, voted negative. Again Austria and Switzerland abstained.[9]

After studying the replies, the Committee of Experts reported to the Council of the League that seven subjects were "ripe for codification." In September, 1927, the Assembly acted on the report and resolved that conferences should be held, starting in 1929 to examine three subjects, including that of territorial

---

5 *Ibid.*, pp. 63, 129, 134–141.
6 *Ibid.*, ("Report of the Sub-Committee on Exploitation of the Products of the Sea," Dr. José Léon Suarez of Argentina, Rapporteur), p. 230.
7 League of Nations, *Third Session of the Committee of Experts for the Progressive Codification of International Law* ("Report to the Council of the League of Nations on the Questions which Appear Ripe for International Regulation"), pp. 8–11.
8 *Ibid.*, pp. 12–13.
9 *Ibid.*, pp. 34–35.

waters. The resolution also referred the question on exploitation of sea products to the League's Economic Committee for further study. Finally the resolution provided for the appointment of a Preparatory Committee to prepare detailed bases of discussion for the conference questions.[10]

The Preparatory Committee. The Preparatory Committee met in February, 1928, and prepared a "Schedule of Points" which was circulated to the governments on February 15th, with the request that comments be provided. Point III requested each state's views on the "breadth of territorial waters subject to the Sovereignty of the State (three miles, six miles, range of cannon, etc.)," and its claims, if any, to jurisdiction beyond territorial waters.[11]

The Preparatory Committee met again in January and February, 1929, to examine the replies of twenty-two states. Although not unanimous, the majority favored the three-mile limit. Great Britain and Japan refused to recognize claims of other states beyond three miles. France rejected the idea of one breadth for all purposes. Germany neither claimed nor recognized any claims beyond three miles, but indicated her willingness to consider a change. The United States claimed a certain amount of control over foreign ships within four leagues of the coast for fiscal and customs purposes. Italy claimed "special rights" within twelve miles.[12]

On the strength of these replies, the Preparatory Committee drew up bases of discussion for use by the conference delegations, including the following:

Basis of Discussion No. 3
The breadth of the territorial waters under the sovereignty of the coastal State is three nautical miles. . . .
Basis of Discussion No. 5
On the high seas adjacent to its territorial waters, the coastal State may exercise the control necessary to prevent, within its territory or territorial waters, the infringement of its customs or sanitary regulations or interference with its security by foreign ships.
Such control may not be exercised more than twelve miles from the coast.[13]

This latter basis of discussion formally introduced on an international level the concept, already practiced by many states, of a twelve-mile zone for special jurisdiction, a concept which Great Britain strongly opposed, and one which was to deadlock the conference, that of the contiguous zone.

10 Eighth Assembly of the League of Nations, Resolution of September 27, 1927, "Codi-fication of International Law," reproduced in Special Supplement to *A.J.I.L.*, vol. XXII, pp. 231–233.
11 League of Nations, *Conference for the Codification of International Law, Bases of Discussion Drawn up for the Conference by the Preparatory Committee*, p. 27.
12 *Ibid.*, pp. 27–28; Brierly, "The Doctrine of Contiguous Zone and the Dicta in *Craft v. Dunphy*," p. 156.
13 League of Nations, *Bases of Discussion*, pp. 28–29.

The Harvard Research. One of the most comprehensive and valuable contributions to the codification and understanding of international law was precipitated by the League's Committee of Experts. In 1927, the faculty of the Harvard Law School, collaborating with experts invited from numerous other universities and institutions, undertook to draft international conventions on each of the subjects to be considered by the Codification Conference. Virtually every well-known American expert on international law—forty-four jurists and scholars—contributed to the research. The work of the research was conducted with reference to the "Schedule of Points" circulated by the Preparatory Committee, but without regard to the replies by the governments. The draft conventions were based on international practice and usage and included extensive documentation and commentary. Pertinent articles are excerpted as follows:

Article 2

The marginal sea of a state is that part of the sea within three miles (60 to the degree of longitude at the equator) of its shore measured outward from the mean low water mark or from the seaward limit of a bay or river-mouth. . . .

Article 20

The navigation of the high seas is free to all states. On the high seas adjacent to the marginal sea, however, a state may take such measures as may be necessary for the enforcement within its territory or territorial waters of its customs, navigation, sanitary, or police laws or regulations, or for its immediate protection.[14]

Unlike the *Bases of Discussion*, the *Harvard Research* draft convention did not set this zone at twelve miles, but in its annotation, documented fully the numerous twelve-mile precedents in the practice of states.

THE CONFERENCE

With such meticulous and exhaustive preparation as the *Bases of Discussion* and the *Harvard Research*, the delegates from forty-eight governments assembled at The Hague in March, 1930. While fifteen members of the League did not participate, nine nonmembers were represented, including an observer from the Soviet Union. The rules of procedure provided that drafts would be approved by a two-thirds majority of the delegates voting in the committee, although only a simple majority would be required in the plenary session of the conference for final approval.

By the time the delegates met, having fully digested the controversial preliminary paperwork, and those of the small, new, and nonmaritime states having come to the realization that they were actually being given the option to vote as they saw fit, there was little chance to obtain the required two-thirds majority required in committee. Although a majority of the state delegations did prefer three miles, some delegations flatly refused to consider claims beyond

14 Harvard Law School, *Research in International Law*, pp. 250, 333–334.

three miles. Others refused to establish a single extent of territorial sea for all purposes. When it was proposed as a compromise to establish a contiguous zone adjacent to the territorial sea for special controls out to twelve miles, still other states objected. Several states found this compromise attractive but it failed because of the strong opposition of Great Britain. The British position advanced by Sir Maurice Gwyer was as follows:

> The British Delegation firmly supports Basis No. 3—that is to say, a territorial belt of three miles without the exercise, as of right, of any powers by the Coastal State in the contiguous zone, and they do that on three grounds, which I will express in as few words as I can: First, because in their view the three-mile limit is a rule of international law already existing adopted by maritime nations which possess nearly 80% of the effective tonnage of the world; secondly, because we have already, in this committee, adopted the principle of sovereignty over territorial waters; and thirdly, because the three-mile limit is the limit which is most in favour of freedom of navigation.[15]

The positions of the states. Because of the widely divergent views, formal voting was not attempted in the Conference's Second Committee (Territorial Sea). On the occasion of the last meeting of the committee, however, the Japanese delegate proposed:

> I do not think that we should vote. I think however . . . that it is desirable to learn the views of the different delegations. I propose, therefore, that each delegation should in turn state its attitude on the question without any vote being taken. . . .[16]

This was agreed upon and thirty-seven states, in order, announced their "position in principle." Ten states declared for the three-mile limit: Union of South Africa, United States, Great Britain, Australia, Canada, China, Denmark, India, Japan, and the Netherlands. Two states, Greece and the Irish Free State, also declared for the three-mile limit, but added that they could accept a contiguous zone. Seven states voted for three miles provided a contiguous zone was added: Germany, Belgium, Chile, Egypt, Estonia, France, and Poland. Three states chose four miles: Iceland, Norway, and Sweden. Finland also voted for four miles but insisted on a contiguous zone beyond. Six states chose six miles: Colombia, Italy, Romania, Uruguay, Yugoslavia, and Brazil; and six others voted for six miles and a contiguous zone: Cuba, Spain, Latvia, Persia, Portugal, and Turkey. Czechoslovakia and the Soviet Union did not vote. In summary, the tally stood at: three miles: 19; four miles: 4; six miles: 12; and two abstentions.[17]

It should be noted that none of the states which voted for six miles were

---

15 League of Nations, *Final Act, Conference for the Codification of International Law, The Hague, March-April, 1930*, pp. 169–181, p. 254.
16 *Ibid.*, p. 253.
17 *Ibid.*, pp. 253–257.

major maritime states, and three of them—Cuba, Latvia, and Yugoslavia—were newly independent. Some of the individual state positions are worthy of specific comment. Portugal's first choice was twelve miles but her delegation was willing to accept six territorial and six contiguous. Chile, similarly, chose six miles but would have accepted three with a contiguous zone. The German position, from the advantage of hindsight, was probably the most reasonable:

> The German Delegation is in favor of the three-mile rule, together with the existence of an adjacent zone, in the hope that the acceptance of the principle of the adjacent zone may facilitate the acceptance of the three-mile rule by other countries.[18]

Had the British not been so fervent in their opposition to the contiguous zone, and had they been able to accept the German view, it seems altogether possible that the three-mile limit, together with a contiguous zone of nine additional miles, might have been codified.

Such was not the case, however, and no doubt it gave the Soviet Union a fair measure of satisfaction to observe the inability of the Western states to obtain agreement on a rule of three miles. Yet, not being in a position to support or enforce their own twelve-mile claim at the time, the Soviet delegation abstained, but not without taking the opportunity to comment on ". . . the great diversity of views . . ." and to cite the existence of claims to three, four, six, ten, and twelve miles.[19] Czechoslovakia, also abstaining, frankly stated her position:

> The Czechoslovak Delegation desires the greatest possible freedom of navigation, but not having any coast line they consider that they should abstain from proposing a definite extent for the zone of territorial waters.[20]

It is not difficult to read into this statement Czechoslovakia's support of the three-mile limit, especially with the knowledge that the 1919 peace treaties gave her guaranteed access to the sea via internationalized rivers, but without coastlines of her own.

The Final Act. The draft presented by the Second Committee to the plenary session was stripped of the substance which was included in the *Bases of Discussion* with which the conference began. The residual articles were appended to the *Final Act* as an Annex entitled "The Legal Status of the Territorial Sea." Some are quoted below:

Article 1

The territory of a State includes a belt of sea described in this Convention as the territorial sea.

Sovereignty over this belt is exercised subject to the conditions provided by the present Convention and other rules of international law.

18 *Ibid.*, p. 254.
19 *Ibid.*, p. 257.
20 *Ibid.*, pp. 256–257.

Article 2

The territory of a Coastal State includes also the air space above the territorial seas, as well as the bed of the sea, and the subsoil. . . .

Article 4

A Coastal State may put no obstacle in the way of the innocent passage of foreign vessels in the territorial sea. . . .

Article 5

The right of passage does not prevent the Coastal State from taking all necessary steps to protect itself in the territorial sea against any act prejudicial to the security, public policy or fiscal interests of the State. . . .[21]

The *Final Act* then recommended to the Council of the League that it convene "a new conference . . . on all questions connected with the territorial sea. . . ."[22] But such a conference was never held.

THE AFTERMATH AND EFFECTS OF THE CONFERENCE

The utter failure of the conference surprised many of the participants. The delegates had gone to The Hague with a spirit of international cooperation and goodwill, generated in part by the conclusion of the Kellogg-Briand Pact of Paris, only two years earlier. But this turned to disillusionment and disappointment as was evidenced by several of the U.S. delegates, such as Jesse Reeves, Manley Hudson, and David Hunter Miller who, writing after the conference, offered various explanations for its failure. Jesse S. Reeves (1872–1942), professor and publicist, attributed the failure of the conference primarily to the unwillingness of the states to compromise. He added another reason:

This failure may be ascribed in the second place to what is believed to have been an erroneous view of the work and aim of the Commission. Following the instructions to the conference, the Commission did not undertake to agree upon statements of existing international law, and so to limit itself, but it proceeded into the field of international law-making.[23]

Manley Hudson (1886–1960), publicist, member of the United States delegation, and director of the *Harvard Research*, attempted vainly to show the brighter side as he wrote:

In conclusion, it may be said that the conference did not wholly fail in its dealing with the subject of territorial waters; it conducted a very useful exploration; it brought into the open the existing divergencies of views. . . .[24]

Even the title of Hudson's essay ("The First Conference for the Codification of International Law") reflected the contemporary, but unwarranted, optimism

21 *Ibid.*, pp. 184–185.
22 *Ibid.*, p. 184.
23 Reeves, "The Codification of the Law of Territorial Waters," p. 488.
24 Hudson, "The First Conference for the Codification of International Law," p. 458.

that a subsequent conference would be held, presumably with more favorable results.

David Hunter Miller, Editor of Treaties, U.S. Department of State, and Chairman of the U.S. Delegation, explained the conference's failure in these terms:

> The program of the Conference was too extensive. The time allotted for its work was one month. . . . It is not desirable that international conferences should be conducted under such pressure.[25]

Of the reasons offered, that of unwillingness to compromise appears the most valid. There seems to have been a naïveté on the part of the great powers in assuming that if given the chance to "vote" on the three-mile limit, the lesser powers would rubberstamp approval of the rule in respectful obedience. There is no other logical explanation for their willingness to permit the matter to be thrown open to discussion so unrestrictedly. Following this, the great powers failed, once they had seen the fragmenting effects of such a discussion, to recoup their losses by accepting a compromise. Instead, they permitted the conference to fail, and in so doing the great maritime powers ended their oligarchical maintenance of the maximum *mare liberum*. The conference suggested to all that the great powers were no longer committed to enforcement of the three-mile limit. From 1930 on, the rule was subjected to increasing criticism, and its significance became diminished by the rapid development of the concept of the contiguous zone.

The contiguous zone. The doctrine of the contiguous zone is as old as the British Hovering Acts and the case of *Church v. Hubbart.* Nevertheless, the contiguous zone was not known by that name until the Hague Conference; and the conference can be credited with coining the phrase and popularizing the concept. The term *contiguous* used in this sense is not generally found in writings before the 1920s. It was not used, for example, by either Fulton or Jessup in their very thorough monographs on territorial and adjacent waters, written in 1911 and 1927 respectively.[26]

It was, however, adopted for use by the Preparatory Commitee for the Hague Conference. And in 1928, the Institute of International Law adopted the principle of a ". . . contiguous, supplementary zone . . ." adjacent to territorial waters for the purposes of ". . . security, neutrality, sanitation, customs, and fishing . . ." the extent of which ". . . cannot exceed nine miles."[27] Since that time the term has become standard parlance, used widely in international instruments and in writing on international maritime law. The rapid adherence of states to the concept during the interwar period will be shown in the following section.

25 Miller, "The Hague Codification Conference," p. 693.
26 Fulton, *Sovereignty of the Sea;* and Jessup, *Territorial Waters.*
27 Institute of International Law, "Projet de règlement relatif à la mer territoriale en temps de paix," p. 758. Translation by the author.

The Interwar Practice of States: The
Contiguous Zone

THE UNITED STATES AND THE CONTIGUOUS ZONE

The interwar experiences and practice of the United States, more than any-thing else, influenced the growth of the doctrine of the contiguous zone. The 1920s gave the Americans a taste of what the British had been through a century earlier during their "Golden Age of Smuggling." (See pages 70–71.) The American smuggling problem centered around alcoholic beverages and was triggered by the ratification of the famous Eighteenth Amendment to the United States Constitution. The Amendment was proposed by Congress December 19, 1917, and was proclaimed adopted on January 29, 1919. Section I provided: "After one year from ratification of this article the manufacture, sale, or transportation of intoxicating liquors within, the importation thereof into, or the exportation thereof from the United States and all territory subject to the jurisdiction thereof for beverage purposes is prohibited."[28] The ensuing "Prohibition Era" was one of the most colorful periods of American history. Its rumrunners created many problems for the U.S. Coast Guard, the courts, and for the U.S. Department of State. Considerable legal literature appeared during the 1920s and 1930s dealing with these problems, bearing the names of such eminent scholars as Philip C. Jessup, William E. Masterson, T. S. Woolsey, James Brown Scott, Edwin D. Dickinson, J. L. Brierly, H. A. Smith, and others. For citations, see bibliography.

National Prohibition Act of 1919. The United States enacted several laws in order to implement the Eighteenth Amendment, the first of these being the National Prohibition Act of 1919, also known as the Volstead Act, intro-duced by Andrew J. Volstead. The Act provided that:

> No person shall . . . manufacture, sell, barter, transport, import, export, deliver, furnish, or possess any intoxicating liquor . . . and all provisions of this Act shall be liberally construed to the end that the use of intoxi-cating liquor as a beverage may be prevented.[29]

The act also gave enforcement officials authority to seize any boat or vehicle unlawfully employed in the transportation of liquor, and if the transporter were convicted, to sell the boat or vehicle at public auction.[30] In 1921 a loop-hole was covered by the passage of a supplemental law by which the Volstead Act was made applicable ". . . not only to the United States, but to all territory subject to its jurisdiction" [including territorial waters].[31]

In 1922, enforcement of the law against foreigners was put to the test.

---

28   Norton, *The Constitution of the United States,* p. 254.
29   Section 3, Title II of "National Prohibition Act of October 28, 1919," 41 *U.S. Statutes at Large* 305, reproduced in Jessup, *Territorial Waters,* p. 212.
30   "National Prohibition Act," Section 26, *ibid.*
31   Section 3, "Act of November 23, 1921," 42 *U.S. Statutes at Large* 222.

Thirsty Americans had become willing to pay exorbitant prices for a bottle of liquor, prices high enough to make the risks seem worthwhile to enterprising British subjects from nearby Canada, Bermuda, and the West Indies, who became smugglers to capitalize on such a lucrative and demanding market. In February of that year, the British vessel *Grace and Ruby* was seized by U.S. coastal authorities four miles from land after having transshipped liquor to a small boat and thence to the Massachusetts shore under cover of darkness. The U.S. court denied the claims for damages by the vessel's owners on the grounds that the participation by the crew of *Grace and Ruby* in the act of delivering the liquor ashore by small boat amounted to "constructive presence" of the mother vessel within the territorial jurisdiction of the United States.[32] The justice delivering the findings of the court referred to the U.S. position in *Church v. Hubbart* (see pages 93–94), in defending the court's position:

> The line between territorial waters and the high seas is not like the boundary between us and a foreign power. There must be, it seems to me, a certain width of debatable waters adjacent to our coasts. . . .[33]

The Tariff Act of 1922. The British protests that logically followed brought about an attempt by the United States to legalize such seizures and to define further those "debatable waters" contiguous to the territorial sea. This was accomplished by passing another statute, the Tariff Act of 1922,[34] which in effect would enable American authorities to enforce the Volstead Act within a zone of twelve miles. Specifically, the new Act authorized federal officials at any time to

> . . . go on board of any vessel . . . within four leagues of the coast of the United States, to examine the manifest and to inspect, search and examine the vessel . . . and every part thereof, and any person, trunk or package on board, and to this end to hail and stop such vessel or vehicle, if under way, and use all necessary force to compel compliance. . . .[35]

This act obviously went a good deal further than the four-league Act of 1799 (see pages 93–94), and it led to the seizure of many British vessels and also vessels of other foreign flags. In the period of one single year—fiscal year 1924–1925—the following seizures of foreign vessels were made:[36]

British	28	Italian	1
French	4	Cuban	1
Honduran	2	Costa Rican	1
Norwegian	2		

32 *The Grace and Ruby*, 283 *Federal Reporter* 475 (1922), in Fenwick, *Cases*, p. 501; and Hudson, *Cases*, p. 633.

33 *The Grace and Ruby, loc. cit.*

34 "Tariff Act of September 21, 1922, 42 *U.S. Statutes at Large* 858.

35 *Ibid.*, Section 581, reproduced in part in Jessup, *Territorial Waters*, pp. 212–213, and in Masterson, *Jurisdiction in Marginal Seas*, pp. 228–233.

36 U.S. Department of Justice, *Annual Report of the Attorney General*, December 9, 1925, cited in Masterson, *Jurisdiction in Marginal Seas*, p. 211.

This action by the Treasury Department was the source of much international friction and created serious problems for the State Department.

Another related source of international friction had developed concurrently. U.S. courts had interpreted the law as prohibiting foreign ships from transporting liquor through American territorial waters, even under seal. This came into direct conflict with the laws of certain states such as Denmark, Belgium, and Italy, which required the supply of drink to the crew and passengers.[37] The lead case in this regard was *Cunard v. Mellon* (1923), wherein the U.S. Supreme Court upheld the action of the New York authorities in confiscating the liquor aboard a British luxury liner, the liquor having been intended for passenger consumption.[38] This decision drew foreign criticism as being inconsistent with the time-honored practice under international law, wherein states abstained from interfering with the internal discipline or administration of a ship unless the peace, tranquility, or public safety of the host state was involved.

The Anglo-American Treaty of 1924. In the days shortly after this Supreme Court decision, there was considerable activity in Washington with respect to negotiations with foreign powers to settle the differences in the application of a state's laws on vessels from another state in territorial waters. On June 12, 1923, draft treaties proposing means whereby U.S. authorities might search vessels out to twelve miles were urgently circulated to the British, Spanish, Japanese, French, and Italians. This rush appeared to some as a U.S. plan to adopt a twelve-mile limit, and was quite annoying to the British. On June 12, 1923, the *New York Herald* printed:

> Proposed Extension of Three Mile Limit—In the midst of the confusion over the ship liquor ruling of the U.S. Supreme Court and the Treasury regulations, the Harding Administration has formulated a plan which, its authors hope, may wipe out international complications and solve the problems of smuggling along American shores.

A few days later, the British Foreign Secretary, Lord Curzon, speaking in the House of Lords on June 28, 1923, also interpreted the American draft treaty as a proposed extension of territorial waters and declared: "There is no chance of our agreeing in any circumstances whatever to the American proposal for a twelve-mile territorial limit."[39]

Although the British, too, had once zealously enforced their customs laws well beyond the three-mile limit (see pages 70–71), in 1876 they had abandoned all their former claims to jurisdiction beyond three miles. In responding to the American draft treaty, the British somewhat sarcastically rebuked the United States for proposing a twelve-mile customs zone by citing the 1876

---

37 Colombos, *Law of the Sea*, p. 129, and Jessup, *Territorial Waters*, p. 217.

38 *Cunard Steamship Company et al. v. Mellon et al.* (1923) 262 U.S. 100; Fenwick, *Cases*, p. 354.

39 Wescott, "British Reject Twelve-Mile Limit," pp. 1579–1580; and Jessup, *Territorial Waters*, p. 234.

Customs Consolidation Act ". . . by which British Municipal legislation is made to conform with international law."[40]

Nevertheless, negotiations were undertaken that cleared up the misunderstandings and led to the conclusion of the Anglo-American Treaty of 1924, wherein the two states reached a compromise. The opening article declared that both states upheld the principle of the three-mile limit for territorial waters. For their part, the British agreed that U.S. authorities could board, search, and seize offending British vessels, provided that this right was not to be exercised

> . . . at a greater distance from the coast of the United States, its territories or possessions than can be traversed in one hour by the vessel suspected of endeavoring to commit the offence.[41]

Such a provision was not entirely novel; in 1651 Loccenius had recommended a territorial sea equal to two day's journey. (See page 27.) The Anglo-American Treaty of 1924 also included this language:

> His Britannic Majesty agrees that he will raise no objection to the boarding of private vessels under British flag outside the limits of territorial waters by the authorities of the United States, its territories or possessions. . .

and permitted examination of the vessel's papers, a search if warranted, and if the law was found to be broken, seizure of the vessel.[42] The *quid pro quo* of the treaty was the U.S. concession that foreign-flag vessels might be allowed to enter American territorial waters with liquor for passenger consumption provided it remained under seal as long as the ships remained within territorial waters.

Between 1924 and 1930, fifteen such treaties were concluded between the United States and other maritime states: France, Germany, Italy, Norway, Sweden, Denmark, Holland, Spain, Belgium, Poland, Greece, Cuba, Chile, Panama, and Japan.[43] These treaties greatly reduced the friction. In *Cook v. United States* (1933), the Supreme Court upheld the sanctity of the new treaties by declaring illegal the U.S. seizure at a distance of eleven and one-half miles from shore of a vessel capable of only ten knots, in spite of the fact that the Tariff Act of 1922 provided jurisdiction out to twelve miles.[44] Without

---

40 British Government memorandum of July 14, 1923, Ms. Records, Department of State, cited in Jessup, *Territorial Waters*, pp. 79, 283.

41 United States and Great Britain, "Convention between the United States of America and Great Britain to Aid in the Prevention of Smuggling of Intoxicating Liquors into the United States, Washington, January 23, 1924," Article II (3), reprinted in Supplement to *A.J.I.L.*, XVIII (July, 1924), pp. 127–130, and in Masterson, *Jurisdiction in Marginal Seas*, pp. 346–352.

42 *Ibid.*

43 Colombos, *Law of the Sea*, p. 130, and Masterson, *Jurisdiction in Marginal Seas*, pp. 352–353.

44 *Cook v. United States*, 288 U.S. 102 (1933), in Briggs, *The Law of Nations*, pp. 362–371.

a doubt, another "limit" of jurisdiction to seaward for a special purpose had been introduced—a variable limit depending on the speed of the craft. A thirty-knot craft could be seized thirty miles from shore; whereas a boat under oars, probably no more than a mile or two. Another link had been forged, moreover, in the development of the concept of the contiguous zone.

The Anti-Smuggling Act of 1935. The Roosevelt Administration, as one of its first orders of business, began the task of repealing prohibition. The Twenty-first Amendment, repealing the Eighteenth, was proposed by the Congress February 20, 1933, and proclaimed adopted on December 5, 1933. Section 2 of Article XXI reads:

> The transportation or importation into any State, Territory, or Possession of the United States for delivery therein of Intoxicating Liquors, in violation of the laws thereof, is hereby prohibited.[45]

This left the door open for individual states to remain "dry" and to continue to enforce antismuggling procedures locally; some did.

Although repeal of prohibition essentially put an end to liquor smuggling, customs enforcement officials did not fancy losing their newly gained authority for enforcement of laws in the case of the other dutiable items. As it worked out, they lost no authority. In fact, a U.S. District Court in 1934 held that repeal of prohibition did not abrogate the right of the United States to search under the Anglo-American Treaty of 1924.[46] Then the following year, the United States enacted the Anti-Smuggling Act of 1935, which gave even greater flexibility and authority to customs enforcement officials. This law was remarkably bold in its scope of jurisdiction over the high seas. The law provided for the proclamation of "customs-enforcement areas" on an as-required basis. A customs-enforcement area was a mobile zone, changing in size, shape, and location, at the President's discretion. It could be ordered upon detection of a smuggling vessel hovering off the coasts of the United States. The spatial extent was prescribed as follows:

> . . . No customs-enforcement area shall include any waters more than one hundred miles from the place or immediate area where the President declares such vessel or vessels are hovering or are being kept . . . and . . . shall not include any waters more than fifty nautical miles outwards from the outer limit of customs waters.[47]

Only five customs-enforcement areas were proclaimed under the act, all in 1935. Sixteen vessels were seized under its provisions. Fifteen seizures were

---

45 Norton, *Constitution*, p. 261.
46 *The Golmaccam*, 8 *F. Supp.* 338 (D. Maine, N.D. 1934), in Hackworth, *Digest*, vol. I, p. 690.
47 United States Anti-Smuggling Act of August 5, 1935, 49 *U.S. Statutes at Large* 517, reprinted in Briggs, *Law of Nations*, pp. 371–372.

in conformity with international law, i.e., ships of U.S. registry, or foreign ships within twelve miles of the coast. The other, a British flag vessel, was seized between fifteen and thirty-six miles off the coast; the British offered no protest.[48]

NORWAY AND THE CONTIGUOUS ZONE

Just as the United States locked horns with Great Britain when the former sought to enforce its customs laws beyond three miles, the Norwegians came in conflict with the British when Norway undertook similarly to exclude foreign fishermen from the contiguous high seas.

Norway had traditionally claimed as "historical bays" several fairly large fjords such as Varanger Fjord and Vest Fjord. One of the reasons the Kingdom of Sweden and Norway had been unwilling to adhere to the North Sea Fisheries Convention of 1882 was the refusal of the other powers to accept Norway's position on the fjords. Norway, on the other hand, was unwilling to accept the ten-mile baseline for bays, saying it was inadequate in the case of her coastline.[49]

Her claim to Varanger Fjord started creating international problems in 1934. During that year, the Norwegian Supreme Court upheld the conviction by a lower court of a German national for "illegal" fishing in Varanger Fjord. The prosecution and conviction was adjudged proper by the high court inasmuch as the German had been fishing within three miles of a baseline drawn thirty and one-half miles across the fjord from cape to cape.[50]

The following year Norway issued her to-become-famous Royal Norwegian Decree of July 12, 1935,[51] wherein her territorial waters—those from the Soviet border in Varanger Fjord to Traena just south of Vest Fjord—were delimited by a series of arbitrary straight baselines drawn between forty-eight fixed points, consisting of rocks, spits, islands, capes and the like. The longest baseline was forty-four miles.[52] To seaward of these baselines, then, the Norwegians measured their four-mile belt of territorial waters. Landward of the baselines, according to the decree, the waters were internal waters. With this baseline construction, certain areas of the high seas more than twenty miles from the nearest land were designated as internal and/or territorial waters.

These Norwegian claims for areas beyond traditional territorial waters were occasioned by a concern for fisheries, not customs enforcement as in the U.S. case. The decree led to a protracted dispute with Great Britain, which was

---

48   Jessup, "The Anti-Smuggling Act of 1935," pp. 101–106.
49   Jessup, *Territorial Waters*, p. 421.
50   *Varanger-Fjord Case*, Norway, Supreme Court, August 24, 1934 *Norsk Retstidende* (1934), 727 in Briggs, *Law of Nations*, pp. 288–290.
51   United Nations, *Laws and Regulations on the Territorial Sea*, pp. 25–28.
52   Shalowitz, *Shore and Sea Boundaries*, U.S. Department of Commerce, Coast and Geodetic Survey, vol. I, pp. 68–69. This work provides a chart showing each of the 48 points and the connecting baselines.

not settled until after World War II, and which will be discussed in Chapter 11.

OTHER STATES AND THE CONTIGUOUS ZONE

The foregoing instances—U.S. Prohibition and the Norwegian Decree of 1935—were the two most celebrated interwar extensions of national jurisdiction to seaward. But to illustrate how widely and rapidly the doctrine of the contiguous zone was accepted during the decade following the Hague Conference, several examples of national laws, regulations, and treaties have been compiled and arranged in Table 3. The claims varied in extent between five miles and one hour's sailing distance, but the most common claim was twelve miles. The purposes were many and diverse, but the majority had to do with customs. At least two of the states—Ecuador and France—utilized the vehicle of the contiguous zone doctrine, like Norway, to extend fishery zones. Five states capitalized on the political climate by actually increasing their territorial waters beyond the three-mile limit. Although the list is by no means complete, it is definitely representative of the variety of claims, both in extent and purpose.

One other interwar claim should be noted. Mexico, which had claimed a nine-mile territorial sea during the nineteenth century, and which had adopted the three-mile limit in 1902 (see page 115), abstained from expressing any view at the 1930 Hague Conference.[53] But afterwards, feeling the time was opportune to revert to her nine-mile limit, she issued a decree to that effect in 1935. The United States protested against this decree which read:

> Sole Article. Section I of Article 4 of the Law of Immobile Properties of the Nation of December 18, 1902 is amended to read as follows: I. The Territorial Waters, for a distance of nine nautical miles (16,668 kilometers), counted from the mark of the lowest tide on the coasts of the mainland or on the shores of the islands forming part of the national territory.[54]

INTERWAR PUBLICISTS

The damage rendered the three-mile limit by the 1930 Hague Conference and its aftereffects was soon reflected in the writings of publicists. The British writers, as might have been expected, went on the defensive. Herbert A. Smith (1885–1961) challenged the actions of states that had extended their fisheries into the contiguous zone. Smith declared flatly that ". . . the doctrine of the contiguous zone cannot be interpreted to justify a claim to monopolize the fisheries outside territorial limits."[55]

J. L. Brierly (1881–1955) criticized the doctrine of the contiguous zone because it created uncertainties as to the intentions of states. Brierly, who

---

53 Heinzen, "Three-Mile Limit," p. 638.
54 "Mexican Decree of August 30, 1935," in Hackworth, *Digest*, vol. I, p. 639; Fenwick, *International Law*, p. 376.
55 Smith, "The Contiguous Zone," p. 123.

Table 3   Miscellaneous State Contiguous Zone Claims (1930–1940)*

State	Extent	Purpose of Claim	Means and Date of Implementation
Bulgaria	6 miles	Territorial waters	Decree-Law of 25 August 1935
China	12 miles	Customs	Customs Preventive Law of 19 June 1934
Colombia	20 kilometers	Customs	Customs Law of 19 June 1931
Cuba	5 miles	Sanitation	General Law on Fisheries of 28 March 1936
Czechoslovakia	12 miles	Anti-smuggling	Treaty with Finland, 21 March 1936
Denmark	12 miles	Anti-smuggling	Act No. 316 of 28 November 1935
Dominican Republic	3 leagues	Naval security area	Law No. 55 of 27 December 1938
Ecuador	15 miles	Fishing	Decree No. 607 of 29 August 1934
El Salvador	12 miles	Police and security	Law of Navigation and Marine of 23 October 1933
Finland	6 miles	Customs	Customs Regulation of 8 September 1939
France	20 kilometers	Fishing (Indo-China)	Presidential Decree of 22 September 1936
Greece	6 miles	Territorial seas	Law No. 230 of 17 September 1936
Guatemala	12 miles	Port authority jurisdiction	Regulations of 21 April 1939
Honduras	12 miles	Territorial seas	Constitution of 28 March 1936
Hungary	12 miles	Anti-smuggling	Treaty with Finland of 23 November 1932
Iran	6 miles	Territorial waters	Act of 19 July 1934
	12 miles	Marine supervision zone	
Italy	12 miles	Customs	Customs Law No. 1424 of 25 September 1940
Lebanon	20 kilometers	Customs	Order No. 137/LR of 15 June 1935
Norway	10 miles	Customs	Royal Resolution of 28 October 1932
Poland	12 miles	Customs	Customs Law of 27 October 1933
Romania	6 miles	Territorial seas	Royal Decree No. 296 of 7 February 1934
Syria	20 kilometers	Customs	Customs Code of 15 June 1935
United Kingdom	1 hour's sailing distance	Customs	Treaty with Finland of 13 October 1933
U.S.S.R.	12 miles	Sovereignty over air space	Air Code of 7 August 1935†
Venezuela	12 miles	Security, customs, sanitation	Presidential Decree of 15 September 1939

* Data in this table is from United Nations, *Laws and Regulations on the Regime of the High Seas*, pp. 53–168, *passim;* and United Nations, *Laws and Regulations on the Regime of the Territorial Sea*, pp. 45–46.

† This Code provided for Soviet sovereignty in the air space over her maritime belt, which had been fixed earlier at twelve miles.

served as a member of the League's Committee of Experts, published the first edition of his well-known *Law of Nations* in 1928, the second edition in 1936, and the fifth edition in 1955, just before his death. (A sixth, posthumous edition, edited by Sir Humphrey Waldock, appeared in 1963.) In commenting on the growing competition between the contiguous zone and the three-mile limit Brierly wrote:

> Great Britain has always resisted the doctrine of the Contiguous Zone, though some of the powers which we claimed in the Hovering Acts of the last century, for the protection of the customs, are difficult to reconcile with this attitude. . . . [I]t is not always clear in these cases whether a state is claiming a width of marginal sea exceeding three miles as its territorial waters, or whether it is satisfied with that limit and merely claiming certain special rights of jurisdiction *outside* its territorial waters. At the Hague Codification Conference of 1930 no agreement on the matter could be reached.[56]

After the United States repealed Prohibition, C. John Colombos (born 1886) wrote of the U.S. interwar deeds rather like those of a prodigal son returned home, pretending he had never gone astray. Colombos used the following language:

> Another striking illustration of the American adherence to the marginal belt of three miles is to be found in the fact that when the United States government sought to extend its liquor Prohibition Laws . . . it sought and obtained the consent of the other maritime nations by the conclusion of . . . treaties. . . .[57]

The French publicist, Gilbert Charles Gidel (1880–1959), like several other French writers, and following French national practice, strongly supported the concept of a contiguous zone with special limits for special purposes and rejected the sanctity of the three-mile limit. Gidel was one of the most active and prolific of all publicists on the law of the sea. He had published three volumes of his multivolume work on the law of the sea (*La haute mer* [1932], *Les eaux intérieures* [1932], and *La mer territoriale* [1934]) when, ironically, the manuscript and notes for the remaining volumes, including one on maritime warfare, were lost at sea, sunk in a ship carrying them to England early in World War II.[58] He subsequently published a volume on the continental shelf (see Bibliography). Concerning the three-mile rule, he would go only so far as to allow that the three-mile limit "is a rule of international law . . . of negative content," in the sense that "no State can refuse to respect the zone of territorial waters established by another State when the width of the zone does not exceed three miles."[59]

56 Brierly, *The Law of Nations*, pp. 165–166.
57 Colombos, "The Unification of Maritime International Law in Time of Peace," p. 97.
58 "Gilbert Gidel—In Memorium," *Proceedings of the Society of International Law at its Fifty-third Annual Meeting*, p. 328.
59 Gidel, *Le droit international public de la mer*, vol. III, pp. 123, 134, translated in Briggs, *Law of Nations*, p. 283.

Charles G. Fenwick of the United States (born 1880) acknowledged the three-mile limit as the "more authoritative practice," but matter-of-factly observed that the consensus was withering away. Fenwick, contemporary publicist, professor of political science, and director of the Pan American Union's Department of International Law, published the first and second editions of his *International Law* during the interwar period. Concerning the extent of territorial waters, Fenwick wrote:

> At the Hague Conference of 1930 no agreement could be reached upon a fixed distance; and the conclusion must be drawn that there was then and is now no generally acknowledged width of the marginal sea. . . .[60]

In marked contrast were the vividly expressive writings of certain other Americans. Philip Marshall Brown (1875–1966) colorfully described it ridiculous for states to restrict themselves to a three-mile limit. Brown, writing in his capacity as one of the editors of the *American Journal of International Law*, attacked the three-mile rule:

> [The three-mile limit] . . . would seem to be regarded as a kind of floating fence patrolled by a lone and lonely policeman who is forbidden to act until someone attempts to step through, very much like a small boy at a baseball game. But this attempt to apply a single arbitrary limit of jurisdiction to utterly different situations results, as the Institute of International Law has pointed out, in much needless confusion. . . . A strict adherence to the 3-mile limit as in the case of a spawning bed extending 4 or 5 miles out to sea would render this task of protection impossible. The extension of the right of jurisdiction to six miles recommended by the Institute of International Law would of course aid materially in the conservation of fisheries on which the livelihood of the poor inhabitants of the neighboring shores may depend. . . . States should not be required to adhere to an interpretation which would reduce them to the undignified, impotent, ridiculous role of playing hide-and-seek within an imaginary three-mile limit with swift craft waiting a favorable opportunity to dart through, violate national laws, and slip out immediately with impunity.[61]

Joseph Walter Bingham (born 1878) denounced the three-mile limit in strong language, claiming that it served only the selfish, short-term interests of the great powers, and was completely inadequate for conservation of fisheries. Professor Bingham, a contemporary publicist, made several astute, interesting observations in his *Report on the International Law of Pacific Coastal Fisheries*, including the following:

> The chief pragmatic reasons for advocacy of the three-mile limit today are: (1) fullest range for operations of belligerent naval powers; (2) free fishing on foreign coasts; and (3) freedom of commerce on the seas—but this third reason could be satisfied by liberal exemptions of commerce

60 Fenwick, *International Law*, p. 376.
61 Brown, "The Marginal Sea," pp. 90–91, 93–94.

from restrictions within a wider territorial zone under the limiting doctrine of free innocent passage. . . . Indeed the utter failure of the sanguine effort under the auspices of the League of Nations at the Hague in 1930 to codify the international law of territorial waters . . . was in large part due to irreconcilable fishery claims. Claims on the part of great states interested in fishing off foreign coasts, and therefore supporting the British doctrine limiting territorial control to a narrow sea zone of three miles and control over coast fisheries to territorial waters, opposed claims by other states to control of fishing off their coasts over a wider zone of the sea.[62]

He went so far as to say:

To an unprejudiced student of history and of present world affairs, it is abundantly apparent . . . that there never has been and is not today any general agreement on the extent of territorial waters . . . [and] . . . that it always has been the opinion of realistic experts that if definite limits are set to marginal seas jurisdiction over those limits should be different for different purposes. . . .[63]

On first reading, the above passage seems to overstate the case. Certainly the three-mile limit existed as a rule of international law by the mid-1920s. True, it may well be that it had been a law for the many dictated by the few. The great maritime powers had been in a position to manipulate adherence, or at least compliance, with the three-mile rule. Doubtlessly there were several, perhaps many, states that did not necessarily agree with the rule which they obeyed; for in 1930, when given a gentlemen's chance to be heard, the lesser countries spoke out against the rule. Professor Bingham was saying that there never had been general *agreement*, and in this latter sense, he was probably right.

62 Bingham, *Report on the International Law of Pacific Coastal Fisheries*, p. 9.
63 *Ibid.*

CHAPTER 10

World War II and the Three-Mile Limit

The events during the years of World War II, 1938–1945, had a great effect on the three-mile limit, significantly accelerating its decline which had commenced during the interwar period. The practice of states—both in proclaiming extensive neutrality zones and in making far-reaching claims over the resources of the sea and its bed—further eroded the concept of a narrow limit of territorial seas. Moreover, out of the many major political upheavals of the war, there re-emerged the once-obscure twelve-mile claim of Russia, and there occurred an unprecedented proliferation of new, non-industrial, independent states, which, in general, were not especially kindly disposed to the past and its international legal practice, and who wished to make their own way and their own decisions. These several developments will be addressed in this chapter.

NEUTRALITY AND SECURITY ZONES

THE DECLARATION OF PANAMA

Early during the war, the first meeting of the Ministers of Foreign Affairs of the American Republics was held in Panama during September and October, 1939. On October 3, the foreign ministers of the twenty-one states adopted a general declaration which ". . . solemnly ratified their netural status in the conflict which is disrupting the peace of Europe."[1] The ministers, who could see ". . . no justification for the interests of the belligerents to prevail over the rights of neutrals . . . which by their neutrality in the conflict and their distance from the scene of events, should not be burdened with its [the war's] fatal and painful consequences," resolved and declared:

> As a measure of continental self-protection, the American Republics, so long as they maintain their neutrality, are as of inherent right entitled to

1 United Nations, *Laws and Regulations on the High Seas*, p. 144.

have those waters adjacent to the American continent . . . free from the commission of any hostile act by any non-American belligerent nation, whether such hostile act be attempted or made from land, sea, or air.[2]

The waters were then defined as those enclosed by ten rhumb lines starting at the Maine–New Brunswick boundary, proceeding south, around Cape Horn and then north, terminating at the Washington–British Columbia border. (A rhumb line is a navigational line, drawn on a chart or map, which maintains a constant compass direction and crosses all meridians at the same angle.) These lines disclose an open sea neutrality belt generally between 500 and 900 miles in width, and at one point off the Chilean and Peruvian coasts, it extends to 1200 miles. Several writers have described this zone as extending to a limit of about three hundred miles, including, C. John Colombos, F. V. Garcia Amador, and Joseph Walter Bingham.[3] This is true in the case of the California coast only. A carefully constructed geographic plot reveals most of the neutrality zone to be much wider, as indicated above.

Although Canadian coasts and waters were expressly excluded, the promulgation of the declaration caused an immediate reaction in Great Britain. In a note dated ten days later, the Admiralty recalled the position taken by the British in opposition to the American Prohibition laws, and made the point that the 1939 Pan American Neutrality Declaration was not to be construed as intending to extend the three-mile limit of territorial waters.[4]

The declaration was invoked by its authors on at least three occasions to protest hostile incidents within the zone. Joint notes were submitted to the European belligerents by the American Republics on December 23, 1939, March 16, 1940, and May 24, 1940.[5]

UNITED STATES SPECIAL SECURITY ZONES

Under the Hague Convention of 1907, a neutral power was obligated to be impartial to belligerent powers with respect to the use of its harbors and roadsteads. The right of innocent passage could normally be assumed with the understanding that:

> . . . a neutral Power may forbid a belligerent vessel which has failed to conform to the orders and regulations made by it, or which has violated neutrality, to enter its ports or roadsteads.[6]

2 "Declaration approved at Panama, at the First Meeting of the Ministers of Foreign Affairs of the American Republics, 3 October 1939," Article 1, in *ibid.,* p. 145, citing Pan American Union, *Congress and Conference Series* No. 29, p. 19.

3 Colombos, *Law of the Sea,* p. 627; Amador, *The Exploitation and Conservation of the Resources of the Sea,* p. 62; and Bingham, "The Continental Shelf and the Marginal Belt," p. 174.

4 British Admiralty Note of October 13, 1939, reproduced in U.S. Naval War College, *International Law Situations 1939,* pp. 68–69.

5 United Nations, *Laws and Regulations on the High Seas,* p. 146.

6 Article 9, Hague Convention XIII, Concerning the Rights and Duties of Neutral Powers in Maritime War, U.S. Department of the Navy, *Law of Naval Warfare,* p. B-3.

The practice of the United States while still a neutral during early World War II was inconsistent with the Hague rules. Under the Act of March 4, 1917, the President had been authorized to establish "defensive sea areas" by executive order "for purposes of national defense."[7] Invoking this authority, between May, 1939, and November, 1942, the President ordered naval defensive sea areas (some were called simply "defensive sea areas") at no less than thirty-four naval installation sites in the United States and its overseas bases: Kiska, Unalaska, and Kodiak, Alaska; Manila Bay and Subic Bay, Philippines; Pearl Harbor, Honolulu, and Kaneohe, Hawaii; Culebra, Puerto Rico and Guantanamo, Cuba in the Caribbean; the islands of Palmyra, Johnston, Midway, Wake, Kingman Reef, Rose, Tutuila, and Guam in the Pacific; and Portland, Maine, Portsmouth, New Hampshire, Narragansett Bay, San Diego, San Francisco, Columbia River Entrance, Puget Sound, Juan de Fuca Strait, New York, New London, Delaware Bay-River, Chesapeake Bay-Norfolk, Charleston, Buzzards Bay and Vineyard Sound, Massachusetts, and Matagorda Bay, Texas.[8] The executive orders establishing these areas went considerably further than the Hague Convention rules:

> At no time shall any person, other than persons or public vessels of the United States enter any of the naval defensive sea areas herein set apart and reserved, nor shall any vessel or other craft, other than public vessels of the United States, be navigated into any of said areas, unless authorized by the Secretary of the Navy.[9]

Concurrently, airspace reservations were established at the same locations, similarly restricting air navigation:

> At no time shall any aircraft, other than public aircraft of the United States, be navigated into any of the naval airspace reservations herein set apart and reserved, unless authorized by the Secretary of the Navy.[10]

The defensive sea areas and the airspace reservations conformed fairly closely to territorial waters within the three-mile limit; hence, their significance was in their denial of free navigation in areas normally open for innocent passage. The so-called "maritime control areas," however, established after the U.S. entry into the war, were not limited to waters within the three-mile limit. By six proclamations issued between December, 1941, and November, 1942, President Roosevelt established seventeen maritime control areas, all of which included waters of the high seas. These areas were justified by the President in terms of national defense

> . . . by virtue of the authority vested in me as President of the United States, and as Commander-in-Chief of the Army and Navy of the United

7   Whiteman, *Digest*, vol. IV, p. 389, citing 39 *U.S. Statutes at Large*, 1194.
8   U.S. Naval War College, *International Law Documents 1948–49*, pp. 157–169.
9   U.S. Navy Department, *Defensive Sea Areas and Airspace Reservations*, p. 7.
10 *Ibid.*

States, and in accordance with the principle of self-defense of the Law of Nations.[11]

As shown in Table 4, the seaward extent varied between 11 miles (Portsmouth, New Hampshire) and 65 miles (Prince William Sound, Alaska). The Hawaiian Maritime Control Area proclamation served as the model for the others and imposed restrictions as follows:

> A vessel not proceeding under United States naval or other United States authorized supervision shall not enter or navigate the waters of the Hawaiian Maritime Control Area except during daylight, when good visibility conditions prevail, and then only after specific permission has been obtained. . . .
>
> Even though permission has been obtained, it is incumbent upon a vessel entering the said Area to obey any further instructions received from the United States Navy, or other United States authority. . . .
>
> Should any vessel or person within the said Area disregard these regulations . . . such vessel or person may be subjected to the force necessary to require compliance, and may be liable to detention or arrest, or penalties or forfeiture, in accordance with law. . . .[12]

All of the maritime control areas were discontinued by proclamations issued in September, 1945, and May, 1946.

THE TRUMAN PROCLAMATIONS

With the end of the war, the wide neutral zone and the maritime control areas were no longer useful. But the end of the war also brought new types of claims over areas of the high seas to take their place. The two Truman Proclamations of 1945 concerning the continental shelf and fisheries conservation stimulated a voluminous international legal literature. Both of these subjects are generally beyond the parameters of this study. Yet they both impinged negatively on the three-mile rule in the sense that they contributed to its demise. These aspects, plus certain background information for purposes of continuity, will be presented in this section.

BACKGROUND

The idea of states reserving certain rights for themselves in the adjacent seabed was not new in 1945. The British nineteenth-century claims to the pearl banks in Ceylon, the oyster beds in Ireland, the offshore coal deposits at Cumberland, and the shell and bêche-de-mer fisheries of Australia have already been mentioned.

11   U.S. Naval War College, *International Law Documents 1948–49*, p. 170.
12   *Ibid.*, pp. 170–171.

Table 4
Seaward Extent of U.S. Maritime Control Areas
(World War II)

Maritime Control Area	Seaward Extent*
Hawaiian	53
Cristobal (Panama)	36
Gulf of Panama	50†
Boston	24
San Francisco	24
Columbia River	50
Puget Sound	50
Southeastern Alaska	50
Prince William Sound (Alaska)	65
Kodiak (Alaska)	50‡
Unalaska	50
Casco Bay (Maine)	12
Portsmouth, New Hampshire	11
Cape Hatteras	17
Key West	35
Los Angeles	15
San Diego	12

* Distances are in nautical miles, determined by plotting co-ordinates of latitude and longitude prescribed in the several proclamations, as reproduced in U.S. Naval War College, *International Law Documents 1948–49*, pp. 170–176.

† More accurately, the Gulf of Panama Maritime Control Area included all waters north of 8° N latitude (which passes 50 miles south of the Pacific entrance to the canal). The Panama Maritime Control Areas proclamation (Proclamation No. 2536 of 16 January 1942, 56 *Stat.* 1932) also cited, as authority, Article 10 of the General Treaty of 2 March 1936 (U.S. Treaty Series No. 945) which provided:

> In cases of an international conflagration or the existence of any threat of aggression which would endanger the security of the Republic of Panama or the neutrality or security of the Panama Canal, the Governments of the United States of America and the Republic of Panama will take such measures of prevention and defense as they may consider necessary for the protection of their common interests. [*Ibid.*, p. 169.]

‡ All waters within a 50-mile radius of Kodiak City.

Portugal appears to have been the next state to stake a claim to the resources of the continental shelf:

> Whereas deep trawling by steam vessels at depths of under 100 fathoms within the limits of the continental shelf is extremely harmful to fisheries, because this method destroys the feeding grounds on the sea bed and therewith the young fry feeding, sheltering and developing there, a process rapidly leading to the destruction of the marine life along the coasts affected since, as a consequence, it becomes impossible to replace the stocks of fish at depths of over 100 fathoms, the habitat of the fully developed fish, so that an important source of wealth is destroyed; . . .
>
> Whereas deep trawling by steam vessels is not harmful at depths of over 100 fathoms; . . .
>
> Article 2. Fishing by this method may only be carried out beyond the bathymetric line of 100 fathoms. . . .[13]

This enlightened 1910 enactment by Portugal occurred "forty years too soon." The nations of the world did not become generally and collectively concerned about the matter until midcentury.

Publicists. In 1923—the same year that the oil-drilling industry was automated with the successful introduction of the electric rotary deep oil well drill in California—Philip Marshall Brown wrote concerning the British submarine mines and the California coastal oil fields:

> A strictly technical interpretation of the three-mile limit in these instances would doubtless lead to serious complications.[14]

The British publicist Cecil Hurst concurred in the coastal states' exploitation of the riches of the continental shelf, provided such exploitation were based on prescription. Also writing in 1923, he held:

> So far as Great Britain at any rate is concerned . . . where effective occupation has been long maintained of portions of the bed of the sea outside the three-mile limit, those claims are valid and subsisting claims, entitled to recognition by other states.[15]

The French publicist Gilbert Gidel, writing in 1932, seemed to be of the opinion that the construction of offshore devices and rigs—presumably such as the "Texas Towers"—should not be undertaken unilaterally:

> Their establishment [installations more or less fixed which for purposes other than fishing occupy a certain amount of the high seas other than

---

13 Portugal, "Degree Regulating Fishing by Steam Vessels, 9 Nov., 1910," in United Nations, *Laws and Regulations on the High Seas*, pp. 19–20, citing "Coleçao oficial de Legislaçao Portuguesa," 1910, vol. 2, p. 76.
14 Brown, "The Marginal Sea," p. 91.
15 Hurst, "Bed of the Sea" p. 43.

the subsoil seabed] ought to be subject to agreement, express or tacit, of all States.[16]

Action by the U.S. Congress. Meanwhile, fishing interests in the United States were beginning to be heard. In 1937, identical bills were introduced in both houses that would have excluded foreign fishermen from the Alaskan continental shelf:

> The salmon which are spawned and hatched in the waters of Alaska are hereby declared to be the property of the United States, and it shall be unlawful for any person . . . to fish for, take, or catch any of the said salmon in the waters adjacent to the coast of Alaska . . . east of the international boundary in Bering Sea between the United States and the Union of Soviet Socialist Republics, the depth of which is less than one hundred fathoms. . . .[17]

These bills would have been a drastic departure from international law not only from the standpoint of ownership of the fish but also from that of the extent of seaward jurisdiction. The Alaskan continental shelf—within the 100-fathoms line—covers about half the Bering Sea east of the international boundary and extends over 400 miles from the Alaskan mainland. But neither bill passed. The following year, however (1938), a watered down version did pass in one house, the Senate. That bill explained that "the shallow depth of the Bering Sea must be regarded as a slightly submerged margin of the American Continent" and that "geologists have concluded that this part of the Bering Sea does not partake of the qualities of a true ocean basin and that the so-called "continental shelf" is no more or less than another of the several old Alaska beach deposits." The bill then recited the need to protect the fish and minerals of the area and provided:

> . . . that jurisdiction of the United States is hereby declared to extend to all the waters and submerged land adjacent to the coast of Alaska lying east of the international boundary in the Bering Sea . . . and lying within the limits of the continental shelf, the edge of such continental shelf having a depth of water of one hundred fathoms, more or less.[18]

Philip Jessup disapproved of both attempts:

> It would be immediately apparent to any student of international law that the enactment of either of the above bills would raise a very serious question of the infringement of the traditional freedom of the seas. It scarcely needs to be argued that under existing international law a state

16 Gidel, *La haute mer* (vol. I of *Le droit international public de la mer*), p. 502, translated and quoted in Whiteman, *Digest*, p. 741.
17 H.R. 8344, November 15, 1937, supplanting H.R. 7552 of June 17, 1937, both introduced by Mr. Dimond, the delegate of Alaska, reproduced in Jessup, "The Pacific Coast Fisheries," p. 130.
18 S. 3744, May 5, 1938, introduced by Senator Copeland, reproduced in *ibid.*, p. 129.

. . . has no right to endeavor to exclude aliens from fishing on the high seas.[19]

Action by Louisiana and Texas. The failure of the U.S. Congress to enact continental shelf legislation did not discourage individual states of the Union. In June, 1938, the Legislature of Louisiana enacted the following:

> Section 1. Be it enacted by the Legislature of Louisiana, that the gulf-ward boundary of the State of Louisiana is hereby fixed and declared to be a line located in the Gulf of Mexico parallel to the three-mile limit as determined according to said ancient principles of international law, which gulfward boundary is located twenty-four marine miles further out in the Gulf of Mexico than the said three-mile limit.[20]

Three years later, a similar 27-mile-limit law was passed by Texas, and like that of Louisiana, employed the rationale of increased cannon range.

> Since the said three (3) mile limit was so established as the seaward boundary of each sovereign State, modern cannon have been improved to such an extent that now many cannon shoot twenty-seven (27) miles and more, and by the use of artillery located on its shores a State can now make its authority effective at least twenty-seven (27) marine miles out to sea. . . .[21]

The oil-rich continental shelf of Louisiana and Texas extends roughly from 50 to 130 miles into the Gulf; that of California's oil-producing coast extends only to about 10 or 15 miles into the Pacific. California's State Constitution of 1849 had provided for ownership of the seabed out to three miles; consequently, that state felt no pressing need to pass additional legislation at the time.[22]

But several years later, and following the 1945 Truman Proclamation, California (in 1947), Louisiana (in 1950), and Texas (in 1950) all failed in their attempts to uphold their maritime claims. In three decisions, the Supreme Court held that the Federal Government, not the states, possessed the paramount rights over the lands and minerals beyond the low-water mark. (See pp. 98 and 238.) So unpopular, and allegedly inconsistent with the law, was the Texas case that a joint memorandum was submitted to the U.S. Supreme Court, urging that the case be reheard. The memorandum was signed by

19 *Ibid.*, p. 131.
20 "Act No. 55, to declare the sovereignty of Louisiana along its seacoast and to fix its present seacoast boundary and ownership, 30 June 1938," United Nations, *Laws and Regulations on the High Seas*, pp. 114–115, citing *Acts Passed by the Legislature of the State of Louisiana*, 1938, p. 169.
21 "Act Declaring the Sovereignty of Texas along its Seacoast, 16 May 1941," in *ibid.*, p. 41, citing *General and Special Laws of the State of Texas*, 47th Legislature (1941), chap. 268, p. 454.
22 Constitution of the State of California, Article XXI, Section 1, 1849, reproduced in United Nations, *Laws and Regulations on the Regime of the Territorial Sea*, pp. 56–57.

United States, British, French, Spanish, and Austrian publicists including: Joseph Walter Bingham, C. John Colombos, Gilbert Gidel, Manley O. Hudson, Charles Cheney Hyde, Hans Kelsen, William E. Masterson, Roscoe Pound, Stephan A. Riesenfeld, Felipe Sanchez Roman, and William W. Bishop, Jr.[23]

United Kingdom and Venezuela. In 1942, England and Venezuela divided between themselves the petroleum resources of the continental shelf in the Gulf of Paria. The Gulf is a shallow area of the high seas measuring about 150 miles long and 40 miles wide between the coast of Venezuela and the island of Trinidad. The treaty provided for "sovereignty or control" of the "sea-bed and sub-soil outside of territorial waters" of the Gulf of Paria.[24]

PROCLAMATION ON THE CONTINENTAL SHELF

World War II emphasized to both Allied and Axis powers alike the great importance of oil. By the end of the war, oil interests in the United States had made it clear to the government that the oil resources offshore must be tapped. In 1945, the Executive branch was prepared to accomplish by proclamation what the Congress had chosen not to enact before the war. Two proclamations were prepared by the Departments of State, Justice, and Interior in collaboration. The first of these declared:

> Whereas the Government of the United States of America, aware of the long range world-wide need for new sources of petroleum and other minerals . . . and . . .
> Whereas it is the view of the Government of the United States that the exercise of jurisdiction over the natural resources of the subsoil and sea bed of the continental shelf by the contiguous nation is reasonable and just, since the effectiveness of measures to utilize or conserve these resources would be contingent upon cooperation and protection from the shore, since the continental shelf may be regarded as an extension of the land-mass of the coastal nation and thus naturally appurtenant to it, since these resources frequently form a seaward extension of a pool or deposit lying within the territory, and since self-protection compels the coastal nation to keep close watch over activities off its shore which are of the nature necessary for utilization of these resources;
> [T]he Government of the United States regards the natural resources of the subsoil and sea bed of the continental shelf beneath the high seas but contiguous to the coasts of the United States as appertaining to the United States, subject to its jurisdiction and control. . . . The character

23 "Joint Memorandum of July 14, 1950," *Baylor Law Review,* III (Winter, 1951), pp. 319–335. For an excellent coverage of the arguments advanced by both sides in the Texas case, see this issue of *Baylor Law Review,* which is entitled, "Symposium on the Texas Tidelands Case." See also Ireland, "Marginal Seas Around the States," and Vallot, "Ownership of the Sea-Bed: *United States v. California,*" pp. 382–385.
24 United Kingdom and Venezuela, "Treaty Relating to the Submarine Areas of the Gulf of Paria, 26 February 1942," reproduced in United Nations, *Laws and Regulations on the High Seas,* p. 44, citing *British Treaty Series,* No. 10 (1942).

as high seas of the waters above the continental shelf and the right to their free and unimpeded navigation are in no way thus affected.[25]

The width of the continental shelf varies widely from about one-half mile to over 600 miles. By definition, it is the shallow, gently sloping, almost flat area of the seabed rimming the continents. At its seaward edge, the sea bottom drops off sharply to the ocean floor; this sharp incline is called the continental slope. The depth of water at the edge of the continental shelf is generally about 100 fathoms, and this depth figure—or that of 200 meters—has become commonly accepted, although somewhat imprecise, as the outer limit of the continental shelf.[26]

THE FISHERIES PROCLAMATION

The fisheries industry, too, continued to press the United States Government during the war. This is reflected in a 1943 letter from the Secretary of the Interior to the White House:

> The Continental Shelf extending some 100 or 150 miles from our shores forms a fine breeding place for fish of all kinds; it is an excellent hiding place for submarines; and since it is a continuation of our continent, it probably contains oil, and other resources similar to those found in our States.
>
> I suggest the advisability of laying the ground work now for availing ourselves fully of the riches in this submerged land and in the waters over them. The legal and policy problems involved, both international and domestic, are many and complex. In the international field, it may be necessary to evolve new concepts of maritime territorial limits beyond three miles. . . .[27]

President Roosevelt agreed:

> I think Harold Ickes has the right slant on this [continental shelf]. For many years, I have felt that the old three-mile limit or twenty-mile limit should be superseded by a rule of common sense. . . .[28]

An interdepartmental board was set up to study the matter. Its efforts culminated in the Fisheries Proclamation of 1945:

> Whereas for some years the Government of the United States of America has viewed with concern the inadequacy of present arrangements

25 Proclamation No. 2667, "Policy of the United States With Respect to the Natural Resources of the Subsoil and Sea Bed of the Continental Shelf," September 28, 1945, 10 *Fed. Reg.* 12303, 3 CFR, 1943–1948 Comp., p. 67, reproduced in Whiteman, *Digest,* pp. 756–757.
26 Mouton, *The Continental Shelf,* pp. 6–7, 22–32.
27 Secretary of the Interior Harold L. Ickes letter to President Roosevelt of June 5, 1943, in Whiteman, *Digest,* p. 946, citing MS. Department of State, file 811.0145/367.
28 President Franklin D. Roosevelt letter to Secretary of State Cordell Hull of June 9, 1943, in Whiteman, *Digest,* citing MS. Department of State, file 811.0145/11-2844.

for the protection and perpetuation of the fishery resources contiguous
to its coasts . . . ; and

Whereas such fishery resources have a special importance to coastal
communities . . . ; and . . .

Whereas there is an urgent need to protect coastal fishery resources
from destructive exploitation, having due regard to conditions peculiar to
each region and situation . . . ;

[T]he Government of the United States regards it as proper to establish conservation zones in those areas of the high seas contiguous to the
coasts of the United States wherein fishing activities have been or in the
future may be developed and maintained on a substantial scale. . . . The
character as high seas of the areas in which such conservation zones are
established and the right to their free and unimpeded navigation are in no
way thus affected.[29]

The proclamation provided, in addition, that the conservation zones would
be established and maintained through agreement with those states whose subjects traditionally fished the areas in question.

Professor Joseph Bingham, who before the war had strongly advocated conservation measures (see pp. 150–151), quickly lauded the Truman Proclamations:

These two proclamations radically alter the practice of our Government
for over a century and a quarter. . . .

Both as a wise preparation for protection of important American interests and as a contribution to the economic and social welfare of the international community, the fisheries proclamation should be commended
heartily.

The proclamation concerning the minerals and other bedded resources
of the continental shelf also should meet with approval. . . .[30]

INTERNATIONAL REACTION TO THE PROCLAMATIONS

Whatever good or bad may be said concerning the Truman Proclamations,
it must be acknowledged that they dealt a crippling blow to the three-mile
limit, and they were the second in a series of five major developments or
events leading to the demise of the three-mile rule. They precipitated a series
of claims by states to jurisdiction over wide expanses of the high seas which,
in turn, led to protracted international fisheries disputes in both hemispheres.
Moreover, as a result, several states abandoned their claims to a three-mile
territorial sea in favor of a much greater width.

Argentina. Mexico was the first state to react to the proclamations, issuing
a declaration the following month much like that of the United States.[31] But
Argentina, one year later, issued a most far-reaching decree. She described

29 Proclamation No. 2668, "Policy of the United States With Respect to Coastal Fisheries
    in Certain Areas of the High Seas," Sept. 28, 1945, 10 *Fed. Reg.* 12304; 3 CRF,
    1943–1948 Comp., p. 68; in Whiteman, *Digest*, pp. 954–956.
30 Bingham, "The Continental Shelf and the Marginal Belt," pp. 173, 177.
31 "Presidential Declaration with Respect to Continental Shelf, 29 October 1945," in
    United Nations, *Laws and Regulations on the High Seas*, p. 13, citing *El Universal*
    (Mexico City), vol. 116, No. 10,541 (30 October 1945), pp. 1, 17.

Table 5
Post-World War II Continental Shelf Claims
of Selected States*

Year	State	Width of Shelf†
1946	Panama	5–80 miles
1947	Chile	5–40 miles
1947	Peru	15–60 miles
1949	Costa Rica	5–35 miles
1950	Nicaragua	30–45 miles
1950	El Salvador	30–50 miles
1952	South Korea	5–200 miles
1957	Cambodia	140 miles

* See Whiteman, *Digest*, vol. IV, pp. 22–24, 27, 29–30.

† Figures for the continental shelf are approximate measurements in statute miles from *National Geographic Atlas of the World, passim.*

the waters over her continental shelf as "transitory zones of mineral reserves . . . characterized by extraordinary biological activity, owing to the influence of the sunlight, which stimulates plant life (algae, mosses, etc.) and the life of innumerable species of animals, both susceptible of industrial utilization." Then in an obvious misconstruction of the U.S. and Mexican declarations, she proclaimed:

> Whereas . . .
> [T]he Governments of the United States of America and of Mexico have issued declarations asserting the sovereignty of each of the two countries over the respective peripheral epicontinental seas and continental shelves . . . ,
> It is hereby declared that the Argentine epicontinental sea and continental shelf are subject to the sovereign power of the nation. . . ."[32]

Argentina is favored with one of the most extensive continental shelves in the world. It averages about 200 miles in width, varying between 100 and 300 miles. Hence, this was a most sweeping assertion of sovereignty; and in July, 1948, the United States protested the scope of the decree, especially Argentina's use of the word "sovereignty" as applied to "epicontinental seas."[33]

During the next decade, eight other states declared sovereignty over the continental shelf and the superjacent waters. These claims, as listed in Table 5, involved shelves as narrow as 35 miles (Costa Rica) and as wide as 200 miles (Korea).

32 "Decree No. 14,708 concerning National Sovereignty over Epicontinental Sea and the Argentine Continental Shelf, 11 October 1946," in United Nations, *Laws and Regulations on the High Seas*, pp. 4–5.
33 United States note of July 2, 1948, to Argentina, in *ibid.*, p. 5.

The 200-mile limit. The assertion of sovereignty over the continental shelf was not sufficient, in the view of certain west coast Latin American states, to provide for adequate fishery conservation measures. Along the Pacific coast of South and Central America, the continental shelf is very narrow, in most places only about 10 miles. Accordingly, between 1947 and 1955, five states declared 200-mile limits for exclusive fishing rights: Chile, Peru, Costa Rica, Ecuador, and El Salvador.[34] The following example is taken from the Chilean decree:

> Protection and control [of whaling and deep sea fishery] is hereby declared immediately over all the seas contained within the perimeter formed by the coast and the mathematical parallel projected into the sea at a distance of 200 nautical miles from the coasts of Chilean territory.[35]

In 1951 the Honduran Congress decreed a similar 200-mile limit, but only with respect to her Atlantic waters.[36]

Chile, El Salvador, and Guinea. Three states, it seems, used the issue actually to assert claims to increased territorial seas. It may or may not be a coincidence, but the Chilean continental shelf extends in its widest part at a location off Magallanes State to an average width of about 50 kilometers; and in 1948 Chile enacted:

> Article 3. The adjacent sea, up to a distance of fifty kilometers, measured from the low-water mark, constitutes the territorial sea and belongs to the national domain; but the right of policing, with respect to matters concerning the security of the country and the observance of fiscal laws, extends up to a distance of 100 kilometers measured in the same manner.[37]

Thus, Chile abandoned her claims of three and twelve miles for claims of 50 and 100 kilometers, respectively. El Salvador, in 1950, dropped her three-mile claim:

> Article 7. The territory of the Republic within its present boundaries is irreducible; it includes the adjacent sea within a distance of two hundred marine miles measured from the line of lowest tide, and it embraces the air space above, the subsoil, and the corresponding continental shelf.[38]

34 Chilean Presidential Declaration of 23 June 1947; Peruvian Presidential Decree No. 781 of 1 August 1947; Costa Rican Regulation No. 363 of 11 January 1949 as amended by Decree No. 739 of 4 October 1949; Ecuadorian Decree No. 1085 of 14 May 1955; and El Salvadorian Decree No. 1961 of 25 October 1955, in United Nations, *Laws and Regulations on the Territorial Sea,* pp. 4, 39, 462, 490, and 491.
35 *Ibid.,* p. 5.
36 Honduran Congressional Decree No. 25 of 17 January 1951 approving Presidential Decree No. 96 of 28 January 1950 in *ibid.,* pp. 22–23.
37 Chilean Water Code, annexed to Law No. 8,944, 21 January 1948, in United Nations, *Laws and Regulations on the High Seas,* p. 61, citing *Diario Oficial,* vol. 71, No. 20,975 (11 February 1948), p. 258.
38 Constitution of the Republic of El Salvador of 7 September 1950 in United Nations, *Laws and Regulations on the Territorial Sea,* p. 14, citing Pan American Union, *Law and Treaty Series,* p. 1.

Under this law, El Salvador's territorial sea measures almost 36,000 square miles, or about four and one-half times the landed portion of the state itself (8,268 square miles). Some years later, the newly independent state of Guinea declared a territorial sea 130 miles wide.[39] Her continental shelf extends to 130 miles at its widest point.

Santiago Declaration on the Maritime Zone (1952). Following their tripartite conference in Santiago, on August 19, 1952, Chile, Ecuador, and Peru issued a joint declaration that specified as its purpose the conservation and preservation ". . . for their respective peoples, the natural riches of the zones of the sea which bathed their coasts." In order to accomplish this, the declaration stated:

> The Governments of Chile, Ecuador, and Peru proclaim as the standard of their international maritime policy, that to each one of them belongs the sovereignty and exclusive jurisdiction over the sea that washes their respective coasts, up to the minimum distance of two hundred (200) nautical miles from the said coasts.[40]

Although the contracting parties used the term "maritime zone" rather than "territorial sea," their resolve to enforce their newly claimed sovereignty was manifested in 1954, when the three states commenced seizing vessels as far from shore as 160 miles. In November, 1954, Peruvian naval and air units seized five of Mr. Aristotle Onassis' whaling vessels flying the Panamanian flag. Two were captured 160 miles off the Peruvian coast. The other three were attacked at 300 and 364 miles from the coast. Peru claimed that these latter ships had been pursued from within the 200-mile limit, invoking the doctrine of the right of "hot pursuit."[41]

VIEWS OF THE CONTEMPORARY PUBLICISTS

F. V. Garcia Amador, Cuban publicist and member of the International Law Commission, justified the 200-mile "maritime zone" from both a scientific and a moral approach. He cited the existence of a complex ecological system, averaging 200 miles in width off the coast of western South America, the whole of which must be considered as one fishery for purposes of conservation. His moral argument is much more articulate. It is commonly theorized that a massive intercontinental evolutionary shifting process has been going on for millions of years. This theory has also served hypothetically to explain why there are generally wide continental shelves on the east coasts of the American continents and virtually none on their western coasts. The more fortunate east

---

39 Guinean Presidential Decree No. 224, June 3, 1964, cited in Whiteman, *Digest*, p. 34.
40 "La Declaración sobre Zona Marítima de Santiago, 19 de Agosto, 1952, in Alvarado-Garaicoa, *El Domino del Mar*, pp. 89–90; translation by the author.
41 Colombos, *Law of the Sea*, p. 89. See also Chapter 11.

coast states with continental shelves have understandably undertaken to exploit them for the common well-being of their subjects. But Amador says:

> There can be no reason in justice . . . why many countries should have a broad submarine zone as a result of prehistoric geological upheavals while others should have none.[42]

He pointed up the argument that the 200-mile limit may be considered compensation to those countries which have no continental shelf (keeping in mind that the Argentinean continental shelf averages about 200 miles in width):

> The important thing is not the contour of the submarine areas but the maritime resources that will produce that wellbeing. . . . In the case of the countries of the west coast of South America, we know that these countries have a narrow continental shelf but that, at the same time, a broad current running parallel to their coasts creates one of the most prodigious sources of fish in the world.[43]

It was inevitable that this politically charged issue would draw sharply contrasting views from the publicists of various states. The U.S. position, as defined in the Truman Proclamations themselves, was defended by Myres McDougal and William Burke, who held that the continental shelf can be best exploited only by the littoral state while offshore fisheries can be exploited by anyone. Concerning the Latin American argument that exploitation of fisheries should be placed on the same basis as exploitation of mineral resources, they wrote:

> The reasons for rejecting the purported similarity between oil exploitation and fishery activity need not be reviewed again, but at least it bears repetition that in the absence of exploitation by means of more or less permanent installations the above position can have no basis whatsoever.[44]

The U.S. counter-argument reduces essentially to this. Foreign fishermen, fishing offshore in fishing boats, are transitory and pose no threat or encroachment on the coastal state's sovereignty. A permanent offshore foreign installation, such as an oil rig, an oceanographic research platform, or in the extreme case, a military installation, could be construed as an encroachment, and would therefore be unacceptable.

Although the United States had clearly disavowed any sovereignty over the waters above the continental shelf, the distinguished Briton, Sir Hersch Lauterpacht, expressed his doubt that exploitation of the resources of submarine

---

42 Amador, *The Exploitation and Conservation of the Resources of the Sea* pp. 74–76; also see Chapter 11.

43 *Ibid.*, p. 75, quoting *La Plataforma Submarina: Falso Límite Marítimo de los Estados,* an Ecuadorian Technical Study, Document 69, p. 8.

44 McDougal and Burke, *The Public Order of the Oceans,* pp. 412, 662.

areas could be accomplished without contradicting the concept of freedom of the seas. On the issue of "sovereignty," he wrote:

> It is probable that while for reasons of its constitutional law and of attachment to consistency in its diplomatic practice the United States may have resorted to a terminology intended to dispel the appearance of assumption of sovereignty, it used words and assumed powers which in fact can have no other result.

Then, concerning the Latin American claims, he observed:

> . . . the claim to sovereignty over submarine areas may be—and has been—abused for the purpose of advancing pretensions to sovereignty over the high seas as such or the exclusive exploitation of their resources. . . . It was perhaps unfortunate that the United States on the day on which it issued the Proclamations as to the continental shelf also issued the Proclamation relative to the conservation zone in the matter of fisheries.[45]

The Argentinean professor Teresa H. I. Flouret went a step further, arguing that sovereignty over the subsoil and the waters above were inseparable and accused the United States of duplicity in her announced policy. In *La Doctrina de la Plataforma Submarina*, Flouret wrote:

> The distinction between the legal status of the soil and that of the waters is in our opinion, practically impossible. "The sovereignty over the subsoil of the continental shelf would demand correlative rights over the respective waters," says Mateesco, "even if these rights were attenuated by the necessity to reconcile the national interest with that of international freedom of navigation." He considers also that "in spite of the affirmation in the proclamation, it is difficult to believe that the waters can remain absolutely free when the subsoil of the continental shelf is extensively exploited." And in a footnote, he adds: "On the day when the U.S.A. is conducting submarine petroleum operations," wonders Mr. Feith, "will they permit Japanese or Russian cruisers to pass freely through their oil fields?"
>
> Nevertheless, the United States has been careful to establish it clearly that they do not intend by their proclamation, to extend their sovereignty beyond territorial waters over the high seas. Consequently, on 2 July, 1948, they sent separate notes of protest to the Governments of Argentina, Chile, and Peru, expressing disagreement with the extent of their declarations.
>
> These notes maintained that while the fundamentals of the declarations were identical to those of the United States, the declarations greatly exceeded the principles of international law, for which reason that Government reserved its rights, previously exercised, over the waters of the continental shelves of each of the three countries. It is necessary to point out that the United States has important fishing interests endangered by these State declarations which they are challenging.[46]

---

45 Lauterpacht, "Sovereignty over Submarine Areas," p. 389.
46 Flouret, *La Doctrina de la Plataforma Submarina*, pp. 63–64. Translation by the author.

Another publicist, the Ecuadorian Teodoro Alvarado-Garaicoa, contended that the 200-mile limit is the product of a logical legal evolution and traced its development through the cannon-shot rule, the three-mile limit, and the continental shelf claim. Jurist and prolific writer on international affairs, Alvarado-Garaicoa published a monograph, *El Domino del Mar*, on the law of the sea in 1968, strongly oriented toward Latin American practice. In it he contended that:

> International law, influenced by the progress of modern armaments, and now by the discovery of new natural resources, has become obliged to modify the classic delimitation of the territorial sea, at the same time, to incorporate within its fundamental rubrics the so-called submarine platform or continental ledge. . . . The zone of the territorial sea, fixed at three miles—at the initiative of Galiani—has remained unalterable for many years. . . . With the passage of time, however, the fixed limit has come to be considered illogical, relegating it to the status of an historic fact.[47]

The Trinidadian, Barry B. L. Auguste, agreed with Amador's thesis that the Latin Americans have a strong moral basis for their claims, but he cautioned that a legal basis is lacking. He wrote:

> [I]t must be stated that the Latin American practice in terms of the continental shelf is *unlawful*, because, when all is said and done, it does involve unilateral claims to exercise jurisdiction over areas that are admittedly high seas; and even though the concept of the Maritime Zone is a realistic entity and marks the development of a new legal tendency, this does not per se make it lawful. The reasonability of the concept of the Maritime Zone only alleviates the basically unlawful situation. . . .[48]

The Spaniard Juan A. C. Salcedo made the interesting suggestion that the American continental-shelf and 200-mile claims, based as they are on unilateral proclamations, may represent a new source of customary international law. Salcedo, a professor of international law at the University of Seville, Spain, wrote:

> Outside of conventional procedures, there has appeared a new customary international rule, product of a series of unilateral declarations: that of the continental shelf. The acquiescence of third states, the limited forcefulness of their protests, and the effectiveness of the pretensions are the basis of this new customary international rule.[49]

The writings of the proponents of the 200-mile limit have at least one common feature; they all point to the wide divergence in contemporary interna-

---

47 Alvarado-Garaicoa, *El Domino del Mar*, pp. 70–71. Translation by the author.
48 Auguste, *The Continental Shelf: The Practice and Policy of the Latin American States with Special Reference to Chile, Ecuador, and Peru*, pp. 355–356.
49 Salcedo, "Funciones del Acto Unilateral en el Régimen Jurídico de los Espacios Marítimos," in Arias, *Estudios de Derecho Internacional Marítimo*, p. 26. Translation by the author.

tional practice as to the extent of the territorial sea. Some of these writers even rely on this divergence of practice as a veiled defense of the 200-mile limit. One is led to the conclusion that the very existence of the 200-mile limit is a consequence of, and dependent upon, the major powers' inability to agree, even between themselves, as to what the extent of the territorial sea should be.

IMPACT OF THE TRUMAN PROCLAMATIONS

Whatever may have been the motives and legal rationale underlying the 1945 Truman Proclamations, and no matter how emphatically the United States may deny any intention to have extended her sovereignty or jurisdiction over the high seas thereby, those proclamations provided the basis for the 200-mile limit, virtually on a cause and effect basis. The Latin Americans had become concerned about the modern U.S. fishing vessels seen off their coasts. Whether or not their concern was well-founded, they feared that their waters might be "overfished" by foreigners, and they wished to extend their exclusive fishing boundaries to eliminate the outside competition. But such a bold departure from customary law would require a suitable pretext; it was fortuitous for them that the Truman Proclamations came when they did.

The U.S. arguments rejecting the 200-mile limit did not impress the Latin Americans. To them, the arguments seemed selfish and lopsided in favor of industrialized states with continental shelves. What, they may challenge, is the criterion which determines who may exploit any particular area of the continental shelf? Is it the proximity of the exploited area to the mainland? If this be the case, then Cubans could exploit the western part of the Floridian continental shelf because their mainland is closer to it. For the same reason, Norway could exploit the British shelf under the North Sea; Italy, that of Tunisia; Japan, that of China; ad absurdum. And what of the Greek Islands located on the continental shelf of Turkey? In short, it is difficult for the Latin American jurist or politician to discern the legal or moral difference, for example, in denying a Mexican oil firm the right to drill an oil well on the shelf 130 miles off the Texas coast and in denying an Argentinean tuna boat the right to work the fishery 130 miles off the coast of Chile.

RESURGENCE OF RUSSIA'S TWELVE-MILE CLAIM

World War II made it clear to all that the United States stood supreme among the great powers. Hers was the greatest fleet, both naval and merchant. She had inherited from the British the role of "mistress of the seas," and if there were to continue to be a strong champion of the three-mile limit it would have to be the United States. During the initial years after the war, the U.S. position of strength was much like that of England after the Napoleonic Wars. Her atomic weapons gave her unprecedented relative military superiority. But Russia, too, had emerged from the war a victor. After the war, rather than demobilize, Russia maintained in the field the world's most formidable army. Within a short time, she managed to achieve a centuries-old goal of securing her western frontier by means of a belt of subservient buffer satellites. And in 1949, Russia satisfactorily tested her own atomic weapon—in the parlance of the early American West, "the great equalizer." America's nuclear monopoly was broken and her military superiority was greatly reduced. The world had entered its Cold War, and many of the nations tended to polarize around one or the other of the then two superpowers.

But the superpower Soviet Russia was different in several respects from the superpower United States. Of significance to this study, Russia had traditionally been a land power, not a sea power. During the 1940s she had virtually no merchant fleet, especially when compared with the United States and the British Commonwealth. Table 6 shows the Soviet Union in seventh place among the maritime states in 1946. However, much of that 1946 merchant fleet was composed of U.S. lend-lease assets; even counting those ships, the Soviet total came to only one-thirtieth of the American figure. Virtually, the same was true with respect to the Soviet Navy. It was by and large a coastal patrol

Table 6
World Merchant Fleets at the Close of
World War II (1946)*

State	Gross Tonnage (in thousands)
United States	38,587
British Commonwealth	16,055
Norway	2,752
Netherlands	1,563
Sweden	1,438
France	1,277
U.S.S.R.	1,238
Japan	1,083
Spain	879
Germany	801
Panama	687
Denmark	641
Italy	576
Greece	519
Others	2,904
Total	71,000

* From "Shipping: Merchant Ships of the World," *Encyclopaedia Britannica* (1953 edition), XX, 549. The figures include privately owned vessels of 1000 gross tons and over. The U.S. figure includes 3¼ million gross tons operating under foreign flags. The U.S. Maritime Commission is quoted as the source.

Table 7
Warships of the Powers in 1946*

State	Battleships, Carriers, Cruisers	Frigates, Destroyers, Escorts	Submarines	Patrol Craft
U.S.A.	197	663	200	423
U.K.	86	400	119	943
U.S.S.R.	11	57	100	409
France	15	49	14	132
China	2	4	—	23
Italy	6	22	—	22
Japan	18	104	58	74
Germany	2	15	30	94

* From *Jane's Fighting Ships 1946–47*, pp. 23–77, 146–151, 175–197, 213–220, 268–285, 329, 378–381, 413–421. The figures for Italy do not include 3 battleships, 6 cruisers, 8 destroyers, 7 submarines and 46 patrol craft surrendered to the Allies. The figures for Japan are the ships surrendered to the United States. The figures for Germany are the surviving seaworthy ships surrendered and divided between the U.S.A., the U.K., and the U.S.S.R.

force, suitable only for policing the fisheries. Seventy-five percent of the vessels were under 100 feet in length. Table 7 compares this unimposing 1946 Soviet Navy with the navies of the other contemporary powers.

Under such conditions of maritime and naval inferiority, it is understandable that Russia would loudly reassert her 1927 twelve-mile claim, in the interest of security, to keep the ships and aircraft of her adversaries as far from her coasts as possible. To give real meaning to her twelve-mile claim, the Soviet Union commenced seizing foreign vessels. Between 1948 and 1950, her coastal patrol craft seized several Swedish fishing boats in the Baltic. Of these, the *Larex* and the *Marion* were seized at eleven and ten and one-half miles, respectively, from the Soviet coast, taken into port under threat of arms, confiscated, and their crews were imprisoned. This led to a bitter exchange of diplomatic notes, culminating in a Soviet refusal to submit the Swedish charges to the International Court of Justice.[50] Not long afterwards, Russia started shooting down foreign aircraft over her twelve-mile belt; this will be discussed in the following chapter.

In 1951 Bulgaria and Romania parroted the Soviet twelve-mile claim in the form of state acts.[51] During the ensuing decade, the Soviet Union organized a block of votes from communist states in the United Nations in support of her twelve-mile policy: Ukrainian S.S.R., Yugoslavia, Albania, Bulgaria,

50 Glenn, "The Swedish-Soviet Territorial Sea Controversy in the Baltic," pp. 942–949.
51 Whiteman, *Digest*, pp. 21, 30.

Table 8
Warships of Selected Navies in 1968*

State	Carriers, Cruisers	Frigates, Destroyers, Escorts	Submarines	Patrol Craft
U.S.A.	92	613	201	44
U.S.S.R.	25	200	380	775
U.K.	9	92	44	7
France	6	48	19	14
Italy	4	21	8	47
Japan	—	42	9	30
Germany (West)	—	30	12	46
China	—	19	33	312

* From Blackman, *Jane's Fighting Ships 1968–1969*, p. 520. Figures include ships in reserve but not those under construction.

Byelorussian S.S.R, Czechoslovakia, Hungary, Poland, and Romania. In addition, communist nonmembers of the United Nations, specifically China and North Korea, declared a twelve-mile zone of territorial seas.[52] Communist China's "Declaration on China's Territorial Sea" of September 4, 1958, read:

> The breadth of the territorial sea of the Peoples Republic of China shall be 12 nautical miles. This provision applies to all the territories of the Peoples Republic of China, including the Chinese mainland and its coastal islands, as well as Taiwan and its surrounding islands. . . ."[53]

Although no specific state act can be found documenting the North Korean claim to 12 miles, it is listed as such in the Soviet *Manual of International Maritime Law*.[54]

Even more important, the Soviet Union, in her international diplomacy, actively encouraged the emerging states of the world not to consider themselves as bound by the three-mile rule. (See pages 179–80, 208, 245.) Many of them, recently released from western colonial status and wishing to industrialize and modernize, were influenced by the Soviet example and adopted the twelve-mile limit. Nothing in Soviet practice, however, enhanced the twelve-mile limit so much as did her rise to status as a first rank maritime power. By 1968, as shown in Table 8, Russia had worked her way up to second place in naval strength. Her program in developing a merchant fleet was equally impressive. Table 9 shows that by 1967, she had risen to fifth place,

52   U.S. Department of State, *Sovereignty of the Sea*, p. 27.
53   Tao Chen, "Communist China and the Law of the Sea," pp. 47, 53, citing *Peking Review*, No. 28 (September 9, 1958), p. 21.
54   Barabolya, [Soviet] *Manual of International Maritime Law*, vol. II, pp. 386–387.

Table 9
World Merchant Fleets in 1967*

State	Gross Tonnage (in thousands)	State	Gross Tonnage (in thousands)
United Kingdom	21,716	India	1,887
United States	20,333	Brazil	1,305
Norway	18,382	Argentina	1,240
Japan	16,883	Poland	1,211
U.S.S.R.	10,617	Yugoslavia	1,196
Greece	7,433	Finland	1,064
Italy	6,219	Belgium	940
West Germany	5,990	Australia	803
France	5,576	Communist China	772
Netherlands	5,123	East Germany	756
Panama	4,756	Portugal	755
Sweden	4,635	Philippines	720
Denmark	3,014	Israel	688
Spain	2,571	Others	6,208
Canada	2,306	Total	155,099

* From "Transportation," *Britannica Book of the Year 1969*, p. 746. The figures include merchant ships of 100 tons and over. *Lloyd's Register, Statistical Tables (1967)* is cited as source. It is interesting to note that the fourteen states listed in the 1946 table, *supra*, were still the top fourteen in 1967; but the ranking had changed considerably. And between 1967 and 1969 the top five again had reranked themselves: first was Japan, with 23,987; second, U.K., 23,844; third, Norway, 19,679; fourth, U.S., 19,550; and fifth, U.S.S.R., 13,705. *Lloyd's Register* (1969).

with a merchant marine half the size of that of the United States. And from the following comparative gross tonnage figures (thousands), it is easy to see that the Soviet merchant fleet could overtake that of the United States during the 1970s if the present trend continues:[55]

	1946	1956	1965	1970
U.S.A.	46,753	33,674	28,283	18,400
U.S.S.R.	2,699	3,439	9,561	13,900

This situation, wherein Russia, having emerged as one of the victorious powers at the close of World War II, had risen to status as a maritime superpower and had reasserted her claim to twelve miles, was the third in the series of five major events or developments leading to the demise of the three-mile

55 Heine, Coe, and Gulick, "The Soviet Merchant Marine," p. 386. Figures include privately-owned and government-owned merchant-type ships. Russian figures include, and U.S. figures exclude, ships transferred under lend-lease.

rule. The Soviet claim had created for the United States—the new apparent defender of the three-mile rule—a set of circumstances far more perplexing than those facing Great Britain in 1815.

THE PROLIFERATION OF SOVEREIGN STATES

Just as new states proliferated after World War I, many new states made their debut in the world community after World War II, and in most cases, as a direct product of the war. Only forty-nine states signed the United Nations Charter in 1945. By 1972, there were over 140 sovereign states, with approximately forty small territories—the last remnants of the colonial empires—being considered for statehood and membership in the community of nations. One of the issues each new state has had to consider is whether or not it will claim a territorial sea, and if so, to what extent. Not all the new states have made claims. Some of the new states followed the practice of their colonial sovereigns and adopted a three-mile rule. But more of them, feeling no particular obligation or attachment to the traditional body of international law, chose a limit greater than three miles, many of them selecting twelve miles.

REMNANTS OF THE AXIS POWERS

Mussolini's interwar imperial adventures won Italy several protectorates, none of which selected the three-mile limit following their liberation. Instead, Ethiopia,[56] Libya,[57] and Somalia[58] adopted a twelve-mile limit, and Albania— showing something of a flair for originality—proclaimed a ten-mile limit in 1952.[59] Japan also lost her territories acquired by earlier conquests. The southern portion of Sakhalin, taken from Russia in the Russo-Japanese War of 1904–1905, was returned to Russia. In addition, the Kurile Islands were also awarded to Russia, placing in all some 2,000 miles of former three-mile coastlines under Russian twelve-mile practice. Moreover, Japan lost Korea, both the north and south of which subsequently adopted the twelve-mile limit—and more.[60] Even though Germany had no colonial possessions, she herself was partitioned, following which, West Germany abandoned the three-mile rule. (East Germany retained the three-mile limit.[61]) The Bonn Government made

56 Ethiopian Maritime Proclamation No. 137 of 1953, in United Nations, *Laws and Regulations on the Territorial Sea*, pp. 128–134.
57 Whiteman, *Digest*, p. 28.
58 U.S. Department of State, Office of the Special Assistant to the Secretary of State for Fisheries and Wildlife, *Breadth of Territorial Sea and Fishing Jurisdiction Claimed by Members of the United Nations System*, p. 2.
59 Whiteman, *Digest*, p. 21.
60 U.S. Department of State, *Sovereignty of the Sea*, loc. cit. See also pp. 183–190, 202–3.
61 *Ibid.*

a most ingenious diplomatic move considering her particular situation, with coasts on both the North Sea and the Baltic. She advised the United Nations:

> There are no national laws and regulations in force which define the territorial sea. The practice as regards the territorial sea is determined by the rules of international law. . . .[62]

In this way West Germany placed herself out of the territorial waters dispute and into a position whereby she could enjoy the best of both sides in the dispute. The United States and other three-mile states could interpret Germany's language as meaning three miles, while the Soviet Union and the other twelve-mile states could similarly interpret it as twelve. Meanwhile, Germany's subjects could fish the coasts of three-mile states as close as three miles, those of twelve-mile states beyond twelve miles, and she could expect reciprocal treatment along her own coasts from states of both limits.

COLONIES OF STATES DEFEATED BY THE AXIS

The colony-holding states defeated by Germany—Netherlands, Denmark, and France—were so badly devastated and weakened that they had little chance of retrieving and holding their former colonies after liberation. The East Indies, which had figured so prominently in the Seldon-Grotius dispute during the seventeenth century, achieved independence from Holland in 1950, and seven years later as Indonesia adopted a twelve-mile limit.[63] In 1944, even before Denmark was liberated from German occupation, Iceland renounced the Danish crown and proclaimed herself a republic. Turning the clock back more than a century to the days when Denmark had claimed four leagues around Iceland, Iceland in 1958 discarded the Danish three-mile zone and adopted a twelve-mile fishing limit.[64] Of the former French mandates and colonies, virtually all of them adopted the twelve-mile limit with the exception of Cameroon, which proclaimed a territorial sea of eighteen miles. Two former French mandates (Togo and Syria) and nine former colonies (Algeria, Dahomey, Gabon, Ivory Coast, Madagascar, Mauritania, Morocco, Senegal, and Tunisia) adopted the twelve-mile limit. In the case of Ivory Coast, Morocco, and Tunisia, the twelve-mile zone was for fishing only, Morocco claiming three and the other two, six miles for territorial seas.[65]

---

62 Note of 9 February 1956 from the Permanent Observer of the Federal Republic of Germany to the United Nations, in United Nations, *Laws and Regulations on the Territorial Sea*, p. 17.
63 Whiteman, *Digest*, p. 26.
64 *Ibid.*
65 U.S. Department of State, *Breadth of Territorial Sea*, pp. 1–2, 5.

Table 10
Post-World War II Twelve-Mile Claims
of Selected States*

State	Year	Territorial Sea	Fishery Zone
Venezuela	1956	12	12
Saudi Arabia	1958	12	12
United Arab Republic	1958	12	12
Iraq	1958	12	12
Panama	1958	12†	12†
Iran	1959	12	12
Sudan	1960	12	12
Thailand	1966	12	12
Yemen	1967	12	12
Dominican Republic	1967	6	12
Liberia	1967	12	12
Brazil	1969	12	12

* From current "Country Files," Office of the Special Assistant to the Secretary of State for Fisheries and Wildlife, U.S. Department of State, Washington, D.C., 10 March 1970.

† Panama later increased her limits to 200 miles; see Chapter 11, p. 187.

POSSESSIONS AND COLONIES OF VICTORIOUS POWERS

Although England "won" the war, she was so exhausted that it was only a matter of time before the Empire would dissolve. She did have an advantage that France did not have—enough time to grant independence to her colonial possessions on a reasonable time schedule. Even so, better than half of them rejected the traditional British three-mile practice. These included India and Israel, the most significant maritime states among the former British possessions. To summarize, only nine former British colonies, mandates, and possessions retained the three-mile limit: Gambia, Guyana, Jordan, Kenya, Malaysia, Maldive Islands, Malta, Singapore, and Trinidad and Tobago. Two adopted the six-mile rule: Ceylon and Israel. Ten opted for twelve miles: Burma, Cyprus, Ghana, India, Jamaica, Kuwait, Nigeria, Pakistan, Sierre Leone, and Tanzania.[66] Ghana's Territorial Waters and Continental Shelf Act of 1963 also provided for a 100-mile fishing and conservation area.[67] Likewise, Ceylon and Pakistan have claimed similar conservation rights out to 100 miles.

The United States granted independence to the Philippines in 1946. Later the Philippines adopted the archipelago doctrine, wherein she claimed as in-

66 *Ibid.*, pp. 1–5.
67 Whiteman, *Digest*, p. 34.

ternal waters the entire area enclosed within a line drawn about the outermost islands of the archipelago. This will be discussed further in the next chapter.

OTHER STATES

Newly independent states were not the only ones to adopt the twelve-mile limit. Several of the more senior states increased their limits, apparently influenced by the Soviet example and/or a desire to extend their exclusive fishing zones. Table 10 lists twelve states that took such action during the Cold War decades; still others will be discussed in Chapter 13.

In summary, the events of World War II provided the basis for the resurgence of the twelve-mile limit and gave rise to the 200-mile limit. This in turn triggered an international controversy concerning territorial seas that was to trouble the states for at least a quarter of a century. The nature of this controversy will be considered in the following chapter.

CHAPTER 11

The Post-World War II Territorial
Seas Controversy

In 1969 an article appeared in the *United States Naval Institute Proceedings* entitled, "The Great Territorial Sea Squabble." In it, the author colorfully summed up the territorial seas situation during the quarter-century following World War II with these words:

> As 20th century men continue their seemingly interminable debate as to the width of their territorial seas, there is more than a passing resemblance to the passengers in the 15th century "Ship of Fools," who frittered away the future in pointless bickering about the past.[1]

Certainly the period from 1945 to 1970 was one of bitter dispute and controversy over the matter of the extent and nature of territorial seas. Numerous states abandoned the three-mile limit and announced claims to extensive areas of the high seas; indeed, it seemed that the world was headed toward something of a neo-*mare clausum*. Every principal maritime area and state was affected by the controversy. Its symptoms were manifested in a great number and variety of international incidents and confrontations, a representative selection of which will be surveyed in this chapter. In virtually every incident there appeared one of two key elements: concern over fishing rights and concern over national security. Accordingly, this study will consider the controversy from each of these two standpoints.

THE FISHERIES CONTROVERSY

The fisheries controversy, it appears, was more bitter and more widespread than that concerning security. The security controversy evolved largely around

---

[1] Meade, "The Great Territorial Sea Squabble," p. 45.

the differing views and the mutual fears of the principal antagonists in the Cold War. The fisheries controversy, however, not only involved a clash of interests between Moscow-oriented and Washington-oriented states, but also divided and vexed relationships between states that were military allies in the Cold War. Professor Bingham, writing just before World War II, had evaluated the fisheries controversy thus:

> Indeed, there is no phase of the history of international affairs which evidences more strikingly the part which selfish national interests play in the development of the doctrines of international law than the history of fishery claims and their effects on legal opinions concerning the law of jurisdiction over sea areas.[2]

Ironically, this strongly worded passage was written after a period of relative calm in the matter of international fishing rights, i.e., as compared to the period following World War II and the 1945 Truman Proclamations.

SUBSTANCE OF THE FISHERIES CONTROVERSY

The eagerness of states to extend their exclusive fishing rights beyond the three-mile limit was strongly encouraged by the so-called communist bloc nations. Using the forum of the United Nations Conference on the Law of the Sea at Geneva in 1958, the Ukrainian delegate advanced the position that each state should fix its own territorial sea limit ". . . in accordance with historical and geographical circumstances as well as economics and security requirements."[3] Even landlocked Czechoslovakia, who at the 1930 Hague Convention had logically indicated her preference for as narrow a territorial sea as possible, obediently recited the Cold War "party line" that:

> Each state was competent to fix the breadth of its own territorial sea in the exercise of its sovereign powers, taking into account its genuine needs.[4]

The other landlocked communist state, Hungary, took the similar position that "the act of delimitation was necessarily unilateral. . . ."[5] Certainly, this position was illogical in the case of the landlocked states which, if they were to take fish, would have to rely on the fisheries of other coastal states, and clearly did not, in the Czechoslovak delegate's own words, quoted above, take into account the genuine needs of either Czechoslovakia or Hungary. Com-

2 Bingham, *Report on the International Law of Pacific Coastal Fisheries*, p. 1.
3 United Nations, *Conference on the Law of the Sea*, vol. III, *First Committee (Territorial Sea and Contiguous Zone)*, p. 67, quoting statement by Mr. Koretsky, March 19, 1958.
4 *Ibid.*, p. 61, quoting Mr. Zourek, head of the Czechoslovak delegation, March 18, 1958.
5 *Ibid.*, p. 63 quoting Mr. Ustor, March 18, 1958.

munist China, too, echoed the bloc view that each state was sovereign to fix the extent of its territorial seas.[6]

At Geneva in 1958, the Soviet delegate noted that there were many recently independent countries participating "on an equal footing with other states, in the drafting of international rules for the law of the sea," and implied that dropping the three-mile limit and adopting a twelve-mile limit might help them cure some of their domestic ills:

> The attitude of the Soviet Union concerning the delimitation of the territorial sea was prompted not only by the fact that it had itself adopted the twelve-mile limit, but also by its policy of helping small and economically less advanced countries to develop their national economies and improve their standards of living.[7]

This attitude, taken by Soviet Russia since the end of World War II, found fertile soil among many of the underdeveloped states, especially those that counted heavily on the sea for their protein. At the third meeting of the Inter-American Council of Jurists, meeting in Mexico City in January and February, 1956, a resolution was adopted denouncing the three-mile limit (15 in favor, 1 opposed [the United States], 5 abstentions):

> 1. The distance of three miles as the limit of territorial waters is insufficient, and does not constitute a general rule of international law. Therefore, the enlargement of the zone of the sea traditionally called "territorial waters" is justifiable.
> 2. Each state is competent to establish its territorial waters within reasonable limits, taking into account geographical, geological and biological factors, as well as the economic needs of its population, and its security and defense.[8]

This Latin American disaffection with the three-mile rule was paralleled in other areas where underdeveloped states sought to protect their fishing grounds from the fishing fleets of the industrialized nations.

Arguments to extend fishing limits beyond three miles. The states that argued the loudest against the three-mile fishing limit were Iceland, Ecuador, and Korea, who wished, respectively, to exclude the fishermen from Great Britain, the United States, and Japan. Iceland complained that the equipment, techniques, and nets used by British fishermen had the effect of overfishing the area with ruinous results to Iceland's economy, which relied on fishing to

---

6 Edwards, "Chinese Communist Territorial Water Claims," p. 157, citing a May 1960 editorial in *Jen-min Jih-pao* (*People's Daily*).
7 United Nations, *Conference on the Law of the Sea*, pp. 31–32, quoting Mr. Tunkin, March 12, 1958.
8 Whiteman, *Digest*, vol. IV, pp. 69, 72, quoting "Principles of Mexico on the Juridical Regime of the Sea," February 3, 1956.

an extent five times that of any other state.[9] Ecuador insisted that its 200-mile zone was necessary for the protection of her fisheries.[10] U.S. fishermen from California had become fond of fishing in Ecuadorian waters, and the concern of the latter state may have been well-founded. In 1967, following the Ecuadorian seizure of certain United States tuna boats, Senator Thomas Kuchel of California proposed in Congress that U.S. Navy warships be deployed to protect the tuna boats beyond the three-mile limit of Ecuador. A tuna boat captain from San Diego, where much of the tuna fleet is based, was interviewed concerning Senator Kuchel's proposal:

> "This is the thing owners and captains fear most. They know Navy men would be so disgusted at the way huge purse seiners are cleaning out offshore fishing grounds off Peru and Ecuador, that they would immediately make those methods public," said "Capt. Nemo," a name given him in this article to protect him and his family from reprisals.
>
> "I am sure the senator and the congressmen are protesting in good faith," he said, "but no one will tell them the real truth. They have run into a wall of lies."
>
> He said a large number of million-dollar vessels carrying seines 600 fathoms in length are being built in West Coast shipyards.
>
> "And that means a circle 3,600 feet in circumference. Everything within this circle," he said, "is caught: tuna, all kinds of other fish, sharks, even small whales. It is heart-rending to hear the squeals of almost-human sounding porpoises as they struggle to get out of the meshes of the net.
>
> "Almost all of the creatures are smothered to death by the time they are dumped on the deck," Nemo said. . . .
>
> "Then the tuna are sorted out, and the rest of the dead fish are dumped back into the sea. . . . Is it any wonder that Peruvian and Ecuadorian seamen are furious when they sail through miles of water covered with the bodies of dead fish? . . .
>
> "Do you know what our fishermen call the big purse seiners?" Nemo asked. "They call them 'vacuum cleaners.' And when a vacuum cleaner gets through with an area, there's nothing left."
>
> William Bravo, Ecuadorian consul in San Diego, substantially agreed with these statements. . . .
>
> Both countries [Peru and Ecuador] license American fishing vessels to fish in their waters, more an attempt to control methods of fishing than to make money. . . .
>
> "But many captains won't buy licenses," he [Nemo] said. "They are taking no chances. If they aren't caught, they're ahead the cost of the licenses. If they are caught, their fines will be repaid from funds authorized by the Fisherman's Protective Act." . . .
>
> "The captains and owners don't give a hoot about conservation," he claimed. "By the time the tuna's wiped out, they'll be retired with nice fat nest eggs. . . .
>
> "Last year, there were crew members who made more than $20,000. . . ."[11]

9 United Nations, *Conference on the Law of the Sea*, p. 59, quoting Mr. Anderson, delegate from Iceland.
10 *Ibid.*, p. 62, quoting Mr. Ponce y Carbo, delegate from Ecuador.
11 Lockwood, "Tuna Boat Owners Fear Navy Escorts," *San Diego Independent*, February 5, 1967, p. 1.

Korea, too, has been similarly concerned with the Japanese beam trawlers. Beam trawlers tend to destroy the bottom feeding grounds and sea grasses. The Korean fishermen, conversely, do not trawl, but use the more primitive methods of hand fishing, which have no adverse effects on the fishery.[12] It follows that "the Korean representative at the United Nations Conference on the Law of the Sea would and did state that the three-mile limit was inadequate to meet Korea's economic needs.[13]

Marine biological science has found that, by and large, it is the shallow waters of the continental shelf adjacent to the land masses that provide the most suitable combinations of light, temperature, nutrient elements, and other factors conducive to the development of intense fish concentration. It is here that the world's great fisheries are chiefly located.[14] Coastal states adjacent to wide continental shelf fisheries have increasingly asserted their "right" and "obligation," by virtue of proximity, to establish and maintain conservation measures throughout the fishery. On this basis, Iceland in 1948, and Korea in 1952 established protective conservation zones on their continental shelves.[15]

Widening the littoral state's exclusive fishing zone not only provides the obvious advantage of reducing competition, but also provides a technical advantage. Certain efficient fishing techniques require the fishing vessel or vessels to proceed shoreward from deeper into more shallow waters. With an exclusive fishing zone as wide as twelve miles, for example, the littoral state's fishermen could proceed from deep water all the way in to the shore; whereas foreigners would be restricted to less efficient sweeps outside the twelve-mile limit.[16]

This argumentation supports the claims of states like Iceland and Korea, but not the so-called CEP (Chile, Ecuador, and Peru) states of Pacific-coast Latin America where there is very little continental shelf. To defend their claim to their 200-mile-wide fishery they propounded the *bioma* theory (see pages 165–166):

> Modern biologists and ecologists have called the sum of non-biotic factors, mainly climatological and hydrological, which are capable of creating a particular situation, that will permit an aggregate of vegetable and animal beings to live within it, an "eco-system."
> Within an "eco-system" many living communities, including man, may co-exist in a particular chain, or succession, constituting a whole which is called a "bioma." Therefore the term "bioma" designates the whole of the complex of living communities of a region, which under the influence of

12   Brittin and Watson, *International Law for Seagoing Officers*, p. 91.
13   United Nations, *Conference on the Law of the Sea*, p. 44, citing Mr. Kim's statement of March 14, 1958.
14   McDougal and Burke, *Public Order*, p. 485.
15   Iceland, "Law No. 44, Scientific Conservation of the Continental Shelf Fisheries, 5 April 1948," United Nations, *Laws and Regulations on the High Seas*, vol. I, pp. 12–13; Republic of Korea, "Presidential Proclamation of Sovereignty over Adjacent Seas, 18 January 1952," United Nations, *Laws and Regulations on the Territorial Sea*, pp. 30–31; see also Kunz, "Continental Shelf and International Law: Confusion and Abuse," p. 833.
16   McDougal and Burke, *Public Order*, p. 478.

the climate and in the course of centuries, becomes constantly more homo-
geneous, until, in its final phase, it becomes a definite type.

An "eco-system" may sustain one or more "biomas," but each one of
these will maintain its unity within the system, except in the areas of contact where there may be an intermixing. . . . All the complexes that may
form a "bioma" are in a state of dynamic equilibrium which is subject to
the laws of Nature. . . .

[Thus] a perfect unity and inter-dependence exists between the communities that live in the sea, which supports their life, and the coastal population which requires both to survive.

This is, in short, the concept of biological unity from which is derived,
in the scientific field, the preferential right of coastal countries. According to this concept, the human population of the coast forms part of the
biological chain which originates in the adjoining sea, and which extends
from the microscopic vegetable and animal life (fitoplankton and zoo-
plankton) to the higher mammals, among which we count man.

These "biomas" are proper to each region . . . and it is, therefore, a
prime duty of every coastal State to insure that they are not destroyed in
the only way that this is possible, which is by the depredations of man.[17]

In effect, this theory contends that to permit nonlittoral fishermen to catch
fish, and to remove them from the *bioma* or the *biomas* of the eco-system
is in defiance of the law of nature.

Arguments against extending the limits of fisheries. During the Santiago
Conference of 1955, the United States rejected the *bioma* theory.[18] The United
States delegation argued that stocks of fish, such as the tuna, roam widely
over the oceans and do not respect the limits of the *biomas*. Fish populations,
being highly migratory, move at random throughout wide ocean areas. Most
fisheries do not conform to three-mile, twelve-mile, or to 200-mile limits. The
fish concentrations are influenced by major world-wide meteorological and
oceanographic forces, such as the Humboldt Current, the Equatorial Currents,
and the California Current, and as a result, migrate both in and out of the
coastal waters, and laterally along the coast between the waters of various
states. Additionally, fish migrate vertically, from one depth to another.

This argument contends, then, that no uniform width for the territorial
sea could encompass the range within which fish move in all their life phases,
and that no unilateral conservation or exploitation could make sense under
such circumstances.[19] For any type of conservation to be effective, measures
must be taken throughout the entire fishery, by multilateral agreement, if
possible, and not unilaterally within the narrow confines of the territorial

---

17 Reiff, *The United States and the Treaty Law of the Sea*, pp. 307–308, quoting
    from Department of State, *Santiago Negotiations on Fishery Conservation Problems*,
    1955, pp. 31–32. For a discussion in defense of this *bioma* theory, see Amador,
    The Exploitation and Conservation of the Resources of the Sea, pp. 73–79.

18 Reiff, *Treaty Law*, p. 308.

19 *Ibid.*, pp. 308–309; and McDougal and Burke, *Public Order*, pp. 259–260, citing
    Netherlands Economic Institute, *The Development of Offshore Fisheries and the
    Economics of Choice* (1958), p. 25.

waters of individual states. It would follow, then, that the narrower the territorial sea, the greater the area that might benefit from any multilateral measures.

The foregoing argument, simply stated, concludes that there is no fixed limit better suited to solve the fisheries conservation problem than the three-mile limit, presuming that a conservation problem exists—unless it be an even narrower one.

Another argument against wider fishery zones is based on the premise that there is no problem in the first place. This argument rejects as invalid the claims that "overfishing" will cause "extinction" of the species, and that ". . . there need not be concern with protecting them [the fish] against being driven to such low levels that they can never recover." This argument "rests in part, on the fact that a fish population is an open-ended biological system which replenishes itself from the effects of losses."[20]

Those who take this stand deny any validity to the allegations that reduced catches are evidence of depletion or overfishing, on the grounds that the fish population in any given area is subject to cyclical fluctuations. It is suggested also that many of the state actions to extend their fisheries have been based on political motives and have no basis in economic fact. For example, in justifying her claim to twelve miles for fisheries, Libya averred that she faced a serious problem of foreign fishermen wrongfully exploiting her coastal waters.[21] Yet, investigation in 1953 by the United Nations Technical Assistance Program revealed that the Libyan territorial sea is, in fact, underfished, and that the Libyans do practically no inshore fishing.[22]

THE FISHERIES CONTROVERSY IN AMERICA

Latin America and the United States. In 1953, Mexico embarked on a policy of enforcing her nine-mile zone. Shrimp boats from the United States and other nations were seized by Mexican authorities.[23] Emboldened by her success and by that of her neighbors to the south, Mexico in 1969 increased her territorial waters from nine miles to 12 miles.[24] Panama, too, which has claimed exclusive

20 McDougal and Burke, *Public Order*, p. 467, quoting from Schaefer, "Scientific Investigation of the Tropical Tuna Resources of the Eastern Pacific" in United Nations, *Papers Presented at the International Technical Conference on the Conservation of the Living Resources of the Sea*, pp. 15–16.
21 United Nations, *Official Records of the Second United Nations Conference on the Law of the Sea*, p. 53.
22 McDougal and Burke, *Public Order*, p. 551, citing United Nations, Technical Assistance Program, *The Economic and Social Development of Libya*, p. 51.
23 "U.S. Shrimp Boats Seized by Mexico," news item in *New York Times*, February 22, 1953.
24 "Mexican Waters," news item in *Washington Post*, September 2, 1969, p. A21. Two years earlier, Mexico had adopted a fishing zone of twelve miles: Law of January 20, 1967, cited in Windley, "International Practice regarding Traditional Fishing Privileges of Foreign Fishermen in Zones of Extended Maritime Jurisdiction," p. 498.

fishing rights over the continental shelf since 1946,[25] seized the United States tuna clipper *Star Crest* in 1953.[26] But these were fairly isolated cases and frictions of much greater magnitude developed between the United States and Ecuador. In 1952 the CEP states declared their sovereignty over a 200-mile limit. In the spring of 1953, Ecuador seized four American tuna vessels; this led to a conference between the two states that could agree only that the legal problem was too broad in scope to be resolved at the U.S.-Ecuador level.[27]

Rather than send warships to enforce the three-mile limit and to strain further her relationships with her allies, the United States enacted the so-called Fishermen's Protective Act of 1954.[28] Under this act, the U.S. government reimbursed fishermen for fines paid and for losses sustained in connection with seizures under Latin American laws adjudged by the United States as infractions of international law. The act was intended to secure the speedy release of seized American vessels and to support U.S. fishermen who wished to fish off Latin America. After funding the fines and losses, the United States would then seek reimbursement at the diplomatic level from the country imposing the fine.

During the same year, the CEP powers put more teeth into their 1952 declaration by agreeing that the proceeds from seizures of vessels and cargos, regardless of where and by whom seized, would be distributed "in equal shares among the Contracting Parties. . . ." In other words, an Ecuadorian naval vessel could theoretically apprehend a U.S. tuna boat in Peruvian waters, and the fine would be split between Ecuador, Peru, and Chile. It was also agreed that each party "undertakes not to enter into any agreements, arrangements or conventions which would imply a diminution of the sovereignty over the said [200-mile] zone.[29] The agreements went on to provide for a twelve-mile exclusive fishery zone for the nationals of the respective states, within the multilaterally protected and policed 200-mile zone.

The following year, Ecuador seized two U.S. vessels, the *Arctic Maid* and the *Santa Ana*, some 14 to 25 miles west of the Ecuadorian island of Santa Clara. An American fisherman was seriously wounded by Ecuadorian gunfire; fines of $49,000 were imposed; strong U.S. protests were ignored.[30] Subse-

25 Whiteman, *Digest*, p. 30.
26 "Confiscated U.S. Ship Returned by Panama," news item in *New York Times*, July 5, 1953.
27 Department of State, "Conference on U.S.-Ecuadorian Fishery Relations," pp. 759–761.
28 United States Congress, House of Representatives, *Protecting the Rights of Vessels of the United States on the High Seas and in the Territorial Waters of Foreign Countries.*
29 United Nations, *Laws and Regulations on the Territorial Sea*, pp. 729–735, quoting Agreements between Chile, Ecuador, and Peru, signed at the Second Conference on the Exploitation and Conservation of the Maritime Resources of the South Pacific, Lima, 4 December 1954.
30 Phleger, "Recent Developments Affecting the Regime of the High Seas," pp. 934, 937.

quently, the CEP states declined a U.S. proposal to submit the dispute to the International Court of Justice.[31]

In May, 1963, Ecuador seized the San Diego tuna boats *White Star* and *Ranger* and levied fines of over $20,000.[32] In January, 1967, Peru seized the tuna boats *Hornet* and *Caribbean* 20 miles offshore and fined them $20,000. At the same time, Ecuador seized the *Sea Preme* 60 miles from shore. California Congressman Lionel Van Deerlin condemned the Ecuadorians and Peruvians as "modern pirates on the high seas" operating "under the thin cloak of legality. . . ." Senator George Murphy termed the seizure "another outrageous affront to the integrity and honor of our nation."[33]

In December, 1968, Ecuador seized the U.S. fishing vessel *Day Island;* two months later, Peru seized the *Mariner*. In reprisal, the United States suspended all military sales to the two countries.[34] This notwithstanding, the following month, March, 1969, Peru seized and fined the U.S. tuna boats *San Juan* and *Cape Anne*.[35] This seizure provoked demands in the U.S. Congress for immediate recall of the U.S. destroyer *Isherwood* on loan to Peru.[36] In June, 1969, the CEP states issued a joint communique:

> [Chile, Ecuador and Peru] see with profound concern the application by the United States government of forceful measures aimed at obliging the countries of the South Pacific region to back down from their legal position on the 200-mile territorial jurisdiction.[37]

Peru, speaking for the others, agreed to discussions with the United States concerning the 200-mile limit fishing controversy, provided the arms sanctions were terminated. This was agreed upon and the ban was lifted.

Nevertheless, the problem was far from solved. Between 1961 and early 1968, over 50 U.S. fishing boats had been seized by Ecuador and Peru. By early 1970, this figure had risen sharply to 92, with fines, damages, and losses totaling $775,000.[38] Moreover, those states seemed determined to defend their 200-mile limit. At the First Latin American Parliament, representing the congresses of 13 nations, held in July 1965, a resolution was adopted, recommending that all the southern republics with seacoasts adopt a 200-mile limit

31 Reiff, *Treaty Law*, pp. 311–312.
32 "Tuna Boats Are Fined by Ecuador," news item in *The Washington Post*, June 5, 1963, p. A15.
33 Shepard, "Peru Gunboats Seize 2 S.D. Tuna Clippers," *San Diego Union*, January 27, 1967, pp. A1–A2; and Shepard, "Tunaboats Reported Fined, Released By Peru, Ecuador," *San Diego Union*, January 28, 1967, pp. B1, B7.
34 "Arms Ban on Ecuador, Peru Lifted," news item in *Washington Post*, July 4, 1969, pp. A1, A12.
35 "Peru seizes 2 U.S. Tuna Boats; Frees Them After Levying Fine," news item in *New York Times*, March 20, 1969.
36 "Destroyer's Return Sought," news item in *New York Times*, March 20, 1969.
37 "Peru Offers to Discuss Fishing Limit," news item in *The Washington Post*, June 19, 1969, p. A29.
38 "U.S. Offers Solution to Tunaboat Seizures," news item in *San Diego Union*, April 19, 1968; "U.S. Tuna Boats Fear New Clashes," news item in *New York Times*, January 6, 1970.

of territorial waters.[39] Nicaragua adopted a new constitution that year that claimed the 200-mile limit for exclusive fishing rights.[40] Panama responded in early 1967 when the Panamanian Congress passed legislation creating a 200-mile territorial sea, specifically citing the CEP agreement and sharing its principles and purpose.[41] Next to react was Uruguay in December, 1969, when she extended her territorial sovereignty from 12 to 200 miles, claiming jurisdiction over fishing, air space, and the continental shelf to that limit.[42]

Canada. The Latin American fishery claims to the south were not the only claims of concern to the United States in the American hemisphere. As early as 1957, the Canadian Parliament had favored the adoption of a twelve-mile fishing limit. This limit would be applied to a series of baselines from the Atlantic to the Pacific, including the Canadian Arctic Archipelago.[43] This scheme, which combined features of the Norwegian Baseline Decree of 1935 (see pages 146–7) and the archipelago doctrine of Indonesia and the Philippines, to be discussed presently, would have incorporated all the waters within Queen Charlotte Sound, Hecate Strait, Dixon Entrance, the Arctic Archipelago (all of the District of Franklin of the Northwest Territories which includes the Northwest Passage), Hudson Bay and Strait, Notre Dame Bay, Placentia Bay, the Gulf of Saint Lawrence, the Bay of Fundy, and other large areas traditionally regarded as high seas.

In June, 1963, Canadian Prime Minister Lester Pearson announced his government's plan to adopt the twelve-mile fishing limit and the baseline principle, to be effective the following May.[44] The baseline principle encountered the resistance of the United States during discussions that were undertaken following Pearson's announcement. As a result, only the twelve-mile fishing zone was placed into effect,[45] with adoption of the straight baselines being held in abeyance. In June, 1970, Canada went a step further, enacting legislation extending her jurisdiction, for purposes of pollution control, 100 miles to seaward. This followed an oil-spill by a U.S. tanker while transiting the Northwest Passage in 1969.

THE FISHERIES CONTROVERSY IN EUROPE

Swedish-Soviet dispute. The Soviet seizures of 1948 to 1950 were noted in the preceding chapter. In those cases, Swedish vessels were apprehended

39 "Latins Ask Widening of Offshore Limits," news item in *New York Times,* July 20, 1965.
40 Windley, "Privileges of Foreign Fishermen," p. 498.
41 *Ibid.,* p. 499, citing Panamanian Law No. 31 of February 2, 1967 (unnamed) in *Gaceta Oficial,* February 14, 1967.
42 "200-Mile Limit," news item in *The Washington Post,* December 4, 1969, p. A25.
43 United Nations, *Conference on the Law of the Sea,* pp. 51–52.
44 "Canada Sets 12-Mile Fishing Zone," news item in *The Washington Post,* June 5, 1963, p. A17; and Whiteman, *Digest,* pp. 1239–1240.
45 Whiteman, *Digest,* p. 1240, quoting the Canadian "Territorial Sea and Fishing Zones Act" of 1964, Section 4 (1) and (2).

fishing for salmon within the twelve-mile limit off the Soviet coast. The fishermen were imprisoned and were not released until after they had confessed to charges of espionage and had paid heavy fines. The Swedish note of protest pointed out that for centuries the Baltic territorial sea had been three or four miles. The Soviet Union replied, denying the existence of a three- or four-mile rule under international law, and asserted that the Soviet territorial sea in the Baltic was twelve miles. Then in April, 1955, Soviet fleet units seized four Swedish trawlers that had been forced into Russian waters in search of shelter from an unusually severe Baltic storm. Although the fishermen denied they had fished within the twelve-mile limit, they were imprisoned and fined, and their fishing catch and equipment were confiscated.[46]

Anglo-Norwegian Fisheries Case. The dispute between Great Britain and Norway, originating with the Norwegian Baseline Decree of 1935, came before the International Court of Justice in 1951. The agent of the United Kingdom argued that Norway was entitled only to the fixed width of four [!] miles; that baselines could be drawn only across fjords and bays ten miles wide and less; and that Norway should pay compensation for certain arrests made under the 1935 baseline decree.[47]

Professor C. H. M. Waldock referred to this British recognition of Norway's claim to a four-mile limit as ". . . something of a landmark in the law of the sea, since it is the first time that the United Kingdom has recognized any limit larger than three miles."[48] Bernard Heinzen referred to it as an acknowledgement on the part of the three-mile states that the four-mile limit was as valid as, and for all practical purposes, tantamount to, the three-mile limit.[49] Nevertheless, it was not Norway's claim to four miles that was on trial here; it was Britain's charge that baselines were in conflict with customary international law of territorial waters. Disregarding a considerable body of customary law, opinions of publicists, and judicial precedent, the court held that

> . . . the method employed for the delimitation of the fisheries zone by the Royal Norwegian Decree of July 12, 1935, is not contrary to international law; and . . . that the base-lines fixed by said decree in application of this method were not contrary to international law.[50]

The court added that, along rugged coastal areas, baselines need not necessarily follow the low-water mark but may be determined by lines "reasonably drawn" conforming to the general direction of the coast. Judge Green Hackworth of the United States concurred in the judgment on the basis that he

---

46 Glenn, "The Swedish-Soviet Territorial Sea Controversy in the Baltic," pp. 942–947.
47 International Court of Justice, *Reports of Judgments, Advisory Opinions and Orders, 1951*, pp. 119–121.
48 Waldock, "The Anglo-Norwegian Fisheries Case," p. 126.
49 Heinzen, "The Three-Mile Limit," p. 619.
50 International Court of Justice, *Reports 1951*, p. 143.

considered that the Norwegian government had proved the existence of an historic title to the disputed areas of water.[51] The British member, Sir Arnold McNair, dissented.[52] This was clearly a debilitating blow to the three-mile limit and furnished legal precedent for the closing off of additional areas of the high seas. This decision was soon reflected in baseline claims by Iceland and by Denmark (for Greenland).[53]

Anglo-Icelandic "Fish War." The considerable volume of debate and dialogue in favor of the twelve-mile limit during the 1958 United Nations Conference on the Law of the Sea provided Iceland with adequate pretext to adopt a twelve-mile limit. Two months after the conference, Iceland adopted the twelve-mile limit for fishing, together with a set of 47 baselines surrounding the entire country and its fringe islands.[54] British fishermen were the foreigners most affected, having fished those waters up to the four-mile limit since 1836. As a result, there began the eighteen and one-half month Anglo-Icelandic "Fish War," during which time British trawlers fished in groups under protective naval escort. Reminiscent of the Anglo-Spanish "fish war" a century earlier, forty-nine different British warships—frigates and destroyers—were deployed to Iceland, spending 1,854 ship-days on patrol through two gale-swept winters and a foggy summer. They thwarted 59 attempts by Iceland's seven gunboats to board the "poaching" British trawlers.[55]

The British declared a three-month "truce," withdrawing all forces in March, 1960, in order to clear the atmosphere for the Second United Nations Conference on the Law of the Sea. The conference did not, however, resolve the controversy over the extent of territorial seas and fishing rights, and Britain continued to deny recognition to the Icelandic claim; nevertheless, since 1960 the British have strictly observed the twelve-mile limit applied along Iceland's cape-to-cape straight baselines.[56]

THE FISHERIES CONTROVERSY IN ASIA

The Rhee-Line (Japan-Korea) Dispute. During the years that Korea was under Japanese rule, Japanese fishermen had become accustomed to fishing along the Korean coasts. During the years of American occupation, the occupation commander, General MacArthur, had excluded Japanese fishermen from a very large sea area surrounding Korea. Following the U.S.-Japanese peace

51 *Ibid.*, p. 144.
52 *Ibid.*, pp. 158–185.
53 Iceland, "Regulations of 19 March, 1952 Concerning Conservation of Fisheries off the Icelandic Coasts," United Nations, *Laws and Regulations on the Territorial Sea*, pp. 516–517; and "Notice No. 292 of 11 November 1953 Respecting Commercial Trapping, Fishing, and Hunting in Greenland and Exports from Greenland," *ibid.*, pp. 476–477.
54 Ibid.; and Davis, *Iceland Extends its Fisheries Limits*, pp. 28–34. The baselines are plotted on a chart on p. 137.
55 Goldsworthy, "More Fun than Fury in the Fish War," pp. 58–59.
56 *Ibid.*, p. 67.

treaty of 1952, modern Japanese trawlers swarmed into the Korean waters denied them for seven years. President Rhee of Korea immediately reinstituted the MacArthur protective zone. Rhee also established a Korean Coast Guard, which utilized ex-Japanese minesweepers and was tasked with excluding foreigners from the protective zone, seizing them if necessary for trial in Korean courts.[57]

The new Korean fishery conservation zone was geographically the same as the former MacArthur protective zone, and included all waters within a perimeter delimited by a series of nine straight lines—the *Rhee Line*—from the Korean-Soviet Border, through the Sea of Japan, the Korea Strait, and the Yellow Sea to the Korean-Chinese border.[58] The sea area within this zone is more than three times greater than South Korea itself, and at one point the Rhee-Line boundary is 175 miles distant from the adjacent South Korean shoreline.

The Korean law defines the maritime area within the Rhee Line as a fishery conservation zone and provides for three years imprisonment or a fine of 500,000 hwan and confiscation of vessel, catch, and equipment in the case of any person fishing within the conservation area without permission of the Korean government. The Rhee Line, needless to say, has been the source of intense ill-feeling between Japan and Korea since its inception of 1954.

Indonesia. In December, 1957, Indonesia adopted the archipelago doctrine, applying it as the delimitation of her national frontiers:

> . . . [T]he Government states that all waters around, between and connecting, the islands or parts of islands belonging to the Indonesian archipelago irrespective of their width or dimension are natural appurtenances of its land territory and therefore an integral part of the inland or national waters subject to the absolute sovereignty of Indonesia. . . . The delimitation of the territorial sea, with a width of 12 nautical miles, shall be measured from straight base lines connecting the outermost points of the islands of the Republic of Indonesia.[59]

Connecting the outermost points with a series of baselines as prescribed creates a geometric figure in the nature of a parallelogram about 3000 miles in length and larger than the area of the continental United States. The latter government felt compelled to protest this remarkable assumption of national sovereignty over areas of the high seas.[60]

A few months later, during the 1958 United Nations Conference on the

57 Brittin and Watson, *International Law for Seagoing Officers*, pp. 89–91.
58 Republic of Korea, "Fishery Resources Conservation Law No. 298," December 12; 1954, in United Nations, *Laws and Regulations on the Territorial Sea*, pp. 523–524.
59 Indonesia, "Announcement on the Territorial Waters of the Republic of Indonesia, December 14, 1957," reproduced in part in Whiteman, *Digest*, p. 284.
60 Whiteman, *Digest, loc. cit.*, citing United States note of December 31, 1957.

Law of the Sea, the Indonesian representative, Mr. Subardjo, commented that he had

> . . . been distressed to hear the United States representative assert that the actions of the Indonesian Government amounted to unlawful appropriation because the seas were held in common for the benefit of all mankind. The fact that the seas were the common property of all nations did not preclude the possibility of a special regime for archipelagos of a unique nature.

He pointed out the complexity of attempting to determine the limits of the territorial sea where some 13,000 islands were involved and added:

> In the opinion of the Indonesian Government, an archipelago should be regarded as a single unit, the water between and around the islands forming an integral whole with the land territory.[61]

Philippines. The policy of the Republic of the Philippines, also an archipelagic state, has been almost parallel to that of Indonesia, except that the Philippines has not formally superimposed a twelve-mile limit about her archipelago baseline.

> The position of the Philippine Government in the matter is that all waters around, between and connecting the different islands belonging to the Philippine Archipelago, irrespective of their widths or dimensions, are necessary appurtenances of its land territory, forming an integral part of the national or inland waters, subject to the exclusive sovereignty of the Philippines. All other water areas embraced in the imaginary lines described in the Treaty of Paris of December 10, 1898 . . . are considered as maritime territorial waters of the Philippines for purposes of protection of our fishing rights, conservation of our fishing resources, enforcement of revenue and anti-smuggling laws, defense and security, etc.[62]

This note antedated by two years the Indonesian announcement of 1957. The similarity between the two suggests that the Philippine position may have served as the model for that of Indonesia.

During the 1958 Conference on the Law of the Sea, the Philippines' representative referred to the three-mile limit as one of the "old rules of international law."[63] The Philippine delegation to the second conference did not conceal the Philippine preference for the twelve-mile limit. It voted for the twelve-mile proposal and abstained in the voting on the U.S. proposals.[64] Also,

61 United Nations, *Conference on the Law of the Sea*, pp. 43–44.
62 Philippine Minister of Foreign Affairs Note to Secretary-General of the United Nations, December 12, 1955, quoted in Whiteman, *Digest*, pp. 282–283.
63 United Nations, *Conference on the Law of the Sea*, p. 5.
64 United Nations, *Second United Nations Conference on the Law of the Sea, Summary Records of the Plenary Meetings and Meetings of the Committee of the Whole*, pp. 30, 151.

during the Second Conference, the Filipino delegation explained the reasoning behind its claim to all the waters of the archipelago:

> Countless generations of Filipinos had derived a large part of their food supply from the waters between and around the islands making up the archipelago[;] and all those waters, irrespective of their width or extent, had always been regarded as part of the inland waters of the Philippines.[65]

Although the United States has objected to this Philippine archipelago claim, it is interesting to note that during the 1907 Hague Conference, the U.S. delegation argued with the British that an unrestricted application of the three-mile limit was inadequate for the extensive island array in the Philippines and desired special baseline delimitation arrangements there. (See pages 116–17.)

THE SECURITY CONTROVERSY

Those who have adopted the archipelago doctrine not only defend it on the basis of providing sea food for the islanders, but also claim that it is required in the interest of their security. This introduces the second key aspect of the post-World War II territorial seas controversy. Security claims have generally been couched in vague terms pointing to the inadequacy of the three-mile limit in meeting security requirements of modern states in the nuclear and space age. This is reminiscent of the nineteenth century French publicists who recommended continuously extending the territorial sea as the range of weapons increased.

SUBSTANCE OF THE SECURITY CONTROVERSY

Arguments to extend territorial seas beyond three miles for security purposes. The Soviet Union—and the entire Soviet Bloc—especially during the initial years following the war, held the view that three miles was insufficient for security. As that of a land power, the Soviet logic is not hard to follow. The United States made no secret of its determination to maintain the principle of *mare liberum*, depending on fleet mobility as one of the main pillars in her national security structure. By widening the territorial sea from three to twelve miles, the Soviet Union could frustrate that mobility, and restrict visual and electronic surveillance.

A fundamental adjunct of the Soviet twelve-mile claim is her view on innocent passage of warships. The Soviet view on innocent passage is relatively new, and although it has been shared by some writers in this century, it is a break with the traditional practice of previous centuries. To review, the

---

65 *Ibid.*, p. 52.

Hague Convention of 1907 seemed to offer no impediment to the innocent passage of warships:

> Article 10. The neutrality of a Power is not affected by the mere passage through its territorial waters of ships of war or prizes belonging to belligerents.[66]

This article reflected the historic concept of neutral waters, wherein belligerents were allowed to enter neutral ports but were prohibited from committing hostile acts under the guns of neutral fortresses. Later, with the advent of submarine warfare, international practice evolved to restrict the activities of submarines within the neutral zone. Article 4 of the report of the Second Commission (Territorial Sea) of the 1930 Hague Conference reads:

> A coastal state may put no obstacles in the way of the innocent passage for foreign vessels [other than warships] in the territorial sea.
> Submarine vessels shall navigate on the surface. . . .
> As a general rule, a coastal state will not forbid the passage of foreign warships in its territorial sea and will not require a previous authorization or notification.[67]

This article did not say enough to suit the Soviet Union. To her, the twelve-mile limit and the right to control navigation are inseparable. This was documented formally when the Soviet Union ratified the 1958 Convention on the Territorial Sea and the Contiguous Zone; she attached the following reservation:

> The Government of the Union of Soviet Socialist Republics considers that a coastal state has the right to establish procedures for the authorization of the passage of foreign warships through its territorial waters.[68]

Each of the Communist states that ratified the convention made a similar reservation. The intent was obvious, that of keeping American warships, or those of her allies, out of the communist states' twelve-mile territorial sea. India, one of the Cold War "neutrals," adopted the Soviet view, while Ghana advanced the view that innocent passage of warships need be subject only to prior notification. Neither of these positions was acceptable to the United States, which maintained that neither authorization nor notification was required.[69]

---

66 Thirteenth Hague Convention of 1907, "Convention Concerning the Rights and Duties of Neutral Powers in Maritime War," in Department of the Navy, *Law of Naval Warfare*, p. B-3.
67 League of Nations, *Final Act*, pp. 241, 246.
68 McDougal and Burke, *Public Order*, p. 1180, quoting "Declarations and Reservations to the Convention."
69 United Nations, *Conference on the Law of the Sea*, pp. 84–113 *passim;* and Dean, "The Second Geneva Conference on the Law of the Sea: The Fight for Freedom of the Seas," p. 771.

Arguments against extending the territorial seas for reasons of security. The principal argument against an extension of territorial seas is scarcely no more than a rejection of the preceding argument that national security is enhanced by excluding foreign warships (and aircraft) from an increased width of territorial seas. As pointed out by Professors McDougal and Burke, the current state of ordnance is such that no width of territorial waters—even 1,000 miles or more—could provide a safe measure of national security.[70] Even a resort to an arbitrary solution such as a fifteenth-century papal-bull partition of the ocean surfaces could not protect a state from U.S. Minuteman and Soviet SS-9 intercontinental multiple-warhead ballistic missiles. Submarine-launched ballistic missiles—Poseidon and "Yankee" class—further complicate the issue. With such weapons in the arsenals of states, the concept of territorial waters, in effect, has become irrelevant in terms of providing military or naval security to the littoral state. Likewise, the Bynkerskoek maxim that a state can claim the waters as far as its ordnance will carry is equally irrelevant for the same reason.

It was argued by the U.S. delegation to the Geneva Conferences that a twelve-mile limit would impose an additional burden on neutral states in time of war.[71] A twelve-mile zone, it was contended, would provide a neutral haven for belligerent submarines while the neutral state faced the difficult problem of detecting and prohibiting such violations. This argument, it is true, has legal validity, but it is weak when examined on a practical basis, especially when the actual conduct of submarine warfare during both World Wars is considered. It would be a futile mental exercise to suppose that submarine commanders might voluntarily restrict their operations and deny themselves the tactical advantage of stealth for which their craft were conceived and built.

THE SECURITY CONTROVERSY IN AMERICA

Nuclear testing. In pursuit of national security, the United States in 1946 embarked on a series of nuclear tests involving the detonation of nuclear devices at, over, and under several Pacific islands and atolls under U.S. trusteeship. Elaborate safety and range clearance procedures were instituted to minimize the possibilities of casualties to ships and seamen due to the effects of the blast, radiation, or fallout. Detailed warnings were published internationally by the Atomic Energy Commission and the U.S. Hydrographic Office.[72]

Nevertheless, these tests ran afoul of Cold War adversaries, neutrals, and allies. The Russian delegate to the 1958 Geneva Conference declared that

> [n]uclear tests were a patent violation of the principle of freedom of the seas and, consequently, of the freedom of navigation and fishing, as

70   McDougal and Burke, *Public Order,* pp. 482–485.
71   Dean, "Second Geneva Conference," p. 755.
72   Whiteman, *Digest,* pp. 543–631.

well as of the principle of conservation of the living resources of the sea. They should, accordingly, be declared illegal in order to reinforce that fundamental freedom, and, at the same time, safeguard international peace and security.[73]

The Indian delegate brought up the admittedly unproven argument that "such explosions not only interfered with the freedom of navigation on the high seas, but also destroyed and contaminated the living resources of the sea and caused extensive pollution of the water."[74] The Indonesian delegate pointed to the harmful effects of such devices as one of the justifications for Indonesia's having adopted the archipelago doctrine.[75] On the occasion of one of the nuclear tests:

> . . . [T]he Japanese Ministry of Foreign Affairs stated that the Government and People of Japan regretted that the United States continued its tests in the Eniwetok area and that a new danger zone would be further set up in a wide area around Johnston Island, and requested once again of the United States Government early suspension of nuclear tests.[76]

The United States responded to this widespread unfavorable criticism by pointing out that the temporary use of areas of the high seas for gunnery and bombing practice had never been considered unlawful and insisted

> . . . that its nuclear weapons testing activities in and around the Marshall Islands in the Pacific Ocean have not violated the principle of the freedom of the seas or any other principle of international law.[77]

This was further amplified:

> The United States has not closed any portion of the high seas in the Pacific Ocean, and, in fact, has strongly maintained the doctrine of the freedom of the seas. . . .
> Closure of waters in the Eniwetok Proving Ground in the Trust Territory of the Pacific Island[s] has been specifically limited to territorial waters.[78]

In any event, the problem ceased to exist with the conclusion of the Limited Nuclear Test Ban Treaty in Moscow on August 5, 1963.

Air defense identification zones. The Soviet Union was not alone in its search for security along its maritime boundaries. The United States, after

73   United Nations, *Conference on the Law of the Sea*, p. 32.
74   *Ibid.*, p. 15.
75   *Ibid.*, p. 44.
76   The American Ambassador at Tokyo (MacArthur) to Secretary Dulles, telegram, July 1, 1958, Ms. Department of State, file 711.5611/7-158 in Whiteman, *Digest*, p. 593.
77   Whiteman, *Digest*, p. 546, quoting a paper prepared for the use of the United States delegation to the 1958 Conference on the Law of the Sea.
78   *Ibid.*, p. 596, citing a U.S. State Department letter of April 25, 1958.

World War II, was still mindful of the surprise attack on Pearl Harbor. Not long after the beginning of the Cold War, when there was great mutual distrust and fear between the two superpowers, the United States established an early warning system as a defense against incoming aircraft. In December, 1950, the *Code of Federal Regulations* was modified to provide for Air Defense Identification Zones (ADIZ).[79] These zones extend approximately 400 nautical miles into both the Atlantic and Pacific Oceans. Under the regulations, no aircraft may fly in the ADIZ without prior clearance. Foreign aircraft must

> . . . make position reports as prescribed for United States aircraft . . . when the aircraft is not less than one hour and not more than two hours average cruising distance via the most direct route from the United States.[80]

Violators are subject to a $10,000 fine, one year imprisonment, or both. United States military aircraft are routinely employed to enforce and police the ADIZ.[81] If an unidentified aircraft penetrates the ADIZ, fighters, based along the coast, are "scrambled" to intercept the incoming aircraft and to escort it to a landing site. The ADIZ is operated in coordination with Canada, which maintains a very similar ADIZ system.[82]

Although the Soviet Union has not objected specifically to the ADIZ, at the 1958 Conference on the Law of the Sea, the U.S.S.R., Albania, and Bulgaria submitted a joint proposal that

> No naval or air ranges or other combat training areas limiting freedom of navigation may be designated on the high seas near foreign coasts or international routes.[83]

It is interesting to note that the Soviet Union has not proclaimed an ADIZ-type security zone in the Pacific. Although Soviet military aircraft would be intercepted entering the U.S. ADIZ, United States Strategic Air Command

79   Part 620 (Security Control of Air Traffic), Title 14 (Civil Aviation), *Code of Federal Regulations of the United States of America*, as modified by Executive Order No. 10197 dated December 20, 1950 and printed in United States Archives, Federal Register Division, *The Federal Register*, Wednesday, December 27, 1950, vol. XV, pp. 9319–9321; and U.S. Department of Commerce, *Regulations of the Administration*, Part 620, reprinted in MacChesney, U.S. Naval War College, *International Law Situations and Documents, 1956: Situations, Documents and Commentary on Recent Developments in the International Law of the Sea*, pp. 578–592. Diagrams plotting the ADIZ are available in *ibid.*, p. 578 and in Brittin and Watson, *International Law for Seagoing Officers*, p. 74.

80   *The Federal Register*, vol. XV, p. 9320.

81   McDougal and Burke, *Public Order*, p. 626.

82   MacChesney, *International Law Situations and Documents 1956*, pp. 592–600, reproducing Canadian Department of Transport, Air Services Branch, 22/55 Rules for the Security Control of Air Traffic (Superseding NOTAM 22/54) effective December 1, 1955.

83   McDougal and Burke, *Public Order*, p. 786, citing U.N. Doc. No. A/CONF. 13/C.2/L. 32 in United Nations, *Conference on the Law of the Sea*, vol. IV, *Second Committee (High Seas)*, p. 124.

bombers could approach unmolested within twelve miles, for example, of the Petropavlovsk Naval Base.

The ADIZ is not an extension of territorial seas as such. Nevertheless, under the regulations, foreign pilots are required to conform with U.S. and Canadian laws while flying over large areas of the high seas. Moreover, the declared purpose of the regulation is ". . . to identify, locate, and *control* U.S. and *foreign aircraft* operated within . . . [the] ADIZ."[84] There can be no doubt, therefore, that this does represent the extension of jurisdiction for special security purposes over a rather wide contiguous zone.

Antisubmarine hydrophone array. Prompted by the growing Soviet submarine fleet, the United States designed and installed a complex underwater array of computer-monitored hydrophones. Arrays of linked hydrophones have been installed on the continental shelf of both the Atlantic and Pacific coasts. This hydrophone array installation is designed to identify and locate enemy submarines approaching the coast.[85]

As in the case of the ADIZ, the use of these hydrophones is not necessarily an extension of territorial rights. But it is another instance of special actions taken by states in ocean areas beyond territorial waters to enhance their national security. In this case, as in the installation of "Texas-Tower" oil rigs, U.S.-owned property is installed on the continental shelf; presumably both would be defended against hostile foreign action.

THE SECURITY CONTROVERSY IN EUROPE

Corfu Channel Case. As early as 1946 there commenced post-war attempts on the part of certain littoral states to exclude foreign warships from waters traditionally considered international. In that year, Albania mined the North Corfu Strait, resulting in loss of lives and damage to ships of the British Royal Navy. The case was referred to the International Court of Justice—the court's first contentious case.

The North Corfu Strait is about two miles wide and is bounded on the east by the Albanian mainland and on the west by the Greek island of Corfu. The Albanians claimed the strait was of secondary importance and did not belong to the class of international straits endowed with the right of passage. They maintained that the British warships had no right to pass through the strait. The British contention was that the Albanians had illegally mined an international strait.

The court decided in favor of the British and ordered Albania to pay damages[86]—damages which, in the Cold War atmosphere, they refused to pay.

84 *The Federal Register,* vol. XV, p. 9319. Italics are the author's.
85 Finney, "Secret Underseas System Guards U.S. Against Hostile Submarines," *New York Times,* September 14, 1965.
86 *The Corfu Channel Case,* United Kingdom-Albania, International Court of Justice, *Reports of Judgments, Advisory Opinions and Orders,* 1949, pp. 4 ff.

The Baltic Sea. The Soviet Union's enforcement of her twelve-mile fishing limit in the Baltic has already been discussed. In 1952, the Soviet government displayed its resolve to defend her twelve-mile air space by force as well. In June of that year, within a period of three days, two unarmed Swedish reconnaissance planes were shot down with the loss of the crew of one plane. The Russians charged that the Swedish aircraft had penetrated to within four miles of the shore; the Swedish declared that the aircraft did not approach closer than 15 miles.[87]

The Soviet policy with respect to the Baltic was more involved than a mere enforcement of her twelve-mile claim. In 1947, the Soviet Union officially embraced the idea of a Baltic *mare clausum*, closed to all states save those littoral to the Baltic. The plan was published in a Soviet Justice Department handbook.[88] This concept was elaborated by Dr. S. V. Molodtsov in 1950. Molodtsov maintained that Baltic states possessed the historic and legal right to blockade the entrance to all foreign warships. "Baltic agreements" should be revised, he wrote, in order to ". . . throw a monkey wrench into the British and American plans of conquest."[89] The project did not materialize, chiefly as a consequence of the Western orientation of Denmark and West Germany and the neutrality of Sweden. Similar Soviet diplomatic efforts were launched to close the Sea of Japan and the Black Sea except to littoral states. These, too, failed due to the resistance of Japan and Turkey, supported by the United States.[90] Still, Soviet diplomacy continued to carry this theme at least as late as 1959. Speaking in Riga, Latvia, Premier Khrushchev proposed that the Scandinavian states join with the Soviet Union in converting the Baltic into a "sea of peace . . . free of atomic and rocket weapons."[91]

The Arctic Ocean. The Sovet Union entered a head-on confrontation with the United States on the issue of territorial waters in 1960. On July 1, the Russians shot down an RB-47 reconnaissance aircraft in the Barents Sea. The Soviet Union claimed that the aircraft was downed over Soviet territorial waters after it disobeyed an order to land. The United States countered that the aircraft had not approached within thirty miles of the Russian coast and that Soviet fighters had tried to force the RB-47 into Soviet airspace before shooting it down.[92]

It is not clear in this case whether the Soviet Union was enforcing her twelve-mile territorial sea or her claim to all Arctic waters north of the Russian

87 Glenn, "Swedish-Soviet Territorial Sea Controversy," p. 946; Morgan, "Soviet Policy in the Baltic," pp. 86–87.
88 Glenn, "Swedish-Soviet Territorial Sea Controversy," p. 947, citing *Mezdunarodnoe Pravo (International Law)*, Moscow, 1947, p. 262.
89 *Ibid.*, citin Molodtsov's dissertation published in the Russian journal *Sovetskoe Gosudarstvo i Pravo*, Moscow, 1950, No. 6.
90 Murphy, "A Soviet Naval Goal: Satellite Seas," pp. 37–40.
91 *Ibid.*, p. 38, quoting a speech of June 11, 1959.
92 Lissitzyn, "Some Legal Implications of the U-2 and RB-47 Incidents," pp. 139–140.

coast. This latter claim dates from 1926 when Russia embraced the "sector principle." The Soviet decree of April 15, 1926, provided:

> Are declared forming part of the territory of the Union of Soviet Socialistic Republics all lands and islands already discovered, as well as those which are to be discovered in the future . . . which lie in the Northern Frozen Ocean north of the coast of the Union of Soviet Socialistic Republics up to the North Pole. . . ."[93]

This decree disturbed certain Soviet jurists and publicists, especially E. A. Korovin, who noted that the wording only included "lands and islands." Korovin believed the intent of the decree was to include also "the ice blocks and waters washing the lands and islands."[94] Following World War II, Soviet jurists developed theories to support government claims to the whole of the Arctic "sector" north of their coasts. The 1966 Russian *Manual of International Maritime Law* lays complete and sovereign Soviet claim to the entire Northern Sea Route.[95] At least two well-known contemporary Soviet publicists, A. N. Nikolaev and S. A. Vyshnepolskii, have written that the Kara, Laptev, East Siberian, and Chukchi Seas must all be considered as closed, or "historic," seas or bays.[96] In 1967, the Soviet Ministry of Foreign Affairs advised the United States that passage of U.S. Coast Guard icebreakers through the Vilkitsky Straits, between the Kara and Laptev Seas, would be a violation of Soviet frontiers. It has been speculated that the Soviet authorities in this instance considered the icebreakers to be warships.[97]

THE SECURITY CONTROVERSY IN ASIA

The Sea of Okhotsk. Soviet maritime policies with respect to her Pacific coast have been equally restrictive. In 1956, the Soviet Union, by unilateral action, closed the Sea of Okhotsk behind an artificial frontier known as the Bulganin Line.[98] This line runs from the Kamchatka Peninsula, along the Kuriles Island chain, and thence to Sakhalin. Soviet jurists consider that the Okhotsk Sea is both a closed and historic sea and would prohibit foreign

---

93 Lakhtine, "Rights over the Arctic," p. 709.
94 Butler, *The Law of Soviet Territorial Waters*, p. 80, citing Korovin, "SSSR i poliarnye zemli" (The USSR and Polar Lands), 1926 *Sovetskoe pravo* (*Soviet Law*), No. 3, p. 46.
95 *Ibid.*, pp. 81–83, citing Barabolya, *Manual of International Maritime Law*, pp. 288–289.
96 Whiteman, *Digest*, pp. 240–241, citing Nikolaev, *Problema territorialnykh vod v mezhdunarodnom prave* (*The Problem of Territorial Waters in International Law*), pp. 207–208; and Butler, *The Law of Soviet Territorial Waters*, pp. 81–82, citing Vyshnepolskii, "K probleme provogo rezhim arkticheskoi oblasti," (On the Problem of the Legal Regime of the Arctic Region), *Sovetskoe gosudarstvo i pravo*, No. 7, 1952, pp. 36–45.
97 Pharand, "Soviet Union Warns United States Against Use of Northeast Passage," pp. 927, 931, citing U.S. State Department Statement of August 31, 1967.
98 Guill, "The Regimen of the Seas," p. 1317.

warships from navigating it,[99] in spite of the fact that its southern reaches wash the shores of Japan. When a U.S. flag airliner misnavigated across the Bulganin Line on July 1, 1968, Soviet fighters forced it to land at the Soviet air base on Iturup Island in the Kuriles. The airliner was released following a United States apology.[100]

Peter the Great Bay. In 1957 the Soviet Union similarly closed Peter the Great Bay, a shallow indentation of the Sea of Japan, and the site of the port of Vladivostok. The Decree of July 21, 1957 proclaimed that

> Navigation of foreign ships as well as flights of foreign planes in the region of Peter the Great Bay can take place only by permission of the competent authorities of the USSR. . . .[101]

The decree defined the closed portion of the bay as those waters within a cape-to-cape baseline 115 miles long. Peter the Great Bay does not have the configuration of a bay; it does not even come close to satisfying the United Nations definition of a bay, and by no stretch of the imagination can it be conceived of as an "historic bay." This was essentially the tenor of the notes of protest delivered by the Japanese and the Americans, and yet the Soviet Union replied that she did in fact regard the Bay as "historic."[102]

Gulf of Aqaba dispute. The Gulf of Aqaba is 98 miles long and is from seven to 15 miles wide. It is bounded on the west by Egypt, on the north by Israel and Jordan, and on the east by Saudi Arabia. The Strait of Tiran, four miles wide, connects the Gulf with the Red Sea. The Gulf gives to Israel a sea access to the Orient, and to Jordan, her only sea access.

Applying the three-mile limit to the Gulf of Aqaba leaves a high seas passage from end to end; even a six-mile limit leaves some high seas areas in the gulf. However, under the traditional rules of international law, the overriding consideration is the international nature of the body of water. All four littoral states would be free to transit the gulf; and the Strait of Tiran would be regarded as an international strait. Yet the events since 1955 make it appear that traditional rules of international law have become irrelevant in the Gulf of Aqaba, having been replaced by rules of sheer military force.

In 1955, Egypt, replying to an inquiry by the International Law Commission,

---

99   Butler, The Law of Soviet Territorial Waters, p. 79. For a strategic appraisal of the Sea of Okhotsk, see Swarztrauber, "Alaska and Siberia: A Strategic Analysis," pp. 138–165.

100   "Chartered Airliner on a Flight From U.S. May Have Strayed," news item in *New York Times,* July 1, 1968, p. 1; and "U.S. Concedes Intrusion," news item in *New York Times,* July 4, 1968, p. 2.

101   Whiteman, *Digest,* pp. 250–251.

102   Japanese note of July 26, 1957; United States note of August 12, 1957; Soviet note of January 7, 1958, in *ibid.,* pp. 251–256.

had expressed its strong preference for a six-mile territorial sea. A six-mile limit, the Egyptian letter read, would

> . . . safeguard the principle of the freedom of the open sea, over which the international law forbids the acquisition of sovereignty.[103]

"Freedom of the open sea for everyone," the letter may well have gone on to say, "except for Israel." For, that same year President Nassar took steps to deny the Gulf of Aqaba to Israel. In September, 1955, Egypt put into effect a regulation requiring all ships desiring to enter the gulf of obtain a permit from the Regional Boycotting Office for Israel.[104] In 1956, Israel invaded Egypt and occupied Sharm el-Sheikh, on the Egyptian shore of the Tiran Strait. Israeli forces did not withdraw until 1957, when it was agreed that a United Nations Emergency Force would be stationed at Sharm el-Sheikh, thus guaranteeing Israel's access to the gulf.[105]

An intense build-up of Israeli port facilities and oil pipelines on the Gulf of Aqaba, occasioned by President Nassar's closure of the Suez Canal to Israeli ships, soon provided an alternate Israeli route between the Mediterranean and the Red Seas, adding fuel to the heated Israeli-Arab dispute. On October 2, 1957, the Saudi representative to the United Nations addressed the General Assembly:

> The Gulf of Aqaba is a national inland waterway, subject to absolute Arab sovereignty. . . . The Gulf is so narrow that the territorial areas of the littoral States are bound to overlap among themselves. . . .
> . . . [T]he Gulf of Aqaba is of the category of historical gulfs that fall outside the sphere of international law. The Gulf is the historical route to the holy places in Mecca. . . .
> Israel . . . has no right to any part of the Gulf.[106]

The Arab states argue that the Gulf of Aqaba, like the Gulf of Fonseca (see pp. 121–23), consists of territorial waters of the littoral states only, denying that Israel has any legitimate right to be considered one of the littoral states, on the grounds that Israel forcibly and illegally occupied her present northern Gulf coast in 1949. Israel argues that she is legally a littoral state according to the original partition plan of 1947 and the Israel-Jordan armistice of 1949.

Supplementing his legal argument, the Saudi delegate rejected a proposal to submit the issue to the International Court of Justice on religious grounds!

103 Letter from the permanent United Nations delegate from Egypt to the International Law Commission, dated May 4, 1955, annexed to "Report of the Seventh Session," in United Nations, *Yearbook of the International Law Commission 1955*, vol. II, p. 45.
104 Whiteman, *Digest*, p. 470, quoting "Egyptian Circular to Shipping No. 4," of September 4, 1955.
105 *Ibid.*, pp. 472–475.
106 Selak, Jr., "A Consideration of the Legal Status of the Gulf of Aqaba," p. 679, quoting from United Nations, *Official Records*, 12th Session, 697th Plenary Meeting, October 2, 1957, p. 233.

As Keeper of the Holy Places, His Majesty King Saud is not prepared to expose to question any matter touching upon the Holy shrines and the free passage of pilgrims to Mecca.[107]

Finally, he rejected the suggestion that Israeli ships be granted innocent passage in the gulf with his argument that the gulf was internal waters where the right of innocent passage does not exist. Then, in 1958, presumably to strengthen their legal position, both Saudi Arabia and Egypt adopted the twelve-mile limit of territorial seas.[108]

The dispute over the Gulf of Aqaba lay dormant for ten years. Then in May 1967 the United Nations Emergency Force was withdrawn.[109] Egyptian troops immediately occupied the positions at Sharm el-Sheikh, vacated by the U.N. troops, and on May 22, President Nassar announced that the Gulf of Aqaba would be closed to Israeli ships and to any others carrying strategic goods to Israel.[110] In an announcement the next day, Egypt declared:

There is a state of war between us and Israel. International law gives us the right to ban the passage of Israeli ships through our territorial waters. U.S. and British talk about innocent passage is unacceptable in a state of war.[111]

The "state of war" of which Egypt spoke became a "shooting war" less than two weeks later when Israel again invaded Egypt, Jordan, and Syria in what became well-known as the Six-Day War. Again Israel occupied Sharm el-Sheikh, but this time she did not withdraw. At the time of this publication, Israel forces remain there to insure access to the Gulf of Aqaba.

North Korea. Although North Korea has apparently not made a formal declaration as to the extent of her territorial sea, both the United States and the Soviet Union attribute to her a twelve-mile limit. (See page 172.) But events of the late 1960s indicate that North Korea intends, obviously in the name of national security, to exercise her jurisdiction beyond twelve miles. The USS *Pueblo* was seized by North Korean naval units on January 23, 1968, in the Sea of Japan, between 15 and 16[112] miles from the North Korean coast while engaged in an electronic surveillance mission there. North Korea rejected U.S. demands for the immediate return of the ship and crew, claiming that the *Pueblo* had committed "intolerable provocations" and charged that

107   *Ibid.*
108   Saudi Arabia, "Decree No. 33 Defining the Territorial Waters of the Kingdom," 16 February 1958, in United Nations, *Supplement to the Laws and Regulations on the Regime of the High Seas (Vols. I and II) and Laws Concerning the Nationality of Ships,* pp. 29–30; and Whiteman, *Digest,* p. 32.
109   "Issues Before the 22nd General Assembly" (Middle East), *International Conciliation* No. 564, Sept., 1954, pp. 14–16.
110   *Ibid.,* p. 16, citing *New York Times,* May. 23, 1967.
111   Salans, "Gulf of Aqaba and Strait of Tiran—Troubled Waters," p. 60, quoting Egyptian announcement of May 23, 1967.
112   Statement by Commander Lloyd M. Bucher, Commanding Officer, *USS Pueblo,* December 23, 1968, in "Pueblo Captain Tells His Story of Capture—and Captivity," *U.S. News and World Report,* January 6, 1969, p. 30.

the ship had "illegally infiltrated into North Korean waters on an espionage mission."[113] The following day, the North Korean Communist Party newspaper described the North Korean action as a "proper self-defense measure" and warned that if there were a repetition of such "provocation," North Korea would "strongly punish the aggressor," adding:

> The criminals who encroach upon other's sovereignty and commit provocative acts must receive deserving punishment.
> These criminals must be punished by law.[114]

The *Pueblo's* commanding officer, Lloyd Bucher, stated that his ship had never approached the North Korean coast closer than 13 miles, in compliance with the orders he had been given,[115] ruling out the application of the right of hot pursuit.

Further evidence that North Korea considered it her right to exercise peacetime security measures beyond twelve miles came on April 15, 1969, when North Korean air forces shot down an unarmed United States EC-121 reconnaissance aircraft over the Sea of Japan some 90 miles from the North Korean coast. The United States protest stated:

> The aircraft commander was under orders to maintain a distance of 50 nautical miles from the coast of North Korea. All evidence confirms that the plane remained far outside your claimed territorial airspace.[116]

The several situations, arguments, and incidents cited in this chapter by no means represent the complete list. They have been selected and included to demonstrate the scope and degree of deterioration of international agreement on the extent and nature of territorial waters that occurred in the years following World War II. Not only did states abandon the three-mile practice in large numbers, but there was also a tendency to reinterpret liberally, and unilaterally in some cases, the rights that coastal states enjoyed in their territorial sea. Also during this period there did occur a major effort to resolve the differences concerning the territorial sea, and to fix its extent and define its nature. This took place in 1958 and 1960 at the United Nations Geneva Conferences on the Law of the Sea. Some consider this effort also as the last major attempt by the traditional maritime powers to salvage what they could of the three-mile limit. The United Nations Conferences will be examined in the following chapter.

113 Statement by Major General Pak Chung-Kuk, senior North Korean delegate to the United Nations Command, Panmunjom, January 24, 1968, in "North Korea Rejects U.S. Demand For Seized Navy Ship's Return," news item in *San Diego Union*, January 24, 1968, pp. A1–A2.

114 "Ready for U.S. Retaliation, N. Korea Says," news item in *San Diego Union*, January 26, 1968, p. A1, citing *Rodong Shinmoon*, January 26, 1968.

115 "Pueblo Captain Tells His Story . . . ," *loc. cit.;* and Bucher, *Bucher: My Story*, pp. 180–181, 420–421, quoting U.S. Navy Task Force 96 Sailing order, USS *Pueblo*, 5 Jan. 1968.

116 Department of State, Press Release No. 87 of April 17, 1969, quoting the text of the statement by Major General James B. Knapp, U.S.A.F., at the 290th meeting of the Military Armistice Commission, Panmunjom, Korea, April 17, 1969.

CHAPTER 12

Role of the United Nations

At first glance, the efforts of the United Nations to codify the law of territorial waters in 1958 and 1960 appear painfully analogous to those of the League of Nations three decades earlier. There was a significant difference however; the League effort had assumed that there was wide consensus among the states and that it would be essentially a matter of reducing that consensus to suitable language, whereas the United Nations effort was an attempt to reach agreement where there was admittedly little. Another difference lay in the fact that the League of Nations had to create its Committee of Experts to prepare for the Hague Conference, whereas the United Nations was able to call upon its International Law Commission, a permanently constituted body, to lay the groundwork for the Geneva Conference.

Contribution of the International Law Commission

The Charter of the United Nations requires the General Assembly to ". . . initiate studies and make recommendations for the purpose of . . . encouraging the progressive development of international law and its codification. . . ."[1] Pursuant to this obligation, the General Assembly established the International Law Commission during its second session in 1947,[2] and elected fifteen members to the commission during its third session in 1948. Members were chosen from Panama, Brazil, U.K., Mexico, Netherlands, China, U.S.A., Syria, U.S.S.R., India, Sweden, France, Greece, Colombia, and Czechoslovakia. The first chairman was the American publicist, Manley O. Hudson.[3] The commission met for its first session at Lake Success, New York, in April, 1949.

---

1 Article 13.1.a., Goodrich and Hambro, *Charter of the United Nations*, p. 101.
2 United Nations General Assembly Resolution 174 (II), November 21, 1947, United Nations, *Yearbook of the International Law Commission, 1949*, p. 278, citing *Official Records of the General Assembly, Second Session, Resolutions*, p. 105.
3 *Ibid.*

In compliance with its statute which required the commission to ". . . survey the whole field of international law with a view to selecting topics for codification,"[4] fourteen topics were selected, among which were included "the high seas" and "territorial waters." First priority was given to the high seas; Mr. J. P. A. François of the Netherlands, was named rapporteur. Study was undertaken during the second (1950) and third (1951) sessions leading to draft articles on the continental shelf, fisheries, and the contiguous zone. At the third session, it was also decided to initiate work on the topic of territorial waters, Mr. François being appointed special rapporteur for this closely related study.[5] During the several years leading up to the 1958 Conference, Mr. François served in both capacities and his name became intimately associated with the law of the sea.

THE FRANÇOIS REPORTS

In his first report on the regime of the territorial sea, presented to the fourth session of the International Law Commission in 1952, François included a compilation of the various limits of territorial waters claimed by states, as evidenced by state legislation then in effect. He also included a proposed draft article:

Limits of the Territorial Sea
Article 4—Breadth
The breadth of the zone of sea designated in the first article [the territorial sea] will be fixed by the littoral State, but it cannot exceed six nautical miles.[6]

François felt it necessary to comment on his decision to propose a limit of six miles. He cited the failure of the 1930 Hague Conference to agree on three miles and the great diversity of practice and opinion existing in 1952 as shown by his compilation.[7]

The following year, Francois presented his second report to the fifth session (1953) of the commission. This report was more extensive than the first and included a revised draft position on the extent of the territorial sea:

Article 4—Breadth
The breadth of the territorial sea will be fixed by the littoral State, but it cannot exceed 12 nautical miles from the baseline of the territorial sea. . . .
Exclusive fishing rights may not be claimed by the littoral State for its nationals beyond a distance of 3 nautical miles, measured from the baseline of the territorial sea. Beyond this limit of three miles, fishing in the terri-

4 Ibid., p. 279.
5 United Nations, Yearbook of the International Law Commission, 1951, vol. II, p. 140.
6 United Nations, Yearbook of the International Law Commission, 1952, vol. II, p. 28, reproducing François' Project de règlement [de la mer territoriale], included in his "Premier rapport," Translation by the author.
7 Ibid., pp. 28–30.

torial sea may be subjected by the littoral State to regulations having the sole purpose of protecting the resources of the sea. No discrimination must be made to the detriment of the nationals of any foreign States.[8]

Something of the frustration that must have faced François in searching for a suitable compromise solution is revealed in the tortuous wording of this almost ambiguous draft. The commission did not approve the draft but it appointed a group of experts to assist François. The experts were from Sweden, the United States, France, the United Kingdom, and the Netherlands.[9]

A third report was prepared by François reflecting the observations of the experts and containing an even more complex draft article on the breadth of the territorial sea:

Article 4
Breadth of the territorial sea

1. The breadth of the territorial sea will be 3 nautical miles measured from its baseline.
2. However, the littoral State is authorized to extend the territorial sea up to a maximum of twelve miles from the baseline, subject to the following conditions:[10]

[The conditions provided for free passage throughout the territorial sea, nondiscriminatory fishery conservation regulations, and conciliation or arbitration in the event of disputes.]

PROVISIONAL ARTICLES CONCERNING THE REGIME OF THE TERRITORIAL SEA

All three François reports were used as the basis for plenary discussions on the territorial sea during the International Law Commission's sixth (1954) session. But unable to agree on three, four, six, or twelve miles, the commission submitted to the General Assembly "Provisional Articles Concerning the Regime of the Territorial sea," which included:

Limits of the Territorial Sea
Article 3
Breadth of the territorial sea
(Postponed)[11]

The Provisional Articles were circulated to the member governments for comment. Only eighteen replies were received; the Soviet Union was conspicuous by its silence. The United States replied:

> Among the articles for which no text has yet been drafted is Article 3 concerning the breadth of the territorial sea. With respect to this Article,

8 United Nations, *Yearbook of the International Law Commission, 1953*, vol. II, p. 59, reproducing "Deuxième rapport de M. J. P. A. François, rapporteur spécial, 19 février 1953." Translation by the author.

9 United Nations, *Yearbook of the International Law Commission, 1954*, vol. II, p. 152.

10 *Ibid.*, p. 2, reproducing "Troisième rapport de J. P. A. François, rapporteur spécial, 4 fevrier 1954." Translation by the author.

11 *Ibid.*, p. 154.

the Commission requested views and suggestions which might help it to formulate a concrete proposal. . . .

That the breadth of the territorial sea should remain fixed at three miles is without any question the proposal most consistent with the principle of freedom of the seas. The three-mile limit is the greatest breadth of territorial waters on which there has ever been anything like common agreement. Everyone is now in agreement that the coastal State is entitled to a territorial sea to that distance from its shores. There is no agreement on anything more.[12]

Three states favored three miles: U.S., U.K., and the Netherlands; Sweden, four miles; Yugoslavia, South Africa, Haiti and Egypt, six miles; Mexico, nine miles; India, 12 miles; El Salvador, 200 miles; Philippines, the archipelago; Thailand, Norway, Australia, Brazil, Belgium, and Iceland reserved comment.

DRAFT ARTICLES ON THE REGIME OF THE TERRITORIAL SEA

The response to the provisional articles not only had been unenthusiastic, but also most of those states that did reply made guarded, general statements, providing little in the way of specific material for the commission to use. Reflecting this inconclusive response, the commission adopted a set of "Draft Articles on the Regime of the Territorial Sea" at its seventh session (1955) that included the following:

Article 3
Breadth of the territorial sea
1. The Commission recognizes that international practice is not uniform as regards the traditional limitation of the territorial sea to three miles.
2. The Commission considers that international law does not justify an extension of the territorial sea beyond twelve miles.
3. The Commission, without taking any decisions as to the breadth of the territorial sea within that limit, considers that international law does not require States to recognize a breadth beyond three miles.[13]

The commission forwarded the draft articles to the General Assembly, asking that the governments again be requested for comments, especially on Article 3, in order that a more detailed and useful codification document could be prepared.

This time, twenty-five states commented. But again, the replies were very cautious, diverse, and indefinite. Most replying states did not commit themselves to a specific width of territorial waters, apparently leaving themselves maneuvering room for any subsequent negotiations. The Belgian reply was typical:

[Provided adequate safeguards are taken to protect fishing interests of littoral states] . . . [i]t will then be possible, by means of international

12 United Nations, *Yearbook of the International Law Commission, 1955*, vol. II, pp. 59–60.
13 *Ibid.*, p. 35.

agreements, to arrive at the solution of fixing a limit other than the three-mile limit, provided that it is less than twelve miles.[14]

Still there was no reply fom the Soviet Union. The Soviet member of the International Law Commission, Mr. S. B. Krylov, who had suggested that Article 3 read, "The breadth of the territorial sea shall be determined by the national legislation of each coastal State,"[15] reserved "the right to refer to the question later."[16]

DRAFT CONVENTION ON THE LAW OF THE SEA

The twenty-five replies were evaluated, incorporated where practicable, and a draft convention was drawn up and submitted to the United Nations General Assembly following the International Law Commission's eighth session in 1956. The draft article on the width of the territorial sea pessimistically read as follows:

Breadth of the territorial sea
Article 3
1. The Commission recognizes that international practice is not uniform as regards the delimitation of the territorial sea.
2. The Commission considers that international law does not permit an extension of the territorial sea beyond twelve miles.
3. The Commission, without taking any decision as to the breadth of the territorial sea within that limit notes, on the one hand, that many States have fixed a breadth greater than three miles, and on the other hand, that many States do not recognize such a breadth when that of their own territorial sea is less.
4. The Commission considers that the breadth of the territorial sea should be fixed by an international conference.[17]

The General Assembly, acting on the report of the commission, resolved in 1957 to convene an international conference of plenipotentiaries to consider further the draft convention prepared by the commission.[18]

The conference convened in Geneva the following year. As bases for discussion, the conference delegates had available to them the draft convention, the François reports, the recorded deliberations of the International Law Commission, and the replies of the several governments. Moreover, at the instigation of the International Law Commission, several volumes were prepared in time

14 United Nations, *Yearbook of the International Law Commission, 1956*, p. 39.
15 United Nations, *Yearbook of the International Law Commission, 1955*, vol. I, p. 156.
16 United Nations, *Yearbook of the International Law Commission, 1956*, vol. I, p. 165.
17 *Ibid.*, vol. II, p. 256.
18 United Nations General Assembly Resolution 1105 (XI), February 21, 1957, reproduced in United Nations, *General Assembly Official Records, Twelfth Session*, Supplement No. 1, pp. 120–121.

Table 11
Territorial Sea Claims of Selected States, Showing
the Diversity of International Practice in 1958*

State	Extent of Territorial Sea Claimed
Australia	3 miles
Finland	4 miles
Cambodia	5 miles
India	6 miles
Mexico	9 miles
Albania	10 miles
Ethiopia	12 miles
Chile	50 kilometers
El Salvador	200 miles
Korea	Continental Shelf
West Germany	In accordance with international law

* From the Society of Comparative Legislation and International Law, *The Law of the Sea*, pp. 36–42.

for the conference by the United Nations Secretariat on the *Laws and Regulations on the Regime of the High Seas* and . . . *of the Territorial Sea*, which have been cited extensively in this book. Following the Geneva Conferences, the commission did very little more work on territorial waters. A study was initiated in 1960 concerning the "Juridical Regime of Historic Waters, including Historic Bays," and was published in 1964.[19] The remainder of this chapter will be devoted to the Geneva Conferences.

THE 1958 UNITED NATIONS CONFERENCE ON THE LAW OF THE SEA

When the United Nations Conference opened in February, 1958, it faced an almost staggering range of claims. As tabulated in Table 11, they varied between three and two hundred miles and included such cryptic pronouncements as West Germany's "in accordance with international law." It is a monotonous process to read through the official records of the First Committee (Territorial Sea and Contiguous Zone), observing that the delegates, in most cases, repeated over and over their initial stands, rewording the same arguments. There were, it is true, some most interesting proposals, but by and large, after three months the delegates were no closer to an agreement on the extent of the territorial sea than they were at the beginning.

Out of the scores of proposals submitted, only a few need be mentioned

19 United Nations, *Yearbook of the International Law Commission, 1962*, vol. II, pp. 1–26.

in this study, because most of the proposals and discussions revolved around three-, six-, and twelve-mile limits and variations thereon. The United States at first proposed a three-mile limit with an exclusive fishing zone out to twelve miles. Canada and Greece, mindful of their archipelagos, separately proposed a three-mile limit drawn around baselines. Six-mile limits were proposed by Ceylon, Italy, and Sweden. Ceylon's proposal included the use of straight baselines. Colombia proposed a twelve-mile limit.[20]

Variations on the twelve-mile limit were also suggested by the Soviet Union and jointly by several states. The Soviet Union proposed that "[e]ach State shall determine the breadth of its territorial waters . . . within the limits . . . of three to twelve miles. . . ." A joint Indian-Mexican proposal submitted in March read almost the same, providing for any limit up to twelve miles.[21] Then the following month eight countries—Burma, Colombia, Indonesia, Mexico, Morocco, Saudi Arabia, Egypt, and Venezuela—jointly sponsored the so-called "eight power" proposal which was worded identically to the Indian-Mexican proposal:

> Every State is entitled to fix the breadth of its territorial sea up to a limit of twelve nautical miles measured from the baseline which may be applicable. . . ."[22]

While this optional limit feature seemed attractive to some as a possible compromise, it failed on the practical and logical grounds that it would eventually force all states to claim the maximum limit. Otherwise fishermen of State A, for example, which claimed twelve miles, might fish up to the three-mile limit of State B, while fishermen from State B would not enjoy the same reciprocal advantage.

Peru, "spokesman" for the CEP states, proposed that:

> Each State is competent to fix its territorial sea within reasonable limits. . . .
> The States shall endeavor to fix the breadth of the territorial sea preferably by regional agreements."[23]

20 United Nations, *Conference on the Law of the Sea*, vol. III, p. 249, U.S. proposal, Document A/CONF. 13/C.1/L.140 of 1 April 1958; p. 232, Canadian proposal, Document A/CONF. 13/C.1/L.77/Rev. 1 of 29 March 1958; p. 248, Greek proposal, Document A/CONF. 13/C.1/L.136 of 1 April 1958; p. 212, Swedish proposal, Document A/CONF. 13/C.1/L.4 of 10 March 1958; p. 248, Italian proposal, Document A/CONF. 13/C.1/L.137 of 1 April 1958; p. 244, Ceylonese proposal, Document A/CONF. 13/C.1/L.118 of 1 April 1958; p. 233, Colombian proposal, Document A/CONF. 13/C.1/L.82 and Corr. 1 of 31 March 1958.
21 *Ibid.*, p. 233, Soviet proposal, Document A/CONF. 13/C.1/L.80 of 31 March 1958; Indian-Mexican proposal, Document A/CONF. 13/C.1/L.79 of 29 March 1958.
22 United Nations, *Conference on the Law of the Sea*, vol. II, p. 128, Document A/CONF. 13/L.34 of 25 April 1958.
23 United Nations, *Conference on the Law of the Sea*, vol. III, p. 247, Peruvian proposal, Document A/CONF. 13/C.1/L.133 of 1 April 1958 with Addendum 1 of 15 April 1958.

As the conference went on, both the United States and the United Kingdom recognized the futility of pressing their position on the three-mile limit. The movement for a greater territorial sea had developed too much momentum. In order to salvage what they could, and to prevent adoption by the conference of a twelve-mile limit, the United States and the United Kingdom decided to attempt a compromise at six miles. The British proposed a six-mile limit with a right of innocent passage for aircraft and vessels, including warships, between three and six miles.[24] The U.S. proposal provided for a territorial sea of six miles and exclusive fishing rights for another six miles, with the proviso that foreign states whose nationals had traditionally fished those coastal waters (for at least the previous five years) could continue to do so, but only in the outer six-mile belt.[25] This latter proviso was unacceptable to Canada, who tabled a similar proposal for a six-mile territorial sea and an additional six-mile exclusive fishing zone, but without any qualifications.

None of the many proposals obtained the necessary two-thirds majority vote. The U.S. "six and six" proposal came closest, polling forty-five out of the eighty-six possible votes, seven shy of the required number.[26]

CONVENTION ON THE TERRITORIAL SEA AND THE CONTIGUOUS ZONE

In plenary session, the conference adopted the Convention on the Territorial Sea and Contiguous Zone, which included many long-needed clarifications concerning the international law of territorial seas. Conspicuous by its absence, of course, was an article establishing the breadth of the territorial sea. Several very useful articles on the delimitation of the territorial sea were adopted and will be discussed in a subsequent section.

Innocent passage. The convention embodies a comprehensive codification of the rules concerning the right of innocent passage, including the following:

Article 14

1. Subject to the provisions of these articles, ships of all States, whether coastal or not, shall enjoy the right of innocent passage through the territorial sea. . . .

4. Passage is innocent so long as it is not prejudicial to the peace, good order or security of the coastal state. . . .

5. Passage of foreign fishing vessels shall not be considered innocent if they do not observe such laws and regulations as the coastal State may make and publish in order to prevent these vessels from fishing in the territorial sea.

6. Submarines are required to navigate on the surface and to show their flag. . . .

---

24 *Ibid.,* pp. 247–248, U.K. proposal, Document A/CONF. 13/C.1/L.134 of 1 April 1958.
25 *Ibid.,* pp. 253–254, U.S. proposal, Document A/CONF. 13/C.1/L.159/Rev. 2 of 19 April 1958; Dean, "The Geneva Conference on the Law of the Sea: What Was Accomplished," pp. 614–616.
26 Dean, "The Geneva Conference on the Law of the Sea . . . ," *loc. cit.*

Article 15

1. The coastal State must not hamper innocent passage through the
territorial sea. . . .

Article 16

4. There shall be no suspension of the innocent passage of foreign ships
through straits which are used for international navigation between one
part of the high seas and another. . . .

Article 17

Foreign ships exercising the right of innocent passage shall comply with
the laws and regulations enacted by the coastal State in conformity with
these articles and other rules of international law. . . .

Article 23

If any warship does not comply with the regulations of the coastal State
concerning passage through the territorial sea and disregards any request for
compliance which is made to it, the coastal State may require the warship
to leave the territorial sea.[27]

The contiguous zone. The conference also codified the concept of the contiguous zone, popularized by the Hague Conference of 1930:

Article 24

1. In a zone of the high seas contiguous to its territorial sea, the coastal
State may exercise the control necessary to:
   (a) Prevent infringement of its customs, fiscal, immigration or sanitary
       regulations within its territory or territorial sea;
   (b) Punish infringement of the above regulations committed within its
       territory or territorial sea.
2. The contiguous zone may not extend beyond twelve miles from the
baseline from which the breadth of the territorial sea is measured.[28]

Several of the lesser powers, notably Korea, Poland, and Yugoslavia, wished
to add "security" as one of the categories of competence in the contiguous
zone,[29] but their proposals could not muster sufficient support. It can only
be surmised that the major powers and a majority of the states did not see
a twelve-mile zone as sufficient to meet their security needs.

As late as 1955, Great Britain had held out against the doctrine of the
contiguous zone. In commenting on the International Law Commission's 1954
draft articles, Great Britain averred:

Her Majesty's Government have not themselves found it necessary to
claim a contiguous zone, and wish to place on record their emphatic opposition as a matter of principle to any increase, beyond limits already recognized, in the exercise of jurisdiction by coastal States over the waters off
their coasts. . . .[30]

27 United Nations, *Conference on the Law of the Sea,* vol. II, pp. 133–135. See Chapter
    11 for Soviet reservation.
28 *Ibid.,* p. 135.
29 United Nations, *Conference on the Law of the Sea,* vol. III, pp. 226, 232, 234.
30 United Nations, *Yearbook of the International Law Commission, 1955,* vol. II, p.
    57.

The British reply added that the only way Britain could accept an article establishing a contiguous zone would be on the condition that such an article be coupled ". . . with another article stating that the territorial waters of a State shall not extend more than three miles from the coast. . . ."[31] It must have been somewhat painful for the British to retreat from this position only five years later when they ratified, in March, 1960, the Convention of 1958, which included a twelve-mile contiguous zone but remained silent on the three-mile—or any—limit of territorial waters.

The Convention on the Territorial Sea and the Contiguous Zone went into effect on September 10, 1969, one month after the Dominican Republic deposited the required twenty-second ratification. As of January, 1972, forty states had ratified the Convention: Australia, Bulgaria, Cambodia, Czechoslovakia, Denmark, Dominican Republic, Fiji, Finland, Haiti, Hungary, Israel, Italy, Jamaica, Japan, Kenya, Malagasy Republic, Malawi, Malaysia, Malta, Mauritius, Mexico, Netherlands, Nigeria, Portugal, Romania, Senegal, Sierra Leone, South Africa, Spain, Swaziland, Switzerland, Thailand, Tonga, Trinidad and Tobago, Uganda, U.S.S.R., U.K., U.S.A., Venezuela, Yugoslavia. (The Byelorussian S.S.R. and Ukrainian S.S.R. also ratified the convention.)

OTHER CONVENTIONS

Fisheries. The several attempts to include a twelve-mile fishing limit in the Convention on the Territorial Sea and the Contiguous Zone failed. The delegates could not agree on a limit for exclusive fishing rights, inextricably entwined, as such a limit is, with the territorial sea issues. In the case of conservation of fisheries, however, a separate convention was drafted and adopted, the "Convention on Fishing and Conservation of the Living Resources of the High Seas."[32] It embodies an important feature of the 1945 Truman Proclamation, namely that conservation programs should be undertaken on a multilateral basis and should extend over the whole of the fishery. The convention does permit unilateral conservation action in cases where negotiations are unfruitful, and provides for settlement of conservation disputes by a special commission. The special commission must consider the dispute in terms of scientific evidence demonstrating the need for conservation measures.

High seas. Also adopted by the 1958 Conference was the "Convention on the High Seas." It relates to this study in that it provides that hot pursuit may be commenced in the contiguous zone as well as within territorial waters and may continue until the pursued ship reaches the territorial waters of its own country or that of a third state.[33]

31 *Ibid.*
32 United Nations, *Conference on the Law of the Sea,* vol. II, pp. 139–142, Document A/CONF. 13/L.54.
33 *Ibid.,* pp. 135–139, Document A/CONF. 13/L.53.

Continental shelf. Another product of the 1958 Conference was the "Convention on the Continental Shelf." It provides for the exploitation of the natural resources of the seabed and subsoil and the sedentary life on the seabed beyond the territorial sea ". . . to a depth of 200 meters or, beyond that limit, to where the depth of the superjacent waters admits of the exploitation of the natural resources. . . ."[34] Article 3, which rules out any claims of sovereignty over the shelf's superjacent waters or air space, implies that the Latin American 200-mile claims are illegal. The convention, which inherently discriminates against nonlittoral states as well as against states with narrow shelves, does not have the concurrence of the three Latin American CEP states, nor of others claiming wide seas.

The three Conventions went into effect on the dates indicated:

High Seas	September 30, 1962
Continental Shelf	June 10, 1964
Fisheries	March 20, 1966

THE 1960 UNITED NATIONS CONFERENCE ON THE LAW OF THE SEA

THE INTERCONFERENCE PERIOD

As the 1958 Conference adjourned, it adopted a resolution requesting the General Assembly to study the possibility of calling a second conference to consider the questions left unsettled, those of the territorial sea and fishing zones.[35] The General Assembly responded in the fall of 1958 and called for a new conference in 1960.[36]

At the time, a general understanding was reached in the General Assembly that governments should not take any action that might prejudice the success of the Second United Nations Conference. This notwithstanding, Iraq, Panama, Iran, Libya, and Iceland enacted twelve-mile legislation during the interval between the conferences.[37]

The interconference period was a busy period for the U.S. State Department. The 1958 Conference had ended with the satire of Dr. Bocobo, the Philippine delegate, who lamented the death of Mr. Three-Miles, who had served the international community so well and so long, and said that his heirs, Mr. Six-Miles and Mr. Twelve-Miles, were quarreling over his estate. This was not an unrealistic evaluation. The three-mile limit, while perhaps not dead, could no longer be considered a rule of international law; at best it could

34 *Ibid.*, pp. 142–143, Document A/CONF. 13/L.55.
35 Resolution of 27 April 1958, in United Nations, *Conference on the Law of the Sea*, vol. II, p. 145.
36 United Nations General Assembly Resolution 1307 (XIII), 10 December 1958, reproduced in United Nations, *Second United Nations Conference on the Law of the Sea*, p. xi.
37 Whiteman, *Digest of International Law*, vol. IV, pp. 117–118.

be described as the *de jure* practice of about one-third of the states of the world. The issue that would be central in the forthcoming 1960 Conference would be a test of strength between the U.S. six-mile proposal and the Soviet twelve-mile limit. So the United States sent teams of representatives from the Defense and State Departments to Asia, Europe, South America, and Africa to line up support for the "six-and-six" formula it would again table at Geneva.[38]

THE CONFERENCE PROPOSALS

When the Conference on the Law of the Sea opened at Geneva in March, 1960, the Soviets reintroduced their optional three- to twelve-mile limit, only this time with exclusive fishing rights to twelve miles. The most interesting proposal tabled was that of Mexico. It combined the optional feature of the Soviet proposal with a sliding-scale fishery limit, designed to reward states that chose narrow territorial seas by permitting them a greater exclusive fishing zone. If a state chose a territorial sea of three to six miles, it could enjoy exclusive fishing rights out to eighteen miles; if it chose a territorial sea of seven to nine miles, it could claim a fishing zone of fifteen miles; if it chose ten or eleven miles, its exclusive fishing rights would extend only to twelve miles.[39]

The "eighteen-power" proposal. Both the Soviet Union and Mexico withdrew their active support from their individually sponsored proposals in favor of the so-called "eighteen-power" proposal, termed by Mr. Arthur Dean, head of the U.S. delegation, as a "grave threat."[40] The "eighteen-power" proposal had the advantage of being sponsored by eighteen underdeveloped states, many of which were attempting to maintain a neutral position in the Cold War. Its provisions were almost verbatim the same as the Soviet proposal:

Article 1
Every State is entitled to fix the breadth of its territorial sea up to a limit of twelve nautical miles measured from the applicable baseline.
Article 2
When the breadth of its territorial sea is less than twelve nautical miles measured as above, a State is entitled to establish a fishing zone . . . to a limit of twelve nautical miles.[41]

38 Rubenstein, Codding, Hardy, and Powers, "How Wide the Territorial Sea," p. 68, 70–71.
39 United Nations, *Second Conference on the Law of the Sea*, p. 164, quoting Soviet proposal, Document A/CONF. 19/C.1/L.1 of 21 March 1960, and Mexican proposal, Document A/CONF. 19/C.1/L.2 of 21 March 1960.
40 Dean, "The Second Geneva Conference on the Law of the Sea: The Fight for Freedom of the Seas," p. 774.
41 United Nations, *Second Conference on the Law of the Sea*, pp. 165, proposal of Ethiopia, Ghana, Guinea, Indonesia, Iran, Iraq, Jordan, Lebanon, Libya, Mexico, Morocco, Philippines, Saudi Arabia, Sudan, Tunisia, United Arab Republic, Venezuela, and Yemen; Document A/CONF. 19/C.1/L.2/Rev. 1 of 11 April 1960.

This proposal was rejected by 39 votes to 36, with 13 abstentions.

The Canada-United States joint proposal. Both the United States and Canada resubmitted their six-mile proposals from the 1958 Conference, but withdrew them after they agreed on a joint proposal combining features of both:

> 1. A State is entitled to fix the breadth of its territorial sea up to a maximum of six nautical miles measured from the applicable baseline.
> 2. A State is entitled to establish a fishing zone contiguous to its territorial sea extending to a maximum limit of twelve nautical miles from the baseline. . . .
> 3. Any State whose vessels have made a practice of fishing in the outer six miles of the fishing zone . . . for . . . five years . . . may continue to do so for . . . ten years.[42]

This is the only proposal that received wide support at the conference. It was adopted in the committee of the whole by a vote of 43 to 33 with 12 abstentions. Under the rules of procedure adopted by the conference, substantive decisions required a two-thirds majority of the representatives present and voting.[43] In order to gather the additional support needed, the United States and Canada agreed to an amendment sponsored by Brazil, Cuba, and Uruguay, providing that:

> the coastal State has the faculty of claiming preferential fishing rights in any area of the high seas adjacent to its exclusive fishing zone when it is scientifically established that a special situation or condition makes the exploitation of the living resources of the high seas in that area of fundamental importance to the economic development of the coastal State or the feeding of its population.[44]

When the joint Canadian-U.S. proposal, as amended, came to the vote in plenary session, it received 54 affirmative votes, 28 negative votes, and 5 abstentions, one vote short of the required number:

> In favor—Argentina, Australia, Austria, Belgium, Bolivia, Brazil, Cameroon, Canada, Ceylon, China, Colombia, Costa Rica, Cuba, Denmark, Dominican Republic, Ethiopia, Finland, France, Ghana, Greece, Guatemala, Haiti, Holy See, Honduras, Ireland, Israel, Italy, Jordan, South Korea, Laos, Liberia, Luxembourg, Malaysia, Monaco, Netherlands, New Zealand, Nicaragua, Norway, Pakistan, Paraguay, Portugal, San Marino, South Africa, Spain, Sweden, Switzerland, Thailand, Tunisia, Turkey, U.S.A., U.K., Uruguay, Vietnam, West Germany.
> Against—Albania, Bulgaria, Burma, Byelorussian S.S.R., Chile, Czechoslovakia, Ecuador, Guinea, Hungary, Iceland, India, Indonesia, Iraq, Libya,

42 *Ibid.*, p. 169, proposal of Canada and United States, Document A/CONF. 19/C.1/L.10 of 8 April 1960.
43 *Ibid.*, p. xxx.
44 *Ibid.*, p. 173, Brazil, Cuba, and Uruguay proposal, Document A/CONF. 19/L.12 of 22 April 1960.

Mexico, Morocco, Panama, Peru, Poland, Romania, Saudi Arabia, Sudan, Ukrainian S.S.R., U.A.R., U.S.S.R., Venezuela, Yugoslavia, Yemen.
Abstaining—Cambodia, El Salvador, Iran, Japan, Philippines.[45]

Arthur Dean attributed this failure to a last-minute withdrawal of promised support by Japan, Ecuador, and Chile.[46] Japan abstained in the voting because of the Brazil-Cuba-Uruguay amendment, which she felt favored Korean fishing interests. Yet this was a vicious circle because Korea had insisted on the amendment as a prerequisite to her support! Chile had offered her support, provided the United States could agree to the Brazil-Cuba-Uruguay amendment, but subsequently withdrew her support, claiming she could not get Peru to release her from her 1952 and 1954 CEP commitments. (See pages 165 and 185.) Ecuador withdrew her promised support on the day of the voting after the United States refused to release her from the claims for seizures of tuna boats dating back to 1953. (See pages 184–86.) Dean remarked that if either Ecuador or Chile had merely abstained, the proposal would have carried.

Emotions were running high by the end of the conference and there were some last minute "sour grapes" on both sides. Just prior to the final vote, it appeared likely to the Russians that the joint Canadian-United States proposal would succeed. The Soviet delegate then denounced the conference rules of procedure and declared that whatever the outcome of the conference, the Soviet Union would adhere to the twelve-mile territorial sea.[47] After the final vote, Mr. Dean announced that since the compromise failed, the United States would continue to adhere to the three-mile limit. The six-mile proposal, he said, had been no more than an offer and that its nonacceptance left the preconference situation unchanged. His country was satisfied with the three-mile rule and would continue to regard it as established international law. Three miles, he added, was the only breadth on which there had ever been anything like common agreement, and there was no obligation on the part of states adhering to the three-mile rule to recognize claims of other states to a greater width.[48]

Later, Mr. Dean wrote:

> The U.S.-Canadian compromise "joint proposal" was sincerely designed to find a rule acceptable to the Conference, though admittedly at considerable expense to U.S. fishing interests.[49]

The conference had closed with no plans for a third attempt. And thus, for the third time since 1930, the representatives of the states of the world had been unable to reach agreement on the extent of the marginal sea. The cumulative debilitating effect of the two conferences on the three-mile limit is con-

45 Whiteman, *Digest*, p. 135.
46 Dean, "Second Geneva Conference," pp. 779–782.
47 *Ibid.*, p. 782.
48 United Nations, *Second Conference on the Law of the Sea*, pp. 33–34.
49 Dean, "Second Geneva Conference," p. 775.

sidered by this writer to be the fourth in the series of five major developments leading to the demise of the three-mile rule.

DELIMITATION OF THE TERRITORIAL SEA

The abject failure of the Geneva Conferences to reach agreement on a limit for the territorial sea tends to overshadow the remarkable progress made there in codifying the delimitation of the territorial sea. The matter of defining the baseline from which the territorial sea is measured had been quite controversial during the nineteenth century. For example, although the United States and Great Britain agreed on a three-mile limit, the two states could not agree on the baseline from which it was to be measured. The resulting North Atlantic fisheries dispute lasted almost a century.

THE LOW-WATER LINE

In documents of the eighteenth and early nineteenth centuries, the words "shore" and "coast" appeared frequently in connection with both the cannon-shot and three-mile measurements. Both terms were adequate under the cannon-shot rule because an exact baseline was irrelevant; the distance to seaward depended on the location and range of the cannon. But in measuring a belt of specific width, such as three or four miles, a more exact point of departure was needed. This is especially essential in certain areas where the rise and fall of tide is great, as in the Bay of Fundy. In several places there, there is well over a mile between the high-water and low-water lines; the range of spring tide is over 50 feet. An extreme example is found in the Bristol Channel estuaries such as that at Loughor, Wales, where the tidal flats are over five miles wide. In such an area, without a clearly defined baseline, laying off a three-mile limit could lead to obvious absurdities. A standard international practice developed during the nineteenth century—that of using the low-water line. The low-water line maximizes the extent of territorial sea for the littoral state. Table 12 indicates when the low-water mark or its equivalent first appeared in state documents of the maritime nations. It was adopted at least as early as 1812 in the case of the Kingdom of Denmark and Norway. By 1909, when it was adopted by Italy, it had been accepted in the practice of all the maritime states. The obvious consensus that had thus developed during the nineteenth century over the choice of the low-water mark has continued to the present. It was included in the *Bases of Discussion* for the 1930 Hague Conference:

Basis of Discussion No. 6
Subject to the provisions regarding bays and islands, the breadth of territorial waters is measured from the line of low-water mark along the entire coast.[50]

50 League of Nations, *Bases of Discussion*, p. 30.

Table 12
Adoption of the Principle of the Low-Water Line by the Maritime States, Showing
Year of Adoption and Terminology Used*

State	Year	Terminology Used
Argentina	1869	low-water mark
Belgium	1832	extreme land frontier
	1882	low-water mark
Chile	1855	low-water line
China	1899	line of low tide
Denmark and Norway	1812	". . . outermost islands or islets which are not over-flowed by the sea"
Denmark	1882	low-water mark
Ecuador	1857	low-water mark
El Salvador	1860	low-water mark
France	1839	low-water mark
Germany	1882	low-water mark
Great Britain	1839	low-water mark
Honduras	1880	low-water mark
Italy	1909	low-water mark
Japan	1870	". . . any part of the coast whatsoever . . ."
Mexico	1885	low-water mark
Netherlands	1882	low-water mark
Portugal	1885	low-water mark at neap tides
Russia	1893	extreme coast line at neap tides
Spain	1885	low-water mark at neap tides
Sweden	1871	". . . coasts which are not constantly submerged by the sea"
United States	1859	low-water mark

* From Crocker, *Marginal Sea*, pp. 486, 511–513, 519, 524, 601, 604–605, 618, 621, 627, and 652. The documents in the case of Argentina, Ecuador, El Salvador, and Honduras may be found in United Nations, *Laws and Regulations on the High Seas*, pp. 51, 67, 71, and 80.

The low-water line was formally codified in 1958 by the United Nations:

Article 3
Except where otherwise provided in these articles, the normal baseline for measuring the breadth of the territorial sea is the low-water line along the coast as marked on large-scale charts officially recognized by the coastal state.[51]

51 United Nations, *Conference on the Law of the Sea*, vol. II, *Plenary Meetings*, p. 132, quoting "Convention on the Territorial Sea and the Contiguous Zone," Document A/CONF. 13/L.52.

THE OUTER LIMIT OF THE TERRITORIAL SEA

Once the baseline is defined, there are essentially two ways to determine the seaward boundary of the territorial sea:[52]

1. The *trace parallele*, a line parallel to the general trend of the coast, following the sinuosities of the baseline.

2. The *courbe tangante*, or "envelope line," also referred to as the "arcs of circles line"; a line all points of which are precisely three miles (or any other width) from the nearest point of land.

The trace parallele method. Along a relatively straight and uninterrupted coast, there is no difficulty in utilizing the *trace parallele*. This system was the earliest, least sophisticated, and most expedient means to define the seaward boundary; it was generally implied in much of the writing and in many of the documents of the nineteenth century. It was expressly used in an 1893 Anglo-Russian document:

> Within a zone of ten marine miles following the sinuosities of the Russian coasts. . . .[53]

As late as 1909, the United States went on record as favoring this method. The United States, in the North Atlantic Fisheries Arbitration, contended that the marginal seas of three miles ". . . must be measured from low-water mark following the indentations of the coast."[54] This system runs into difficulties when the seaward boundary line must run around a point, a cape, or a cluster of coastal islands. A ship might be located three miles to seaward from the corresponding "parallel" point on the coast, but within two miles, e.g., of a protruding spit or an island.

The courbe tangante method. The *courbe tangante* method, on the other hand, solves the problem of points, islands, and otherwise irregular coasts. This line is constructed by striking arcs to seaward from every point on the coast, which results in a line, every point of which is at a distance equal to the marginal belt from the nearest point of land. For the navigator, this method assures him that if he is within three miles, say, from a point or islet, he is within territorial waters. Another advantage is that one, and only one, such line can be drawn from any given coast; this cannot be said of the *trace parallele*. The *courbe tangante* was utilized by Russia in her 1893

---

52 Boggs, "Delimitation of the Territorial Sea," p. 543.

53 Great Britain and Russia, "Draft Agreement Relative to the Seal Fisheries," April 30-May 12, 1893, reproduced in Crocker, *Marginal Sea*, p. 578.

54 United States Congress, Senate, *North Atlantic Coast Fisheries Arbitration*, vol. I, pp. 10, 248.

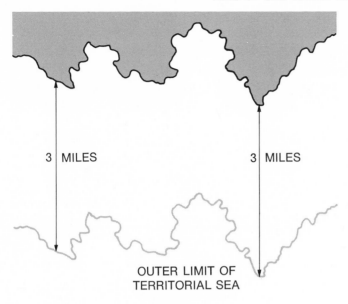

3 | MILES   3 | MILES

OUTER LIMIT OF
TERRITORIAL SEA

TRACE PARALLELE Application of Three-Mile Limit.

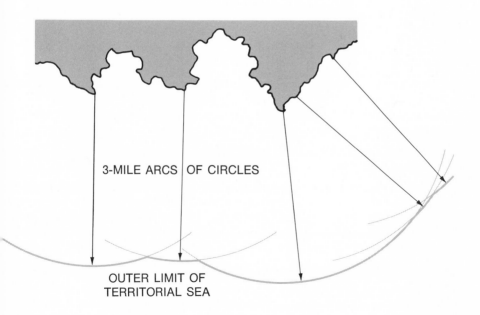

3-MILE ARCS | OF CIRCLES

OUTER LIMIT OF
TERRITORIAL SEA

COURBE TANGANTE Application of Three-Mile Limit.

"Instructions to Cruisers." This directive proclaimed that the extent of territorial waters along the Arctic coast included all waters within

> a radius of three marine or Italian miles from the extreme coast line at low tide or from the farthermost islands, rocks, stone banks, or reefs which project above the level of the water.[55]

The United States proposed this method at the 1930 Hague Convention:

> Except as otherwise provided in this Convention, the seaward limit of the territorial waters is the envelope of all arcs of circles having a radius of the three nautical miles drawn from all points on the coast (at whatever line of sea level is adopted in the charts of the coastal state), or from the seaward limit of those interior waters which are contiguous with the territorial waters.[56]

Although no action was taken on this recommendation at The Hague, it was again recommended by the International Law Commission in its 1956 Draft Convention and was approved by the United Nations Conference in 1958. The wording adopted was somewhat stilted inasmuch as no agreement had been reached on the extent of the territorial sea:

> Outer Limit of the Territorial Sea
> Article 6
> The outer limit of the territorial sea is the line every point of which is at a distance from the nearest point of the baseline equal to the breadth of the territorial sea.[57]

In view of its advantages, there was little opposition to this article. Moreover, use of this "arcs of circles" method tends to increase the area within the maritime belt by "straightening out" the seaward boundary. On a highly irregular "sawtooth"-type coast, it could easily increase the expanse of water in the marginal belt by fifty percent over that enclosed by a line following every sinuosity. On a straight coast, obviously there is no difference in the area enclosed by the two different systems.

BAYS

Another problem solved by the 1958 Geneva Conference was that of bays. Since the earliest days of the concept of territorial waters, publicists and states had considered the problem of bays but had never been able to agree on how to define them. In the early nineteenth century, it was generally agreed that a bay could be closed off as interior waters at the point where its mouth narrowed to a distance that equalled twice the extent of territorial waters.

55   Crocker, *Marginal Sea*, p. 621.
56   Boggs, "Delimitation of the Territorial Sea," p. 544.
57   United Nations, *Conference on the Law of the Sea*, vol. II, p. 133.

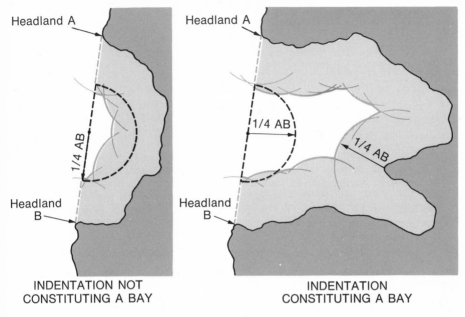

Delimitation of Bays: U.S. Proposal, 1930 Hague Conference

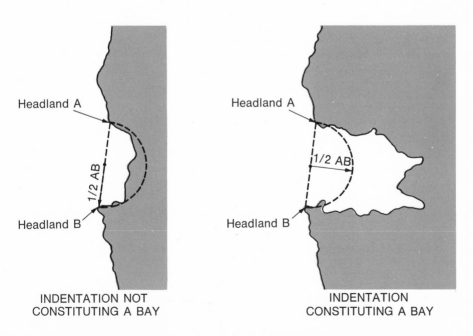

Delimitation of Bays: Article 7 of the 1958 U. N. Convention
on the Territorial Sea and the Contiguous Zone

(See page 93.) Later it was agreed that a bay could be closed off at the point where its mouth narrowed to ten miles. (See pages 65, 120–21.) But there was no agreement as to how a body of water must be configured, that is, in terms of breadth, width, area, length, mouth, and other factors, in order to be classified as a bay.

Hague Conference of 1930. Serious consideration was given to the problem of bays at the time of the 1930 Hague Convention. The Preparatory Committee "codified" the ten-mile bay baseline rule as Basis of Discussion No. 7:

> In the case of bays the coasts of which belong to a single State, the belt of territorial waters shall be measured from a straight line drawn across the opening of the bay. If the opening of the bay is more than ten miles wide, the line shall be drawn at the nearest point to the entrance at which the opening does not exceed ten miles.[58]

Aware that this did not define the term "bay," the committee observed:

> It is agreed that the base line constituted by the sinuosities of the coast should not be maintained for every bay. The suggested exception, however, contemplates, not a mere curvature of the shore line, but an indentation presenting the characteristic features of a bay, showing in particular a well-marked entrance and a certain proportion (which it will be for the Conference to fix) between the breadth of such entrance and the depth of the indentation.[59]

The United States rose to the occasion and proposed a rather wordy and complicated procedure for defining a bay with rules for incorporating certain bays into internal waters. Even though complex, it served as a first step in satisfying the long-standing requirement to define a bay for purposes of determination of baselines. The definitive criteria was to be applied to indentations which had openings of ten miles or less, and would separate bona fide bays from indentations too shallow to be considered bays, hence, too shallow to be incorporated into internal waters. Following application of the ten-mile baseline:

> (2) The envelope of all arcs of circles having a radius equal to one-fourth the length of the straight line across the bay or estuary shall then be drawn from all points on the coast of the mainland (at whatever line of sea-level is adopted on the charts of the coastal state) but such arcs of circles shall not be drawn around islands in connection with the process which is next described;
> (3) If the area enclosed within the straight line and the envelope of the arcs of circles exceeds the area of a semi-circle whose diameter is equal to one-half the length of the straight line across the bay or estuary, the waters of the bay or estuary inside of the straight line shall be regarded, for the

58 League of Nations, *Bases of Discussion,* p. 31.
59 *Ibid.*

purposes of this convention, as interior waters; otherwise they shall not be so regarded.[60] (See figure, page 223.)

The proposal went on to point out that if the bay was determined by this procedure to be internal waters, then the territorial sea would be measured to seaward from the ten-mile (or less) baseline across the bay entrance.

France also prepared a similarly complex system for defining a bay.[61] Because of the failure of the conference to agree on rules for measuring the marginal sea, the American and French proposed amendments also failed to be adopted.

International Law Commission. Next, the International Law Commission undertook to define the term "bay." In his third report, Mr. François attempted definition as follows:

Article 8
Bays

1. The waters of a bay will be considered as interior waters if the line drawn across the mouth does not exceed 10 miles.

2. The term "bay" as used in the first paragraph, is understood to be an indentation, the area of which is equal to or greater than the area of a semicircle having as its diameter the length of the line drawn across the mouth of the indentation. . . .[62]

This is believed to be the first formal appearance of the semicircle rule (as it later was called). The International Law Commission espoused it at once. Nevertheless, the commission felt moved to propose a baseline longer than the traditional ten miles in François' report:

As an experiment the Commission suggests a distance of twenty-five miles; thus, the length of the closing line will be slightly more than twice the permissible maximum width of the territorial sea as laid down in paragraph 2 of article 3. Since, firstly, historical bays, some of which are longer than twenty-five miles, do not come under this article and since, secondly, . . . it is possible that some extension of the closing line will be more readily accepted than a widening of the territorial sea in general.[63]

The semicircle bay definition with a twenty-five-mile baseline was circulated to the governments for comment. A plurality of the twenty-five replies objected to twenty-five miles as excessive and recommended either ten or twelve. Only Nationalist China agreed with 25 miles. Belgium, Brazil, Israel, Turkey, U.K. and U.S.A. suggested either ten or twelve miles. The other states were silent or noncommittal on the issue: Austria, Cambodia, Canada, Chile, Denmark,

60 League of Nations, *Final Act*, pp. 249–250.
61 *Ibid.*, p. 250.
62 United Nations, *Yearbook of the International Law Commission, 1954*, vol. II, p. 4, reproducing "Troisième rapport." Translation by the author.
63 United Nations, *Yearbook of the International Law Commission, 1955*, vol. II, p. 37.

Dominican Republic, Iceland, India, Ireland, Italy, Lebanon, Nepal, Netherlands, Norway, Phillipines, Sweden, South Africa, and Yugoslavia. As a result of this reaction, in its final draft convention, the commission included the semicircle bay definition with a fifteen-mile bay baseline.[64]

The 1958 Conference on the Law of the Sea. The semicircle rule was adopted and codified as international maritime law by the 1958 United Nations Conference on the Law of the Sea. After a century and a half of imprecision, doubt, and controversy on the issue of bays, clear rules were approved by which bays are defined and incorporated into the internal waters of a state. The conference made one important change to the International Law Commission draft convention, however—that of increasing the fifteen-mile bay baseline to twenty-four miles. (See figure, page 223.) Article 7 of the Convention on the Territorial Sea and the Contiguous Zone reads:

> 2. For the purposes of these articles, a bay is a well-marked indentation whose penetration is in such proportion to the width of its mouth as to contain landlocked waters and constitute more than a mere curvature of the coast. An indentation shall not, however, be regarded as a bay unless its area is as large as, or larger than, that of the semi-circle whose diameter is a line drawn across the mouth of that indentation.
> 3. For the purpose of measurement, the area of an indentation is that lying between the low-water mark around the shore of the indentation and a line joining the low-water mark of its natural entrance points. Where, because of the presence of islands, an indentation has more than one mouth, the semi-circle shall be drawn on a line as long as the sum total of the lengths of the lines across the different mouths. Islands within an indentation shall be included as if they were part of the water area of the indentation.
> 4. If the distance between the low-water marks of the natural entrance points of a bay does not exceed twenty-four miles, a closing line may be drawn between these two low-water marks, and the water enclosed thereby shall be considered as internal waters.
> 5. Where the distance between the low-water marks of the natural entrance points of a bay exceeds twenty-four miles, a straight baseline of twenty-four miles shall be drawn within the bay in such a manner as to enclose the maximum area of water that is possible with a line of that length.[65]

The twenty-four-mile line, or shorter as appropriate, drawn across the bay, becomes the baseline from which the territorial sea is measured. At the conference it had been suggested that the bay baseline should be double the width of the territorial sea—the early nineteenth century practice. The Soviet delegate proposed that a twenty-four-mile rule be adopted so as to put all states on the same footing with respect to bays, regardless of the breadth they

64 United Nations, *Yearbook of the International Law Commission, 1956*, vol. II, pp. 37–102, 257.
65 United Nations, *Conference on the Law of the Sea*, vol. II, p. 133.

chose for their territorial sea.[66] The adoption of this Soviet proposal—a bay closing line that was exactly double the Soviet twelve-mile territorial sea—was a clear victory for the Soviet Union and for the twelve-mile limit and at the same time a defeat for the advocates of the three-mile limit.

It is interesting to note that the twenty-four-mile rule makes irrelevant the "historic bay" status of such bays as Chesapeake, Delaware, Conception, and Fonseca, for they became *ipso facto* internal waters with the new rule. Monterey Bay in California became internal waters. But the new rule did not enhance the Canadian claim to "historic" status for Hudson Bay, whose entrance measures fifty miles, or for that matter, Norway's claim to Varanger Fjord (thirty miles). British writers, both before and after Canadian independence have asserted that Hudson Bay is internal waters.[67] The United States has disagreed. Thomas Balch challenged the Canadian view in his article, "Is Hudson Bay a Closed or an Open Sea?", and answered his own question in another article a year later entitled, "The Hudsonian Sea Is a Great Open Sea."[68] Nor is Russia's claim to Peter the Great Bay validated by the new rule. That body of water fails to qualify under both the twenty-four-mile and the semicircle critieria.

STRAIGHT BASELINES

Irregular coastlines. The use of straight baselines along irregular coastlines is relatively new. It was introduced by Norway in 1935, and in spite of strong British opposition, was "approved" by the International Court of Justice in 1951. (See pages 146–47, 188–89.) Because of the 1951 judicial precedent, this concept was readily approved by the 1958 Geneva Conference. François had included it in each of his three reports.[69] The International Law Commission had recommended such a provision in its draft convention. The 1958 Conference approved the following procedure:

Article 4

1. In localities where the coastline is deeply indented and cut into, or if there is a fringe of islands along the coast in its immediate vicinity, the method of straight baselines joining appropriate points may be employed in drawing the baseline from which the breadth of the territorial sea is measured.

2. The drawing of such baselines must not depart to any appreciable extent from the general direction of the coast. . . .

3. Baselines shall not be drawn to and from low-tide elevations. . . .[70]

66 United Nations, *Conference on the Law of the Sea*, vol. III, p. 32.
67 See Johnston, "Canada's Title to Hudson Bay and Hudson Strait," pp. 1–20.
68 Balch, "Is Hudson Bay a Closed or an Open Sea?" pp. 409–459; and "The Hudsonian Sea Is a Great Open Sea," pp. 546–565.
69 United Nations, *Yearbook of the International Law Commission, 1952*, vol. II, pp. 32–33, reproducing "Premier rapport"; *Yearbook of the International Law Commission, 1953*, vol. II, p. 65, reproducing "Deuxième rapport"; and *Yearbook of the International Law Commission, 1954*, vol. II, p. 3, reproducing "Troisième rapport."
70 United Nations, *Conference on the Law of the Sea*, vol. II, p. 132.

While under this procedure waters on the landward side of the straight base-lines become internal waters, the Convention of 1958 made the following qualification:

Article 5
2. Where the establishment of a straight baseline in accordance with article 4 has the effect of enclosing as internal waters areas which previously had been considered as part of the territorial sea or of the high seas, a right of innocent passage . . . shall exist in those waters.[71]

Archipelagos. The convention adopted by the 1958 Conference gave no encouragement to the proponents of the archipelago doctrine:

Article 10
2. The territorial sea of an island is measured in accordance with the provisions of these articles.[72]

This has annoyed the states who have adopted the archipelago doctrine. Indonesia's delegate to the conference, Mr. Subardjo, complained:

The final decision on the question of archipelagos was a matter solely for the Conference. The fact that the nations most directly interested in the question were few and comparatively weak was no reason for leaving the problem unsolved.[73]

As of the time of publication, Indonesia and the Philippines have not ratified the 1958 Convention. Moreover, Canada, concerned about her Arctic Archipelago and Hudson Bay; Norway, similarly concerned about the Spitzbergen Archipelago and Varanger Fjord; and Greece, with her Aegean Archipelago, have not ratified the convention. Japan, conversely, an archipelagic state that does not adhere to the doctrine, did ratify the convention, but not until 1968. Neither the United States, with her lesser archipelagos, the Aleutians and the Hawaiians, nor the Soviet Union, with her small Arctic icebound archipelagos, found Article 10 to be an impediment to ratification.

In sum, the failure of the 1958 and 1960 Conferences to reach agreement on the extent of the territorial sea did mortal damage to the three-mile rule. Yet, in spite of the gloom and pessimism with which the three-mile advocates view the conferences, the 1958 Conference produced a very useful codification of the mechanics of the international law of the sea. No matter what specific limit becomes the ultimate successor to the three-mile limit—if any—it will be well-served by the comprehensive delimitation procedures laid down in the Convention on the Territorial Sea and the Contiguous Zone.

71 *Ibid.*, p. 133.
72 *Ibid.*
73 United Nations, *Conference on the Law of the Sea,* vol. III, p. 44.

CHAPTER 13

The Demise of the Three-Mile Limit

———◆———

THE TWELVE-MILE FISHING LIMIT

The United Nations Conference on the Law of the Sea at Geneva in 1958 prompted Iceland, as pointed out earlier, to declare a twelve-mile fishing limit. The Second Conference, which followed two years later, precipitated an almost worldwide adoption of the twelve-mile limit for fisheries. Among the first to react were Norway and Denmark. By unilateral action, Norway adopted a twelve-mile fishing limit on September 1, 1961.[1] Denmark did likewise in the case of Greenland and the Faeroes in 1963.[2]

FISHERIES CONVENTION OF 1964

The unilateral pronouncements by Iceland, Norway, and Denmark created a stir of concern among the states of western Europe and triggered an international fisheries conference,[3] which convened at London in December, 1963. By March, the delegates of sixteen states had completely revised the eighty-two-year-old North Sea Fisheries Convention, which had upheld the three-mile limit since 1882. All six of the 1882 signatories, together with ten other western European states and the Commission of the European Economic Community (Common Market), participated. Although the new convention is more accurately referred to as the North-East Atlantic Fisheries Convention, it has become widely and commonly known as the European Fisheries Convention,

---

1 Whiteman, *Digest of International Law*, vol. IV, p. 34.
2 Danish Announcement No. 192, Ministry for Greenland, May 27, 1963, effective June 1, 1963, and Danish Foreign Ministry's Regulation No. 156 (Faeroe Islands) of April 24, 1963, effective March 12, 1964, *ibid*.
3 Feron, "16 Nations Split on Fishing Code," *New York Times*, January 18, 1964, p. 36M.

or simply as the Fisheries Convention. The convention provides for a twelve-mile fishing zone among the signatories, qualified as follows:

Article 2
The coastal state has the exclusive right to fish and exclusive jurisdiction in matters of fisheries within the belt of six miles measured from the baseline of its territorial sea.

Article 3
Within the belt between six and twelve miles measured from the baseline of the territorial sea, the right to fish shall be exercised only by the coastal state and by such other Contracting Parties, the fishing vessels of which have habitually fished in that belt between 1st January, 1953 and 31st December, 1962.[4]

Drafting states included Austria, Belgium, Denmark, France, West Germany, Iceland, Ireland, Italy, Luxembourg, The Netherlands, Norway, Portugal, Spain, Sweden, Switzerland, and the United Kingdom. Norway and Iceland refused to sign the convention, being unwilling to share the outer six-mile belt. Switzerland, whose only international waters are those of Lake Geneva, which she shares with France, likewise did not sign the convention.[5] Denmark became a signatory but excluded, by annex, the application of the convention to Greenland and the Faeroes.[6]

Thus, in 1964, Great Britain terminated her almost century-old practice of adhering to the three-mile limit as the only limit for all purposes. In 1964, Britain also enacted a Continental Shelf Act, which became effective in April; the next month she ratified the 1958 United Nations Convention on the Continental Shelf.[7]

THE UNITED STATES AND THE TWELVE-MILE FISHING LIMIT

Internal pressures. In the United States, too, pressures were mounting to abandon the three-mile fishing zone in favor of a twelve-mile zone. The Alaskans had been the most outspoken in their desire to extend fishing limits before World War II. (See page 158.) In the postwar period they were joined by the Washington State and New England fishing interests. In 1963, Warren G. Magnuson, U.S. Senator from Washington and chairman of the Senate Commerce Committee, announced that the United States might be forced to extend its fishing limits in order to push back the large Russian

---

4 *Final Act of the European Fisheries Conference*, p. 1071, citing text of the Ministry of Agriculture, Fisheries, and Food, U.K.
5 "13 Nations Extend Their Fisheries Jurisdiction," news item in *The Washington Post*, March 4, 1964, p. D4.
6 *Final Act of the Fisheries Conference*, p. 1074.
7 Great Britain, *Continental Shelf Act 1964*, reproduced in *American Journal of International Law*, vol. LVIII, pp. 1085–1090; ratification, May 11, 1964, United Nations Document A/CONF. 13/L.55 (1958).

and Japanese trawling fleets encircling the American coasts. He noted that some states claimed fishing limits as great as 200 miles out to sea, and added:

> We might want to keep up with the Joneses, . . . We might not want to, but may be forced to.[8]

Concurrently, Senator Ernest Gruening of Alaska was seeking an extension to protect the Alaska king crab industry:

> Now, the Russians are invading these king crab fishing grounds, [and] have depleted the traps of our American fishermen. . . .
> It is true that many of these traps are outside the 3-mile limit and therefore in international waters. Two remedies, of course, are immediately available: The first would be to extend the fishing limits for all fisheries to 12 miles, and the second—but even more pertinent—would be to extend the limits for the taking of crustacea and shellfish to the Continental Shelf. . . .[9]

Senator Gruening, three months later, criticized the three-mile limit policy which:

> . . . permits the fishing vessels of other nations to make themselves at home in our waters, gorge themselves with our fish, and sometimes, ironically, to even compound their profits as they sell to U.S. consumers the very product which has been taken from our waters.[10]

More recently, Massachusetts fishing interests have become concerned with the routine appearance of over 300 modern foreign fishing vessels off their coast, 200 of which were identified as Russian, the rest mostly German and Polish.[11] Sentiment among the New England fishermen is in favor of greatly expanded exclusively fishing limits, as expressed by Captain Henrique Duarte of Provincetown:

> The government should set the limit 200 miles offshore, and keep the foreign fishing boats from inside that line.[12]

A 1969 editorial in the *Cape Cod Standard Times* read:

> One lone United States Coast Guard patrol boat can't keep tabs on more than 300 foreign vessels off the Cape area. . . . Cape fishermen say that the

8 "Extension of Limit on Fishing is Seen," news item in *New York Times*, September 7, 1963.
9 Gruening, "The Russian Raids on Alaskan Fishermen Should be Stopped," *Congressional Record*, November 5, 1963, p. 20005.
10 *Congressional Record (Senate)*, February 25, 1964, p. 3340.
11 Gordon, "Foreign Vessels Fishing Illegally Irk Coast Guard," *Boston Globe*, September 14, 1969, p. 37.
12 Nickerson, "Cape-tip Skipper Fears Squeeze-out," *Cape Cod Standard-Times*, September 15, 1969, p. 1.

big boats by their very presence force area fishermen to pull up their drags to save them from damage. Many fishermen have reported over the years that their nets have been ruined and cut by the foreign vessels cutting across them. And the big boats roil the bottom and drive the fish away. . . . [T]he federal government must consider limiting foreign vessels to a much greater distance than 12 miles. Many nations now claim a 200-mile limit. This seems much more feasible than 12 miles, which practically permits foreign fishing right in the frontyard of our area fishermen. The day when a nation based its claim of territorial waters on the distance a cannon ball could carry went out with the dodo.[13]

Testifying in favor of proposed legislation to increase the United States fisheries limit to twelve miles, Robert Simon, Alaska Fish and Game official, told the U.S. Senate:

Admittedly, a 12-mile fisheries limit is not adequate to give our coastal fisheries the full protection they need. It will, however, be a necessary step in the right direction. . . .[14]

Act of 1964. The U.S. Government responded to the internal pressures from fishing interests by passing a series of three laws, the first of which was the so-called "Bartlett Act" of 1964.[15] The act has been referred to in this way because of its sponsor, Senator E. L. Bartlett of Alaska. The law prohibited foreign vessels from taking any of the living resources of the U.S. continental shelf out to a depth of 200 meters. The law was expected to have its greatest impact on Russian, Japanese, and Cuban trawlers.[16] The Japanese, who had not become a party to the Convention on the Continental Shelf, objected to the new law, claiming it would have a serious effect on their king crab industry.[17]

Twelve-Mile Fishery Act of 1966. An act to extend United States fishing limits was introduced into the Senate in June, 1966, jointly by Alaska Senator Bartlett, Washington Senator Magnuson, and Massachusetts Senator Kennedy. Subsequently, senators from Oregon, Maine, Rhode Island, and Connecticut joined as cosponsors. The legislation was strongly supported by fishing interests all over the country, with the conspicuous exception of those of southern California. It is pertinent to recall that the fishing fleet of southern California

13 "Fishing Industry Faces Extinction," editorial in *Cape Cod Standard-Times*, September 18, 1969, p. 4.
14 United States Congress, Senate, *Twelve-Mile Fishery Zone*, p. 2.
15 United States Congress, "Act to Prohibit Fishing by Foreign Vessels in the Territorial Waters of the United States and in Certain other Areas," May 20, 1964, (Public Law 88-308), 78 *U.S. Statutes at Large*, 194, reproduced in *A.J.I.L.*, LVIII (October, 1964), pp. 1090–1093.
16 "Trawler Penalty is Voted by House," news item in *New York Times*, May 5, 1964, p. 1.
17 "Alien Trawler Bill Signed by Johnson," news item in *New York Times*, May 21, 1964.

fishes primarily off the shores of other states; consequently, extension of U.S. limits would serve no purpose for the San Diego–Los Angeles tuna fleet and could possibly be counterproductive to its long-term interests. Ironically, the twelve-mile legislation encountered much opposition from the Pacific Northwest and New England, where it was argued that twelve miles was too little, and that the limit should be set at 200 miles, or at least should extend to the 100-fathom line.[18] Nevertheless, the law was passed. It provided simply and briefly an exclusive fishing zone of nine miles contiguous to the three-mile belt of territorial seas.[19] Out of the law's brevity, there soon became apparent a legal loophole. On July 26, 1968, President Johnson signed into law a supplemental act,[20] which prohibited also the activities of foreign fishing support ships that did no actual fishing themselves. The amending statute bars, within the twelve-mile limit, support activities such as the freezing, packing, and processing of fish caught by other fishing vessels and prohibits the transfer of fish, tackle, personnel, and fuel between fishing vessels and support ships.[21]

JAPAN AND THE TWELVE-MILE FISHING LIMIT

The twelve-mile fishing limit is viewed much differently by the Japanese. The United States, which has extensive, lucrative fishing grounds, relies only moderately on fish in its national diet. Japan, conversely, with a relatively small coastline of her own, counts on seafood for almost 70 percent of its animal protein.[22] Even though most of the Japanese fishing fleet had been destroyed during World War II, by 1959 Japan had risen to the status of the most important fishing state in the world. She was engaged in overseas fishery enterprises in 35 foreign countries and had 200 Japanese fishing vessels homeported abroad.[23]

Because of this reliance on foreign fishing grounds, Japan became a consistent and strong defender of the three-mile limit for all purposes as early as the Hague Conference of 1930. In 1969, however, Japan, too, became affected by the rapidly growing Soviet fishing fleet, which had begun to appear outside the three-mile limit of Japan's Pacific coast mackerel fishing grounds. Since that time, the Japanese fishing industry has urged the government to extend its territorial sea to 12 miles.[24]

18 United States Senate, *Twelve-Mile Fishery Zone*, pp. 1, 10.
19 United States Congress, "An Act to Establish a Contiguous Fishery Zone Beyond the Territorial Sea of the United States, October 14, 1966" (Public Law 89-658), 80 *U.S. Statutes at Large*, 908, reproduced in *International Legal Materials: Current Documents*, vol. V, p. 1103.
20 Public Law 90-427, July 26, 1968, 82 *U.S. Statutes at Large*, 445.
21 "New Ban Applies in 12-Mile Limit," news item in *San Diego Union*, July 27, 1968, p. 47.
22 "Fisheries," *Britannica Book of the Year 1964*, p. 366.
23 "Fisheries," *Britannica Book of the Year 1960*, p. 247.
24 "12-Mile Sea Limit Studied by Tokyo," news item in *New York Times*, March 19, 1969, p. 6.

OTHER STATES

Norway, Denmark, and the United States were not the only states to adopt unilaterally the twelve-mile fishing limit during the post-Conference fishing grounds "rush." There were also the twelve-mile claims of roughly forty newly independent and miscellaneous states, listed in Chapter 10. (See pp. 174–177.) And in addition to the claims already discussed or mentioned, Albania proclaimed twelve-miles for fishing in 1960.[25] South Africa proclaimed a twelve-mile fishing limit in 1963, applicable not only to her own coasts but also to those of her mandate, Southwest Africa.[26] This Act also provided for a territorial sea of six miles. Turkey followed the twelve-mile suit in 1964.[27] New Zealand and Australia, in 1966 and 1968 respectively, placed in effect twelve-mile fishing limits,[28] and Cambodia increased her territorial sea to that limit in 1969.[29]

So many states followed this pattern that by the end of the decade there were only thirteen states remaining that claimed as little as three miles for exclusive fishing rights: Congo, Cuba, Gambia, Guyana, Japan, Jordan, Kenya, Malaysia, Malta, Poland, Singapore, Taiwan, and Trinidad and Tobago.[30] Only Japan among them can be identified as a significant maritime or fishing state. The several significant fishing states—significant because of the volume of their catch or because of the importance they have placed on fishing in their international relations—appear in Table 13, as of 1963. It was during that year that Peru overtook Japan as the state with the largest fishing catch, a position that she has held since. It should be noted that Peru's lead is in volume only; in cash value of catch, Japan still leads by a significant margin. Not since 1945 had the United States lead all the others in volume, and by 1970 she had dropped to sixth place. Conversely, Chile has risen to eleventh place. Peru's rise from twenty-seventh place in 1955 to first place in 1963, with Chile also moving up in the ranks, is important because of the claims of those states to 200-mile limits. Worthy of note also is the fact that Callao, Peru, became the world's leading port in annual tonnage of landed fish catches in 1961.[31]

That most of these states have abandoned the three-mile limit for fishing

25 Whiteman, Digest, p. 34, citing Correction No. 682, March 1, 1960 Monthly Supplement to Adriatic Pilot-East Coast, Oglas za Pomorce (Notices to Mariners).
26 South African Territorial Waters Act, Law No. 87 of 1963, cited in Windley, "Privileges of Foreign Fishermen," p. 502.
27 Whiteman, Digest, p. 35, citing Turkish Official Gazette, May 25, 1964.
28 New Zealand Territorial Sea and Fishing Zone Act of 1965 (Law No. 11 of September 10, 1965) and Australian Fisheries Act 1967 (Law No. 116 of November 17, 1967) in Windley, "Privileges of Foreign Fishermen," pp. 502–503.
29 Cambodia, Declaration on Territorial Sea and on the Continental Shelf, published 27 September 1969, U.S. State Department Airgram A-45 of October 2, 1969, Chargé d'Affaires L. M. Rives, American Embassy, Phnom Penh, to U.S. Secretary of State.
30 United States Department of State, Office of the Special Assistant to the Secretary of State for Fisheries and Wildlife, Breadth of the Territorial Sea and Fishing Jurisdiction Claimed by Members of the United Nations System, pp. 1–5.
31 "Fisheries," Britannica Book of the Year 1962, p. 255.

Table 13
Leading Fishing States of the World (1963)*

Rank	Country	Annual Catch (in 100 metric tons)
1	Peru	6901
2	Japan	6698
3	China	4933
4	U.S.S.R.	3977
5	U.S.A.	2712
6	Norway	1388
7	Canada	1191
8	Spain	1089
9	India	1046
10	Denmark	985
11	U.K.	951
12	Indonesia	936
13	Iceland	785
14	Chile	763
15	France	742
16	West Germany	647
17	South Africa	591
18	Philippines	565
19	Portugal	540
20	South Korea	444

* From "Fisheries," *Britannica Book of the Year 1966*, p. 308, citing United Nations Food and Agriculture Organization (FAO), *Yearbook of Fishery Statistics*. For comparison, the ranking of the top six states in 1970: Peru, 12,600; Japan, 9300; U.S.S.R., 7300; China, 5800; Norway, 3000; and U.S., 2700. (News item, *Washington Post*, 7 January 1972, p. A15)

is especially significant when considered in historical context. Since the days of Grotius and Selden, the territorial sea's two most important *raisons d'être* have been fishing rights and neutral rights. That of fishing has been the dominant of the two, if the number and nature of disputes, arbitrations, conventions, treaties, and court cases can be considered a fair indication. The primacy of fishing rights in this regard is most logical from a practical and economic point of view as well. Fish are tangible assets, capable of exploitation for the nourishment of the fishermen and for profitable sale to others. Indeed, to many states, particularly less-developed states and those which rely heavily on the living resources of the sea, virtually the sole significance of the legal regime of littoral waters—whether they are termed the territorial sea, the contiguous zone, or the maritime belt—is the extent to which they provide exclusive fishing rights. This was true in the past and is still true today. To states that view the territorial sea primarily as a source of food, the fact that the three-mile limit has been abandoned so far as fishing is concerned, removes all pith and meaning from the rule. As the world's population continues to expand at its present, seemingly uncontrolled rate, it may well be that the food-producing aspect of the territorial sea will become foremost in the view of all states.

Yet at the present time, there are still states that place value on the intangible benefits accruing from the territorial sea, such as security, privacy, neutrality rights, and rights of passage. To them, the fact that the three-mile limit has been abandoned as the seaward limit for fishing is insufficient reason to abandon it completely. The supreme naval powers—first Great Britain, then the United States—are in this category. They have been referred to as the "champions of the three-mile limit."

The United States as Champion of the Three-Mile Limit

Great Britain championed the three-mile limit to its interwar paramountcy by employing two methods. First, she adopted the three-mile limit—and only that limit—for all purposes. She climaxed this policy with her Customs Consolidation Act of 1876, wherein she repealed all outstanding laws that might conflict with her three-mile limit. By adhering strictly to one limit, she provided a very clearly understood standard for the other states to observe, and at the same time, she could not be accused of duplicity in her foreign policy. Second, she utilized her position of naval superiority to force other states to comply with the three-mile rule. She forced Russia to back down from her 100-mile ukase of 1821. She deployed the Royal Navy to guarantee the right of fishermen—French and German, as well as British—to fish off the coasts of Portugal and Spain from the middle of the nineteenth century until the early twentieth century. She did the same in the case of Iceland even as late as the mid-twentieth century.

UNITED STATES PRACTICE

The United States, on the other hand, used neither of these methods after her post-World War II succession to the role of champion of the three-mile limit. First, the United States did not consider that it would serve her interests to observe the three-mile limit for all purposes as had Great Britain. Second, the use of forceful measures against a territorial-sea adversary in possession of nuclear weapons was ruled out as too risky a course of action. These decisions by the United States can best be examined in terms of a review of the various limits of maritime jurisdiction, as practiced by the United States.

Security. Although many states have considered security as one of the more important benefits of a belt of territorial sea, in U.S. practice, three miles has been considered inadequate. As a result, security measures have been taken well beyond the three-mile limit. Early in World War II, the United States established Maritime Control Areas as far as 65 miles out to sea. During the postwar nuclear war scare, Air Defense Identification Zones (ADIZ) were established to monitor all aircraft, foreign and domestic, within a maritime belt 400 miles wide.

At about the same time—the early 1950s—the Soviet Union, with the self-confidence of having developed her own atomic weapon, embarked on a program of aggressive enforcement of her twelve-mile territorial sea. If the Russian twelve-mile bid were to be challenged, it would have had to have been the United States who made the challenge. Yet, there was the risk of nuclear war in any direct confrontation between the two powers. U.S. naval units might have been deployed to penetrate the twelve-mile limit in a deliberate and obvious attempt to discredit the Russian claim. It will probably never be known if this could have succeeded. But the United States chose the less dangerous course. Her ships and aircraft were instructed to remain outside the twelve-mile limit of not only the Soviet Union, but of China and other allied communist states that also claimed 12 miles. The orders for the USS *Pueblo* to remain at least thirteen miles from North Korea, and for the ill-fated EC-121 to remain beyond 50 miles, were noted earlier. The extent of the U.S. Government's commitment not to provoke China over the issue of territorial seas was vividly revealed in February, 1968, when a U.S. Navy pilot was shot down by Chinese fighter aircraft after he had violated Chinese airspace. The pilot parachuted into the sea five miles off the Chinese coast, where he transmitted emergency radio signals for at least seven hours. Orders from Washington, however, prevented Seventh Fleet rescue helicopters and ships in the vicinity from penetrating the twelve-mile limit to make the pick-up. The pilot was presumed captured by the Chinese.[32] In this case the United States tacitly, but unmistakably, acknowledged the right of China to a reciprocal measure of security against incoming aircraft, the purpose for which the ADIZ had been created.

Neutrality. The United States has never been content with a belt of three miles for purposes of neutrality. Thomas Jefferson and early American publicists such as James Kent advocated much wider neutral zones. In 1896, Secretary of State Olney indicated the interest of the United States in extending the neutrality zone to six miles. Then during World War II, the United States, with other American states, jointly proclaimed a neutral zone several hundred miles wide.

Customs. The United States has maintained since 1799 that three miles is insufficient to provide for customs enforcement. This was reemphasized during Prohibition with the passage of the Tariff Act of 1922, extending broad author-

32 "Unarmed Navy Plane Downed by a Chinese Communist MIG," news item in *New York Times*, February 15, 1968; and "Ships Ordered to Stay Clear of Red Territory: Aid to Downed Pilot Barred," news item in *San Diego Union*, February 16, 1968, pp. A1, A6.

ity to customs officials out to twelve miles. The Act of 1935 extended customs jurisdiction to 62 miles.

Fishing. Very early in U.S. history, the three-mile limit was considered adequate for fishing because of the favorable terms of the Convention of 1818. But dissatisfaction started to develop during the days of the Bering Sea pelagic sealing disputes late in the century. The Truman Fisheries Proclamation of 1945 made public the U.S. intention "to establish conservation zones in those areas of the high seas" as required to "protect coastal fishery resources from destructive exploitation." During the Geneva Conferences of 1958 and 1960, the United States indicated her willingness to adopt a twelve-mile fishing zone. Then in 1964, she declared her exclusive rights to the living fishery resources of the continental shelf and followed this two years later with a twelve-mile fishing limit for her own coasts.

With respect to the more extensive fishing claims of other states, the United States practiced considerable restraint. The government resisted the urgings of congressmen to send warships to protect U.S. fishermen from Ecuadorian and Peruvian gunboats. It would seem that this decision not to use force to challenge the 200-mile limit was made in the interest of preserving the integrity of the Rio Pact, considered essential to the U.S. Cold War strategy. Too, in its postwar diplomatic relations with Latin America, the United States was attempting to steer clear of the interventionist policy and tactics so characteristic of the past. So instead, she enacted the Fisherman's Protective Act and attempted to resolve differences at the diplomatic level.

Seabed and subsoil. The Truman Proclamation of 1945 on the continental shelf did not define the continental shelf or its extent. A White House press release issued the same day, September 28, did define the shelf as that submerged, contiguous land that is covered by no more than 100 fathoms of water.[33] Its breadth was defined by the Secretary of the Interior as between 20 and 250 miles on the east coast and from 1 to 50 miles on the west coast.[34] On May 22, 1953, Congress further delimited the U.S. title to the natural resources of the seabed and subsoil. The Submerged Lands Act of 1953 relinquished to the coastal states the property rights to the seabed and subsoil out to three miles, but confirmed the rights of the federal government to the resources of the seabed and subsoil beyond the three-mile limit, to the outer edge of the shelf, or to the 100-fathom line. (The Supreme Court later interpreted this act to grant Texas and Florida a three-league limit based on their claims to three leagues dating to the mid-nineteenth century.[35])

33 White House Press Release, September 28, 1945, reproduced in Whiteman, *Digest*, pp. 757–758, citing *State Department Bulletin*, XIII (September 30, 1945, No. 327), pp. 484–485.
34 Whiteman, *Digest*, p. 760, quoting *Annual Report of the Secretary of the Interior, Fiscal Year Ended June 30, 1945*, pp. ix–x.
35 Submerged Lands Act, May 22, 1953, 67 *U.S. Statutes at Large*, 29, reproduced in part in Whiteman, *Digest*, pp. 783–784.

Navigation. The three-mile limit has not provided an adequate width, as far as the United States has been concerned, for the proper application of its navigation laws. The United States Inland Rules of the Road were approved by Congress on June 7, 1897, and became effective four months later.[36] These rules, somewhat different from the International Rules of the Road applicable elsewhere in the world, provide the rules and regulations for the safe navigation of ships at sea, in and near the United States and its territories. The rules prescribe the visual and sound signals to be used by vessels and the rules by which ships in the vicinity of one another must maneuver.

The boundary line for the application of these rules, oddly, does not conform to U.S. territorial waters. Rather, it follows the shoreline in most cases, and in the vicinity of ports, harbors, and rugged coastlines, it follows a series of sea buoys, lighthouses, and lightships. On the landward side of the boundary line, U.S. Inland Rules apply to the navigation of ships; on the seaward side of this boundary, the International Rules apply. In many places, the boundary line for Inland Waters extends well beyond the three-mile limit. Along the New England coast and in the vicinity of the Florida Keys, the line plots about 15 miles from the shore.[37] Theoretically, a foreign ship involved in a collision on the high seas off New England, but within the boundary for Inland Rules, could be tried in a U.S. admiralty court and be found guilty of violating the U.S. Rules of the Road, although she may not have violated the International Rules of the Road.

The Inland Rules underwent a revision in 1965 aimed at bringing greater uniformity between the several U.S. navigation laws and between the Inland Rules and the International Rules of the Road. At the time, concerning the boundary line, it was reported that:

> The Coast Guard has no intention of eliminating the demarcation line between the areas where international and inland rules must be applied.[38]

Sanitation and pollution. In the Oil Pollution Act of 1924,[39] the U.S. Congress forbade the discharge of oil by any method within U.S. territorial waters. Pollution of the oceans was of such concern to the United States that the President called an international conference on the subject in 1926. An American proposal that there be an absolute prohibition against the discharge of oil at sea was voted down.[40] Continuing efforts by the United States to extend more rigid international controls over pollution achieved only limited success, and in 1961, the United States enacted a revised Oil Pollution Act making

---

36 Wentworth, *Knight's Modern Seamanship*, p. 297.
37 Farwell, *The Rules of the Nautical Road*, pp. 389–399; United States Coast Guard, *Rules of the Road: International—Inland*, pp. 67–74.
38 "Revision of Navigation Rules in U.S. Waters Nearly Ready," news item in *New York Times*, July 25, 1965.
39 Oil Pollution Act of 1924, 43 *U.S. Statues at Large*, 604–606, quoted in Whiteman, *Digest*, p. 689.
40 Whiteman, *Digest*, p. 690.

it unlawful for oil tankers to discharge wastes in ". . . all sea areas within fifty miles from land."[41]

The several preceding paragraphs point out the great variety and extent of U.S. interests along her ocean frontiers, beyond the three-mile limit. For nearly every advantage or jurisdiction associated with the territorial sea, the United States has found it to be in her national interest to claim a jurisdiction greater than that afforded by the three-mile limit. In effect, the importance that the United States attaches to its "residual" three-mile limit now focuses solely around the right of innocent passage of warships.

ROLE OF THE UNITED STATES NAVY

It is, of course, the U.S. Navy that holds the vested interest in what remains of the three-mile rule. And this is true primarily because of the adamant view of the Soviets that warships do not possess the right of innocent passage through the territorial sea. Under the original concept of innocent passage, this would not have been an issue. The passage of fishing ships and warships through territorial waters was deemed "innocent," and was permitted, so long as they did not fish nor commit acts of war, respectively. The Soviet view, however, holds that a foreign warship, by its very nature and presence in the territorial sea, is less than innocent. The U.S. Navy's position, accordingly, was to resist any extension of the territorial sea, which in turn would reduce the ocean areas available for transit and training maneuvers.

As might be expected, the Navy was the most ardent and most persistent of the voices in Washington promoting the three-mile limit. For example, in March, 1964, Representative Thomas N. Downing of Virginia introduced a bill in the House of Representatives that would have increased the limit of U.S. territorial waters to twelve miles.[42] In commenting on the proposed bill the Navy submitted the following remarks:

> 4. The effect of United States action to extend its territorial sea to twelve miles would understandably lead to worldwide adoption of such a limit. Universal extension of the breadth of the territorial sea to twelve miles would adversely affect the Free World's seapower by reducing the high seas by an area of three million square miles or the entire area of the U.S. including the Great Lakes. In the Mediterranean alone, extending the territorial sea from 3 to 12 miles removes 145,000 square miles from the high seas (an area 1½ times the size of Italy). Of even greater significance is the effect of extension of the breadth of territorial seas on the narrow straits which interconnect the high seas of the world. Extending the territorial sea from 3 to 12 miles would remove some 116 straits as free high seas, placing them under the national sovereignty of the bordering states.

41 Oil Pollution Act, August 30, 1961, Public Law 87-167; 75 *U.S. Statutes at Large,* 402–407; Whiteman, *Digest,* p. 702.
42 H.R. 10492, March 18, 1964, "A Bill Extending the National Sovereignty of the United States over Certain Waters," 88th Congress, 2nd session.

5. The right of "innocent passage" does not provide a guarantee of passage through those straits affected and removed as "high seas" routes. The coastal states, under whose sovereignty they would come, could employ such actions as harassment by patrol activities, "failure" of navigational aids, and a flood of notices to mariners as to obstructions to navigation and mine fields in order to force the abandonment of such waterways; moreover, the Soviets and Communist Bloc countries do not recognize the unqualified "right of innocent passage" of warships but condition it upon *authorization* of the coastal state.

6. Extending territorial waters over straits, furthermore, would adversely affect U.S. *submarine* operations. In territorial waters submarines are required to navigate on the surface and show their flag. National sovereignty over the narrow passages would therefore prevent submerged entry into areas of the high seas and jeopardize the effective deployment of the U.S. submarine fleet and its Polaris weapons system.[43]

The U.S. Air Force shared the Navy's concern in this matter because of transit and overflight requirements. The right of innocent passage has not been interpreted by international agreement to include aircraft.

Positions of United States Navy and Royal Navy compared. As ardent and persistent as the U.S. Navy's voice was, it had nowhere near the influence and impact of that of the Royal Navy during the years that Great Britain championed the three-mile limit. There are some important reasons for this. In 1815, when Great Britain became champion of the three-mile limit, the Royal Navy enjoyed a very high position in the government hierarchy. The First Lord of the Admiralty was one of the members of the so-called "Inner Cabinet," which dealt directly with the sovereign.[44] Conversely, following World War II, when the United States became champion of the three-mile limit, the United States Navy lost its cabinet status, and with it, its immediate and direct access to the President, incident to the establishment of the Defense Department in 1947.

It is not unrealistic to attribute this 1947 downgrading of the U.S. Navy from cabinet status to its comparative lesser importance. During the nineteenth century the very day-to-day survival of the British Empire depended on the Royal Navy and its maintenance of the sea lines of communication between England and all the outlying regions of the Empire. Without the Royal Navy, the Empire would have collapsed; it was as basic as that. But it was not so in the case of the post-World War II United States Navy. The United States was not an empire. Aircraft, unknown during the nineteenth century, provided the United States with an alternative means of international communication. So, important the United States Navy was—but not utterly vital as in the case of the nineteenth century Royal Navy.

The postwar mission of the Navy had a subtle impact on the Navy's ability

---

43 Navy Department, Office of the Chief of Naval Operations, Director, Politico-Military Policy Division to Chief of Legislative Affairs, Memorandum Op-614C/mg ser M1669P61 dated 9 May 1964.

44 "The Cabinet," *Encyclopaedia Britannica* (1953 edition), IV, 499.

to defend the three-mile limit. The United States' postwar strategy of "massive nuclear retaliation" envisioned the use of both Navy carrier-based aircraft and Air Force Strategic Air Command bombers. With the transition to intercontinental ballistic missiles, the importance of the manned bomber, including those on aircraft carriers, started to decrease. The Navy's strategic retaliatory role shifted in the 1960s from carriers to ballistic missile "Polaris" submarines. Inasmuch as the three-mile limit is more important to carrier operations than it is to submarine operations, this change in tasks impaired to some extent the impact of the Navy's arguments to hold fast on the three-mile limit.

United States Navy and the twelve-mile limit. By 1966, the Navy could see that there was no stopping the swing to twelve miles for fishing. Testifying before Congress on the twelve-mile fishery belt, the Navy's Judge Advocate General, Rear Admiral Wilfred Hearn, said that the Navy had traditionally opposed extending fishing limits, but that it had come to accept the State Department position that sovereignty and fishing rights could be separated. He added:

> We believe that our security interests are best served when nations are limited to narrow territorial seas which interfere only slightly with this freedom of navigation.[45]

Less than a year later an article appeared in a professional journal, *The U.S. Naval Institute Proceedings*, entitled "Three-Mile Limit—Obsolete Concept?" In it, the author, a senior naval officer, wrote pragmatically and resignedly:

> The three-mile limit as the only enforceable breadth is no longer a meaningful principle of international law. Adherence to this principle may not be in the best interest of the United States. This is not to say that we should lightly abandon it without receiving something in return. . . .
> . . . It seems that the United States might trade a recognition of 12-mile territorial sea claims for a guaranteed right of *free*, as opposed to *innocent*, passage through international straits.[46]

These words would probably have labeled their author as a heretic twenty years earlier. But out of necessity, and to salvage as much as possible of the freedom of navigation, the Navy agreed to negotiate the three-mile limit. In 1968, the Chief of Naval Operations, Admiral Thomas H. Moorer testified before the House Defense Appropriations Subcommittee:

> . . . [B]efore we would want to agree to expanding the limit to 12 miles we would want a very firm agreement as to passage through the straits and overflights through the straits.[47]

45 "Navy Backs 12-Mile Fish Limit," p. 154, citing *Christian Science Monitor*, June 15, 1966.
46 Carlisle, "Three-Mile Limit—Obsolete Concept?" p. 33.
47 Prina, "12-Mile Sea Limit Expected for U.S.," *San Diego Union*, June 16, 1968, pp. A1, A6.

APPRAISAL OF THE U.S. ROLE

Great Britain, the traditional champion of the three-mile limit, emerged from World War II thoroughly exhausted, with her Empire on the verge of collapse. If any state were to take up the three-mile yoke, it would have to be the United States. The three-mile limit never looked better to the United States than it did after World War II. It offered many advantages to the new "mistress of the seas." Accordingly, the United States assumed a role as spokesman for the rule and engaged her energies in diplomatic efforts to strengthen it.

But the post-World War II United States was not in a position to play a role similar to that of post-Napoleonic War Great Britain. If the three-mile rule were to be preserved, competing claims, such as the twelve-mile limit and the 200-mile limit, would have to be successfully challenged, by force if necessary, as did Great Britain. During the nineteenth century, Britain was not encumbered by alliances. She played the role of "balancer" in her balance of power politics, and could freely and universally bring diplomatic pressure or naval force to bear without embarassment. The United States, on the other hand, had become extensively involved in alliances following World War II. To have forced an issue with Iceland, Norway, Ecuador, Argentina, Korea, or the Philippines, for example, would have been to confront an ally. NATO, SEATO, OAS, and bilateral Cold War alliances were at stake.

The State Department was in the middle of the dilemma. On the one hand, it would have been advantageous to uphold the three-mile limit and thus enhance the U.S. Navy's value as an instrument to extend and implement U.S. foreign policy. But on the other hand, to have challenged forcibly the Russian twelve-mile claim could have risked nuclear war. For these reasons, frequent urging by the Navy to take various positive steps to demonstrate U.S. determination to uphold the rule was overruled.

There were other voices in the United States that carried more weight than the Navy's. These were the strong national interests—petroleum and fishing—in the contiguous waters beyond the three-mile limit. These strong economic interests served as an impediment to the U.S. service as would-be champion of the three-mile limit. Britain had been in a position to point to her own record of strict interpretation and practice when insisting others follow her lead. But not so with the United States. It was difficult for her to build a strong and convincing case against the claim of a state to some special maritime jurisdiction when the United States had so many special-purpose maritime jurisdiction claims of her own.

Prior to World War II, the United States had never been an ardent supporter of the three-mile limit. At least two of her presidents, Thomas Jefferson and Franklin Roosevelt, regarded it as inadequate. U.S. practice and institutions were not inextricably committed to the rule. Even to her newly acquired position of maritime leadership, the three-mile limit was not critically important as it had been to Britain during the nineteenth century. So when the United

States inherited the role of champion of the three-mile limit in 1945, it was a role she could never play with the righteous fervor of Great Britain.

In the final analysis, when the three-mile limit needed a daring, brute-force defense, it was not forthcoming. U.S. diplomatic effort was not enough, and there was no other state in a position to serve as champion. The circumspect U.S. policy concerning the three-mile limit is viewed as the fifth and final in the series of developments that contributed directly to the demise of the three-mile limit. Borrowing a little from the metaphor of Dr. Bocobo: since the United States had served reluctantly as midwife at the birth of Mr. Three-Miles, it was only fitting and proper that she should serve also as the attending physician—again reluctantly—at Mr. Three-Miles' death.

But it would be both inaccurate and unfair to fault the United States for having permitted the demise of the three-mile limit through ineptitude, error, or negligence. Rather, it appears that the key decisions were made with due deliberation, only after careful consideration of the alternatives and consequences, domestic and international. It was simply a matter of national priorities.

THE UNITED STATES-SOVIET UNION TERRITORIAL SEAS RAPPROCHEMENT

To point up the United States Navy's concern about adopting a twelve-mile limit, a few examples may be in order. In December, 1967, the Algerian Government formally protested to the United States that a squadron of warships from the Navy's Sixth Fleet had violated Algerian territorial waters, claiming the ships sailed within seven miles of the coast off Cherchell.[48] These waters had been sailed by the Sixth Fleet continuously for twenty years; Algeria had declared a twelve-mile limit in 1963.

But there was developing among the major naval and maritime powers a far more serious concern over the very wide claims of the Latin American states and the archipelago states. In August, 1964, a U.S. aircraft carrier task force transited certain "internal" waters of the Indonesian Archipelago—the Java Sea and the Sunda Strait. Indonesia reacted by announcing that henceforth all foreign shipping transiting the waters of the Indonesian Archipelago would be required to obtain prior written permission.[49]

Meanwhile, Soviet ships—naval, merchant, and fishing—were also plying the many oceans of the world, far from their home ports. One of them, a Soviet government hydrographic survey ship, was apprehended by the Indonesian Navy for "violating" those "internal" waters near Natuna Island. The Soviet ship was interned in an Indonesian port but she managed to get underway and escape, with her Indonesian captors in an unsuccessful hot pursuit.[50]

48 News item in *San Diego Union*, December 12, 1967, p. A5.
49 United States Navy, Offices of the Chief of Naval Operations and the Judge Advocate General, *Study on United States Policy on Freedom of the Seas and the Navy's Support of that Policy*, p. 14.
50 *Ibid.*, p. M10.

A few years later the Soviet Union encountered a similar situation in Argentina's 200-mile territorial sea. In June, 1968, five Russian trawlers were spotted 120 miles off the coast by Argentine aircraft. Argentine warships were deployed to seize the trawlers. Two were captured and escorted under arms towards Mar del Plata. One of the two, the *Pavlovo*, escaped from its escort, the *Yamana*, when they reached a point 25 miles offshore. Argentine war planes were vectored to the scene. When they located the *Pavlovo*, they opened fire in an abortive effort to force the evading trawler to stop and return.[51]

Incidents such as this were making it clear to the Soviet Union that her initial postwar policy of encouraging states to unilaterally fix their own territorial sea limits had been "misunderstood." The Soviet position was clarified at the 1960 Conference:

> Hitherto, coastal States had themselves fixed the breadth of their territorial sea, with due regard for their own interests and circumstances. With a few exceptions, that breadth nowhere exceeded twelve nautical miles. . . .
> For its part, the Soviet Union delegation had proposed that each State should fix the breadth of its territorial sea . . . within the limits . . . of three and twelve miles.[52]

Included in the 1966 Russian *Manual of International Maritime Law* is the following statement:

> . . . [T]he substantial (200-mile) territorial sea which certain Latin American States claim is essentially a special zone for . . . protection of fishing and maritime interests from the predatory activities of United States fishing vessels.
> In this connection it must be noted that the establishment of excessively broad territorial waters is at variance with the authoritative opinion of the United Nations International Law Commission, which in 1956 declared . . . that "international law does not permit extension of the territorial sea beyond the 12-mile limit."[53]

By the late 1960s it was obvious to the Russians that the 200-mile and archipelago claims of the lesser powers were a product of the superpowers' failure to agree on the international law of the sea. The spectacular growth of the Soviet fleets had brought many of their maritime interests and objectives into alignment with those of the United States. If the two superpowers could reach an agreement on the breadth of the territorial sea, with the support of their allies, something on the order of a two-thirds majority consensus—85 or more states—might be achieved. Accordingly, in 1967, Soviet representatives in Washington suggested that a new conference on the law of the sea be

---

51 "Soviet Trawler Eludes Capture by Argentina," news item in *San Diego Union*, June 23, 1968, p. A-10.
52 United Nations, *Second United Nations Conference on the Law of the Sea*, p. 39, quoting Soviet delegate, Mr. Tunkin, March 22, 1960.
53 Barabolya, *Manual of International Maritime Law*, vol. I, p. 21.

scheduled and that the United States and the Soviet Union enter the conference with an agreed, twelve-mile position. The United States reaction was generally favorable, subject to an important condition:

> In return for the right of innocent passage in all international straits, the Navy probably would go along with the wishes of the Soviet Union to establish a uniform 12-mi. territorial limit for all coastal states.
> This was the view volunteered by the Navy's top legal officer, Rear Adm. Joseph B. McDevitt, during a question-and-answer session following a speech by Donald McKernan, special assistant to the Secretary of State for fisheries and wildlife, at a luncheon meeting of the Marine Technology Society's law committee in Washington, D.C., on Tuesday.
> The right of innocent passage for Naval vessels through certain straits will be in jeopardy, McDevitt said, so long as coastal states are in control of these waters. The Navy "could live with" uniform 12-mi. limits if it was sure of no interference in the straits by coastal states, he added. The Soviet Union has, without much success, been urging that an international conference be convened to establish uniform boundaries for territorial seas, preferably 12 mi.[54]

Concurrently, pressures for a twelve-mile limit were building up in the U.S. Congress. In 1968, Senator Robert P. Griffin of Michigan introduced an amendment to a pending Senate bill, S. 2269, which proposed a variable territorial sea that would have placed the United States in a position similar to that of West Germany. (See pages 174–75.) The amendment read:

> Sec. 4(a). The territorial sea of the United States is hereby established as extending three nautical miles from the coastline of the United States: *Provided,* that in the case of any coastal country (including ships and nationals thereof) which claim a territorial sea extending more than three nautical miles from its coastline, the territorial sea of the United States shall be equal in distance to that claimed by such other country, but not to exceed twelve nautical miles.[55]

It was also during 1968 that representatives from the United States and the Soviet Union quietly reached tentative agreement on the twelve-mile limit. Legal experts from the two superpowers prepared a draft convention on the breadth of the territorial sea. The key article granted each state the right to establish the breadth of the territorial sea up to the limit of twelve miles, as long advocated by Russia. The *quid pro quo* took the form of two additional articles. One of them—*free* passage, as opposed to *innocent* passage—guaranteed the right of all ships and aircraft—naval and military included—to pass through all international straits connecting areas of the high seas. The other one recognized a state's right to adopt unilateral, nondiscriminatory fishery conservation measures as envisioned in the 1945 Truman Proclamation and the 1958 United Nations Fisheries Convention. It included complex procedures

54 "Navy Would Make Concessions for Right of Innocent Passage in Straits," p. 149.
55 *Congressional Record*, April 3, 1968, vol. 114, part 7, pp. 8872–8873.

for determining the scientific necessity for such measures and machinery for international arbitration in case of disputes. During 1969, these draft articles were circulated widely by the Soviet Union and the United States in their respective spheres in order to generate support. Strong opposition, as might be expected, was encountered from the CEP states. In December, the CEP states conferred at Lima to determine their course of action. Following the conference, Peruvian Foreign Minister Mercado was quoted in a joint communique:

> He [Mercado] said that the Soviet Union and the United States have given every country in the world a copy of the agenda of the proposed conference. The agenda calls for limiting territorial waters to 12 miles. . . .
> In brief, the Peruvian Foreign Minister said that the proposal tends to disregard the right of exclusive jurisdiction over a 200-mile maritime area. It also disregards rights of fiscal jurisdiction, patrol, and control in this area. . . .
> The Peruvian Foreign Minister said that they [the CEP states] will seek the support of all countries that have extended their jurisdiction to 200 miles and of the developing nations. . . .[56]

This appeal for support was followed on March 25, 1970, by a Brazilian decree extending her territorial waters to 200 miles.[57] This decree by Brazil was followed a few weeks later by the Montevideo Declaration on the Law of the Sea, May 8, 1970, in which Argentina, Brazil, Chile, Ecuador, El Salvador, Nicaragua, Panama, Peru, and Uruguay multilaterally extended their sovereignty seaward to a distance of 200 miles.[58]

The Ecuadorian press, too, strongly opposed the U.S.-U.S.S.R. twelve-mile draft convention, pointing out that it would limit the right of coastal states to regulate fishing off their shores. In caustic anti-United States and Soviet Union terms, it denounced the procedures for compulsory arbitration of fishing disputes, complaining bitterly that

> . . . powerful nations always attempt to impose their own designs instead of observing established rights. The great gulf between rich and poor remains. . . . Ecuadorian aspirations have been defrauded; Ecuador has a duty to defend herself.[59]

On February 18, 1970, U.S. State Department Legal Advisor John R. Stevenson publicly announced United States support of the twelve-mile limit.[60] Then two months later, in April, 1970, the United States, jointly with the Soviet

---

56 *Agence France-Presse* (AFP) Bulletin, Lima, Peru, December 12, 1969.
57 "Brazil Extends Waters to 200 Miles," news item in *The Washington Post*, March 26, 1970, p. A25.
58 See *American Journal of International Law*, LXIV (October, 1970), pp. 1021–1023.
59 Editorial in Quito [Ecuador] *El Commercio*, December 14, 1969, and in Guayaquil [Ecuador] *El Telegrapho*, December 14, 1969.
60 "U.S. Shifts Position on Territorial Limit," news item, in *The Washington Post*, February 19, 1970, p. A16.

Union, introduced a draft treaty in the United Nations which forbade placing, launching, storing, testing, or using nuclear weapons on or under the sea bed beyond the twelve-mile limit.[61]

This section might well have been captioned, "The Genesis of the Twelve-Mile Rule." Although the three-mile limit is surely defunct as a rule of law, it has yet to be replaced formally by a new rule. In the words of Dr. Bocobo, "Mr. Twelve-Miles" seems to be a much stronger contender than "Mr. Six-Miles" in their quarrel over the estate of the late "Mr. Three-Miles." The twelve-mile limit needs only to be codified by international convention; this seems a reasonable possibility. On December 17, 1970, the United Nations resolved to convene a new law of the sea conference in 1973 to deal, among other things, with the breadth of the territorial sea.[62]

VIEW OF CONTEMPORARY PUBLICISTS

The view of several contemporary Spanish-language publicists were considered in Chapter 10. Representative opinions of the writers of other selected literature groups will be examined in this section.

RUSSIAN

P. D. Barabolya, in collaboration with *S. V. Molodtsov* and other Soviet legal experts, prepared the 1966 Soviet *Manual of International Maritime Law,* which takes the following position:

> The United States, Great Britain and some other imperialist States are endeavoring against the will of other countries, to establish as a rule of international law a breadth of the territorial sea which would enable their warships and fishing vessels to navigate as close as possible to the coastlines of other States. For quite some time they have been proposing a 3-mile limit for the territorial sea. However, the imperialist States cannot and never have been able to justify this.[63]

FRENCH LANGUAGE

Charles de Visscher, Belgian professor, international arbiter, president of the Institute of International Law, and judge of the International Court of Justice, wrote concerning the three-mile rule, significantly, in the past tense:

> There is no doubt that the attachment of the great maritime Powers to the three-mile limit regarded as a maximum is largely explained by the fact that, having no great interest in a legal extension of their own terri-

61 For the text of the draft treaty see U.N. Document A/7741, 3 November 1969, Annex A.
62 United Nations, General Assembly Resolution 2750C (XXV), 17 Dec. 1970.
63 Barabolya, *Manual of International Maritime Law,* vol. 1, p. 20.

torial waters owing to the *de facto* superiority that their means of action give them over vast expanses of ocean, they object to establishing the exclusive jurisdiction of other States over parts of the high sea, where, in peace, their ships are subject only to the law of the flag, while in time of war their fleets exercise rights there that would be restricted by any extension of the zone of neutrality. Defense of the principle of freedom of the sea was thus for them a matter of national interest.[64]

GERMAN LANGUAGE

Hans Kelsen, German jurist and successively a professor at Cologne, Geneva, and Prague, has published extensively in German and English. Born in 1881, he has lived since 1941 in the United States, where he became a professor of political science at the University of California at Berkeley. In his first edition of *Principles,* he wrote:

> Nowadays, the three-mile rule is certainly obsolete. But the principle remains valid that the territorial waters do not extend beyond that part of the sea over which the littoral state can exercise effective control.[65]

In Kelsen's second edition, revised and edited by Professor Robert Tucker of The Johns Hopkins University, his view was expressed more fully:

> It has for some time been apparent that the one-league or three-mile limit of territorial waters can no longer be regarded as expressive of the law governing the width of the territorial sea. Though quite generally accepted by states during the nineteenth century and the early years of the present century, the limit formerly set to the territorial sea has been progressively abandoned in recent decades. . . .
> . . . [I]t is not possible to state that there is any specific width of territorial waters presently sanctioned by a general rule of international law.[66]

Josef L. Kunz, Austrian-born naturalized American, is professor emeritus in the College of Law at the University of Toledo, and is the author of numerous books in German, English, French, and Spanish. Whereas most German language—and American—publicists have traditionally devoted much effort and many pages to the extent of territorial waters and freedom of the seas, it is considered significant that Professor Kunz, in his 970-page text on international law published in 1968 scarcely mentioned the three-mile limit at all, and for that matter, then only in another context. He said:

> [E]ven the concurrent attitude of the leading powers cannot create a norm of customary general international law against the resistance of other powers. That is why the three-mile limit of territorial waters, upheld by the leading maritime powers, the United States and Great Britain, has, in

64 de Visscher, *Theory and Reality in Public International Law,* p. 212.
65 Kelsen, *Principles of International Law,* p. 220.
66 Kelsen and Tucker, *Principles of International Law,* pp. 324–325.

the light of non-acceptance by other states, not become a norm of customary general international law. . . . [A] mere majority of states is not enough. The practice must have been applied by the overwhelming majority. . . ."[67]

JAPANESE

Shigeru Oda, professor of international law at Tohoku University, reflects the growing Japanese concern over the extension of foreign fishing limits beyond three miles:

> The eminent scholars of the world are of the opinion that there is no agreed rule of international law as to the width of the territorial sea, so long as the three-mile limit is not considered as established.
> The absence of a uniform limit to the territorial sea has made it difficult to give precise legal evaluation to the claims of various States to coastal waters, especially if asserted within twelve miles from the coast. . . .
> . . . It is no exaggeration to say that the claims of jurisdiction [beyond three miles] have been asserted, in effect, mainly with a view toward securing a national advantage, which was best served by exclusive control of the resources. At most, the idea of conservation was used to cloak the true intent of the claims.[68]

BRITISH

Sir Humphrey Waldock, professor of international law at Oxford and counsel before international tribunals, became editor of J. L. Brierly's *Law of Nations* after the latter's death in 1955. Writing about the Geneva Conferences of 1958 and 1960, Sir Humphrey observed:

> The three-mile states, so far from having the two-thirds majority that they had possessed in 1930, could not now muster one-third of the votes. . . .
> . . . Many other states, however, continue to claim six or twelve miles, and the question of the width of the territorial sea remains a serious potential source of future difficulties.[69]

UNITED STATES

Myres S. McDougal and *William T. Burke*, law professors at Yale and the University of Washington, respectively, collaborated on and produced what is certainly the most comprehensive postwar American work on international maritime law. They speculated:

> What may happen, in the absence of explicit multilateral agreement, is not of course easy to forecast. Some observers predict, it is said, that

67   Kunz, *The Changing Law of Nations*, pp. 339–340.
68   Shigeru Oda, *International Control of Sea Resources*, pp. 15, 18.
69   Brierly, *The Law of Nations*, pp. 208, 211.

without explicit agreement of this type the tendency will be toward wider adoption of the twelve-mile territorial sea and that such distance may achieve recognition in customary international law.[70]

H. B. Jacobini, professor of government at Southern Illinois University wrote in 1968:

> There is steady and apparently increasing pressure to extend the territorial sea to 12 miles, but at the present writing the matter remains unresolved. It may be pointed out, however, that a consensus of important states can . . . influence the ultimate . . . law.[71]

It is interesting to note that this latter statement and that of Professor Kunz were published concurrently with the United States-Soviet effort to effect such a consensus in order to halt, at twelve miles, the seemingly uncontrolled grab for territorial seas.

Lawrence W. Wadsworth, professor of international law at The American University, evaluated the failure of the three-mile limit in terms of

> . . . the growing recognition that a single limit for the territorial jurisdiction of the state over a maritime belt no longer is a satisfactory solution to the problem of territorial waters. . . .
>
> Of course, it is still desirable to find an agreed limitation on the breadth of territorial seas, for general purposes. . . . In the meantime, however, the idea of special limits for specific purposes offers a hopeful new path for exploration. . . .[T]he time may not be far off when the belt of sea area over which the State maintains jurisdiction may depend entirely upon the reason for the advancement of the claim of jurisdiction.[72]

This chapter has been entitled, "The Demise of the Three-Mile Limit." It has dealt primarily with the events of the 1960s. It may be too early to pick any one of the events of the 1960s and point to it as the one that marks most clearly the demise of the three-mile limit. Other, or subsequent, writers may even argue that the demise occurred in the 1950s or perhaps even the 1940s. But it seems that the signal event was the U.S. decision to follow the European states in adopting the 12-mile fishing limit. This, coupled with the self-imposed restriction of her warships and warplanes from the communist states' twelve-mile belt—which amounted to a *de facto* recognition of the twelve-mile limit—administered the coup de grâce to the three-mile limit. After that, the United States had no practical alternative left but to accept the 1967 Soviet bid and come to terms with the twelve-mile limit.

---

70   McDougal and Burke, *Public Order*, p. 558.
71   Jacobini, *International Law: A Text*, pp. 101–102.
72   Wadsworth, "The Changing Concept of the Territorial Seas," pp. 68–69.

CHAPTER 14

Prospects and Recommendations

In early times—especially during the heyday of the Italian city states, Portugal, and Spain—littoral princes and kings viewed their waters as private property, through which passage of foreign ships might be regulated or prohibited altogether. Later, the territorial sea concept evolved to take on added significances for the coastal sovereign—fishing, customs, security, and the many others. Then, during recent decades, these added special significances were extracted, one by one, with special zones claimed for each, with the end result that the territorial sea was reduced conceptually to its single ancient attribute—private property.

THE TERRITORIAL SEA

Current politics of the problem. It was this aspect of the territorial sea which was the crux of the Soviet-United States territorial seas controversy during the postwar period. The Soviet Union, traditionally a land power, desired the wider twelve-mile zone in order to exclude United States ships, arguing that warships did not enjoy the right of passage in the territorial sea. The United States, a naval power, desired to retain as much freedom of maneuverability as possible for her fleet; this could be best served by a three-mile limit together with general agreement that warships enjoyed the right of innocent passage *without* prior notification or authorization.

But since the early years of the Cold War, the situation between the two superpowers has changed. Russia is no longer strictly a land power. She now supports naval and merchant fleets comparable to those of the United States. Her fishing fleet is larger. Neither of these powers singly rules or controls the seas. Whereas Britain alone enjoyed naval supremacy during the nineteenth century, currently the United States and the Soviet Union share control of the seas in somewhat of an uneasy condominium.

During the 1960's the Soviet Union ventured from the Black Sea into the

Mediterranean where her fleet units have since routinely and literally shared those waters with the United States Navy. Moreover, the Soviet Navy, which was transformed first from a small coastal patrol force to the world's largest submarine force, has since broadened its mission to include operation of air-craft-carrying capital ships. Hence, the Soviet Navy, becoming more and more like the United States Navy, will increasingly note the advantages of a narrow territorial sea belt. It may conceivably develop that the Soviet Union is even more committed to narrow territorial seas than the United States; unlike the United States Atlantic and Pacific Fleets, the Soviet Baltic, Black Sea, and Pacific fleets must rely on passage through the straits and territorial waters of other states to reach the open oceans.

Rising as they have to superpower status, the United States and the Soviet Union have come to share a joint responsibility for world stability. Whether or not they accept the responsibility willingly and cheerfully does not matter, for in any event theirs will be the blame or credit for the result. Great Britain assumed the task in the nineteenth century and succeeded in preventing global war for 99 years. If the United States and the Soviet Union perform their joint obligations with similar skill and responsibility, the so-called Cold War might turn out to be another long-lasting period of relative peace and stability similar to the "Pax Britannica." The "Pax Britannica" and the Cold War thus far compare very interestingly in this regard. During the ninety-nine-year "Pax Britannica" there were literally scores of local wars, uprisings, border clashes, and subversive movements aimed at coup or assassination. There were arms races, ideological clashes, and student riots. For virtually every Cold War crisis, there can be found a "Pax Britannica" parallel. In the present Cold War both superpowers seem to be taking their roles seriously. Even though they are mutual competitors, they have maturely sidestepped serious and direct confrontation which could have led to global war. At the same time, they have both applied military or naval force to check trouble within their respective spheres.

The United States has used naval force in this regard and it is only a matter of time and opportunity until the Soviet Union does likewise. Her effectiveness in doing so could be affected by the breadth of the territorial sea, a case of Soviet chickens coming home to roost. During the early days of the American Cold War "containment" policy, the Soviet Union found herself surrounded by the United States Fleets. Although her insistence on a twelve-mile zone could provide her no positive security advantages, such a limit offered her an advantage in the negative sense that it reduced the effectiveness of the United States' "containment" strategy. By the early 1970s, however, as a result of Russia's largely overcoming her naval inferiority, the twelve-mile limit had become as disadvantageous to the Soviet Union as it was to the United States, imposing annoying restrictions on the fleets of both superpowers, almost equally. In fact, the United States might have logically adhered with alacrity to the twelve-mile limit on the grounds that it is more restrictive to the Soviet Navy than to its own. No doubt, this has occurred to the Kremlin, and it should not be surprising to learn that the Soviet Navy may secretly already favor a three-mile limit over the twelve-mile limit. This awkward situation is ironically unfortunate, because a three-mile limit—in its remaining competence of "private property"—would seem to be in the best interests of both the superpowers. It would provide them with more efficient tools in their world leadership role and as a result would probably better serve the ends of world peace and stability.

Yet, it cannot be expected that the Soviet Union would suddenly do a *volte face* on the three-mile limit. The twelve-mile limit has become a matter of national pride with the Soviet Union and represents a significant diplomatic victory. Even if there is support for a three-mile limit within the Soviet naval ranks, it is not likely to surface.

The most practical solution. Certainly the most practical, logical alternative is the twelve-mile limit. It has become, with few exceptions, the international fishing and customs limit. A plurality of states have already adopted twelve miles as their limit of territorial waters. It is important that the superpowers agree on a limit if they hope to put an end to such claims as 130 miles, 200 miles, or the like. If, conversely, they cannot agree on a limit, there is virtually no end to the extent and variety of limits the lesser states might claim, and the superpowers would have no one to blame for the resulting territorial seas anarchy but themselves. The twelve-mile limit offers a "ready-made" and most expeditious solution. Meanwhile, the 200-mile limit continues to gather support, with more than a dozen adherents. The twelve-mile limit—with free passage—is obviously a better choice, and for the United States, a necessary compromise.

BEYOND THE TERRITORIAL SEA

The three-mile limit failed primarily on the grounds that it did not provide coastal states a wide enough exclusive fishing zone. Failure of the three-mile rule to provide a fully acceptable security zone also figured importantly in its demise; but the security shortcoming was secondary to that of fisheries. Throughout the nineteenth century, the Russians maintained that three-miles was not wide enough for her fishermen; they persisted long enough to have seen their position vindicated. Now, even as twelve miles is becoming the generally accepted international fishing limit, there are heard dissenting states which claim that twelve miles, too, is insufficient. Unless this problem is addressed and solved, it is quite possible that the twelve-mile limit could fail on the same grounds; the seeds for its demise have already been sown. Not that this statement needs further proof—consider the words of Fernandez de Cordoba, Ecuadorian consul in San Diego: "The old twelve-mile claim for territorial waters in the oceans of some nations was to protect ports in time of war. Now we are trying to protect our maritime resources."[1] In defending the 200-mile limit thus, the CEP states are speaking of the twelve-mile limit as already outmoded, just as the Russians defended the twelve-mile limit against the three-mile limit at the beginning of the twentieth century.

Exploitation of the resources of the sea. The situation has changed in certain respects since the nineteenth century. Then the sea yielded primarily food. Now, in addition, it yields minerals. Moreover, the burgeoning population of this century is being forced into a position of increasing reliance on the protein and mineral resources of the sea. This was brought into world focus by the 1945 Truman Proclamations on the continental shelf and fisheries. Although the United States, in its dealings with Latin America, has since emphasized the separateness of the two proclamations, they were issued jointly with "two companion Executive Orders" under a single press release[2]; and in the context of concern over sea resources beyond territorial waters they should be considered on the basis of their joint nature.

The states which claimed 200-mile limits justified them—at least in the earlier cases—largely on the basis of the United States' 1945 Proclamations. After reading carefully all the arguments by both sides, it is believed that the objective student of history or law will agree that the 200-mile fishing claims have as much legal, moral, and logical basis as the claims to the continental shelf. There is no logic—moral or legal—in the claim that crabs and other "sedentary" sea life on the continental shelf are the property of the littoral state when the other fish living there are not. Neither is there any logic in the argument that Argentina, for example, owns the minerals of the seabed 200 miles off her coast when Chile does not. This is not to say that this writer approves of the 200-mile exclusive fishing zones. He does not. But neither does he approve of any *exclusive* rights for the coastal state to exploit the resources of the continental shelf or ocean floor beyond the limit of territorial waters.

The doctrine that a coastal state should enjoy exclusive right to exploit the continental shelf is patently unfair to non-littoral states and to states with little or no continental shelf. Such an inequitable regime over the resources of the sea can be predicted to be a constant source of friction, and with a population expansion problem, an increasing one. For example, the United States 1964 "Bartlett Act," prohibiting foreigners from taking sedentary life from the United States continental shelf triggered difficulties between the United States and both Japan and the Soviet Union.[3] That law creates as much concern among the Japanese and Russian fishermen as the Declaration

1   "200-Mile Limit Upheld by Ecuador Consul," news item in *San Diego Union*, February 27, 1970, p. B5.
2   Whiteman, *Digest*, vol. IV, pp. 757–758, quoting White House press release of 28 September 1945.
3   Windley, "Privileges of Foreign Fishermen," pp. 492–494.

of Santiago does among California fishermen. Left alone, the situation will probably continue to deteriorate. With populations growing, and with ocean technology making great strides, it is only a matter of time until it will be not only possible, but also necessary, to exploit the entire ocean, its seabed, and subsoil and not just those areas where there is a continental shelf. International lawyers have already prepared charts, inherently controversial, dividing the oceans between the coastal states under the procedures laid down in the 1958 Convention on the Continental Shelf.[4] The arrangement envisioned is a geometric partition of the oceans based on the principle of equidistance from the nearest points of the baseline. The political unworkability of such a scheme can be best illustrated by the fact that the Soviet Union, a seagoing superpower with demonstrated technological prowess, would be assigned a disproportionately—and no doubt unacceptably—small share of the seas. Germany would get virtually none. Germany's dissatisfaction with such a means of apportionment has already been articulated.[5] Conversely, less technically advanced Portugal, by virtue of her ownership of the Azores and Cape Verdes, would fall heir to the major share of the North Atlantic Ocean. The balance of the North Atlantic—that off the U.S. east coast—would go mainly to the United Kingdom because of Bermuda and the Bahamas.

A formula for reform. A better solution, it would seem, might be found in the experience and practice of nineteenth century Great Britain. Faced with a serious smuggling problem, Great Britain had increased her customs boundaries successively to two, three, four, eight and even to 100 leagues. Although this solved her domestic customs problems, her extensive customs zones were creating international problems for her, and she withdrew her customs boundaries to within her three-mile limit of territorial waters.

Today, extended claims are being advanced unilaterally by states in the name of conservation. There is little hope that long range conservation of the living and mineral resources of the sea can be accomplished in this uncoordinated manner. But to arrest the present trend, to pull back and start afresh as did Great Britain, would require today a joint effort by the United States and Soviet Russia. These two states would do well to spearhead a plan to renounce all exclusive claims to the sea, the seabed, and subsoil beyond the limit of territorial waters, contingent upon the conclusion of an international convention regulating the exploitation of the living and mineral resources of the sea. Such a convention would establish "rules of the road" for pollution (crude oil, chemicals, sewerage, radioactivity, etc.), safety (navigation, communications, mutual interference, etc.), and conservation (seasons, limits, harm-

4 Reistrup, "Davy Jones' Locker Tempts the World," *The Washington Post*, November 19, 1967, p. B5. The ocean chart is appended also to Alexander, *The Law of the Sea: The Future of the Sea's Resources.*
5 See International Court of Justice, *Reports of Judgements, Advisory Opinions and Orders, 1969: North Sea Continental Shelf Cases:* and/or "Judicial Decisions," *American Journal of International Law*, vol. LXIII, pp. 591–636.

ful techniques and equipment, ocean research regulation, etc.) on, in, and beneath the high seas. Under an international "exploitation rules of the road" agreement such as this, everyone alike would be free to exploit the resources of the ocean beyond the territorial waters of all states, but subject to compliance with the rules. Infractions would be considered in a sense as "piratical," against the laws of all states and could be tried and punished as in the case of the International Regulations for Preventing Collisions at Sea (International Rules of the Road) by the courts of any state, sitting in admiralty.

The high seas beyond territorial waters should be treated as *res communes*, available for the use and common welfare of all states and peoples. The regime of the mineral and living resources beyond the territorial sea, and consequently conservation thereof, is too important to the community of states in general to be left up to the uncoordinated efforts of individual states. A vivid example is the "conservation" area proclaimed by Chile, Ecuador, and Peru which measures 200 by 4000 miles—the better part of a million square miles. Protecting a fishery of that magnitude is a global concern, not limited to the interests of the littoral states. An important adjunct of international regulation of exploitation and conservation would be a narrow territorial sea. For obvious reasons, the narrower the territorial sea, the larger and more effective the conservation areas.

The contiguous zone. Assuming that the twelve-mile limit becomes the ultimate successor to the three-mile limit, the *de jure* doctrine of the contiguous zone becomes irrelevent. The Convention on the Territorial Sea and the Contiguous Zone provides that the contiguous zone cannot extend beyond twelve miles, so the two would become congruent. It should not work any particular hardship on states if they were to confine the enforcement of their customs, navigation, immigration, and sanitation laws within the twelve-mile zone. But then there are the *de facto* contiguous zones exercised by states for security reasons, occasioned by and large out of Cold War mutual distrusts. Although the Soviet publicist A. N. Nikolaev writes that ". . . the Soviet Union . . . at the present time has no contiguous zone," he does not deny or clarify the vague Soviet claims in the Arctic "sector."[6] On the United States side, there are the ADIZs, created in 1950 to detect an incoming attack by manned bombers. Perhaps in this day of ICBMs, they may have outlived their cost-effectiveness. If one needs a *quid pro quo*, perhaps unrestricted passage of Soviet airliners through the ADIZ could be bartered for unrestricted passage of American icebreakers through the Northeast Passage. Thus, "security" could be added as one of the competences of the twelve-mile limit.

Although there is no guarantee that an all-purpose twelve-mile limit would serve the states better than one with a contiguous zone, the history of the three-mile limit would make it seem so. The three-mile limit was a stable

6 Nikolaev, *The Territorial Sea* (Moscow, 1959), p. 12, translated and reproduced in part in American Embassy Moscow, State Department Airgram A-1682 of December 31, 1969.

rule of law until the interwar period when the concept of the contiguous zone began to gather momentum. As that concept—with its special limits for special purposes—gained strength, the rule of three miles proportionally lost strength. It would seem advisable, then, if the maritime states desire a stable rule fixing the extent of the territorial sea at twelve miles, that they strive to create in it a package regime representing at once the maximum extent of their sovereignty *and* of the several special jurisdictions they have traditionally claimed over the sea.

BIBLIOGRAPHY

The Bibliography is organized into ten sections as follows: 1. Collected Documents, p. 259; 2. Government Publications, p. 261; 3. Publications of International Organizations, p. 263; 4. Treaties, Conventions, Arbitrations, p. 266; 5. Books, p. 266; 6. Publications of Learned Societies and Universities, p. 280; 7. Periodicals, p. 281; 8. Encyclopedia Articles, p. 296; 9. Newspapers, p. 297; 10. Unpublished Materials, p. 297.

1. COLLECTED DOCUMENTS

Adams, John Quincy. *The Duplicate Letters, the Fisheries and the Mississippi: Documents Relating to Transactions at the Negotiation of Ghent*, Washington, D.C.: Davis and Force, 1822.
———. *Memoirs of John Quincy Adams: Comprising Portions of His Diary from 1795–1848.* 12 vols. Ed. Charles Francis Adams. Philadelphia: J. B. Lippincott and Co., 1874–1877.
Briggs, Herbert W., ed. *The Law of Nations: Cases, Documents and Notes.* Second edition. New York: Appleton-Century-Crofts, Inc., 1952.
British Institute of International and Comparative Law, *British International Law Cases.* 7 vols. London: Stevens and Sons, and Dobbs Ferry, N.Y.: Oceana Publications, 1965.
Cobbett, Pitt. *Leading Cases on International Law with Notes Containing the Views of the Text-writers on the Topics Referred to, Supplementary Cases, Treaties, and Statutes.* Fourth Edition by Hugh H. L. Bellot. 2 vols. London: Sweet and Maxwell, Ltd., 1922–1924.
Crocker, Henry G., ed. *The Extent of the Marginal Sea: A Collection of Official Documents and Views of Representative Publicists.* United States Department of State. Washington, D.C.: Government Printing Office, 1919.
Davenport, Frances Gardiner. *European Treaties Bearing on the History of the United States and its Dependencies to 1648.* Vol. I of 4 vols. Washington, D.C.: Carnegie Institution of Washington, 1917.
Dickinson, Edwin DeWitt, ed. *A Selection of Cases and Other Readings on the Law of Nations Chiefly as It Is Interpreted and Applied by British and American Courts.* New York and London: McGraw-Hill Book Co., Inc., 1929.
Evans, Lawrence B. *Leading Cases on International Law.* Chicago: Callaghan and Co., 1922.
Favé, Le Général Alphonse. *Etudes sur le passé et l'avenir de l'artillerie: ouvrage continué sur le plan de l'empereur: histoire des progrès de l'artillerie.* 6 vols. Paris: Librairie Militaire de J. Dumaine, 1846–1871.
    Volume IV covers the period 1650–1800; volume V focuses on the period between the French Revolution and the Congress of Vienna; volume VI covers the nineteenth century to the Crimean War. This work is also listed under Napolean III, Emperor of the French, with the explanation: "Tomes III–VI continué à l'aide des notes de l'empereur."
Fenwick, Charles G., ed. *Cases on International Law.* Second edition. Chicago: Callaghan and Co., 1951.

Ford, Paul Leicester. *The Writings of Thomas Jefferson.* 10 vols. New York: G. P. Putnam's Sons, 1892–1899.

Green, L. C. *International Law through the Cases.* Second edition. London: Stevens and Sons, Ltd., 1959.

Hackworth, Green Haywood. *Digest of International Law.* 8 vols. Washington, D.C.: Government Printing Office, 1940–1944.

Hertslet, William Lewis, et al., eds. *Hertslet's Commercial Treaties: A Collection of Treaties and Conventions, between Great Britain and Foreign Powers, and of the Laws, Decrees, Orders in Council, &c., Concerning the Same, so far as They Relate to Commerce and Navigation, Slavery, Extradition, Nationality, Copyright, Postal Matters, &c., and to the Privileges and Interest of the High Contracting Parties.* 31 vols. London: Foreign Office, 1827–1925.

Hudson, Manley O., ed. *Cases and Other Materials on International Law.* St. Paul: West Publishing Co., 1929.

———. *International Legislation.* 9 vols. Washington, D.C.: Carnegie Endowment for International Peace, 1931–1950.

Jaeger, Walter H. E., and William O'Brien. *International Law: Cases, Text-Notes, and Other Materials.* 2 vols. Revised edition. Washington, D.C.: Georgetown University Press, 1959–1960.

Malloy, William M., ed. *Treaties, Conventions, International Acts, Protocols, and Agreements between the United States of America and Other Powers, 1776–1909.* Senate Document No. 357, 61st Cong., 2nd sess. 2 vols. Washington, D.C.: Government Printing Office, 1910.

Martens, Fedor Fedorovich de. *Recueil des traités et conventions conclus par la Russie avec les Puissances étrangères.* 15 vols. St. Petersburg, 1874–1909.

Martens, George Friedrich von, ed. *Nouveau recueil général de traités et autres actes relatifs aux rapports de droit international.* Second series ed. and trans. Charles Samever, Jules Hopf, and Felix Stoerk. 35 vols. Gottingue: Dieterich, 1876–1908.

———, ed. *Recueil de traités d'alliance, de paix, de trève, de neutralité, de commerce, de limite, d'échange etc., et plusieurs autres actes servants à la connaissance des relations étrangers des puissances et états de l'Europe.* First edition. 7 vols. plus 4 supplemental vols. Gottingue: Dieterich, 1791–1808. (Second edition, 8 vols., Gottingue: Dieterich, 1817–1835.)

Moore, John Bassett. *A Digest of International Law.* 8 vols. Washington, D.C.: Government Printing Office, 1906.

———. *History and Digest of the International Arbitrations to which the United States Has Been a Party.* 6 vols. Washington, D.C.: Government Printing Office, 1898.

Napoleon III, Emperor of the French. *Etudes sur le passé et l'avenir de l'artillerie.* . . . See entry under Favé, le Générale Alphonse.

Orfield, Lester B., and Edward D. Re. *Cases and Materials on International Law.* Revised edition. Indianapolis, Kansas City, and New York: The Bobbs-Merrill Co., Inc., 1965.

Parry, Clive, ed. *A British Digest of International Law.* 15 vols. (projected estimate). London: Stevens and Sons, Ltd., 1965–. Volume III deals with the law of the sea.

Scott, James Brown, ed. *Argument of the Honorable Elihu Root on behalf of the United States before the North Atlantic Coast Fisheries Arbitration Tribunal at The Hague, 1910.* Boston: The World Peace Foundation, 1912.

———, ed. *The Reports to the Hague Conferences of 1899 and 1907.* Oxford: The Clarendon Press, 1917.

Smith, Herbert Arthur, ed. *Great Britain and the Law of Nations: A Selection of Documents Illustrating the Views of the Government in the United Kingdom upon Matters of International Law.* 2 vols. London: P. S. King and Son, 1932–1935.

Snow, Freeman. *Cases and Opinions on International Law.* Boston: The Boston Book Co., 1893.

Sohn, Lewis B. *Cases and Other Materials on World Law.* Brooklyn: The Foundation Press, Inc., 1950.

Steiner, Henry J., and Detlev F. Vagts. *Transnational Legal Problems: Materials and Text.* Mineola, N.Y.: The Foundation Press, 1968.

Stowell, Ellery C., and Henry F. Munro, *International Cases.* 2 vols. London: Constable and Co., Ltd., and Boston and New York: Houghton Mifflin Co., 1916.

Wharton, Francis. *A Digest of International Law of the United States.* 3 vols. Second edition. Washington, D.C.: Government Printing Office, 1887. Volume I deals with territorial seas.

Whiteman, Marjorie M. *Digest of International Law.* 15 vols. Washington, D.C.: Government Printing Office, 1963–. Volume IV deals with territorial seas; volume XV not published as of May, 1972.

2. GOVERNMENT PUBLICATIONS

Borchardt, Edwin M., ed. *North Atlantic Coast Fisheries Arbitration: Coastal Waters: English Translation of Extracts from Works of French, German, Austrian, Argentinian, Spanish, Swiss, Russian, Italian, and Belgian Publicists.* Washington, D.C.: Government Printing Office, 1910. [Also spelled Borchard.]

The British Information Service. *The Territorial Sea.* London: Central Office of Information (Reference Division Pamphlet No. R. 4872), September, 1961.

Franklin, Carl M., ed. *U.S. Naval War College International Law Studies 1959–1960: The Law of the Sea: Some Recent Developments.* Department of the Navy. Washington, D.C.: Government Printing Office, 1961.

Great Britain, Foreign Office. *British and Foreign State Papers, 1812/14—.* Eds. Lewis Hertslet, *et al.* —— vols. London: H. M. Stationery Office (various printers), 1841–.

——. *Treaty Series,* no. 10 (1942). London: H. M. Stationery Office, 1942.

Great Britain, Parliament. [Hansard's] *Parliamentary Debates.* Fifth series. London: H. M. Stationery Office, 1909–.

MacChesney, Brunson, ed. *U.S. Naval War College International Law Situations and Documents 1956: Situation, Documents and Commentary on Recent Developments in the International Law of the Sea.* Department of the Navy. Washington, D.C.: Government Printing Office, 1957.

Mallison, W. T., Jr. *U.S. Naval War College International Law Studies 1966: Studies in the Law of Naval Warfare: Submarines in General and Limited Wars.* Washington, D.C.: Government Printing Office, 1968.

Shalowitz, Aaron L. *Boundary Problems Associated with the Submerged Lands Cases and the Submerged Lands Acts.* Vol. I of *Shore and Sea Boundaries: With Special Reference to the Interpretation and Use of Coast and Geodetic Survey Data.* (U.S. Department of Commerce, Coast and Geodetic Survey Publication 10-1) 2 vols. Washington, D.C.: Government Printing Office, 1962.

Tucker, Robert W. *U.S. Naval War College International Law Studies 1955: The Law of War and Neutrality at Sea.* Washington, D.C.: Government Printing Office, 1957.

United States Archives, Federal Register Division. *The Code of Federal Regulations of the United States of America.* Washington, D.C.: Government Printing Office, 1939–.

——. *The Federal Register,* Wednesday, December 27, 1950.

United States Coast Guard. *Rules of the Road: International—Inland* (CG-169). Washington, D.C.: Government Printing Office, 1965.

United States Congress. *Congressional Record (Senate)*, February 25, 1964, p. 3340.

———. *Congressional Record* (Volume 114, Part 7, April 3, 1968). Washington: Government Printing Office, 1968.

———, House of Representatives. *The Counter Case of Great Britain as Laid Before the Tribunal of Arbitration, Convened at Geneva under the Provisions of the Treaty Between the United States of America and Her Majesty the Queen of Great Britain, concluded at Washington May 8, 1871*. 42nd Cong., 2nd sess., Ex. doc. 324. Washington, D.C.: Government Printing Office, 1872.

———, House of Representatives. *Protecting the Rights of Vessels of the United States on the High Seas and in Territorial Waters of Foreign Countries*. 83rd Cong., 2nd sess., House Report No. 2449, July 22, 1954. Washington, D.C.: Government Printing Office, 1954.

———. *The Public Statutes at Large*. Ed. Richard Peters, Esq. 8 vols. Boston: Charles C. Little and James Brown, 1850. The series now published by the U.S. government under the title *U.S. Statutes at Large* currently numbers over 80 volumes.

———, Senate. *Coastal Waters and Territorial Sovereignty (Supplement to Extracts Used by Great Britain During the Oral Argument in the North Atlantic Coast Fisheries Arbitration)*. 61st Cong., 3rd sess. Washington, D.C.: Government Printing Office, 1910.

———. *Proceedings in the North Atlantic Coast Fisheries Arbitration*. 12 vols. 61st Cong., 3rd sess., Senate Doc. No. 870. Washington, D.C.: Government Printing Office, 1912.

———. *Proceedings of the Alaska Boundaries Tribunal*. 7 vols. 58th Cong., 2nd sess., Senate Doc. No. 162. Washington, D.C.: Government Printing Office, 1903–1904.

———. *Twelve-Mile Fishery Zone*. 89th Cong., 2nd sess., Senate Report No. 1280. Washington, D.C.: Government Printing Office, 1966.

United States Department of the Army. *International Law*. 2 vols. (Army Pamphlets 27-161-1 and -2). Washington, D.C.: Government Printing Office, 1962–1964.

United States Department of the Interior. *Annual Report of the Secretary of the Interior, Fiscal Year Ended June 30, 1945*. Washington, D.C.: Government Printing Office, 1945.

United States Department of the Navy. "Court-Martial Order 3-1949: Extension of Territorial Waters Beyond Three-Mile Limit Would Be Contrary to Prevalent Concepts of International Law," *Navy Department Court-Martial Orders*, pp. 47–64. Office of the Judge Advocate General, Department of the Navy. Washington, D.C.: Government Printing Office, 1951.

———. *Defensive Sea Areas and Airspace Reservations* (General Order Number 13 of 21 September 1948). Washington, D.C.: Government Printing Office, 1948.

———. Offices of the Chief of Naval Operations and Judge Advocate General. *Study on United States Policy on Freedom of the Seas and the Navy's Support of that Policy*. Washington, D.C.: Navy Department, 1964. (Xeroxed.)

———. Office of the Chief of Naval Operations. *The Law of Naval Warfare* (NWIP 10-2). Washington, D.C.: Government Printing Office, 1955.

United States Department of State, Office of the Special Assistant to the Secretary of State for Fisheries and Wildlife. *Breadth of Territorial Sea and Fishing Jurisdiction Claimed by Members of the United Nations System*. Washington, D.C.: State Department, 15 August 1969. (Xeroxed.)

———. *Papers Relating to the Foreign Relations of the United States*. — vols. Washington, D.C.: Government Printing Office, 1862–.

————. *Press Release Number 87, April 17, 1969*. ("Text of Statement by USAF Major General James B. Knapp at 290th Meeting of the Military Armistice Commission, Panmunjom, Korea, April 17, 1969.")

————. *Sound Dues upon American Commerce to the Baltic: Message from the President of the United States, Transmitting Correspondence in Relation to the Imposition of "Sound Dues" upon our Commerce to the Baltic*. Washington, D.C.: Government Printing Office, 1854.

————. *Sovereignty of the Sea* (Geographic Bulletin Number 3, April 1965). Washington, D.C.: Government Printing Office, 1965.

United States Department of the Treasury. *Fur-Seal, Sea Otter and Salmon Fisheries: Acts of Congress, Presidents' Proclamations, Regulations Governing U.S. Vessels, Acts of Parliament, Orders in Council, Pertaining to the Fur-Seal Fisheries in Bering Sea and North Pacific Ocean, Sea Otter Regulations, Laws as to Salmon Fisheries in Alaska*. Treasury Department (Office of Division of Revenue Cutter Service) Doc. No. 1850. Washington, D.C.: Government Printing Office, 1896.

United States Government. *The American State Papers: State Papers and Publick Documents of the United States from the Accession of George Washington to the Presidency, Exhibiting a Complete View of our Foreign Relations Since that Time*. 10 vols. Second edition. Boston: T. B. Wait and Sons, 1817.

————. *The Federal Cases: Comprising Cases Argued and Determined in the Circuit and District Courts of the United States*. Vol. I of a continuing series. St. Paul: West Publishing Co., 1894.

————. *Fur Seal Arbitration: Proceedings of the Tribunal of Arbitration Convened at Paris under the Treaty Between the United States of America and Great Britain, Concluded at Washington February 29, 1892 for the Determination of Questions Between the Two Governments Concerning the Jurisdictional Rights of the United States in the Waters of Bering Sea*. 16 vols. Washington, D.C.: Government Printing Office, 1895.

United States Naval War College, "Contiguous Zones, Airplanes, and Neutrality," *International Law Situations 1939*. Washington, D.C.: Government Printing Office, 1940.

————. *International Law Discussions 1903: The United States Naval War Code of 1900*. Washington, D.C.: Government Printing Office, 1904.

————. *International Law Documents 1948–49*. Washington, D.C.: Government Printing Office, 1950.

————. "Marginal Sea and Other Waters," *International Law Topics and Discussions 1913*. Washington, D.C.: Government Printing Office, 1914.

————. "Maritime Jurisdiction," *International Law Situations with Solutions and Notes 1928*. Washington, D.C.: Government Printing Office, 1929.

————. "Neutrality and Territorial Waters," *International Law Situations with Solutions and Notes 1931*. Washington, D.C.: Government Printing Office, 1932.

United States Navy Hydrographic Office (originally by Nathaniel Bowditch). *American Practical Navigator (H. O. Pub. No. 9)*. Washington, D.C.: Government Printing Office, 1958.

3. PUBLICATIONS OF INTERNATIONAL ORGANIZATIONS

Comité Jurídico Interamericano. *Mar territorial y cuestiones afines. Resolución del comité jurídico interamericano por la cual mantiene la suspensión de estudio sobre mar territorial y cuestiones afines*. Washington, D.C.: Departamento Jurídico, Unión Panamerica, 1955.

International Court of Justice. *Reports of Judgments, Advisory Opinions and Orders, 1949*. Leyden, Neth.: A. W. Sijthoff's Publishing Co., 1949.

——. *Reports of Judgments, Advisory Opinions and Orders, 1951*. Leyden, Neth.: A. W. Sijthoff's Publishing Co., 1951.

——. *Reports of Judgments, Advisory Opinions and Orders, 1969: North Sea Continental Shelf Cases*. Netherlands: International Court of Justice, 1969.

League of Nations. *Acts of the Conferences for the Codification of International Law*, Vol. III, *Minutes of the Second Committee, Territorial Waters*. Geneva: League of Nations, 1930.

——. *Conference for the Codification of International Law, Bases of Discussion Drawn up for the Conference by the Preparatory Committee*, Vol. II, *Territorial Waters* (League of Nations Doc. C. 73. M. 38. 1929. V.). Geneva: League of Nations, 1929. Reprinted in Supplement to *American Journal of International Law*, XXIV (January, 1930), pp. 1–8, 25–46.

——. *Final Act, Conference for the Codification of International Law, The Hague, March–April, 1930* (Publication of the League of Nations V. Legal Questions, 1930. V. 7.). Geneva: League of Nations, 1930. Reprinted in Supplement to *American Journal of International Law*, XXIV (July, 1930), pp. 169–258.

——. *First Session of the Committee of Experts for the Progressive Codification of International Law*. Geneva: League of Nations, 1925. Reprinted in Special Supplement to *American Journal of International Law*, XX (July, 1926), pp. 12–16.

——. *Report of the Sub-committee (Schücking, de Magalhaes, Wickersham) on Territorial Waters, Committee of Experts for the Progressive Codification of International Law*. Geneva: League of Nations, 1926. Reprinted in Special Supplement to *American Journal of International Law*, XX (July, 1926), pp. 62–147.

——. *Report of the Sub-committee (Suárez) on Exploitation of the Products of the Sea, Committee of Experts for the Progressive Codification of International Law*. Geneva: League of Nations, 1926. Reprinted in Special Supplement to *American Journal of International Law*, XX (July, 1926), pp. 230–241.

——. *Report to the Council of the League of Nations on the Questions which Appear Ripe for International Regulation, League of Nations Committee of Experts for the Progressive Codification of International Law, Third Session, March–April 1927*, Annex, III, *Analysis of Replies Received from Governments to Questionnaires Submitted by Members of the Committee*. Geneva: League of Nations, 1927. Reprinted in Special Supplement to *American Journal of International Law*, XXII (January, 1928), pp. 4–38.

——. *Second Session of the Committee of Experts for the Progressive Codification of International Law*. Geneva: League of Nations, 1926. Reprinted in Special Supplement to *American Journal of International Law*, XX (July, 1926), pp. 17–278.

——. *Third Session of the Committee of Experts for the Progressive Codification of International Law*. Geneva: League of Nations, 1927. Reprinted in Special Supplement to the *American Journal of International Law*, XXII (January, 1928).

Pan American Union. *Congress and Conference Series, Number 29*. (Report on the Meeting of the Ministers of Foreign Affairs of the American Republics, Panama, September 23–October 3, 1939). Washington, D.C.: Pan American Union, 1939.

Schaefer, Milner B. "Scientific Investigation of the Tropical Tuna Resources of the Eastern Pacific," *Papers Presented at the International Technical Conference on the Conservation of the Living Resources of the Sea* (Rome, 18 April to 10 May, 1955) (U.N. Doc. No. A/CONF. 10/7, 1956). New York: United Nations, 1956.

United Nations. *The Economic and Social Development of Libya* (U.N. Doc. No. ST/TAA/K/Libya/3). New York: United Nations, 1953.

————. General Assembly Resolutions 2467 A-D (XXIII) on the "Examination of the question of the reservation exclusively for peaceful purposes of the sea-bed and the ocean floor, and the subsoil thereof, underlying the high seas beyond the limits of present national jurisdiction, and the use of their resources in the interests of mankind, 21 December, 1968," *Decisions of the General Assembly 1968: Peaceful Uses of the Sea-bed and Ocean Floor* (U.N. pub. OPI/350-01690-Jan. 1969-20M). New York: United Nations, 1969.

————. *Laws and Regulations on the Regime of the High Seas.* 2 vols. and Supplement (U.N. Pubs. ST/LEG/SER B/1, 1951; ST/LEG/SER. B/2, 1952; ST/LEG/SER. B/8, 1959). New York: United Nations, 1951–1959.

————. *Laws and Regulations on the Regime of the Territorial Sea* (U.N. Pub. ST/LEG/SER. B/6). New York: United Nations, 1957.

————. *Official Records of the Second United Nations Conference on the Law of the Sea, Geneva, 17 March–26 April 1960, Committee of the Whole, Verbatim Records of the General Debate* (U.N. Pub. A/CONF. 19/9). New York: United Nations, 1960.

————. *Official Records of the General Assembly, Eleventh Session.* New York: United Nations, 1957.

————. *Official Records of the General Assembly, Twelfth Session* (Supplement No. 1). New York: United Nations, 1957.

————. *Papers Presented at the International Technical Conference on the Conservation of the Living Resources of the Sea* (Rome, 18 April to 10 May, 1955) (U.N. Doc. No. A/CONF. 10/7, 1956). New York: United Nations, 1956.

————. *Second United Nations Conference on the Law of the Sea: Summary Records of Plenary Meetings and Meetings of the Committee of the Whole* (U.N. Pub. A/CONF. 19/8). Geneva: United Nations, 1960.

————. *United Nations Conference on the Law of the Sea: Bibliographical Guide to the Law of the Sea* (Preparatory Doc. No. 14; A/CONF. 13/17). New York: United Nations, 1957.

————. *United Nations Conference on the Law of the Sea,* Vol. II of 7 vols., *Plenary Meetings* (U.N. Pub. A/CONF. 13/38). New York: United Nations, 1958.

————. *United Nations Conference on the Law of the Sea,* Vol. III of 7 vols., *First Committee (Territorial Sea and Contiguous Zone)* (U.N. Pub. A/CONF. 13/39). New York: United Nations, 1958.

————. *Yearbook of the International Law Commission, 1949.* (U.N. Pub. A/CN. 4/SER. A/1949). New York: United Nations, 1956.

————. *Yearbook of the International Law Commission, 1950.* 2 vols. (U.N. Pub. A/CN. 4/SER. A/1950 with Add. 1). New York: United Nations, 1957, 1958.

————. *Yearbook of the International Law Commission, 1951.* 2 vols. (U.N. Pub. A/CN. 4/SER. A/1951 with Add. 1). New York: United Nations, 1957.

————. *Yearbook of the International Law Commission, 1952.* 2 vols. (U.N. Pub. A/CN. 4/SER. A/1952 with Add. 1). New York: United Nations, 1958.

————. *Yearbook of the International Law Commission, 1953.* 2 vols. (U.N. Pub. A/CN. 4/SER. A/1953 with Add. 1). New York: United Nations, 1959.

————. *Yearbook of the International Law Commission, 1954.* 2 vols. (U.N. Pub. A/CN. 4/SER. A/1954 with Add. 1). New York: United Nations, 1959, 1960.

————. *Yearbook of the International Law Commission, 1955.* 2 vols. (U.N. Pub. A/CN. 4/SER. A/1955 with Add. 1). New York: United Nations, 1960.

————. *Yearbook of the International Law Commission, 1956.* 2 vols. (U.N. Pub. A/CN. 4/SER. A/1956 with Add. 1). New York: United Nations, 1956, 1957.

———. *Yearbook of the International Law Commission, 1957.* 2 vols. (U.N. Pub. A/CN. 4/SER. A/1957 with Add. 1). New York: United Nations, 1957, 1958.
———. *Yearbook of the International Law Commission, 1962.* 2 vols. (U.N. Pub. A/CN. 4/SER. A/1962). New York: United Nations, 1964.
———. *Yearbook of the United Nations, 1958.* New York: United Nations, 1959.
———. *Yearbook of the United Nations, 1960.* New York: United Nations, 1961.

4. TREATIES, CONVENTIONS, ARBITRATIONS

Agreement Between the United States and Great Britain Adopting with Certain Modifications the Rules and Methods of Procedure Recommended in the Award of September 7, 1910, of the North Atlantic Coast Fisheries Arbitration, Washington, July 20, 1912. Reprinted in Supplement to *American Journal of International Law,* VI (January, 1913), pp. 41–46.

Award of the Tribunal of Arbitration Constituted under the Treaty Concluded at Washington, the 29th of February, 1892, Between the United States of America and Her Majesty the Queen of the United Kingdom of Great Britain and Ireland, Paris, August 15, 1893. Reprinted in *American Journal of International Law,* VI (January, 1912), pp. 233–241.

Convention Between Japan, Great Britain, Russia and the United States for the Protection and Preservation of Fur Seals and Sea Otters in the North Pacific Ocean, Washington, July 7, 1911. Reprinted in Supplement to *American Journal of International Law,* V (October, 1911), pp. 267–274.

Convention Between the United States of America and Great Britain to Aid in the Prevention of the Smuggling of Intoxicating Liquors into the United States, Washington, January 23, 1924, Ratifications Exchanged May 22, 1924. Reprinted in Supplement to *American Journal of International Law,* XVIII (July, 1924), pp. 127–130.

Final Act of the European Fisheries Conference (London, December 3, 1963 to March 2, 1964). Reproduced in *American Journal of International Law,* LVIII (October, 1964), pp. 1068–1081.

The Republic of El Salvador v. The Republic of Nicaragua, Central American Court of Justice, Opinion and Decision of the Court (San Jose, Costa Rica, March 9, 1917). Reproduced in *American Journal of International Law,* XI (July, 1917), pp. 674–730.

5. BOOKS

Abreu y Bertodano, Félix Joseph de. *Tratado juridico-politico sobre pressas de mar, y calidades, que deben concurrir para hacerse legitimamente el corso.* Cadiz: Imprenta real de marina, 1746.

Afflictis, Matthaeus de. *Sanctiones, et Constitutiones Novissima Praelectio.* Venitiis, 1562.

Alessandri, Jean. *Introduction à l'étude du droit de la mer.* Paris: E. de Boccardi, 1924.

Alexander, Lewis M., ed. *The Future of the Sea's Resources* (Proceedings of the Second [1967] Annual Conference of the Law of the Sea Institute). Kingston, R.I.: University of Rhode Island, 1968.

———, ed. *International Rules and Organization for the Sea* (Proceedings of the Third [1968] Annual Conference of the Law of the Sea Institute). Kingston, R.I.: University of Rhode Island, 1969.

————, ed. *Offshore Boundaries and Zones* (Papers of the First [1966] Annual Conference of the Law of the Sea Institute). Columbus: Ohio State University Press, 1967.

————. *Offshore Geography of Northwestern Europe: The Political and Economic Problems of Delimitation and Control.* Chicago: Rand McNally and Co. for the Association of American Geographers, 1963.

Alvarado-Garaicoa, Teodoro. *El dominio del mar.* Guayaquil, Ecuador: Departamento de Publicaciones de la Universidad de Guayaquil, 1968.

Alvarez, Alejandro. *Le droit international nouveau.* Paris: Pédone, 1959.

Amador, F. V. Garcia. *The Exploitation and Conservation of the Resources of the Sea: A Study of Contemporary International Law.* Leyden, Neth.: A. W. Sythoff, 1963. Addendum, 1963.

Aman, Jacques. *De la condition juridique de la mer territoriale.* Paris: Les Presses modernes, 1938.

Anninos, P. C. L. *The Continental Shelf and Public International Law.* The Hague: H. P. de Swart et fils, S.A., 1953.

Antraygues, E. *Notions de droit maritime international.* Paris: Sociéte d'éditions géographiques, maritimes et coloniales, 1923.

Arechaga, Eduardo Jimenez de. *Curso de derecho international publico.* 2 vols. Montevideo: Centro Estudiantes de Derecho, 1961.

Arias, Luis Garcia, ed. *Estudios de derecho internacional marítimo.* Zaragoza: Seminario de estudios internacionales "Jordon de Asso" (C. S. I. C.) de la universidad de Zaragoza, 1963.

Arnold-Forster, W. *The New Freedom of the Seas.* London: Methuen and Co., Ltd., 1942.

Auguste, Barry B. L. *The Continental Shelf: The Practice and Policy of the Latin American States with Special Reference to Chile, Ecuador, and Peru: A Study in International Relations.* Geneva: Librairie E. Droz, and Paris: Librairie Minard, 1960.

Azcárraga y de Bustamante, José Luis de. *El Corso marítimo, concepto, justificación e historia.* Madrid: Consejo Superior de Investigaciones Científicas, Instituto "Francisco de Vitoria," 1950.

————. *La plataforma submarina y el derecho internacional.* Madrid: Instituto Francisco de Vitoria, 1952.

Azuni, Domenico Alberto. *Droit maritime de l'Europe.* 2 vols. Paris: Chez l'auteur, 1805.

————. *The Maritime Law of Europe.* 2 vols. Trans. William Johnson. New York: George Forman, 64 Water-Street, for I. Riley and Co., 1806.

————. *Sistema universale dei principj del diritto marittimo dell' Europa.* 2 vols. Second edition. Trieste: Presso Wage, Fleis e comp., 1796–1797.

Baker, Sir Sherston. *First Steps in International Law.* Boston: Little, Brown and Co., and London: Kegan, Paul, Trench, Trübner & Co., 1899.

Baldoni, Claudio. *Il mare territoriale nel diritto internazionale comune.* Padova: A. Milani, 1934.

Baldus de Ubaldis (Baldo degli Ubaldi or Baldus of Perugia). *Usus Feudorum Commentaria.* Lugduni, 1585.

Barclay, Sir Thomas. *Problems of International Practice and Diplomacy, with Special Reference to the Hague Conferences and Conventions and other General International Agreements.* London: Sweet and Maxwell, Ltd., and Boston: Boston Book Co., 1907.

Bartley, Ernest R. *The Tidelands Oil Controversy: A Legal and Historical Analysis.* Austin: University of Texas Press, 1953.

Bartolus de Saxoferrato (Bartolo di Sassoferrato). *Tractatus: Tyberidis sive de Fluminibus.* In vol. VI of *Opera.* 12 vols. Venitiis: apvd Ivntas, 1570–1571.

Barabolia, P. D., *et al. Voenno-morskoi mezhdunarodno-pravovoi spravochnik* (Naval International Law Manual). Moscow: Voenizdat, 1966.

Barabolya, P. D., *et al. Manual of International Maritime Law.* 2 vols. U.S. Navy Department translation from the 1966 Moscow edition in Russian. Springfield, Va.: Clearinghouse, U.S. Department of Commerce, 1968.

    This is an English version of the preceding entry under the name "Barabolia."

Baty, Thomas. *Britain and Sea Law.* London: G. Bell and Sons, Ltd., 1911.

————. *International Law.* London: John Murray, and New York: Longmans, Green and Co., 1909.

————, ed. *Prize Law and Continuous Voyage.* London: Stevens and Haynes, 1915.

Baxter, R. R. *The Law of International Waterways, with Particular Regard to International Canals.* Cambridge, Mass.: Harvard University Press, 1964.

Bayitch, S. A. *Interamerican Law of Fisheries: An Introduction with Documents.* Dobbs Ferry, N.Y.: Oceana Publications, 1957.

Bernardi, G. *Norme e disposizioni sul mare territoriale.* Rome, 1939.

Bingham, Joseph Walter. *Cases on the Law of Water Rights.* Indianapolis: The Bobb-Merrill Co., 1916.

————. *Report on the International Law of Pacific Coast Fisheries.* Stanford, Calif.: Stanford University Press, and London: Oxford University Press, 1938.

Blackman, Raymond V. B., ed. *Jane's Fighting Ships 1968–1969.* London: Sampson Low, Marston and Co., Ltd., and New York and Scarborough, Ontario: Mc-Graw-Hill Book Co., 1969.

Blondel, Henri. *Du droit de juridiction de l'Etat en matière civile et en matière pénale sur les navires étrangers dans les eaux nationales ou littorales.* Nancy: Berger-Levrault et Cie., 1901.

Bloomfield, L. M. *Egypt, Israel and the Gulf of Aqaba in International Law.* Toronto: The Carswell Co., Ltd., 1957.

Bluntschli, Johann Kaspar. *Le droit international codifié.* Trans. from German M. C. Lardy. Fifth edition revised. Paris: Guillaumin, 1895.

Bodin, Jean. *Les six livres de la république de I. Bodin Anquein.* Paris: Chez I. du Puis, 1583.

Boggs, S. Whittemore. *International Boundaries: A Study in Boundary Functions and Problems.* New York: Columbia University Press, 1940.

Bonfils, Henri J. F. X. *Manuel de droit international public (droit des gens) destiné aux étudiants des facultés de droit et aux aspirants aux fonctions diplomatiques et consulaires.* Seventh edition. Paris: Rousseau, 1914.

Boroughs, Sir John. *The Sovereignty of the British Seas (written in the year 1633).* Ed. Thomas Wade. Edinburgh: W. Green & Son, Ltd., 1920.

    Sir John was Keeper of the Records in the Tower of London; he wrote this work prior to the publication of Selden's *Mare Clausum.*

Boucher, Pierre B. *Institution au droit maritime.* Paris: Levrault, Schoell, et Cie., 1803.

Bouchez, Leo J. *The Regime of Bays in International Law.* Leyden: A. W. Sythoff, 1964.

Bowett, D. W. *The Law of the Sea.* Manchester: Manchester University Press, and Dobbs Ferry, N.Y.: Oceana Publications, Inc., 1967.

Brierly, J. L. *The Law of Nations: An Introduction to the International Law of Peace.* Fourth edition. Oxford: Clarendon Press, 1949.

————. *The Law of Nations: An Introduction to the International Law of Peace.* Sixth edition by Sir Humphrey Waldock. New York and Oxford: Oxford University Press, 1963.

Brittin, Burdick H. *International Law for Seagoing Officers.* Annapolis: U.S. Naval Institute, 1956.

——— and Liselotte B. Watson. *International Law for Seagoing Officers.* Second edition. Annapolis: U.S. Naval Institute, 1960.

Brown, Louise Fargo. *The Freedom of the Seas.* New York: E. P. Dutton and Co., 1919.

Brownlie, Ian. *Principles of Public International Law.* Oxford: Clarendon Press, 1966.

Brüel, Erik. *International Straits: A Treatise on International Law.* 2 vols. Copenhagen: Nyt Nordisk Forlag, and London: Sweet and Maxwell, 1947.

Bucher, Lloyd M. *Bucher: My Story.* Garden City, New York: Doubleday and Co., Inc., 1970.

Burke, William T. *Ocean Sciences, Technology and the Future International Law of the Sea.* Columbus: Ohio State University Press, 1966.

Burlamaqui, Jean Jacques. *Principes du droit de la nature et des gens.* 5 vols. New revised edition by M. Dupin. Paris: B. Warée, 1820–1821.

Bustamente y Sirvén, Antonio Sánchez de. *La mer territoriale.* Trans. Spanish to French Paul Goulé. Paris: Librairie du Recueil Sirey, 1930.

———. *Derecho internacional publico.* 5 vols. Habana: Carasa y Cia., 1933.

Butler, William E. *The Law of Soviet Territorial Waters: A Case Study of Maritime Legislation and Practice.* New York, Washington, D.C., London: Frederick A. Praeger, 1967.

Bynkershoek, Cornelius van. *De Dominio Maris.* Text of 1702–03 trans. by Ralph van Deman Magoffin. In *Classics of International Law,* ed. James Brown Scott. New York: Carnegie Endowment for International Peace, 1923.

———. *Questionum Juris Publici Libri Duo.* Text of 1737 trans. by Tenny Frank. In *Classics of International Law,* ed. James Brown Scott. New York: Carnegie Endowment for International Peace, 1930.

Calvo, Carlos. *Le droit international théorique et pratique: précédé d'un exposé historique des progrès de la science du droit des gens.* 6 vols. Fifth revised edition. Paris: A. Rousseau, 1896.

Canfield, G. L., and G. M. Dalzell. *The Law of the Sea.* London, 1921.

Cansacchi, Giorgio. *L'occupazione dei mari costieri; critica di una dottrina di diritto internazionale.* Torino: G. Giappichelli, 1936.

Carmon, Ramon. *Vigencia de la convención sobre pesca y conservación de los recursos vivos de la mar sus repercusiones nacionales e internacionales.* Caracas: Empressa El Cojo, C.A., 1967.

Carnazza-Amari, Guiseppe. *Traité du droit international public en temps de paix.* Trans. from Italian Montanari Revest. 2 vols. Paris: L. Larose, 1880–1882.

Casaregi, Guiseppe Lorenzo Maria de (Josephi Laurentii Mariae de Casaregis). *Discursus legales de commercio . . . conculatus maris, cum ejusdem explicatione.* 4 vols. Venetiis: Balleoniana, 1740.

Castel B. *Du principe de la liberté des mers et de ses applications dans le droit commun international.* Toulouse: Impr. Causse, 1900.

Castel, J.-G. *International Law Chiefly as Interpreted and Applied in Canada.* Toronto: University of Toronto Press, 1965.

Cauchy, Eugène François. *Le droit maritime international: considérée dans ses origines et dans ses rapports avec les progrès de la civilization.* 2 vols. Paris: Guillaumin, 1862.

Charet, Jules Charles Edouard. *Notions de droit maritime international.* Paris: Berger-Levrault et Cie., 1907.

Christy, Francis T., Jr., and Anthony Scott. *The Common Wealth in Ocean Fisheries.* Baltimore: The Johns Hopkins Press, 1966.

Chucarro, Eduardo M. *Derecho Marítimo: Tiempo de paz.* 2 vols. Montevideo: Castro y Pizarro, impresores, 1931.

Coenen, Hanns Wolf. *Das Küstenmeer im frieden.* Lepzig: R. Noske, 1933.

Collado, Louis. *Platica manual de artilleria, en la qual se tracta de la excelencia del el arte militar, y origen de ella, y de las maquinas con que los antiguos commençaron a usarla*. . . . Milan: P. G. Poncio, 1592.

Colombos, C. John. *The International Law of the Sea*. Fourth revised edition. London, New York and Toronto: Longmans, Green and Co., 1959.

———. *The International Law of the Sea*. Fifth revised edition. New York: David McKay Co., Inc., 1962.

———. *Le tunnel sous la Manche et le droit international*. Paris: Rousseau et Cie., 1917.

Conforti, Benedetto. *Il Regime Guiridico dei Mari: Contributo alla Ricostruzione. dei Principi Generali*. Naples: Dott. Eugenio Jovene, 1957.

Coplin, William D. *The Functions of International Law*. Chicago: Rand McNally and Co., 1966.

Corbett, Percy E. *Law and Society in the Relations of States*. New York: Harcourt, Brace and Co., 1951.

Coulson, H. J. W., and Urquhart A. Forbes. *The Law Relating to Waters, Sea, Tidal and Inland*. Second edition. London: Sweet and Maxwell, Ltd., 1902.

Creasy, Sir Edward Shepherd. *First Platform of International Law*. London: J. Van Voorst, 1876.

Crecraft, Earl Willis. *Freedom of the Seas*. New York and London: D. Appleton-Century Co., Inc., 1935.

Cussy, Baron Ferdinand de. *Phases et causes célèbres du droit maritime des nations*. 2 vols. Leipzig: F. A. Brockhaus, 1856.

David, Robert. *La pêche maritime au point de vue international*. Paris: A. Rousseau, 1897.

Davis, George B. *The Elements of International Law*. Fourth revised edition. New York and London: Harper & Brothers Publishers, 1915.

Davis, Morris. *Iceland Extends its Fisheries Limits*. Norway: Universitetsforlaget, 1963.

De Pauw, Frans. *Grotius and the Law of the Sea*. Trans. P. J. Arthern. Brussels: Editions de l'Institut de Sociologie, 1965.

Despanet, Frantz Clement René. *Cours de droit international public*. Fourth edition revised. Paris: L. Larose et L. Tenin, 1910.

Diaz Cisneros, César. *El mar territorial y la reforma del código civil: la zona de seguridad americana*. Buenos Aires, 1943.

Dumont, Jean. *Corps universel diplomatique de droit des gens*. 8 vols. Amsterdam: Chez P. Brunel, R. et G. Wetstein, etc., 1726–1731.

Durante, Francesco. *La piattaforma litorale nel diritto internazionale*. Milano.: A. Giuffre, 1955.

Elliot, C. B. *The United States and the Northeastern Fisheries: A History of the Fishing Question*. Minneapolis, 1887.

Farwell, Raymond F. *The Rules of the Nautical Road*. Revised edition by Alfred Prunski. Annapolis: United States Naval Institute, 1954.

Fauchille, Paul. *Traité de droit international public*. — vols. Eighth edition by Henri Bonfils. Paris: Rousseau and Co., 1922–.

Fariña, Francisco. *El buque de guerra ante el derecho internacional*. Madrid: Editorial Naval, 1941.

———. *Derecho y legislación marítima*. Revised edition. Barcelona: Bosch, 1955.

Fenn, Percy Thomas. *The Origin of the Right of Fisheries in Territorial Waters*. Cambridge, Mass.: Harvard University Press, 1926.

Fenwick, Charles G. *International Law*. Third edition. New York: Appleton-Century-Crofts, Inc., 1952.

Ferguson, Jan Helenus. *Manual of International Law*. 2 vols. London: W. B. Whittingham and Co., The Hague: Martinus Nyhoff, and Hong Kong: Noronha and Co., 1884.

Ferrero, Raul. *Derecho internacional*. Vol. I. Lima: Tipografia y Offset Peruanas, S.A., 1966.

Ferron, Oliver de. *Le droit international de la mer*. 2 vols. Geneva: Librairie E. Droz and Paris: Librairie Minard, 1958.

Fiore, Pasquale. *International Law Codified and its Legal Sanction; or The Legal Organization of the Society of the State*. Trans. from fifth Italian ed. Edwin M. Borchardt. New York: Baker, Voorhis and Co., 1918.

Florio, Franco. *Il mare territorale e la sua delimitazione*. Milan: A. Giuffrè, 1947.

Flouret, Teresa H. I. *La doctrina de la plataforma submarina*. Madrid: Artes Gráficas Arges, 1952.

Foulke, Roland R. *A Treatise on International Law*. 2 vols. Philadelphia: John C. Winston Co., 1920.

Fruin, Robert. *Een Onuitgegeren werk van Hugo de Groot (An Unpublished Work of Grotius)* in *Verspreide Geschritten*, vol. III. English version in *Biblioteca Visseriana*, Vol. V. Leyden, 1925.

Fulton, Thomas Wemyss. *The Sovereignty of the Sea: An Historical Account of the Claims of England to the Dominion of the British Seas, and of the Evolution of the Territorial Waters, with Special Reference to the Rights of Fishing and the Naval Salute*. Edinburgh and London: W. Blackwood and Sons, 1911.

Funck-Brentano, Théophile, and Albert Sorel. *Précis du droit des gens*. Third edition. Paris: E. Plon, Nourrit, 1900.

Galiani, Ferdinando. *De' doveri di' principi neutrali verso i principi guerreggianti, e di questi verso i neutrali*. Milan, 1782.

Garcia Arias, L. *Historia del principio de la libertad de los mares*. Santiago: de Compostela, 1946.

Garner, James W. *Recent Developments in International Law*. Calcutta: The University of Calcutta, 1925.

Gentili, Alberico. *De Iure Belli Libri Tres*. Trans. of 1612 edition John C. Rolfe. In *The Classics of International Law*, ed. James Brown Scott. Dobbs Ferry, N.Y.: Oceana Publications, Inc., and London: Wildy and Sons, Ltd., reprinted 1964.

―――. *Hispanicae Advocationis Libri Duo (The Two Books of the Pleas of a Spanish Advocate)*. Trans. Frank Frost Abbott. In *The Classics of International Law*, ed. James Brown Scott. Dobbs Ferry, N.Y.: Oceana Publications, Inc., and London: Wildy and Sons, Ltd., text of 1661, reprinted 1964.

Gessner, Ludwig. *Le droit des neutres sur mer*. Berlin: Stilke et van Muyden, 1865.

Gidel, Gilbert Charles. *Le droit international public de la mer*. 3 vols. Chateauroux: les Etablissements Mellotlée, 1932–1934.

―――. *La plataforma continental ante el derecho*. Trans. French to Spanish Alejandro Herrero. Valladolid, Spain: Sever-Cuesta, 1951.

Godey, Paul. *La mer côtière: Obligations réciproques des neutres & des belligérents dans les eaux côtières et dans les ports et rades*. Paris: A. Pedone, 1896.

―――. *Régime international de la mer territoriale: Etat de paix, état de guerre dans les eaux côtières et nationales*. Paris: A. Pedone, 1896.

González López Negrete, C. *Mar continental*. México, D. F., 1942.

Goodrich, Leland M., and Edvard Hambro. *Charter of the United Nations: Commentary and Documents*. Boston: World Peace Foundation, 1946.

Gould, Wesley L. *An Introduction to International Law*. New York: Harper and Brothers Publishers, 1957.

Grotius Hugo. *De Jure Belli ac Pacis*. Text of 1646 trans. by Francis W. Kelsey. In *Classics of International Law*, ed. James Brown Scott. New York: Carnegie Endowment for International Peace, 1925.

————. *The Freedom of the Seas or The Right which Belongs to the Dutch to Take Part in the East Indian Trade. (Mare Liberum)*. Trans. Ralph van Deman Magoffin. In *Classics of International Law*, ed. James Brown Scott. New York: Oxford University Press for Carnegie Endowment for International Peace, 1916.

Guerrero, Jose Gustave. *La codification du droit international: la première conférence*. Paris: A. Pedone, 1930.

Guggenheim, Paul. *Lehrbuch des Völkerrechts*. 2 vols. Basel: Verlag fur Recht und Gesellschaft AG, 1948.

————. *Traité de droit international public*. 2 vols. Geneva: Librairie de l'Université, Georg & Cie., S.A., 1967.

Gullion, Edmund A., ed. The American Assembly, Columbia University. *The Uses of the Seas*. Englewood Cliffs, N.J.: Prentice-Hall, Inc., 1968.

Günther, Karl Gottlob. *Europäisches Völkerrecht*. 2 vols. Altenburg: Richter, 1787–1792.

Gutierrez Olivos, Sergio. *Mar territorial y derecho moderno*. Santiago: Editorial juridica de Chiles, 1955.

Hall, William Edward. *A Treatise on International Law*. Seventh ed. by A. Pearce Higgins. Oxford: The Clarendon Press, and London and New York: H. Milford, 1917.

Halleck, Henry Wagner. *Halleck's International Law or Rules Regulating the Intercourse of States in Peace and War*. 2 vols. Fourth edition by Sir G. Sherston Baker. London: K. Paul, Trench, Trübner, and Co., Ltd., 1908.

Hartingh, France de. *Les conceptions soviétiques du droit de la mer*. Paris: R. Pichon et R. Durand-Auzias, 1960.

Hautefeuille, Laurant Basile. *Code de la pêche maritime*. Paris: Imprimeurs unis, 1844.

————. *Des droits et des devoirs des nations en temps de guerre maritime*. 3 vols. Third edition, corrected and modified. Paris: Guillaumin, 1868.

————. *Histoire des origines des progrès et des variations du droit maritime international*. Second edition. Paris: Guillaumin et Cie., 1869.

Heffter, August Wilhelm. *Le droit international de l'Europe*. Fourth edition. Berlin: H. W. Müller, and Paris: A. Cotillon and Co., 1883.

Heilborn, Paul. *Das system des völkerrechts entwickelt aus den völkerrechtlichen Begriffen*. Berlin: J. Springer, 1896.

Henkin, Louis. *Law for the Seas' Mineral Resources*. New York: Columbia University, 1968.

Hershey, Amos S. *The Essentials of International Public Law*. New York: The Macmillan Co., 1912.

————. *The International Law and Diplomacy of the Russo-Japanese War*. New York: The Macmillan Co., 1906.

Hill, John C., Thomas F. Utegaard, and Gerard Riordan, eds. *Dutton's Navigation and Piloting*. Annapolis, Md.: United States Naval Institute, 1958.

Holborn, Hajo. *The Political Collapse of Europe*. New York: Alfred A. Knopf, 1962.

Holland, Sir Thomas Erskine. *Letters to "The Times" upon War and Neutrality (1881–1909)*. London, New York: Longmans, Green and Co., 1909.

Holtzendorff, Franz von et al. *Handbuch des völkerrechts: Auf grundlage europäisches staatspraxis*. 4 vols. Berlin: C. Habel, 1885–89.

Hyde, Charles Cheney. *International Law Chiefly as Interpreted and Applied by the United States*. 3 vols. Second revised edition. Boston: Little, Brown and Company, 1945.

Imbart de Latour, Joseph Jean Baptiste. *La mer territoriale au point de vue théorique et pratique*. Paris: G. Pedone-Lauriel, 1889.

————. *De la pêche en droit romain et dans les droit international actuel.* Paris: Lebas, 1885.

Jacobini, H. B. *International Law: A Text.* Revised edition. Homewood, Illinois: The Dorsey Press, and Nobeton, Ontario: Irwin-Dorsey Ltd., 1968.

Jane's Fighting Ships 1946–47. London: Sampson Low, Marston and Co., Ltd., and New York and Toronto: The Macmillan Co., 1947.

Jaureguilberry, E. *La mer territoriale.* Paris, 1932.

Jenkins, James Travis. *The Sea Fisheries.* London: Constable and Co., Ltd., 1920.

Jessup, Philip C. *The Law of Territorial Waters and Maritime Jurisdiction.* New York: G. A. Jennings Co., Inc., 1927.

Johnston, Douglas M. *The International Law of Fisheries: A Framework for Policy-Oriented Inquiries.* New Haven and London: Yale University Press, 1965.

Jones, Robert Lee. *The Eighteenth Amendment and our Foreign Relations.* New York: Thomas Y. Crowell Co., 1933.

Junker, W. *Das Küstenmeer.* Kiel, 1925.

Kathan, Manfred. *The Renascence of International Law* (Grotius Society Publication No. 3). London: Sweet and Maxwell, Ltd., 1925.

Kalb y Rubin, J. *El mar territorial desde el punto de vista del derecho internacional.* México, D.F., 1941.

Kelson, Hans. *Principles of International Law.* New York: Rinehart and Co., Inc., 1952.

————, and Robert W. Tucker. *Principles of International Law.* Second edition; New York, Chicago, San Francisco, Toronto, London: Holt, Rinehart and Winston, Inc., 1966.

Kent, James. *Commentaries on American Law.* 4 vols. Fourteenth edition by John M. Gould. Boston: Little, Brown and Co., 1896.

Kenworthy, J. M. (Strabolgi), and George Young. *Freedom of the Seas.* New York: Horace Liveright, 1928.

Khoshkish, Anoushiravan (d'Iran). *The Right of Innocent Passage: A Study in International Maritime Law.* Geneva: Editions Générales, 1954.

Klee, H. *Hugo Grotius and Johannes Selden.* Bern, 1946.

Klüber, Johann Ludwig. *Droit des gens moderne de l'Europe avec un supplément contenant un bibliothèque choisie du droit des gens.* Second edition. Paris: Guillaumin, 1874.

Kreuger, Robert B. (Project Director). *Study of the Outer Continental Shelf Land of the United States.* 2 vols. Los Angeles: Nossaman, Waters, Scott, Krueger and Riordan, 1968.

Kunz, Josef L. *The Changing Law of Nations.* Columbus: Ohio State University Press, 1968.

Lapradelle, Albert Geouffre de. *La frontière: étude du droit international.* Paris, 1928.

————. *La Mer.* Paris, 1934.

Laris Casillas, J. L. *El mar territorial y 429.000 km² de plataforma continental que aumentan al territorio nacional.* México, D.F., 1946.

Latouche, L. *La pêche maritime en droit international public.* Laval, 1904.

Latour: see Imbart de Latour.

Lauterpacht: see Oppenheim.

Lawrence, Thomas Joseph. *The Principles of International Law.* Sixth edition. Boston: D. C. Heath & Co., 1915.

————. *War and Neutrality in the Far East.* Second edition. London and New York: Macmillan Co., 1904.

Le Moine, Frédéric Ange. *Précis de droit maritime international et de diplomatie d'après les documents les plus récents.* Paris: Berger-Levrault et Cie., 1888.

Leonard, L. Larry. *International Regulation of Fisheries.* Washington, D.C.: Carnegie Endowment for International Peace, 1944.

Linares Fleytas, Antonio. *Le plataforma continental en el derecho internacional actual.* Habana, 1953.

Liszt, Franz von. *Das völkerrecht systematisch dargestellt.* Fifth edition. Berlin: O. Häring, 1907.

Lloyd's Register of Shipping. — vols. London: Wyman and Sons, etc., 1883–.

Loccenius, Joannes. *De jure maritimo libri tres.* Holmiae: Nicolai Wankivii, Reg. Maj., typogr., 1674.

López, de Lara Lobo, Diana. *México y su mar territorial, plataforma continental y aguas suprayacentes.* Mexico City, 1956.

Lorimer, James. *The Institutes of the Law of Nations.* 2 vols. Edinburgh and London: William Blackwood and Sons, 1883.

Louter, J. de. *Le droit international public positif.* 2 vols. Oxford: University Press, 1920.

Mackenzie, Norman and Lionel H. Laing, eds., *Canada and the Law of Nations.* Toronto: The Ryerson Press, etc., 1938.

Mahan, Alfred Thayer. *The Influence of Sea Power upon History 1660–1783.* Fifteenth edition. Boston: Little, Brown and Co., 1898.

Maine, Henry Summer. *International Law.* Second edition. London: John Murray, 1894.

Manning, William Oke. *Commentaries on the Law of Nations.* A new edition. London: H. Sweet and Cambridge: Macmillan and Co., 1875.

Manucy, Albert. *Artillery Through the Ages: A Short Illustrated History of the Cannon, Emphasizing Types Used in America.* Washington, D.C.: Government Printing Office (for the National Park Service), 1949.

Martens, Fedor Fedorovich de. *Traité de droit international.* Trans. from Russian by Alfred Leo. 3 vols. Paris: Chevalier-Marescq and Co., 1883–1887.

Martens, Georg Friedrich von. *Précis du droit des gens moderne de l'Europe.* 2 vols. Second edition ed. Ch. Vergé. Paris: Guillaumin, 1864.

———. *Summary of the Law of Nations, Founded on the Treaties and Customs of the Modern Nations of Europe.* Trans. from French by William Cobbett. Philadelphia: Thomas Bradford, Printer, Bookseller, and Stationer, 1795.

Massé, Gabriel. *Le droit commercial dans ses rapports avec le droit des gens et le droit civil.* 6 vols. Paris: Guillaumin, 1844–1847.

Masterson, William Edward. *Jurisdiction in Marginal Seas with Special Reference to Smuggling.* New York: The Macmillan Co., 1929.

Mateesco, Mircea. *Le droit Maritime soviétique face au droit occidental.* Paris: A. Pedone, 1966.

Mateesco, Nicholas Matte. *Deux frontières invisibles: de la mer territoriale a l'air "territoriale."* Paris: A. Pedone, 1965, [Also cited Nicholas M. Matte.]

———. *Vers un nouveau droit international de la mer.* Paris: A. Pedone, 1950.

McDougal, Myres S., and William T. Burke. *The Public Order of the Oceans: A Contemporary International Law of the Sea.* New Haven and London: Yale University Press, 1962.

McFarland, Raymond. *A History of the New England Fisheries.* Philadelphia: University of Pennsylvania, and New York: D. Appleton and Co., 1911.

McFee, William. *The Law of the Sea.* Philadelphia and New York: J. B. Lippincott Co., 1950.

Mérignhac, Alexander Giraud Jacques Antoine. *Traité de droit public international.* — vols. Paris: F. Pichon et Duran-Auzias. 1905–.

Meurer, Christian. *The Program of the Freedom of the Sea: A Political Study in International Law.* Trans. from German by Leo J. Frachtenberg. Washington, D.C.: Government Printing Office, 1919.

Meyer, Christopher B. V. *The Extent of Jurisdiction in Coastal Waters: Illustrated by State Practice and the Opinions of Publicists*. Leyden: A. W. Sijthoff, 1937.

———. *Norway's Usage and Prescription in the Matter of Coastal Fisheries*. Oslo, 1951.

Mochot, Jean. *Le régime des baies et des golfes en droit international*. Paris: Librairie Nizet et Bastard, 1938.

Molen, Gesina H. J. van der. *Alberico Gentili and the Development of International Law: His Life Work and Times*. Second revised edition. Leyden: A. W. Sijthoff, 1968.

Molloy, Charles. *De Jure Maritimo et Navali*. Eighth edition. London: J. Walthoe, 1744.

Molodtsov, S. V. *Mezhdunarodno-pravovi rezhim Baltiiskikh prolivov*. Ipan, 1950.

Moore, Stuart Archibald. *The History and Law of Fisheries*. London: Stevens and Haynes, 1903.

———. *A History of the Foreshore and the Law Relating thereto. With a hitherto Unpublished Treatise [A Narratiue Legall and Historicall Touchinge the Customes] by Lord Hale, Lord Hale's "De Jure Maris," and Hall's Essay on the Rights of the Crown in the Sea-shore*. Third edition. London: Stevens and Haynes, 1888.

Müller, M. *Die völkerrechtliche Stellung des Küstenmeeres*. Wurzburg, 1923.

Münch, F. *Die technischen Fragen des Küstenmeeres*. Kiel, 1934.

Mouton, M. W. *The Continental Shelf*. The Hague: Martinus Nijhoff, 1922.

Nascimento Ceccatto, Gastão do. *L'évolution juridique de la doctrine du plateau continental*. Paris, 1955.

Newlands, V. M. *The International Law of Territorial Waters with Special Reference to the Coasts of Scotland*. Edinburgh, 1940.

Niemeyer, Theodor. *Allgemeines Völkerrecht des Küstenmeeres*. Kiel: Verlag des Instituts für internationales recht an der Universität Kiel, 1926.

Nikolaev, A. N. *Problema territorialnykh vod v mezhdunarodnom prave (The Problem of Territorial Waters in International Law)*. Moscow: Gosiurizdat, 1954.

———. *The Territorial Sea*. Trans. U.S. State Dept. Moscow, 1969.

Norman, A. V. B., and Don Pottinger. *A History of War and Weapons, 449 to 1660*. New York: Thomas Y. Crowell Co., 1966.

Norton, Thomas James. *The Constitution of the United States: Its Sources and its Application*. New York: Committee for Constitutional Government, Inc., 1943.

Nuger, Antoine Louis. *De l'occupation: Des droits de l'état sur la mer territoriale*. Paris: Impr. Moquet, 1887.

Nussbaum, Arthur. *A Concise History of the Law of Nations*. New York: The Macmillan Co., 1950.

Nys, Ernest. *Le droit international: les principes, les théories, les faits*. 3 vols. Brussels: A. Castaigne, 1904–1906.

O'Connell, Daniel Patrick. *International Law*. 2 vols. London: Stevens and Sons, Ltd., and Dobbs Ferry, N.Y.: Oceana Publications, Inc., 1965.

———. *International Law in Australia*. Sydney, Melbourne, Brisbane: The Law Book Co., Ltd., 1965.

Olivos, Sergio Gutierrez. *Mar territorial y derecho moderno*. Santiago: Editorial Juridica de Chile, 1955.

Olivart, Marquis de Ramón de Dalmau y de. *Tratado de derecho internacional público*. 4 vols. Fourth edition revised. Madrid: V. Suárez, 1903–1904.

Oppenheim, Heinrich Bernhard. *System des völkerrechts*. Second edition. Stuttgart and Leipzig, 1866.

Oppenheim, Lassa Francis Lawrence. *International Law, a Treatise*. 2 vols. Second edition. New York and London: Longmans, Green and Co., 1912.
———. *International Law, a Treatise*. 2 vols. Sixth ed. by Sir Hersch Lauterpacht. New York and London: Longmans, Green and Co., 1940.
Ortolan, Théodore. *Règles internationales et diplomatie de la mer*. 2 vols. Second edition revised. Paris: Plon Frères, 1853.
Pallieri, G. Balladore. *Diritto Internazionale Pubblico*. Milano: Dott. A. Giuffrè, 1956.
Parades, Angel Modesto. *El domino de las naciones sobre el mar*. Quito, Ecuador: Editorial Universitaria, 1957.
Pavithran, A. K. *Substance of Public International Law: Western and Eastern*. Madras: A. P. Rajendran, 1965.
Perels, Ferdinand Paul. *Manuel de droit maritime international*. Trans. from German Leo Arendt. Paris: Guillaumin, 1884.
Pfankuchen, Llewellyn. *A Documentary Textbook in International Law*. New York: Farrar and Rinehart, Inc., 1940.
Phillimore, Sir Robert Joseph. *Commentaries upon International Law*. 4 vols. Third edition. London: Butterworths, 1879–1889.
Piédelièvre, Robert. *Précis de droit international public ou droit des gens*. 2 vols. Paris: F. Pichon, 1894–1895.
Piggott, Sir Francis Taylor. *The Freedom of the Seas, Historically Treated*. London and New York: Oxford University Press, H. Milford, 1919.
Plocque, A. H. *De la mer et de la navigation maritime*. Paris, 1870.
Potter, Pitman Benjamin. *The Freedom of the Seas in History, Law and Politics*. New York and London: Longmans, Green and Co., 1924.
Poulantzas, Nicholas M. *The Right of Hot Pursuit in International Law*. Leyden: A. W. Sijthoff, 1969.
Pradier-Fodéré, Paul Louis Ernest. *Traité de droit international public européen et américain, suivant les progrès de la science et de la pratique contemporaine*. 8 vols. Paris: G. Pedone-Lauriel, 1885–1906.
Pufendorf, Samuel. *De Jure Naturae et Gentium Libri Octo* (*On the Law of Nature and Nations*). Trans. from Latin by C. H. and W. A. Oldfather. In *The Classics of International Law*, ed. James Brown Scott. Dobbs Ferry, N.Y.: Oceana Publications, Inc., and London: Wildy and Sons, Ltd., reprinted 1964.
Raestad, Arnold Christopher. *Kongens Strömme: historiske og folkeretslige under-søkelser angaaende sjøterritoriet*. Kristiania: Cammermeyer, 1912.
———. *La mer territoriale: études historiques et juridiques*. Paris: A. Pedone, 1913.
Ralston, Jackson Harvey. *International Arbitral Law and Procedure: Being a Résumé of the Procedure and Practice of International Commissions, and Including the Views of Arbitrators upon Questions Arising under the Law of Nations*. London and Boston: Ginn and Co., for the International School of Peace, 1910.
Rass, H. *Das Küstenmeer nach den Beschlüssen der Haager Kodifikations-Konferenz von 1930*. Kallmunz, 1936.
Rayneval, Joseph Mathias Gérard de. *Institutions du droit de la nature et des gens*. 2 vols. New 1832 edition. Paris: A. Durand, 1851.
———. *De la liberté des mers*. 2 vols. Paris: Treuttel et Wurtz, 1811.
Reiff, Henry. *The United States and the Treaty Law of the Sea*. Minneapolis: University of Minnesota Press, 1959.
Reinkemeyer, Hans-Albert. *Die Sowjetische Zwölfmeilenzone in des Ostsee und die Freiheit des Meeres*. Cologne and Berlin: Carl Heymanns Verlag, 1955.
Renaud, L. M. *L'état et la mer*. Montpellier, 1933.

Riesenfeld, Stefan A. *Protection of Coastal Fisheries under International Law.* Washington, D.C.: Carnegie Endowment for International Peace, 1942.

Ripert, Georges. *Droit maritime.* 3 vols. Third edition. Paris: A. Rousseau, 1929.

———. *Précis de droit maritime.* Paris: Dalloz, 1939.

Riquelme, Antonio. *Apéndice al derecho internacional de España.* Vol. II of *Elementos de derecho público internacional.* 2 vols. Madrid: Impr. de D. S. Saunaque, 1849.

Rivault, Jean. *Les conventions de Londres de 1929 et de 1930 sur la sécurité en mer.* Paris: Librairie générale de droit et de jurisprudence, 1936.

Rivier, Alphonse Pierre Octave. *Principes du droit des gens.* 2 vols. Paris: A. Rousseau, 1896.

Robles, Alfonso Garcia. *La conferencia de Ginebra y la anchura del mar territoriale.* México, 1959.

Ryan, James W. *Freedom of the Seas and International Law.* New York: The Court Press, 1941.

Ryckère, R. de. *La régime légal de la pêche maritime dans la Mer du Nord.* Bruxelles: Ferdinand Larcier, 1901.

——— and A. Bultinek. *Les règles de route en mer.* Bruxelles: Ferdinand Larcier, 1909.

Sandiford, Roberto. *Diritto Marittimo.* Milano: Dott A. Giuffrè, 1960.

Sarpi, Frà Paolo. *Domino del mar Adriatico della serenissima republica di Venetia.* Vol. VI of *Opere del padre Paolo dell' ordine de' servi: e theologo della serenissima republica di Venetia.* 6 vols. Venice: Appresso Roberto Meietti, 1687.

Sayan, Enrique García. *Notas sobre la Soberanía Marítima del Perú: Defensa de las 200 millas de mar peruano ante las recientes transgressiones.* Lima: Talleres Gráficos P. L. Villanueva, 1955.

Scelle, Georges. *Plateau continental et droit international.* Paris: A. Pedone, 1955.

———. *Précis de droit des gens: principes et systématique.* 2 vols. Paris: Librairie du Recueil Sirey, 1932–1934.

Schmalz, Theodor Anton Heinrich. *Le droit des gens européen.* Trans. from German Léopold de Bohm. Paris: N. Maze, 1823.

Schücking, Walther M. A. *Das Küstenmeer im Internationalen Rechte.* Göttingen: Dieterich 'sche univ.-buchdr., 1897.

Schuschnigg, Kurt von. *International Law: An Introduction to the Law of Peace.* Milwaukee: The Bruce Publishing Co., 1959.

Schwarzenberger, Georg. *A Manual of International Law.* Vol. I. Fourth edition. London: Stevens and Sons, Ltd., and New York: Frederick A. Praeger, 1960.

Scott, James Brown. *The Spanish Conception of International Law and of Sanctions.* Washington, D.C.: Carnegie Endowment for International Peace, 1934.

———. *The Spanish Origin of International Law: Lectures on Francisco de Vitoria (1480–1546) and Francisco Suarez (1548–1617).* Washington, D.C.: The School of Foreign Service, Georgetown University, 1928.

Selden, John. *Mare Clausum: the Right and Dominion of the Sea.* Trans. from Latin Marchamont Nedham. Ed. James Howell. London, 1663.

Shigeru Oda. *International Control of Sea Resources.* Leyden: A. W. Sythoff, 1963.

———. *The Structure of the International Law of the Sea.* (Kaiyo no Kokusai-ho-Kozo). Tokyo: Yushindo, 1957.

Smith, Herbert Arthur. *The Law and Custom of the Sea.* Third edition. New York: Frederick A. Praeger, 1959.

Sørensen, Max, ed. *Manual of Public International Law.* New York: St. Martin's Press, 1968.

Starke, J. G. *An Introduction to International Law.* Sixth edition. London: Butterworths, 1967.

Stanton, Stephen Berrien. *The Behring Sea Controversy.* New York: A. B. King, 1892.

———. *The Behring Sea Dispute.* New York: A. B. King, 1889.

Stockton, Charles H. *Outlines of International Law.* New York, Chicago, Boston: Charles Scribner's Sons, 1914.

Stoerk, Felix. "The Legal Regulation of the International Maritime Traffic Outside of the Territory of the Adjacent State," in Franz von Holtzendorff *et al.*, *Handbuch des Völkerrechts.* Berlin: C. Habel, 1885–1889.

Storni, R. *Intereses argentinos en la mar.* Buenos Aires, 1916.

Strang, Lord Williams. *Britain in World Affairs: The Fluctuation in Power and Influence from Henry VIII to Elizabeth II.* New York: Frederick A. Praeger, 1961.

Strohl, Mitchell P. *The International Law of Bays.* The Hague: Martinus Nijhoff, 1963.

Suárez, Francisco. *Selections from Three Works.* 2 vols. In *The Classics of International Law*, ed. James Brown Scott. Dobbs Ferry, N.Y.: Oceana Publications, Inc., and London: Wildy and Sons, Ltd., reprinted 1964.

Tandon, Mahesh Prasad. *Public International Law.* Ninth edition. Allahabad: Allahabad Law Agency, 1963.

Taylor, Hannis. *A Treatise on International Public Law.* Chicago: Callaghan & Co., 1901.

Tecklenborg, Heinrich. *Die Freiheit des Meeres.* Bremen: C. Schünemann, 1870.

Tellez, Benoît, M. E. *La plataforma continental.* Mexico, D.F., 1946.

Teruo Kobayashi. *The Anglo-Norwegian Fisheries Case of 1951 and the Changing Law of the Territorial Sea.* Gainesville, Fla.: University of Florida Press, 1965.

Testa, Carlos. *Le droit public international maritime: Principes généraux, règles pratiques.* Trans. from Portuguese by Ad Boutiron. Paris: A. Durand et Pedone-Lauriel, Editeurs (G. Pedone-Lauriel, Successeur), 1886.

Textor, Johann Wolfgang. *Synopsis of the Law of Nations.* Trans. John P. Bate. In *The Classics of International Law*, ed. James Brown Scott. Dobbs Ferry, N.Y.: Oceana Publications, Inc., and London: Wildy and Sons, Ltd., reprinted 1964.

Thurston, E. *Pearl and Chank Fisheries of the Gulf of Manaar.* Madras, 1894.

Tillier, Maurice. *Les pêcheries de phoques de la mer de Behring: Questions de droit international soumises au tribunal d'arbitrage constitué par l'Angleterre et les Etats-Unis.* Paris: L. Larose et L. Tenin, 1906.

Tomasevich, J. *International Agreements on Conservation of Marine Resources, with Special Reference to the North Pacific.* Stanford, Calif., 1943.

Tung, William L. *International Law in an Organizing World.* New York: Thomas Y. Crowell Co., 1968.

Twiss, Sir Travers. *The Law of Nations Considered as Independent Political Communities: The Rights and Duties of Nations in Time of Peace.* Revised second edition. Oxford: Clarendon Press, 1884.

Ulloa, Alberto. *Derecho Internacional Público.* 2 vols. Lima: Sanmarti y Cia., 1929.

Vahl, M. and G. C. Andrup, eds. *Greenland*, London, 1929.

Valin, René Josué, ed. *Commentaire sur l'ordonance de la marine, du mois d'août 1681.* 2 vols. Second edition. Paris: Joubert, 1841.

———. *Traité des Prises ou Principes de la jurisprudence françoise concernant les prises que se font sur mer . . .* 2 vols. La Rochelle: Chez J. Legier, and Paris: Chez Merigot père, 1763.

Varadi, M. *La liberta del mare e lo stato chiuso moderno.* Firenze, 1922.

Vattel, Emmerich de. *The Law of Nations or the Principles of Natural Law: Applied to the Conduct and to the Affairs of Nations and of Sovereigns.* Trans. Charles G. Fenwick. In *The Classics of International Law,* ed. James Brown Scott. Dobbs Ferry, N.Y. (Oceana Publications, Inc., and London: Wildy and Sons, Ltd., 1758 edition, reprinted 1964.

Velázques, Alvarez Sonia. *La doctrina de Abreu Bertodano y su relación con los límites del mar.* Mexico City, 1957.

Victoria (Vitoria), Franciscus de. *De Indis et de Iure Belli Relectiones. . . . (Relectios on the Indians Lately Discovered, and On the Indians, or On the Law of War Made by the Spaniards on the Barbarians).* Trans. John Bate. Ed. Ernest Nys. In *The Classics of International Law,* ed. James Brown Scott. Dobbs Ferry, N.Y.: Oceana Publications, Inc., and London: Wildy and Sons, Ltd., text of 1696, reprinted 1964.

Vilallonga Ibarra, José de. *La libertad de los mares.* Madrid, 1919.

Villamil, Humberto López. *La plataforma continental y los problemas jurídicos del mar.* Madrid: Talleres Gráficos, 1958.

Villeneuve, Romée de. *De la détermination de la ligne séparative des eaux nationales et de la mer territoriale, spécialement dans les baies.* Paris: A. Rousseau, 1914.

Visscher, Charles de. *Theory and Reality in Public International Law.* Trans. from French by P. E. Corbett. Princeton: Princeton University Press, 1957.

Visser, Lodewijk Ernst. *De Territoriale zee.* Amersfoort: J. Valkhoff, 1894.

Visser 'T Hooft, H. Ph. *Les nations unies et la conservation des ressources de la mer.* The Hague: Martinus Nijhoff, 1958.

Vreeland, Hamilton. *Hugo Grotius: the Father of the Modern Science of International Law.* New York, London, Toronto, Melbourne and Bombay: Oxford University Press, 1917.

Walker, Thomas Alfred. *From the Earliest Times to the Peace of Westphalia.* Vol. I of *A History of the Law of Nations.* Cambridge: Cambridge University Press, 1899.

Ward, Sir A. W., Sir G. W. Prothero, and Sir Stanley Leathes, eds. *The Reformation.* Vol. II of *The Cambridge Modern History.* 13 vols. Cambridge: Cambridge University Press, 1934.

———. *The Wars of Religion.* Vol. III of *The Cambridge Modern History.* 13 vols. Cambridge: Cambridge University Press, 1934.

Weissberg, Guenter. *Recent Developments in the Law of the Sea and the Japanese-Korean Fishery Dispute.* The Hague: Martinus Nijhoff, 1966.

Wenck, Friedrich August Wilhelm. *Codex juris gentium recentissimi.* 3 vols. Leipzig: Apvd haer. Weidmann et Reich, 1781–1795.

Wentworth, Ralph S., *et al.*, eds. *Knight's Modern Seamanship.* Twelfth edition. New York, London, Toronto: D. Van Nostrand Co., Inc., 1953.

Werner, Auguste-Raynald. *Traité de droit maritime: général; éléments et système, définitions, problèmes, principes.* Geneva: Librairie Droz, 1964.

Westlake, John. *International Law.* 2 vols. Second edition. Cambridge: The University Press, 1910–1913.

Wetering, W. van de. *Les eaux territoriales et leur régime en temps de paix et en temps de guerre.* Geneva, 1933.

Wheaton, Henry. *Elements of International Law.* Eighth edition by Richard Henry Dana, Jr. Boston: Little, Brown and Co., 1866.

———. *Elements of International Law.* English edition by A. C. Boyd. London: Stevens and Sons, 1878.

Whitaker, Urban G., Jr. *Politics and Power: A Test in International Law.* New York, Evanston, and London: Harper and Row, 1964.

Wiebringhaus, H. *La question de la zone contiguë devant la conférence de Genève de 1958.* Sarrebruck, 1960.

Wilhelmi, C. *Das Küstenmeer*. Jena, 1914.
Wilson, George Grafton. *Handbook of International Law*. St. Paul: West Publishing Co., 1910.
———. *International Law*. Ninth edition. New York, Boston, Chicago, and San Francisco: Silver Burdett Co., 1935.
Wolff, Christian. *Jus gentium methodo scientifica pertractatum*. Trans. Joseph H. Drake. In *The Classics of International Law*, ed. James Brown Scott. Dobbs Ferry, N.Y.: Oceana Publications, Inc., and London: Wildy and Sons, Ltd., reprinted 1964.
Woolsey, Theodore Dwight. *Introduction to the Study of International Law: Designed as an Aid in Teaching and in Historical Studies*. Boston and Cambridge: J. Munroe and Co., 1860. (Sixth edition revised and enlarged by Theodore Salisbury Woolsey. New York: C. Scribner's Sons, 1901.
Zoričić, Milovan. *Teritorijalno More (Territorial Sea)*. Zagreb: Yugoslav Academy of Arts and Sciences, 1953.
Zouche, Richard. *An Exposition of Fecial Law and Procedure, or of Law Between Nations and Questions Concerning the Same: Wherein Are Set forth Matters Regarding Peace and War between Different Princes or Peoples, Derived from the Most Eminent Historical Jurists*. Trans. from Latin by J. L. Brierly. In *The Classics of International Law*, ed. James Brown Scott. Dobbs Ferry, N.Y.: Oceana Publications, Inc., and London: Wildy and Sons, Ltd., reprinted 1964.

6. PUBLICATIONS OF LEARNED SOCIETIES AND UNIVERSITIES

Akademie der Wissenschatten der Ud SSR Rechtsinstitut. *Völkerrecht*. Berlin: Veb Deutscher Zentralverlag, 1960.
American Society of International Law. *International Legal Materials: Current Documents*, V (No. 6, November, 1966).
Baylor University Law School. "Symposium on the Texas 'Tidelands' Case," *Baylor Law Review*, III (No. 2, Winter, 1951), pp. 115–335.
The British Institute of International and Comparative Law. *Developments in the Law of the Sea 1958–1964*. London: The British Institute of International and Comparative Law, 1965.
Harvard Law School. *Research in International Law: Nationality; Responsibility of States; Territorial Waters*. Cambridge, Mass.: Harvard Law School, 1929. Reprinted in Supplement to *American Journal of International Law*, XXII (April, 1929), pp. 1–380.
Institute of International Law. "Projet de règlement relatif à la mer territoriale en temps de paix," *Annuaire de l'Institut de Droit International*, XXXIV (1928 Stockholm Session), pp. 755–759.
International Law Association. "Amended Draft Convention: Laws of Maritime Jurisdiction in Time of Peace," *Report of the Thirty-Third Conference of the International Law Association*, XXXIII (September, 1924), pp. 285–288.
———. *Report of the Seventeenth Conference of the International Law Association* (Brussels, 1895 Session). London, 1896.
National Geographic Society. *Atlas of the World*. Washington, D.C.: National Geographic Society, 1963.
The Society of Comparative Legislation and International Law. *The Law of the Sea: The Final Act and Annexes of the United Nations Conference on the Law of the Sea, Geneva, 1958, Together with a Synoptical Table of Claims to Jurisdiction over the Territorial Seas, the Contiguous Zone, and the Continental Shelf*. London: Society of Comparative Legislation and International Law, 1958.

7. PERIODICALS

Allen, Edward W. "Fish Can Be International," *U.S. Naval Institute Proceedings*, LXXXII (October, 1956), pp. 1066–1071.

———. "The Fishery Proclamation of 1945," *American Journal of International Law*, XLV (January, 1951), pp. 177–178.

———. "Freedom of the Sea," *American Journal of International Law*, LX (October, 1966), pp. 814–816.

———. "Legal Limits of Coastal Fishery Protection," [Seattle] *Washington Law Review*, XXI (1946), pp. 1–4.

———. "A New Concept for Fishery Treaties," *American Journal of International Law*, XLVI (April, 1952), pp. 319–323.

———. "Territorial Waters and Extraterritorial Rights," *American Journal of International Law*, XLVII (July, 1953), pp. 478–480.

Ancel, J. "Les frontières étude de géographie politique: exemple de frontières maritimes: l'Allemagne du Nord sur la mer du Nord," *Recueil des cours de l'Académie de Droit International*, LV (1936-I), pp. 242–258.

Anderson, Chandler P. "Exploitation of the Products of the Sea," *American Journal of International Law*, XX (October, 1926), pp. 752–753.

———. "The Final Outcome of the Fisheries Arbitration," *American Journal of International Law*, VI (January, 1913), pp. 1–16.

Mr. Anderson served as special representative of the United States in negotiating the final agreement with Great Britain.

Anonymous. "Conference on U.S.-Ecuadorian Fishery Relations," *Department of State Bulletin*, XXVIII (1953), pp. 759–761.

———. "Jurisdicción sobre la plataforma continental," *Bulletin of the Pan American Union*, (March, 1948), pp. 142–146.

———. "Law of the Shallow Seas: Territorial Waters and the Continental Shelf," *Round Table* (London), (June, 1955), pp. 255–263.

———. "Navy Backs 12-mile Fish Limit," *U.S. Naval Institute Proceedings*, XCII (September, 1966), p. 154 citing *Christian Science Monitor*, 15 June 1966.

———. "Navy Would Make Concessions for Right of Innocent Passage in Straits," *Oceanology: The Weekly of Ocean Technology*, V (November 21, 1968; No. 21), p. 149.

———. "Plataforma continental," *Revista de Derecho y Legislación* (Caracas, Venezuela), XLII (1953), pp. 115–135.

———. "Territorial Waters and Continental Shelf: Three-Mile Limit Outmoded: Sovereign Rights over Continental Shelf an Economic Necessity," *Indian Shipping* (Bombay), VIII (1956), pp. 13–17.

———. "U.N. Conference on the Law of the Sea," *The Department of State Bulletin*, XXXVIII (June 30, 1958), pp. 1110–1125.

———. "U.N. to Convene Second Conference on the Law of the Sea," *The Department of State Bulletin*, XL (January 12, 1959), pp. 64–67.

———. "United States Delegations to International Conferences: Second U.N. Conference on the Law of the Sea," *The Department of State Bulletin*, XLII (March 28, 1960), pp. 504–505.

———. "United States Delegations to International Conferences: U.N. Conference on the Law of the Sea," *The Department of State Bulletin*, XXXVIII (March 10, 1958), pp. 404–405.

Aramburu Menchaca, A. "Carácter y alcances de los derechos y ejercidos sobre el mar y zocalo continental," *Revista Peruana de Derecho Internacional*, (September-December, 1952), pp. 153–185.

Aubert, L. M. B. "Définition et régime de la mer territoriale" (Report of the

Third Commission and annex, M. Renault, Reporter), *Annuaire de l'Institut de Droit International*, XI (1891 Hamburg Session), pp. 863–879.

——. "La mer territoriale de la Norvège," *Revue Générale de Droit International Public*, I (1894), pp. 429–441.

Austin, J., and N. A. M. Mackenzie, "A Canadian View of Territorial Seas and Fisheries," *International Law, Rivers and Marginal Seas: University of British Columbia Lecture Series* (Vancouver), No. 27, pp. 35 ff.

Azcárraga y de Bustamente, José Luis de. "Los derechos sobre la plataforma submarina," *Revista Española de Derecho Internacional* (Madrid), II (1949), pp. 47–99.

——. "Régimen jurídico de las aguas históricas," *Anuario Hispano-Luso-Americano de Derecho Internacional* (Zaragoza) (1959), pp. 83–91.

——. "Régimen jurídico de los espacios marítimos," *Revista Española de Derecho International* (Madrid), V (1952), pp. 27–118.

Balch, Thomas Willing. "The Hudsonian Sea Is a Great Open Sea," *American Journal of International Law*, VII (July, 1913), pp. 546–565.

——. "Is Hudson Bay a Closed or an Open Sea?" *American Journal of Intertional Law*, VI (April, 1912), pp. 409–459.

——. "The Marine Belt and the Question of Territorial Waters," *Proceedings of the American Society of International Law*, (1912), pp. 132–142.

Baldoni, C. "Les navires de guerre dans les eaux territoriales étrangères," *Recueil des Cours de l'Académie de Droit International*, LXV (1938-III), pp. 189–303.

Barclay, Sir Thomas (Reporter). "Report of the Sixth Commission: La mer territoriale," *Annuaire de l'Institut de Droit International*, XXV (1912 Christiania Session), pp. 368–389.

——. "Report of the Third Commission: Définition et régime de la mer territoriale," *Annuaire de l'Institut de Droit International*, XII (1892 Geneva Session), pp. 47–96.

——. "Report of the Third Commision: Définition et régime de la mer territoriale," *Annuaire de l'Institut de Droit International*, XIII (1894 Paris Session), pp. 355–393, 448–497, 517–519.

Bartos, M. "Les eaux territoriales et l'ONU," *Revue de la Politique Mondiale Internationale* (Belgrade), V (1954), pp. 1–35; VI (1955), pp. 7–99.

Baty, Thomas. "The Free Sea—Produce the Evidence," *American Journal of International Law*, XXXV (April, 1941), pp. 227–242.

——. "Naval Warfare: Law and License," *American Journal of International Law*, X (January, 1916), pp. 42–52.

——. "The Three-Mile Limit," *American Journal of International Law*, XXII (July, 1928), pp. 503–537.

Baxter, Richard R. "The Territorial Sea," *Proceedings of the American Society of International Law*, (April, 1956), pp. 116–124.

Becker, Lofter. "The Breadth of the Territorial Sea and Fisheries Jurisdiction," *The Department of State Bulletin*, XL (March 16, 1959), pp. 369–374.

Benitez, R. C., and Philip B. Yeager. "The Law of the Sea and the Naval Officer," *U.S. Naval Institute Proceedings*, LXXXII (December, 1956), pp. 1271–1280.

Bernfeld, Seymour S. "Developing the Resources of the Sea—Security of Investment," *The International Lawyer*, II (October, 1967), pp. 67–76.

Bilder, Richard B. "Emerging Legal Problems of the Deep Seas and Polar Regions," *Naval War College Review*, XX (December, 1967), pp. 34–49.

Bingham, Joseph Walter. "The Continental Shelf and the Marginal Belt," *American Journal of International Law*, XL (January, 1946), pp. 173–177.

——. "Juridical Status of the Continental Shelf," *Southern California Law Review*, XXVI (1952–1953), pp. 4–20.

——. "Maritime Jurisdiction in Time of Peace," *Proceedings of the American Society of International Law*, (1940), pp. 54–71.

Blociszewski, J. de (Reporter). "Report of the Seventh Commission: La Navigation en Haute Mer," *Annuaire de l'Institut de Droit International*, (1927 Lausanne Session), vol. I, pp. 103–146; vol. III, pp. 257–267, 339.

Boggs, S. Whittemore. "Delimitation of Seaward Areas under National Jurisdiction," *American Journal of International Law*, XLV (April, 1951), pp. 240–266.

——. "Delimitation of the Territorial Sea," *American Journal of International Law*, XXIV (July, 1930), pp. 541–555.

——. "National Claims in Adjacent Seas," *Geographic Review* (New York), XLI (1951), pp. 185–209.

——. "Problems of Water-Boundary Definition: Median Lines and International Boundaries through Territorial Waters," *Geographic Review* (New York), (1937), pp. 445–456.

Borchardt, Edwin M. "Jurisdiction over the Littoral Bed of the Sea," *American Journal of International Law*, XXXV (July, 1941), pp. 515–519. [Also spelled Borchard.]

——. "Resources of the Continental Shelf," *American Journal of International Law*, XL (January, 1946), pp. 53–70.

Borisov, S. "Mezhdunarodnyi sud o territorial'nykh vodakh," *Sovetskoe Gosudarstvo Pravo* (Moscow), 1952, No. 8, pp. 52 ff.

Bourquin, M. "Le domaine maritime," *Recueil des Cours de l'Académie de Droit International*, XXXV (1931-I), pp. 118–122.

Böye, Thorvald. "Territorial Waters with Special Reference to Norwegian Legislation," *Report of the Thirty-Third Conference of the International Law Association 1924*. London: Sweet and Maxwell, Ltd., 1925, pp. 294–335.

Brierly, J. L. "The Doctrine of the Contiguous Zone and the Dicta in *Craft v. Dunphy*," *British Yearbook of International Law*, XIV (1933), pp. 155–157.

Briggs, Herbert W. "Les Etats-Unis et la loi de 1935 sur la contrebande," *Revue de Droit International et de Législation Comparée* (third series), XX (1939), pp. 338–342.

——. "Jurisdiction over the Sea Bed and Subsoil Beyond Territorial Waters," *American Journal of International Law*, XLV (April, 1951), pp. 338–342.

Brinton, J. Y. "Jurisdiction over Sea-bed Resources and Recent Developments in Persian Gulf Area," *Revue Egyptienne de Droit International*, V (1949), pp. 131–133.

——. "Territorial Sea and the Continental Shelf: A Review of Recent Developments," *Revue Egyptienne de Droit International*, VIII (1952), pp. 103–128.

——. "Territorial Waters," *Revue Egyptienne de Droit International*, VII (1951), pp. 91–96.

Brittin, Burdick H. "Article 3, Regime of the Territorial Sea," *American Journal of International Law*, L (October, 1956), pp. 934–941.

——. "International Law Aspects of the Acquisition of the Continental Shelf by the United States," *U.S. Naval Institute Proceedings*, LXXIV (December, 1948), pp. 1541–1543.

Brock, John R. "Archipelago Concept of Limits of Territorial Seas," *Naval War College Review*, XIX (December, 1966), pp. 34–97.

Brown, Philip Marshall. "The Law of Territorial Waters," *American Journal of International Law*, XXI (January, 1927), pp. 101–105.

——. "The Marginal Sea," *American Journal of International Law*, XVII (January, 1923), pp. 89–95.

——. "Protective Jurisdiction over Marginal Waters," *Proceedings of the American Society of International Law*, XVII (April, 1923), pp. 15–31.

Browning, T. B. "The Behring Sea Question," *Law Quarterly Review* (London), VII (1891), pp. 128–139, 315–336.

Brüel, Erik. "Les détroits danois au point de vue du droit international," *Recueil des Cours de l'Académie de Droit International,* LV (1936-I), pp. 599–695.

Burke, William T. "Some Comments on the 1958 Conventions," *Proceedings of the American Society of International Law,* (1959), pp. 197–206.

Bustamente y Sirvén, Antonio Sánchez de. "El mar territorial cubano," *Revista de Derecho Internacional* (Habana), (no. 44), p. 199.

Butler, William E. "The Legal Regime of Russian Territorial Waters," *American Journal of International Law,* LXII (January, 1968), pp. 51–77.

———. "The Soviet Union and the Continental Shelf," *American Journal of International Law,* LXIII (January, 1969), pp. 103–107.

Carlisle, Geoffrey E. "Three Mile Limit—Obsolete Concept?" *U.S. Naval Institute Proceedings,* XCIII (February, 1967), pp. 24–33.

Carroz, J. E. and A. G. Roche. "The International Policing of High Seas Fisheries," *Canadian Yearbook of International Law,* VI (1968), pp. 61–90.

Castro, Luis V. "The 12-mile Limit: Its Disadvantages," [United States Congress] *Congressional Record,* CV (part 9, June 18–30, 1959), pp. 12160–12162.

Chapman, W. M. "United States Policy on High Seas Fisheries," *Department of State Bulletin,* XX (16 January 1949; no. 498), pp. 67–71, 80.

Charteris, A. H. "Territorial Jurisdiction in Wide Bays," *Yale Law Journal,* XVI (1906-7), pp. 471–496.

Chih-shih Chen. "Is the Three-mile Limit a Rule of Universal International Law?", *The Annals of the Chinese Society of International Law,* I (July, 1964), pp. 65–81.

Chowl-Kewn Chee. "International Aspects of Fishery Conservation Zones and Fishery Treaties of the Nations," *Korean Journal of International Law,* II (1957, no. 1), pp. 101–164.

Christy, Francis T., Jr. "Economic Criteria for Rules Governing Exploitation of Deep Sea Minerals," *The International Lawyer,* II (January, 1968), pp. 224–242.

Clark, G. Norman. "Grotius's East India Mission to England," *Transactions of the Grotius Society,* XX (1934). Dobbs Ferry, N.Y.: Oceana Publications, Inc., and London: Wildy and Sons, Ltd., reprinted 1962. Pp. 45–84.

Cleminson, H. M. "International Unification of Maritime Law," *Journal of Comparative Legislation and International Law* (London), (third series), XXIII (1941), pp. 163–168.

———. "Laws of Maritime Jurisdiction in Time of Peace," *Report of the Thirty-Third Conference of the International Law Association,* (1924, Stockholm Session). London: Sweet and Maxwell, 1925. Pp. 285–293.

———. "Laws of Maritime Jurisdiction in Time of Peace with Special Reference to Territorial Waters," *British Yearbook of International Law,* VI (1925), pp. 144–154.

Cochran, Charles L. "Territorial Waters, Fishing Rights and International Law," *U.S. Naval Institute Proceedings,* XCIII (August, 1967), pp. 132–135.

Cole, Sanford D. "The Highways of the Sea," *Transactions of the Grotius Society,* IV (1918). Dobbs Ferry, N.Y.: Oceana Publications, Inc., and London: Wildy and Sons, Ltd., reprinted 1962. Pp. 15–25.

Colombos, C. John. "Territorial Waters," *Transactions of the Grotius Society,* IX (1923). Dobbs Ferry, N.Y.: Oceana Publications, Inc., and London: Wildy and Sons, Ltd., reprinted 1962. Pp. 89–100.

———. "The Unification of Maritime International Law in Time of Peace," *British Yearbook of International Law,* XXI (1944), pp. 96–110.

——— (Secretary of the Neutrality Committee). "Report of the Neutrality Committee," *Report of the Thirty-Third Conference of the International Law Association*, XXXIII (September, 1924), pp. 259–335.

Conboy, M. "The Territorial Sea," *Proceedings of the Canadian Bar Association*, (1923), pp. 276 ff.

Cosford, Edwin J. "The Continental Shelf, 1910–1945," *The McGill Law Journal*, IV (1958), pp. 245–266.

Craven, John P. "Sea Power and the Sea Bed," *U.S. Naval Institute Proceedings*, XCII (April, 1966), pp. 36–51.

Creamer, Robert A. "Title to the Deep Seabed: Prospects for the Future," *Harvard International Law Journal*, IX (Spring, 1968), pp. 205–231.

Cromie, William J. "Who Will Own the Ocean's Wealth?" *U.S. Naval Institute Proceedings*, XCI (January, 1965), pp. 52–61.

Cumbrae-Stewart, F. W. S. "The Maritime Boundary of Queensland," *Journal of Comparative Legislation and International Law* (London), XII (1930), pp. 299 ff.

Custance, Sir Reginald. "The Freedom of the Seas," *Transactions of the Grotius Society*, V (1919). Dobbs Ferry, N.Y.: Oceana Publications, Inc., and London: Wildy and Sons, Ltd., reprinted 1962. Pp. 65–70.

Daggett, A. P. "The Regulation of Maritime Fisheries by Treaty," *American Journal of International Law*, XXVIII (1934), pp. 693–717.

Dean, Arthur H. "Achievements at the Law of the Sea Conference," *Proceedings of the American Society of International Law* (1959), pp. 186–197.

    Mr. Dean headed the United States delegation to Geneva in both 1958 and 1960.

———. "Department Seeks Senate Approval of Conventions on Law of the Sea," *The Department of State Bulletin*, XLII (February 15, 1960), pp. 251–261.

———. "Freedom of the Seas," *Foreign Affairs*, XXXVII (October, 1958), pp. 83–94.

———. "The Geneva Conference on the Law of the Sea: What Was Accomplished," *American Journal of International Law*, LII (October, 1958), 607–628.

———. "The Law of the Sea," *The Department of State Bulletin*, XXXVIII (April 7, 1958), pp. 574–581.

———. "The Second Geneva Conference on the Law of the Sea: The Fight for Freedom of the Seas," *American Journal of International Law*, LIV (October, 1960), pp. 751–789.

Delay, J. K. "Relation of Federal and State Title of United States to Tidelands," *Michigan Law Review*, L (1951), pp. 114–124.

Dennis, W. C. "The Sinking of the 'I'm Alone'," *American Journal of International Law*, XXIII (1929), pp. 351–362.

Dickinson, Edwin D. "Are the Liquor Treaties Self-Executing?" *American Journal of International Law*, XX (July, 1926), pp. 444–452.

———. "Jurisdiction at the Maritime Frontier," *Harvard Law Review*, XL (November, 1926), pp. 1–29.

———. "Rum Seizures under the Recent Treaties," *American Journal of International Law*, XX (January, 1926), pp. 111–117.

———. "The Supreme Court Interprets the Liquor Treaties," *American Journal of International Law*, XXVII (1933), pp. 305–310.

———. "Treaties for the Prevention of Smuggling," *American Journal of International Law*, XX (April, 1926), pp. 340–346.

Edwards, D. Jay. "Chinese Communist Territorial Water Claims," *U.S. Naval Institute Proceedings*, LXXXIX (October, 1963), pp. 157–158.

Ely, Northcutt. "American Policy Options in the Development of Undersea Mineral Resources," *The International Lawyer*, II (January, 1968), pp. 215–223.

Evans, Alona E., ed. "North Sea Continental Shelf Cases," *American Journal of International Law*, LXIII (July, 1969), pp. 591–636.

Evensen, Jens. "The Anglo-Norwegian Fisheries Case and Its Legal Consequences," *American Journal of International Law*, XLVI (October, 1952), pp. 609–630.

Feith, Jonkheer P. R. "Rights to the Sea Bed and Its Subsoil," *Report of the Forty-Third Conference of the International Law Association*, (1948, Brussels Session). Cambridge: Crompton and Sons, Ltd., 1950. Pp. 183–206.

Fenn, Percy Thomas, Jr. "Justinian and the Freedom of the Sea," *American Journal of International Law*, XIX (October, 1925), pp. 716–727.

———. "Origins of the Theory of Territorial Waters," *American Journal of International Law*, XX (July, 1926), pp. 465–482.

Ferrero Rebagliati, R. "El territorio del estado," *Revista Peruana de Derecho Internacional* (January-December, 1955), pp. 16–35.

Finlay, Luke W. "The Outer Limit of the Continental Shelf: A Rejoinder to Professor Louis Henkin," *American Journal of International Law*, LXIV (January, 1970), pp. 42–72. Louis Henkin's reply is included, pp. 62–72.

Fitzmaurice, Sir Gerald G. "The Case of the 'I'm Alone'," *British Yearbook of International Law*, XVII (1936), pp. 82–111.

———. "The Law and Procedure of the International Court of Justice, 1951–1954: Points of Substantive Law: Maritime Law (Territorial Waters, Internal Waters, The Norwegian Fisheries Case)," *British Yearbook of International Law*, XXXI (1957), pp. 371–429.

———. "Some Results of the Geneva Conference on the Law of the Sea: Part I—The Territorial Sea and Contiguous Zone and Related Topics," *The International and Comparative Law Quarterly*, VIII (January, 1959), pp. 73–121.

Fletcher, Eric G. M. "John Selden (Author of *Mare Clausum*) and his Contribution to International Law," *Transactions of the Grotius Society*, XIX (1933). Dobbs Ferry, N.Y.: Oceana Publications, Inc., and London: Wildy and Sons, Ltd., reprinted 1962. Pp. 1–12.

Focsaneanu, L. "Le droit maritime de l'Océan pacifique et de ses mers adjacentes," *Annuaire Français de Droit International*, VII (1961), pp. 173–214.

François, J. P. A. "El régimen de alta mar," *Revista de Derecho Internacional* (Habana), (no. 60), pp. 60 ff.

———. "Rights to the Sea-bed and Its Subsoil," *Report of the Forty-Fifth Conference of the International Law Association* (1952, Lucerne Session). Great Britain: Cambrian News (Aberystwyth), Ltd., 1953. Pp. 143–178.

Franklin, Carl M. "The Law of the Sea: Some Recent Developments," *Egyptian Review of International Law*, XVIII (1962), pp. 28–52.

Fraser, Henry S. "The Extent and Delimitation of Territorial Waters," *Cornell Law Quarterly*, XI (1925–1926), pp. 455–481.

Frosch, Robert A. "Marine Mineral Resources: National Security and National Jurisdiction," *Naval War College Review*, XXI (October, 1968), pp. 53–60.

Gidel, Gilbert Charles. "La mer territoriale et la zone contiguë," *Recueil des Cours de l'Académie du Droit International*, XLVIII (1934-II), pp. 137–277.

Gihl, Torsten. "The Limits of Swedish Territorial Waters," *American Journal of International Law*, L (January, 1956), pp. 120–122.

Glenn, Gene. "The Swedish-Soviet Territorial Sea Controversy in the Baltic," *American Journal of International Law*, L (October, 1956), pp. 942–949.

Goddard, G. "The Land Under the Sea," *The Indian Year Book of International Affairs*, (1957), pp. 81–103.

Godey, Paul. "Les limits de la mer territoriale," *Revue générale de droit international public*, III (March-April, 1896), pp. 224–237.

Goldie, L. F. E. "Australia's Continental Shelf: Legislation and Proclamations,"

International and Comparative Law Quarterly (London), III (1954), pp. 535–575.

——. "The Ocean's Resources and International Law—Possible Developments in Regional Fisheries Management," *The Columbia Journal of Transnational Law*, VIII (Spring, 1969, No. 1), pp. 1–53.

——. "Sedentary Fisheries and Article 2 (4) of the Continental Shelf Convention," *American Journal of International Law*, LXIII (January, 1969), pp. 86–97.

——. "Sedentary Fisheries and the North Sea Continental Shelf Cases—A Paradox Revealed," *American Journal of International Law*, LXIII (July, 1969), pp. 536–541.

Goldsworthy, Frank. "More Fun Than Fury in the Fish War," *U.S. Naval Institute Proceedings*, LXXXVII (February, 1961), pp. 58–67.

Gotlieb, A. E. "The Canadian Contribution to the Concept of a Fishing Zone in International Law," *Canadian Yearbook of International Law*, II (1964), pp. 55–76.

Green, L. C. "The Anglo-Norwegian Fisheries Case, 1951," *The Modern Law Review*, XV (1952), pp. 373–377.

——. "The Continental Shelf," *Current Legal Problems* (London), IV (1951), pp. 54–80.

Gregory, C. "Jurisdiction over Foreign Ships in Territorial Waters," *Michigan Law Review*, II (1904), pp. 333 ff.

Gros, André. "La convention sur la pêche et la conservation des ressources biologiques de la haute mer," *Recueil des Cours de l'Académie de Droit International*, XCVII (1959-II), pp. 1–89.

Gross, Leo. "Geneva Conference on the Law of the Sea and the Right of Innocent Passage through the Gulf of Aqaba," *American Journal of International Law*, LIII (July, 1959), pp. 564–594.

Gruening, Ernest. "The Russian Raids on Alaskan Fishermen Should be Stopped," *The Congressional Record (Senate)*, November 5, 1963, pp. 20005–20006.

Guill, James H. "The Regimen of the Seas," *U.S. Naval Institute Proceedings*, LXXXIII (December, 1957), pp. 1308–1319.

Guillaume, Baron. "La Convention de La Haye de 1882," *Revue de Droit International et de Législation Comparée*, XXVI (1894), pp. 488–510.

Gushue, R. "The Territorial Waters of Newfoundland," *Canadian Journal of Economics and Political Science*, XIV (1949, no. 3).

Gutierrez, G. "La libertad del mar y las plataformas continental e insular," *Revista de Derecho Internacional* (Habana), (no. 54), pp. 5 ff.

Gutteridge, J. A. C. "The 1958 Geneva Convention on the Continental Shelf," *British Yearbook of International Law*, XXV (1959), pp. 102–123.

——. "The Regime of the Continental Shelf," *Transactions of the Grotius Society*, XLIV (1957). Dobbs Ferry, N.Y.: Oceana Publications, Inc., and London: Wildy and Sons, Ltd., reprinted 1962. Pp. 77–89.

Haight, G. Winthrop. "The Seabed and the Ocean Floor," *The International Lawyer*, III (April, 1969), pp. 642–673.

Hale, Richard W. "Territorial Waters as a Test of Codification," *American Journal of International Law*, XXIV (January, 1930), pp. 65–78.

Hammad, Burhan W. "The Right of Passage in the Gulf of Aqaba," *Revue Egyptienne de Droit International*, XV (1959), pp. 118–151.

Hanna, John. "The Submerged Land Cases," *Baylor Law Review*, III (Winter, 1951, no. 2), pp. 201–240.

Hearn, Wilfred A. "The Law of the Sea: the 1958 Geneva Conference," *Journal of the Navy Judge Advocate General (JAG Journal)*, (March–April, 1960), pp. 3–6.

Heine, Irwin M., Muriel W. Coe, and J. W. Gulick (U.S. Maritime Administration). "The Soviet Merchant Marine," *Naval Review, 1969* ed. Frank Uhlig, Jr. Annapolis, Md.: United States Naval Institute, 1969. Pp. 373–393.

Heinzen, Bernard G. "The Three-Mile Limit: Preserving the Freedom of the Seas," *Stanford Law Review*, XI (July, 1959), pp. 597–664.

Henkin, Louis. See entry, Luke W. Finlay, *supra*.

Hideo Takabayashi. "Historical Background of Maritime Disputes: the Formative Process of Principles of Freedom of the High Seas," *Kyoto Law Review*, LX (1954), pp. 60–93.

——. "Normalization of Relations between Japan and the Republic of Korea: Agreement on Fisheries," *The Japanese Annual of International Law*, X (1966), pp. 16–22.

Hilbert, W. E. "The Three-Mile Limit of Territorial Waters," *U.S. Naval Institute Proceedings*, LXIV (June, 1938), pp. 804–812.

Hill, C. E. "Le régime international des détroits maritimes," *Recueil des Cours de l'Académie de Droit International*, XLV (1933–III), pp. 479–555.

Hirst, F. W. "The American Conception of the Freedom of the Sea," *Transactions of the Grotius Society*, IV (1918). Dobbs Ferry, N.Y.: Oceana Publications, Inc., and London: Wildy and Sons, Ltd., reprinted 1962. Pp. 26–34.

Hittle, James D. "New Soviet Strategy on the High Seas: The Grab for Narrow Waters," *Life*, LIII (December 21, 1962), 83–92.

Honig, F. "International Maritime Law: the Work of the International Law Commission," *Law Journal* (London), CV (1955), pp. 23–24.

Hounshell, C. D., and L. H. Kemp. "Continental Shelf: A Study in National Interest and International Law," *Journal of Public Law* (Emory University, Ga.), V (Fall, 1956), pp. 343 ff.

Houston, Oscar R. "Freedom of the Seas: The Present State of International Law," *American Bar Association Journal*, XLII (March, 1956), pp. 235–238.

Hudson, Manley O. "The First Conference for the Codification of International Law," *American Journal of International Law*, XXIV (July, 1930), pp. 447–466. Mr. Hudson was a member of the U.S. delegation to the Conference.

——. "The Thirteenth Year of the World Court: Anglo-Norwegian Fisheries Case," *American Journal of International Law;* XLVI (1952), pp. 23–30.

Hurst, Sir Cecil. "The Continental Shelf," *Transactions of the Grotius Society*, XXXIV (1948). London, New York, Toronto: Longmans Green and Co., 1949. Pp. 153–169.

——. "The Territoriality of Bays," *British Yearbook of International Law*, III (1922–23), pp. 42–54.

——. "Whose is the Bed of the Sea?" *British Yearbook of International Law*, IV (1923–24), pp. 34–43.

Hyde, Charles Cheney. "The International Law of the Texas Tideland Case," *Baylor Law Review*, III (Winter 1951, no. 2), pp. 172–187.

Ireland, Gordon. "Marginal Seas Around the States," *Louisiana Law Review*, II (1939–1940), pp. 252–293, 436–478.

——. "The North Pacific Fisheries," *American Journal of International Law*, XXXVI (July, 1942), pp. 400–424.

"Issues Before the 22nd General Assembly (Middle East)," *International Conciliation*, No. 564 (September, 1967), pp. 11–28.

Jessup, Philip C. "The Anti-Smuggling Act of 1935," *American Journal of International Law*, XXXI (January, 1937), pp. 101–106.

——. "Civil Jurisdiction over Ships in Innocent Passage," *American Journal of International Law*, XXVII (1933), pp. 747–750.

——. "L'exploitation des richesses de la mer," *Recueil des Cours de l'Académie de Droit International*, XXIX (1929-IV), pp. 401–514.

————. "The Geneva Conference on the Law of the Sea," *American Journal of International Law*, LII (October, 1958). pp. 730–733.

————. "The Pacific Coast Fisheries," *American Journal of International Law*, XXXIII (January, 1939), pp. 129–138.

Johnson, D. H. N. "The Anglo-Norwegian Fisheries Case," *International and Comparative Law Quarterly*, I (1952), pp. 145–180.

————. "Control of Exploitation of Natural Resources in the Sea off the United Kingdom," *International Law Quarterly* (London), IV (1951), pp. 445–453.

————. "Icelandic Fishery's Limits," *International and Comparative Law Quarterly*, I (1952), pp. 71–73, 350–540.

————. "Law of the Sea: Development since the Geneva Conferences of 1958 and 1960: Anglo-Scandinavian Agreements Concerning the Territorial Sea and Fishery Limits," *International and Comparative Law Quarterly*, X (1961), pp. 587–597.

————. "The Legal Status of the Sea-bed and Subsoil," *Zeitschrift für Auslandisches Offentliches Recht und Völkerrecht*, XVI (1956), pp. 451–499.

————. "The Preparation of the 1958 Geneva Conference on the Law of the Sea," *The International and Comparative Law Quarterly*, VIII (January, 1959), pp. 122–145.

————. "Repercussions of the International Court's Judgment in the Anglo-Norwegian Fisheries Case on the Tidelands Dispute in the United States," *International and Comparative Law Quarterly*, I (1952), pp. 213–216.

Johnston, Kenneth V. "Canada's Title to Hudson Bay and Hudson Strait," *British Yearbook of International Law*, XV (1934), pp. 1–20.

Kalijarvi, Thorsten. "Scandinavian Claims to Jurisdiction over Territorial Waters," *American Journal of International Law*," XXVI (January, 1952), pp. 57–69.

Katzenbach, Nicholas DeB. "Sharable and Strategic Resources: Outer Space, Polar Areas, and the Oceans," *Proceedings of the American Society of International Law*, (1959), pp. 206–212.

Kent, H. S. K. "The Historical Origins of the Three-Mile Limit," *American Journal of International Law*, XLVIII (October, 1954), pp. 537–553.

Keishiro, Iriye. "The Status of Peter the Great Bay (Piyotoru-Taitei-Wan no Chiyi)," *Legal Reports* (Horitsu Ziho), XXIX (1957), pp. 1166–1167.

Kenworthy, Hon. J. M., and G. S. Bowles. "Freedom of the Seas," *Transactions of the Grotius Socity*, XIV (1928). Dobbs Ferry, N.Y.: Oceana Publications, Inc., and London: Wildy and Sons, Ltd., reprinted 1962. Pp. 113–130.

Ko Nakamura. "The Japan-United States Negotiations concerning King Crab Fishery in the Eastern Bering Sea," *The Japanese Annual of International Law*, IX (1965), pp. 36–45.

Kraske, E. "Küstenmeer, Meeresboden, und Freiheit des Meeres," *Archiv des Völkerrechtes* (Tübingen), III (1952), pp. 259–274.

Kunz, Josef L. "Continental Shelf and International Law," *American Journal of International Law*, L (October, 1956), pp. 828–853.

La Forest, G. V. "Canadian Inland Waters of the Atlantic Provinces and the Bay of Fundy Incident," *Canadian Yearbook of International Law*, I (1963), pp. 149–171.

Lakhtine, W. "Rights over the Arctic," *American Journal of International Law*, XXIV (October, 1930), pp. 703–717.

Lalive D'Epinay, O. A. "The Developing Law of the Continental Shelf," *Petroleum Times* (London), LVIII (1954), pp. 655–659.

Langeraar, W. "The North Sea," *U.S. Naval Institute Proceedings*, XCIII (January, 1967), pp. 21–32.

Lansing, Robert. "The North Atlantic Coast Fisheries Arbitration," *American Journal of International Law*, V (January, 1911), pp. 1–31.

Lapradelle, Albert G. de. "Le droit de l'état sur la mer territoriale (The Right of the State over Territorial Sea)," *Revue Générale de Droit International Public*, V (1898), pp. 264–344.

Laun, R. "Le régime international des ports," *Recueil des Cours de l'Académie de Droit International*, XV (1926-V), pp. 5–141.

Lauterpacht, Sir Hersch. "Sovereignty over Submarine Areas," *British Yearbook of International Law*, XXVII (1950), pp. 376–433.

Letts, E. S. "Les réunions interamericanas de México y Ciudad Trujillo en relación con la política marítima del Perú," *Revista Peruana de Derecho Internacional*, XVI (1956, no. 49), pp. 3–9.

Lewis, John D. "The Deep Sea Resources," *Naval War College Review*, XXI (June, 1969), pp. 130–151.

Li Tchong-koel. "L'étude sur la Convention Internationale de la Pêche en Haute Mer et la Conservation des Ressources Biologiques de la Mer," *The Annals of the Chinese Society of International Law*, III (July, 1966), pp. 98–107.

Lissitzyn, Oliver J. "Some Legal Implications of the U-2 and RB-47 Incidents," *American Journal of International Law*, LVI (January, 1962), pp. 135–142.

Llorente, Luis Orcasitas. "El mar territorial en la Conferencia de Ginebra de 1958," *Anuario Hispano-Luso-Americano de Derecho Internacional* (Zaragosa), (1959), pp. 70–82.

Macdonald, R. St. J. "Some Aspects of International Fisheries Control in U.S.-Canadian Relations," *Revue Hellénique de Droit International* (Athens), VII (1954), pp. 194–213.

Martens, Fedor Fedorovich de. "Le tribunal d'arbitrage de Paris et la mer territoriale," *Revue Générale de Droit International*, I (January-February, 1894), pp. 39 ff.

Martial, M. "State Control of the Air Space of the Territorial Sea and Contiguous Zone," *Canadian Bar Review*, XXX (1952), pp. 245 ff.

Masterson, William Edward. "Territorial Waters and International Legislation," *Transactions of the Grotius Society*, XIV (1928). Dobbs Ferry, N.Y.: Oceana Publications, Inc., and London: Wildy and Sons, Ltd., reprinted 1962. Pp. 45–68.

McDougal, Myres S., and Norbert A. Schlei. "The Hydrogen Bomb Tests in Perspective: Lawful Measures for Security," *Yale Law Journal*, LXIV (April, 1955), pp. 648–710.

———, and William T. Burke. "Crisis in the Law of the Sea," *Yale Law Journal*, LXVII (February, 1958), pp. 539 ff.

———, and William T. Burke. "The Community Interest in a Narrow Territorial Sea: Inclusive versus Exclusive Competence over the Oceans," *Cornell Law Quarterly*, XLV (Winter, 1960), pp. 171–253.

Meade, James F. "The Great Territorial Sea Squabble," *U.S. Naval Institute Proceedings*, XCV (April, 1969), pp. 45–53.

Miller, Hunter. "The Hague Codification Conference," *American Journal of International Law*, XXIV (October, 1930), pp. 674–693.
   Mr. Miller headed the U.S. delegation to the Hague Codification Conference.

———, et al. "The First Conference for the Codification of the International Law," *Proceedings of the American Society of International Law* (1930), pp. 213–234.

Misra, K. P. "Territorial Sea and India," *The Indian Journal of International Law*, VI (1966), pp. 465–482.

Molina, A. "Los dominios marítimos y submarinos de Guatemala," *Revista de la Facultad de Ciencias Juridicas y Sociales de Guatemala*, IV (1949, no. 3), pp. 15–19.

Moore, James Wm. "Expropriation of the Texas Tidelands by Judicial Fiat," *Baylor Law Review*, III (Winter, 1951, no. 2), pp. 130–171.

Morin, Jacques-Yvan. "Les eaux territoriales du Canada au regard des droit international," *Canadian Yearbook of International Law*, I (1963), pp. 82–148.

———. "La zone de pêche exclusive du Canada," *Canadian Yearbook of International Law*, II (1964), pp. 77–106.

———. "Les zones de pêche de Terre-Neuve et du Labrador à la lumière de l'évolution du droit international," *Canadian Yearbook of International Law*, VI (1968), pp. 91–114.

Moreau, Lucien E. "International Law: Maritime Boundaries of California: Extent of Submerged Lands Granted to the States by Congress," *The Harvard International Law Club Journal*, VII (Spring, 1966), pp. 339–349.

Morgan, Henry G. "Soviet Policy in the Baltic," *U.S. Naval Institute Proceedings*, LXXXVI (April, 1960), pp. 83–89.

Morris, Joseph W. "The North Sea Continental Shelf: Oil and Gas Legal Problems," *The International Lawyer*, II (January, 1968), pp. 191–214.

Mouton, M. W. "The Continental Shelf," *Recueil des Cours de l'Académie de Droit International*, LXXXV (1954-I), pp. 347–465.

Murphy, Frank M. "A Soviet Naval Goal: Satellite Seas," *U.S. Naval Institute Proceedings*, LXXXVII (April, 1961), pp. 36–41.

Nafziger, James A. "International Law: Claim to Waters Beyond Three Mile Limit," *The Harvard International Law Club Journal*, VII (Winter, 1965), pp. 143–149.

Neblett, William R. "Freedom of the Seas—for Fishing," *U.S. Naval Institute Proceedings*, LXXXV (February, 1959), pp. 85–87.

Nguyen Quoc Dinh. "Les revendications des droits préférentiels de pêche en haute mer devant les Conférences des Nations Unies sur le droit de la mer de 1958 et 1960," *Annuaire Français de Droit International*, VI (1960), pp. 77–110.

Nielsen, Fred K. "Is the Jurisdiction of the United States Exclusive within the Three-Mile Limit? Does It Extend Beyond this Limit for Any Purpose?" *Proceedings of the American Society of International Law*, XVII (April, 1923), pp. 32–39.

O'Connell, Daniel Patrick. "L'Australie et sa plataforme sous-marine," *Revue de Droit International, de Sciences Diplomatiques et Politiques* (Geneva), XXXII (1954), pp. 63–66.

———. "Sedentary Fisheries and the Australian Continental Shelf," *American Journal of International Law*, XLIX (April, 1955), pp. 185–209.

Oddini, M. "L'instituto della zona contigua nei suoi recenti sviluppi," *Diritto Marittimo* (Mortara), L (1954), pp. 3–20.

Oppenheim, Lassa Francis Lawrence. "Die Fischerei in der Moray Firth," *Zeitschrift für Völkerrecht* (Breslau), V (1911), pp. 74–95.

———. "Zur Lehre von den territorialen Meerbusen," *Zeitschrift für Völkerrecht* (Breslau), I (1907), pp. 579–587.

——— (rapporteur). "Report of the Sixth Commission: La mer territoriale: La nature de la mer territoriale," *Annuaire de l'Institut de Droit International*, XXVI (1913 Oxford Session), pp. 985–995.

Padwa, David J. "Submarine Boundaries," *The International and Comparative Law Quarterly*, IX (October, 1960), pp. 628–653.

Panayotacos, G. P. "Un cas d'extension arbitraire des limites de la mer territoriale," *Revue Hellénique de Droit International* (Athens), VI (1953), pp. 253–256.

Pankhurst, D. T. "The Fisheries Act and the Pearl Fisheries Act: Note on Pending Australian Legislation on Fisheries," *Sydney Law Review*, I (1953), pp. 96–104.

Parfond, P. "Etude sur la haute mer et la mer territoriale à la Commission du Droit International de l'ONU," *Revue Maritime et Coloniale* (Paris), (1956), pp. 600–604.

Pardo, Arvid. "Whose is the Bed of the Sea" (address), *Proceedings of the American Society of International Law*, (1968), pp. 216–229.

————. "Who Will Control the Seabed?" *Foreign Affairs*, XLVII (October, 1968), pp. 123–137.

Parks, Larry G. "The Law of—and Under—the Sea," *U.S. Naval Institute Proceedings*, XCII (February, 1966), pp. 54–59.

Patry, André. "Le régime des cours d'eau internationaux," *Canadian Yearbook of International Law*, I (1963), pp. 172–212.

Paulus, Dr. J. "La mer territoriale," *Revue de Droit International et de Législation Comparée* (Third Series), V (1924), pp. 397–424.

Pearcy, G. Etzel. "Geographical Aspects of the Law of the Sea," *Annals of the Association of American Geographers*, XLIX (March, 1959), pp. 1–23.

————. "Measurement of the U.S. Territorial Sea," *The Department of State Bulletin*, XL (June 29, 1959), 963–971.

   Mr. Pearcy was writing in his capacity as United States Department of State Geographer.

Pharand, A. Donat. "Innocent Passage in the Arctic," *Canadian Yearbook of International Law*, VI (1968), pp. 3–60.

————. "Soviet Union Warns United States Against Use of Northeast Passage," *American Journal of International Law*, LXII (October, 1968), pp. 927–935.

Phleger, Herman. "Recent Developments Affecting the Regime of the High Seas," *Department of State Bulletin*, XXXII (1955), pp. 934–940.

Pound, Roscoe. "Critique on the Texas Tidelands Case," *Baylor Law Review*, III (Winter, 1951, no. 2), pp. 120–129.

Powell, George Baden. "Rights of Fishery in Territorial and Extra-Territorial Waters," *Association for the Reform and Codification of the Law of Nations, Report of the Fourteenth Conference (1890)*. London: Richard Flint and Co., 1890. Pp. 189–199.

Powers, Robert D., Jr. "The Geneva Conferences on the Law of the Sea," *U.S. Naval Institute Proceedings*, LXXXVI (April, 1960), pp. 133–135.

   Captain Powers served as a member of the United States delegation to the Geneva conference.

Pradier-Fodéré, Paul L. E. "Le Congrès de droit international Sud-Américain et les traités de Montevideo," *Revue de Droit International et de Législation Comparée*, XXI (1889, no. 6), pp. 561–577.

Price, Daniel. "Sovereignty and Ownership in the Marginal Sea and their Relation to Problems of the Continental Shelf," *Baylor Law Review*, III (Winter, 1951, no. 2), pp. 241–266.

"*Pueblo* Captain Tells His Story of Capture—and Captivity," *U.S. News and World Report*, January 6, 1969, pp. 30–31.

Raestad, Arnold Christopher. "La portée du canon comme limite de la mer territoriale," *Revue Générale de Droit International Public*, XIX (July-October, 1912), pp. 598–623.

————. "Le problème des eaux territoriales à la conférence pour la codification du droit international," *Revue de Droit International* (de Lapradelle), VII (1931), pp. 107–146.

————. "Le régime des eaux territoriales devant la codification," *Revue de Droit International et de Législation Comparée* (third series), XI (1930), pp. 147–163.

————. "Tableau des lois et règles actuellement en vigueur dans les pays d'Europe et aux Etats-Unis d'Amerique en ce qui concerne l'étendue de la mer territoriale," *Revue Générale de Droit International Public*, XXI (May-June, 1914), pp. 401–420.

Rao, K. Krishna. "The Legal Regime of the Sea-Bed and Ocean Floor," *The Indian Journal of International Law*, IX (January, 1969), pp. 1–18.

Rao, P. Sreenivasa. "The Law of the Continental Shelf," *The Indian Journal of International Law*, VI (1966), pp. 363–464.

Reeves, Jesse S. "The Codification of the Law of Territorial Waters," *American Journal of International Law*, XXIV (July, 1930), pp. 486–499.

Professor Reeves served as a member of the United States delegation to the Codification Conference.

Renault, L. "L'exercice de la juridiction criminelle d'un état dans la mer territoriale," *Journal de Droit International* (Paris), VI (1879), pp. 238–254.

Ricketts, Claude V., and Stanley L. Beck. "Freedom of the Seas, the Territorial Sea, and the Doctrine of the Continental Shelf," *JAG Journal* (Office of the Judge Advocate General of the Navy), June, 1956, pp. 3–4.

Robertson, Horace B. "A Legal Regime for the Resources of the Seabed and Subsoil of the Deep sea: A Brewing Problem for International Lawmakers," *Naval War College Review*, XXI (October, 1968), pp. 61–108.

Robertson, J. H. "Anti-Smuggling Bill: Jurisdiction on the High Seas," *Michigan Law Review*, XXXV (1937), pp. 1146–1157.

Robin, R. "Le tunnel sous la Manche et le droit des gens," *Revue Générale de Droit International Public*, XV (1908), pp. 50–77.

Robinson, John T. "Ocean Fisheries: National Instrument for International Stability," *Naval War College Review*, XXI (June, 1969), pp. 106–129.

Robledo, Antonio Gómez. "La Convención de Ginebra sobre la plataforma continental," *Anuario Hispano-Luso-Americano de Derecho Internacional* (Zaragosa), (1959), pp. 62–69.

Roque, R. de M. "Plataforma continental," *Revista de la Facultad de Derecho de la Universidad Nacional de Tacunam*, no. 12 (1955), pp. 119–131.

Rubenstein, Alvin Z., George A. Codding, Jr., Leonard R. Hardy, and Robert D. Powers, Jr. "How Wide the Territorial Sea?" *U.S. Naval Institute Proceedings*, LXXXII (February, 1961), pp. 68–77.

Salans, Carl F. "Gulf of Aqaba and Strait of Tiran—Troubled Waters," *U.S. Naval Institute Proceedings*, XCIV (December, 1968), pp. 54–62.

Salcedo, Juan Antonio Carrillo. "Funciones del Acto Unilateral en el Régimen Jurídico de los Espacios Marítimos," *Estudios de Derecho International*, ed. Luis Garcia Arias. Zaragoza, Spain: University of Zaragoza, 1963. Pp. 9–27.

Sambrailo, B. "La liberté des mers et l'ONU," *Revue de la Politique Internationale* (Paris), VI (1955), pp. 12–14.

Scelle, Georges. "Plateau continental et droit international," *Revue Générale de Droit International Public*, LIX (1955), pp. 5–62.

Scerni, Mario. "Les espaces maritimes et le pouvoir des états," *Recueil des Cours de l'Académie de Droit International*, CXXII (1967-III), pp. 107–172.

Schapiro, L. B. "The Limits of Russian Territorial Waters in the Baltic," *British Yearbook of International Law*, XXVII (1950), pp. 439–448.

Schoenborn, W. "Territoire de l'Etat relativement à la surface de la mer," *Recueil des Cours de l'Académie de Droit International*, XXX (1929-V), pp. 135–145.

Scott, James Brown. "The Liquor Treaty Between the United States and Great Britain," *American Journal of International Law*, XVIII (April, 1924), pp. 301–306.

Selak, Charles B., Jr. "A Consideration of the Legal Status of the Gulf of Aqaba," *American Journal of International Law*, LII (October, 1958), pp. 660–698.

———. "Fishing Vessels and the Principle of Free Passage," *American Journal of International Law*, XLVIII (1954), pp. 627–635.

———. "The Proposed International Convention for the High Seas Fisheries of the North Pacific Ocean," *American Journal of International Law*, LXVI (1952), pp. 323–330.

———. "Recent Developments in High Seas Fisheries Jurisdiction Under the Presidential Proclamation of 1945," *American Journal of International Law*, XLIV (1950), pp. 670–681.

Shalowitz, Aaron L. "Where Are our Seaward Boundaries?" *U.S. Naval Institute Proceedings*, LXXXIII (June, 1957), pp. 616–627.

Shear, H. E. "Freedom of the Seas," *U.S. Naval Institute Proceedings*, LXXXIV (June, 1958), pp. 66–68.

Shigeru Oda. "The Concept of the Contiguous Zone," *International and Comparative Law Quarterly*, XI (January, 1962), pp. 130–141.

————. "The Continental Shelf," *The Japanese Annual of International Law*, I (1957), pp. 15–37.

————. "The Extent of the Territorial Sea—Some Analysis of the Geneva Conferences and Recent Developments," *The Japanese Annual of International Law*, VI (1962), pp. 7–38.

————. "The Hydrogen Bomb Tests and International Law," *Friedens-Warte* (Berlin), LIII (1956), pp. 126–135.

————. "Japan and the United Nations Conference on the Law of the Sea," *The Japanese Annual of International Law*, III (1959), pp. 65–86.

————. "Japan and the International Fisheries," *The Japanese Annual of International Law*, IV (1960), pp. 50–62.

————. "Proposals for Revising the Convention of the Continental Shelf," *The Columbia Journal of Transnational Law*, VII (Spring, 1968), pp. 1–31.

————. "The Territorial Sea and National Resources," *The International and Comparative Law Quarterly*, IV (July, 1955), pp. 415–425.

————. "A Zone for Exclusive Fisheries of the Coastal State," *Journal of Political Science* (Kinki University), no. 3 (1954), pp. 55–81.

Siegfried, A. "Les canaux internationaux et les grandes routes maritimes mondiales," *Recueil des Cours de l'Académie de Droit International*, LXXIV (1949-I), pp. 5–71.

Slonim, Solomon. "The Right of Innocent Passage and the 1958 Geneva Conference on the Law of the Sea," The *Columbia Journal of Transnational Law*, V (1966, no 1), pp. 96–127.

Smith, Emory C. "The Three-Mile Limit" (part I), *JAG Journal* (Office of the Judge Advocate General of the Navy), (March, 1949), pp. 4–7.

Smith, Herbert Arthur. "The Contiguous Zone," *British Yearbook of International Law*, XX (1939), pp. 122–125.

Sørenson, Max. "Law of the Sea," *International Conciliation*, no. 520 (November, 1958), pp. 195–256.

Soyer, Jean-Claude. "Les aspects de droit international privé de la réforme du droit maritime," *Journal du Droit International* (Paris), XCVI (July-September, 1969), pp. 610–629.

Sparrow, H. G. "Territorial Waters," *U.S. Naval Institute Proceedings*, XLII (March-April, 1916), pp. 447–460.

Stang, David Phillip. "The Walls Beneath the Sea," *U.S. Naval Institute Proceedings*, XCIV (March, 1968), pp. 33–43.

Svarlien, Oscar. "The Territorial Sea: A Quest for Uniformity," *University of Florida Law Review*, XV (1962), pp. 333–351.

Swarztrauber, Sayre Archie. "Alaska and Siberia: A Strategic Analysis," *Naval Review 1965*, Frank Uhlig, Jr., editor. Annapolis: U.S. Naval Institute, 1964. Pp. 138–165.

Sweitzer, H. B. "Sovereignty and the SLBM," *U.S. Naval Institute Proceedings*, XCII (September, 1966), pp. 32–41.

Tao Cheng. "Communist China and the Law of the Sea," *American Journal of International Law*, LXIII (January, 1969), pp. 47–73.

Takashi Nakamura. "Acquisitive Prescription in International Law and Prescriptive

Acquisition over the Sea Bed of the High Seas," *Journal of Law and Politics* (Hogaku Ronso) (Keio Gijiku University), XXVII (1954, no. 7), pp. 13–38.

Terumichi Kuwabara. "International Law Commission (4th Session) and Problems of the Territorial Sea," *Hitotsubashi Review* (Tokyo), (1954), pp. 29–62.

Toku Ogasawara. "The Freedom of the Seas," *Journal of Law and Politics* (Hogaku Ronso) (Keio Gijiku University), XXVII (1954, no. 7), pp. 39–71.

Vallot, F. A. "The Continental Shelf," *British Yearbook of International Law*, XXIII (1946), pp. 333–338.

———. "Ownership of the Sea-bed: *United States of America* v. *State of California*," *British Yearbook of International Law*, XXIV (1947), pp. 382–385.

Vaughan, R. M. "Delimitation of Norwegian Fisheries Zone," *Geographic Review* (New York), XLII (1952), pp. 302–304.

Verdross, A. "Etendue du territoire de l'Etat"; "La haute mer," *Recueil des Cours de l'Académie de Droit International*, XXX (1929-V), pp. 385–395, 405–408.

Vivaldi Queirolo, A. "La resurrección del mare clausum," *Revista de Derecho* (Concepción), (1955), pp. 3–57.

Vyshnepolskii, S. A. "K probleme pravogo rezhim arkticheskoi oblasti," (On the Problem of the Legal Regime of the Arctic Region), *Sovetskoe gosudarstvo i pravo*, no. 7, (1952), pp. 36–45.

Wadsworth, L. W. "The Changing Concept of the Territorial Seas," *World Affairs*, CXXIII (Fall, 1960), pp. 67–69.

Waldock, C. H. M. "The Anglo-Norwegian Fisheries Case," *British Yearbook of International Law*, XXVIII (1951), pp. 114–171.

Sir Humphrey served as counsel for Great Britain before the I.C.J. during the Anglo-Norwegian Fisheries Case.

———. "Rights to the Sea Bed and its Subsoil," *Report of the Forty-Sixth Conference of the International Law Association*, (1954, Edinburgh Session). Great Britain: Cambrian News (Aberystwyth), Ltd., 1955. Pp. 411–442.

———. "The Legal Basis of Claims to the Continental Shelf," *Transactions of the Grotius Society*, XXXVI (1950). London: The Grotius Society, 1951, pp. 115–148.

Walker, Peter B. "What is Innocent Passage?" *Naval War College Review*, XXI (January, 1969, no. 5), pp. 53–76.

Walker, Wyndham L. "Territorial Waters: The Cannon Shot Rule," *British Yearbook of International Law*, XXII (1945), pp. 210–231.

Wescott, Allan. "British Reject Twelve-Mile Limit," *U.S. Naval Institute Proceedings*, XLIX (September, 1923), pp. 1579–1580.

White, Lawrence A. "A Code of Conduct for the Fishing Grounds," *U.S. Naval Institute Proceedings*, XCI (March, 1965), pp. 76–82.

Whiteman, Marjorie M. "Conference on the Law of the Sea: Convention on the Continental Shelf," *American Journal of International Law*, LII (October, 1958), pp. 629–659.

———. "The Territorial Sea," *Proceedings of the American Society of International Law*, (April, 1956), pp. 125–136.

Wilberforce, R. O. "Some Aspects of the Anglo-Norwegian Fisheries Case," *Transactions of the Grotius Society*, XXXVIII (1952). London: The Grotius Society, 1953. Pp. 151–168.

Wilkey, Malcolm R. "The Deep Ocean: Its Potential Mineral Resources and Problems," *The International Lawyer*, III (October, 1968), pp. 31–48.

Williams, William. "Reminiscences of the Bering Sea Arbitration," *American Journal of International Law*, XXXVII (October, 1943), pp. 562–584.

Mr. Williams was the American counsel before the arbitration tribunal.

Wilson, George Grafton. "Les eaux adjacentes au territoire des états," *Recueil des Cours de l'Académie de Droit International*, I (1923), pp. 127–176.

Windley, David W. "International Practice Regarding Traditional Fishing Privileges of Foreign Fishermen in Zones of Extended Maritime Jurisdiction," *American Journal of International Law*, LXIII (July, 1969), pp. 490–503.

Woolsey, T. S. "The Supreme Court Decision in the Ship Liquor Cases," *American Journal of International Law*, XVII (July, 1923), pp. 504–507.

Yepes, J. M. "Les nouvelles tendances du droit international de la mer et le droit international américain," *Revue Générale de Droit International Public*, LX (1956), pp. 10–79.

Young, Richard. "The Continental Shelf in the Practice of American States," *Anuario Jurídico Interamericano 1950–1951*. Washington, D.C.: Pan American Union, 1953. Pp. 27–36.

———. "Developments Abroad Regarding the Continental Shelf," *American Bar Association Journal*, XL (1954), pp. 431–439.

———. "Further Claims to Areas Beneath the Seas," *American Journal of International Law*, XLIII (October, 1949), pp. 790–792.

———. "The Geneva Convention on the Continental Shelf: A First Impression," *American Journal of International Law*, LII (October, 1958), pp. 733–738.

———. "The International Law Commission and the Continental Shelf," *American Journal of International Law*, XLVI (January, 1952), pp. 123–128.

———. "The Legal Regime of the Deep-Sea Floor," *American Journal of International Law*, LXII (July, 1968), pp. 641–653.

———. "The Legal Status of Submarine Areas Beneath the High Seas," *American Journal of International Law*, XLV (April, 1951), pp. 225–239.

———. "The Limits of the Continental Shelf—and Beyond," *Proceedings of the American Society of International Law*, (April, 1968), pp. 229–236.

———. "Lord Asquith and the Continental Shelf," *American Journal of International Law*, XLVI (1952), pp. 512–515.

———. "The Over-extension of the Continental Shelf," *American Journal of International Law*, XLVII (July, 1953), pp. 454–456.

———. "Pan American Discussion on Offshore Claims," *American Journal of International Law*, L (October, 1956), p. 909.

———. "Recent Developments with Respect to the Continental Shelf," *American Journal of International Law*, XLII (October, 1948), pp. 849–857.

———. "Saudi Arabian Offshore Legislation," *American Journal of International Law*, XLIII (1949), pp. 530–532.

Zengo Ohira. "The Continental Shelf and the Conservation Zone," *Hitotsubashi Review* (Tokyo), XXX (1953, no. 3), pp. 108–128.

———. "The Freedom of the Seas and Japan," *Annals of the Hitosubashi Academy* (Tokyo), I (1954, no. 1), pp. 89–96.

8. ENCYCLOPEDIA ARTICLES

"Alexander," *Encyclopaedia Britannica* (1953 edition), I, 558–561.

"Artillery," *Encyclopaedia Britannica* (1953 edition), II, 463–478.

"The Cabinet," *Encyclopaedia Britannica* (1953 edition), IV, 498–504.

"Coal and Coal Mining," *Encyclopaedia Britannica* (1953 edition), V, 868–883.

"Cornwall," *Encyclopaedia Britannica* (1953 edition), VI, 452–454.

"Fisheries," *Britannica Book of the Year, 1960*. Chicago, Toronto, London: Encyclopaedia Britannica, Inc., 1960. Pp. 256–257.

"Fisheries," *Britannica Book of the Year, 1962*. Chicago, Toronto, London, Geneva: Encyclopaedia Britannica, 1962. Pp. 255–256.

"Fisheries," *Britannica Book of the Year, 1964*. Chicago, Toronto, London, Geneva, Sydney, Tokyo: Encyclopaedia Britannica, Inc., 1964. Pp. 366–367.

"Fisheries," *Britannica Book of the Year, 1966*. Chicago, Toronto, London, Geneva, Sydney, Tokyo, Manila: Encyclopaedia Britannica, 1966. Pp. 307–309.

"Galiani, Ferdinando," *Dizionario Enciclopedico Italiano* (1956 edition; Rome: Instituto dell' enciclopedia italiana), V, 183–184.

"Great Britain," *Encyclopaedia Britannica* (1953 edition), X, 673–729.

"Ordnance," *Encyclopaedia Britannica* (1953 edition), XVI, 856–870.

"Shipping: Merchant Ships of the World," *Encyclopaedia Britannica* (1953 edition), XX, 548–551.

"Transportation," *Britannica Book of the Year, 1969*. Chicago, Toronto, London, Geneva, Sydney, Tokyo and Manila: Encyclopaedia Britannica, 1969. Pp. 744–748.

9. NEWSPAPERS

Agence France-Presse (AFP) Bulletin, Lima, Peru, December 12, 1969.

Cape Cod [Massachusetts] *Standard-Times*, September 18, 1969.

Christian Science Monitor, June 15, 1966.

Feron, James. "16 Nations Split on Fishing Code," *New York Times*, January 18, 1964, p. 36M.

Finney, John W. "Secret Undersea System Guards U.S. Against Hostile Submarines," *New York Times*, September 14, 1965.

Gordon, Herbert. "Foreign Vessels Fishing Illegally Irk Coast Guard," *Boston Globe*, September 14, 1969, p. 37.

[Guayaquil, Ecuador] *El Telegrapho*, December 14, 1969.

Lockwood, Herbert W. "Tuna Boat Owners Fear Navy Escorts," *The* [San Diego] *Independent*, February 5, 1967, p. 1.

New York Herald, June 13, 1923.

New York Times, February and July, 1953; September, 1963; May, 1964; July, 1965; October, 1966; May, 1967; February and July, 1968; March, 1969; January and February, 1970.

Nickerson, Neil G. "Cape-tip Skipper Fears Squeeze-out," *Cape Cod Standard-Times*, September 15, 1969, p. 1.

Prima, L. Edgar. "Ships Ordered to Stay Clear of Red Territory: Aid to Down Pilot Barred," *San Diego Union*, February 16, 1968, pp. A1, A6.

———. "12-Mile Sea Limit Expected for U.S.," *San Diego Union*, June 16, 1968, pp. A1, A6.

[Quito, Ecuador] *El Comercio*, December 14, 1969.

Reistrup, J. V. "Davy Jones's Locker Tempts the World," *The Washington Post*, November 19, 1967.

San Diego Union, December, 1967; January, April, June and July, 1968; February, 1970.

Shepard, Tim. "Peru Gunboats Seize 2 S.D. Tuna Clippers," *San Diego Union*, January 27, 1967, pp. A1–A2.

———. "Tunaboats Reported Fined, Released by Peru, Ecuador," *San Diego Union*, January 28, 1967, pp. B1, B7.

The Washington Post, June, 1963; June, July, September, and December, 1969; February, 1970; March, 1970.

10. UNPUBLISHED MATERIALS

Bisson, G., District Geologist, Institute of Geological Sciences, Exeter, Devon, England, letter to author, GB/LMB/RES/5/4 dated 5 December 1969.

Bruno, Jean, Conservateur, Bibliothèque Nationale (French National Library), Paris, France, letter to author, JB/AKA-78596/70-035 dated 19 January 1970.

Evans, W. B., Institute of Geological Sciences, Leeds, Yorkshire, England, letter to author N/1028/70/1 dated 5 January 1970.

Eytchison, Ronald Marvin. *Contemporary Exclusive Claims of the Latin American States to the Territorial Sea.* Master's thesis. Washington, D.C.: The American University, 1968.

Foster, William Feeny. *Baselines and Freedom of the Seas.* Master's thesis. Washington, D.C.: The American University, 1965.

Munro, P. M., Administrative Assistant, Stanford School of Law, letter to author, dated 29 December 1969.

Nadeson, Alexander Govind. *An Analysis of the Geneva Conferences on the Breadth of the Territorial Sea.* Doctor's dissertation. Washington, D.C.: The American University, 1968.

Piédelièvre, René, Professor, Paris Academy of Medicine, letter to author, dated 4 December 1969.

Senft, Christophe, Editions Droz, Geneva, Switzerland, letter to author, dated 7 January 1970.

Strohl, Mitchell P. "The Navy's Stake in the Three-Mile Limit," *International Law Compendium.* Monterey, Calif.: U.S. Naval Postgraduate School, 1959. (Mimeographed.)

Swarztrauber, Sayre Archie. *Twentieth Century Developments in the Extent of the Territorial Sea.* Master's thesis. Washington, D.C.: The American University, 1963.

Index